The European Nobility
Vol. 1

Noble privilege

M. L. Bush

Noble privilege

Manchester University Press

Published by
Manchester University Press
Oxford Road, Manchester M13 9PL

British Library cataloguing in publication data
Bush, M. L.
  The European nobility.
  Vol. 1: Noble privilege
  I. Europe—Nobility—History
  I. Title
  305.5'223   HT653.E/

  ISBN 0-7190-0913-8

Printed in Great Britain
by Butler & Tanner Ltd, Frome and London

Contents

Introduction

This study examines the European nobility within its natural boundaries of time and place. Only in this way, I felt, could the more important questions be satisfactorily posed and answered. A confinement to one period in the nobility's development or a concentration upon a small number of nobilities would have based the work on too many wobbly assumptions concerning periodisation, perspective and generalisation.[1] Several studies of the European nobility have been published, but they have tended to concentrate upon a limited period, to focus upon only a handful of nobilities and to present a juxtaposition of case studies rather than a systematic comparison.[2] None, to my knowledge, has explored the subject more fully or comparatively than this work.

Its scope creates some natural problems. The study heavily and necessarily depends upon secondary authorities, most of which take a periodised and insulated view of one nobility. Very few of them examine a nobility throughout its history or seek to compare one nobility systematically with another. Furthermore, the very nature of this work allows it no hope of being definitive. Its purpose, as I conceive it, is rather to provide a framework of study within which the nobility at particular times and places can be more adequately researched. Such a work is in danger of producing distilled and rarified generalisations which conceal the differences between nobilities and overlook their capacity to undergo radical changes in character. To counter

[1] See my article 'Place and period in the study of History', *Times Higher Education Supplement*, Sept. 1980.
[2] A. Goodwin (ed.), *The European Nobility in the Eighteenth Century*; D. Spring (ed.), *European Landed Elites in the Nineteenth Century*; J.-P. Labatut, *Les noblesses européennes de la fin du XVe siècle à la fin du XVIIIe siècle*; J. Meyer, *Noblesses et pouvoirs dans l'Europe d'ancien régime* and G. Birtsch, K. Kluxen, H. Roos and E. Weis, *Der Adel vor der Revolution*. P. du Puy de Clinchamps' *La noblesse* escapes periodisation, treating the nobility throughout its life span, but deals mainly with the French nobility, having but a final, brief chapter on 'les noblesses européennes' which is essentially concerned with their twentieth-century demise.

this possibility, emphasis is laid on the range of exception and the changes which occurred with the passing of time. The first stage in writing the work was to compose a similarly structured case study of each European nobility. This was to ensure that individual nobilities received their due consideration.

Essentially the work studies the nobility as a class or order. It makes very little reference to individual nobles and no mention whatsoever of their foibles and eccentricities. Privilege is treated first and foremost, since it is the European nobility's only indispensable characteristic. There were landless nobles and nobles without a ruling function and nobles whose way of life was indistinguishable from the rest of society, but there was no such thing as nobles without privilege. The term 'privilege', as it is used in this study, means neither the informal advantages conferred by the possession of wealth and power nor the rights which subjects enjoyed as citizens of the state. It has a much narrower definition. Essentially it refers to rights which are sanctioned by custom or law, confined to specific social groups and transmissible from one generation to the next. The secondary characteristics of the nobility will be presented in volume two.

Throughout the work the term 'nobility' is preferred to 'aristocracy', except when reference is made to the peers, gentry and baronetcy of England. On these occasions 'aristocracy' is used to label the nobility as a class or order and 'nobility' is reserved for the peerage. In making this exception my intention was not to suggest a difference in kind between English and continental lords, nor to present the gentry and baronetcy as socially distinct from the peerage. Indeed, the work accepts that the English aristocracy and the continental nobilities had much in common and that the gentry and baronetcy were essentially a lesser nobility. This exception was made only to avoid the misunderstanding which might have resulted from a failure to respect a well established convention.

Needless to say, a work of this scale owes a massive debt to other historians. Its progress was promoted by my colleagues in the Modern History section at Manchester University, who tolerated a theme on the subject of aristocracy as a major component of the first-year introductory course and assisted in teaching it. It also owes much to the size of the history department at Manchester and the accumulation within it of a wealth of specialised knowledge on European nobles and other political elites. The easy access which I had to this knowledge and the generosity of my colleagues in dispensing it helped the book along. I need to give special thanks to Graham Burton, who read chapter I and guided me on the subject of the elites of the Roman Republic and Empire; to Patrick Riley, who furnished me with reading and ideas on the Scottish nobility; to Richard Davies, who not only suggested reading on the subject of honorific privileges but also produced the books for me to read; to John Breuilly, who wasted valuable research time in London to select and transcribe for my benefit passages from the Prussian *Algemeines Landrecht* of 1794; to Constantine Brancovan and Peter Gatrell, who advised me on the Russian nobility; to Brian Pullan, who answered my queries on the Venetian patriciate; to Steve Rigby for reading the chapter on seigneurial rights and subjecting its demographic emphasis to telling criticism; to Joe Bergin, who exposed several embarrassing gaps in my reading on the subject; and to Joe Harrison, who gave me bibliographical assistance on the Spanish nobilities. The work also benefited from conversations with Michael Beames and John Ellis and from the encouragement which they discreetly offered me when the study was in its early, uphill stages. The excellence of both the Manchester University and Manchester Central Reference Libraries needs to be acknowledged. For six weeks of 1978 Michael and Miriam Foot allowed me free residence in London, subject to the labour service of feeding their cats. This gave me the opportunity to cope with the reading not available in Manchester. Manchester University generously awarded me two terms leave of absence in 1977-8. I am indebted to my modernist colleagues, especially Terence Ranger, who took over my teaching chores in that time. This leave enabled me to write the first draft of the book. The work is also indebted to certain indelible experiences of childhood, particularly the discovery that a local greengrocer was an Irish peer and an encounter with the family doctor, transformed in an afternoon of leisure from a humble professionalman to a lordly aristocrat simply by virtue of being seated on a high horse with a very tall hat on his head. It is finally indebted to the experience of living in a society where aristocratic values unfortunately remain a potent force.

Didsbury,   M. L. Bush
Manchester
September 1980

I

Noble privileges in general

1 Character

For much of the last thousand years of European history noble privilege was
not merely an expression of social superiority or of economic and political
advantage. It was essentially a juridical fact, conferred or confirmed by royal
grant and existing not because of the laxity of the state but because of a legal
provision. Thus, in failing to pay state taxes, nobles were not necessarily
breaking the law; frequently they were complying with it. In managing to
own much of the land, or to occupy the more important public offices, or to
dominate parliaments, or to dispense private justice, or to avoid penalties
and processes in the law, nobles were not simply asserting their power and
influence; often they were exercising their legal due.

Noble privileges firmly distinguished noble from commoner. The distinction frequently related to both property and person: the privileges assumed
that not only nobles and commoners but also noble and commoner estates
were juridically different.[1] Essentially, the privileges of nobility were held by
hereditary right. Normally a noble could transmit them to his descendants.
However, the nobility was for most of its history far from being a caste, and
commoners-born could easily obtain the privileges either by ennoblement or
the acquisition of a noble estate.

Noble privileges remained remarkably secure until the French Revolution
and its aftermath. Governments traditionally possessed powers to confiscate
them from individual subjects, especially for felony and treason, the failure
to fulfil military obligations, and the pursuit of ignoble occupations. Yet in
practice the Crown had a very limited ability to apply its rights of confiscation. No matter what the law, the stigma of treason and felony tended to be
confined to the perpetrator of the crime. It was not usually imposed upon his
descendants. By the early modern period the failure of noble families to fulfil
their obligations to the ruler no longer resulted in their denoblement. Derogation for the pursuit of ignoble occupations existed in the laws of many
states but in practice was not much of a threat to nobility. In Genoa and

Brittany derogation was not final; it only put nobility into abeyance until the offending occupation had been abandoned. Derogation laws were not often enforced. Moreover, limits were eventually placed upon the range of derogatory occupations. By the eighteenth century they tended to be restricted to manual work or the retail trade. By this time the operation of mines, factories and wholesale or overseas trade had all become legitimate occupations for noblemen.[2]

A greater threat to noble families came of the Crown's right to define noble status. Subjects could lose their privileges through being officially declared non-noble. Especially when financial considerations were at stake—the government gained, for example, from limiting the numbers of subjects with the right not to pay taxes—the Crown could proceed rigorously, as in seventeenth-century France, eighteenth-century Russia and Spain and nineteenth-century Russia and Poland. In each case a weeding out of the so-called spurious element reduced the size of the nobility.[3] Nevertheless, the general, long-term attitude of the Crown towards noble privilege was one of forbearance. Under the old regime the occasional privilege of the noble order could be eliminated, but governments allowed families with a genuine claim to nobility to remain privileged.

The privileges of nobility were held corporately or non-corporately. In other words, they were imparted either by noble status or by landed, titular and lineal qualifications. The former conferred privilege upon every member of the nobility; the latter, upon a part of it. The prevalence of non-corporate privileges meant that a huge amount of noble privilege was unavailable to large sections of the nobility. The privileges were either seigneurial or noble. Seigneurial rights bestowed upon nobles the authority of rulers (*dominium*); noble privileges awarded them the rights of subjects (*libertas*). Seigneurial rights allowed a noble to make exactions of his tenants and other dependants and to exercise some control over their lives, while the noble privileges awarded him rights of political participation and of exemption from the demands of the state. The seigneurial rights mostly sprang from the landlord-tenant relationship, although not entirely, since they could be held quite independently of landownership. They consisted of (1) dues, private taxes and services; (2) patrimonial justice; (3) the administration of state obligations such as taxation and conscription; (4) the appointment of public officials; (5) the monopoly of oven, wine press and mill, as well as of hunting and fishing and of the natural products of the estate, such as minerals, firewood, mushrooms and nuts; (6) commercial rights of pre-emption and of first sale; (7) pre-eminence in public gatherings and (8) control of the tenantry's right to migrate, marry, change occupation and hold land.

The noble privileges were chiefly (1) tax exemption and other fiscal concessions; (2) rights of political participation, consisting of parliamentary membership, the tenure of offices reserved for nobles or the preferential promotion of nobles to offices which could be held by commoners; (3) honorific rights such as armorial bearings, titles, special forms of address, pre-eminence in public gatherings, carrying arms, wearing sumptuous dress and exclusive membership rights to military and chivalric orders or to educational and clerical establishments; (4) the exclusive right to own land; (5) indemnity from some of the judicial and service obligations imposed upon the commonalty either by the state or by private landlords; (6) trading concessions such as the monopoly of alcohol production; and (7) the right to hunt. In contrast to the seigneurial rights, which stemmed from the ownership of land, serfs or regalian authority, the noble privileges could be conferred by noble status alone. Several, however, also derived from the ownership of a noble estate. Others relied upon the possession of a title or upon ancient lineage. Some, notably fiscal exemption and parliamentary membership, were corporate rights in one society and imparted by special qualifications in another. Because the latter type of privilege was so prevalent, the English aristocracy was not exceptional in confining its more important privileges to the peerage. For example, in parts of the Prussian monarchy and in most of the German principalities only the holders of noble estates were traditionally entitled to exemption from direct taxation and to parliamentary representation in the noble chamber. In all the territories of the Austrian Habsburgs, with the exception of Hungary, the parliamentary and office-holding privileges as well as immunity from direct taxation were confined to certain, specially qualified nobles. And even in Hungary, where all the noble privileges were initially enjoyed by corporate right, they came eventually to stratify the nobility, notably because the titled nobility received the exclusive right of personal membership of the national diet in 1608 and because elements within the lesser nobility lost rights of fiscal exemption long before they were taken away from the rest of the nobility. In France membership of, or representation in, the noble chamber of the provincial diets and the Estates General depended not simply upon noble status but upon lineal or landed qualifications; the tenure of certain offices was determined by lineage; and south of the Loire exemption from the *taille* tended to be restricted to the owners of noble estates. In Sweden and Denmark only the owners of noble estates were exempt from the traditional land tax. In Sicily personal membership of parliament and fiscal exemption exclusively belonged to the nobles who were tenants-in-chief. Only in a small minority of states were noble privileges commonly enjoyed by all of noble status. Thus the English aristocracy differed not because of the privileges of its peerage but because the gentry and baronetcy had so few noble privileges. For example, the French nobles who lacked parliamentary privileges and exemption from the *taille* were nonetheless highly privileged, enjoying immunity from certain indirect taxes, access to some reserved offices and a range of honorific and indemnity privileges. Much the same can be said of the German principalities, Austria, Bohemia and Hungary. In contrast, English aristocrats without rights of peerage possessed only the honorific noble privileges of coat of arms and the hereditary titles of esquire or baronet. Privileges which on the continent were corporately held tended in England to be restricted to the peerage. A similar paucity of corporate rights was found in Sicily, where the bulk of noble privilege was confined to the owners of fiefs. In this case the peers who lacked the qualification of tenancy-in-chief were almost as underprivileged as the rest of the non-baronial nobility. Stratified by its peerage privileges, the English aristocracy was a typical European nobility, but in possessing so few corporate privileges it was distinctly peculiar.

Noblewomen usually exercised seigneurial rights in a manner indistinguishable from the noblemen. In some respects, however, the two held their noble privileges differently. The noble privileges of parliamentary membership and of office-holding, in particular, were very much a male preserve. For this reason the peerage act of 1963 which awarded peeresses a seat in the British house of lords was a revolutionary breach of tradition. Furthermore, while all the children of noblemen normally received noble status and its attendant privileges, this was not always true of the offspring of noblewomen. Where nobility passed only by patrilineal descent, as in parts of France, the children of a noblewoman married to a commoner did not inherit noble status. However, as property was generally inheritable on the male and the female side, the inheritance of seigneurial rights and of fiscal privileges conferred by landownership were freed of this restriction. Nonetheless, throughout Europe a female's share of the estate and its privileges tended to occur only in the absence of heirs male.

Laws of primogeniture placed another bar on the inheritance of noble privilege, although corporate rights tended to pass to the whole family rather than to one child and the widely practised partible or preferential transmission of land enabled at least all the male offspring to receive a portion of the estate and its rights. Also excluding nobles from the enjoyment of privilege was the use of legal devices to maintain the integrity of the estate. By the eighteenth century devices of this nature were common and, as a result, large numbers of nobles were denied noble and seigneurial privileges not only because they were females but also because they were younger sons.

Access to the noble privileges was quite easy for commoners-born, especially through ennoblement. The corporate privileges were normally within reach of large numbers of commoners, who obtained them by the purchase of noble status, by royal grant of nobility in reward for service or by securing offices of state which automatically ennobled their holder. A distinction, however, needs to be made between the privileges imparted by a noble title and those conferred by noble status. The former were relatively difficult for non-nobles to obtain because they tended to go to nobles, whereas commoners could easily acquire the latter, largely because the Crown's generosity in dispensing nobility was maintained over the centuries by its need to use it as a form of patronage and to raise revenue from selling honours. In addition, several states allowed an informal means of ennoblement. In France until the late sixteenth century the ownership of a noble estate ennobled; in Spain the rule that only nobles were entitled to membership of the military orders allowed commoners to assume nobility when accepted as a member; while in Poland noble status could be established by its uncontested, long-term enjoyment.

Commoners could also secure the privileges of nobility without ennoblement. Simply by owning noble estates, commoners gained possession of seigneurial and sometimes noble rights. Further privileges of nobility could result from concessions made by the Crown to special groups of favoured commoners. In Spain, for example, large numbers of subjects enjoyed noble privileges, partly because of the nobility's populousness but also because of the multitude of commoners officially permitted to enjoy them: the commoner knights of medieval Castile, the honoured citizens of Valencia and Catalonia, the graduates of certain universities, the wet nurses of noble offspring, the fathers of twelve or more children, medical doctors in the Crown of Aragon after 1626 and wholesale merchants after 1773. In France and Prussia commoner state officials were awarded noble privileges, as were commoner knights in a number of medieval states. In France noble privileges were granted to the residents of certain townships; in the Austrian Empire and Russia a class of honoured citizens was created by the government in the late modern period and awarded noble rights. However, the noble privileges bestowed upon commoners by royal favour were different in character from those which the nobility enjoyed by corporate right. The privileges awarded commoners tended to involve one or two, rather than all, the rights conferred by noble status. Moreover, they were not usually granted on an hereditary basis. Commoners with noble privileges were a social exception; nobles with privileges were the rule. Privilege thus made a juridical distinction between noble and commoner even though the privileges imparted to nobles by the processes of inheritance or ennoblement could be secured by men who remained of commoner status.

2 Origins and extension

The nobility originally acquired its privileges by annexing the hereditary rights of other social groups.[4] Its privileges stemmed from five sources: (1)

the dichotomy commonly found in early societies between the rights of freemen and slaves; (2) the lordship rights associated with men of ruler rather than of subject status; (3) the legacy of hereditary privilege which developed under Roman rule in connexion with consular rank and membership of the equestrian and senatorial orders; (4) the rights associated with knighthood, and (5) the authority acquired by landlords over their tenants. In this respect the privileges of nobility were a compound of princely, official, knightly, freeman and landlord rights.

Essential to the crystallisation of the nobility as a privileged class was a heightening of the juridical distinction between freeman and noble and a blurring of the distinction which had existed originally between, on the one hand, princely subjects or old senatorial families whose privileges were hereditary and free of specific obligations to the state and, on the other, the much lowlier class of knights whose rights had initially depended upon military service and had been personal, not hereditary, in character. By A.D. 1000 these processes had yet to occur; by 1200 they had taken place in parts of France; by 1400 they had produced a distinct noble order throughout most of Europe. Largely responsible was the conversion of the nobility from a caste of rulers divided into clans to a class of subjects composed of separate families. Equally important was the role played by mounted military service in the conferment of hereditary privilege, and the emergence of political organisations centring on the monarchy and administered by national institutions. These developments did not create the noble: nobility existed long before the eleventh century, its members distinguished from the rest of society not only by their power and wealth but also by juridically sanctioned hereditary privileges. They rather transformed a small social group with insubstantial or very general privileges into a relatively large class with an extensive and highly valued range of precisely defined rights.[5]

(a) Roman roots

The Roman contribution to the development of noble privilege was outstanding. It imparted not only the concept of landed lordship, the essence of the seigneurial system, but also the idea that the birthrights of nobles should not be conferred simply by consanguinity but could be created by an act of royal patronage or in reward for state service. In this respect the largely honorific privileges granted to the descendants of consuls under the Republic and to the descendants of senators under the Principate, and the Emperor's extensive use of patrician status as a form of patronage and of senatorial rank as a device for romanising native elites throughout the Empire were important steps in the development of noble privilege. The privileges of nobility also owed something to the social distinction which the Romans made between *pedites* and *equites* and between families of equestrian and senatorial rank, the former distinction associating cavalry service with the enjoyment of special rights, the latter distinction proposing that the ruling elite should be stratified as well as defined by privilege.[6] In addition, Roman example helped to make noble privilege a right of subjects rather than of royalty. In early Germanic societies 'the nobility' was originally a chieftain group, its members distinguished from other freemen by their right of election to the rulership of the tribe. Its privileges were those of royalty. Alternatively, the original nobles were either relatives of the reigning dynasty or ex-kings and their kin who, having been deprived of independent rulership, were allowed to retain some royal privileges, as in the Frankish Empire or in the centralising states of Denmark, Norway and Sweden of the ninth and tenth centuries.[7] In contrast, the senatorial and patrician orders of the Roman Empire were clearly subjects, not royalty.[8]

However, with the fall of the Western Empire the surviving members of the senatorial order became, like the nobility of royal extraction and connexion, a nobility of the blood, with entry to it determined by birth. Consisting of these two basic elements, the nobility for several centuries was predominantly a caste. Entry to it for non-nobles was extremely difficult unless it came of kinship with royalty. Because birthright was central to this nobility's identity, privilege was not an important distinction between noble and commoner. Arguably, noble privileges underwent their major development when the noble order became accessible to commoners and the blood distinction resting on birth ceased to be the hallmark of nobility. Its conversion from a caste to a class encouraged the nobles to value the privileges which set them apart from the community of freemen. This radical change in character occurred in the West in the course of the tenth and eleventh centuries as noble status became attainable through the acquisition of *bannum et iustitia* or as a royal or princely reward. The latter added to the nobility of the blood a service nobility, its members obtaining noble status through the process of dubbing for knighthood or royal creation. Faced by the influx of new nobles in the eleventh and twelfth centuries, the old nobles in the West grew appreciative of those privileges which stratified the nobility, while the new nobles' search for a verifiable noble identity led them to value the idea of a range of privileges which served to distinguish noble from commoner. A basic change in the nobility's composition thus gave its members a compulsive reason for wanting the juridical nature of its privileges emphasised.[9]

(b) Freeman and knighthood rights

Originally the obligation and right to provide military service had lain with the freemen. Apart from military service, the freemen were distinguished by several other rights, notably the right of trial by public, rather than private, tribunal, the right of landownership and the right to wear arms. As heavily armoured cavalry became the main instrument of war in ninth- and tenth-century Western Europe, not all freemen could afford to provide the military service which the ruler now required. Those who could meet the requirement were awarded additional privileges. As a result, the provision of military service came to divide the freemen into two categories of privileged subject. This distinction was enlarged between the ninth and eleventh centuries with the subjection of freemen to private lordship, a consequence of the decay and disappearance of public institutions following the collapse of the Carolingian Empire. Through receiving immunity from the exactions of private lordship, the nobles and knights acquired a privilege which further distinguished them from the commonalty. The extension of serfdom in the same period meant that in some societies free status and nobility became equivalent terms, the non-noble freeman ceasing for a time to exist. When he reappeared in the thirteenth and fourteenth centuries as a result of manumission from serfdom, the process of emancipation preserved a juridical distinction between the freemen of noble and commoner status since it failed to restore to the emancipated the full extent of the freeman's original *libertas*.[10] The feudal system enlarged this distinction by introducing a military obligation which was required only of certain freemen. However, its contribution to the emergence of noble privilege needs careful qualification, especially as privileges could develop out of special military service in areas which at the time were either untouched or only partially affected by feudalism— for example, France south of the Loire, much of Spain, Sweden, Poland and Hungary.[11] Moreover, in feudal regions the development of noble privilege owed less to feudalism than to the transformation of knighthood from a professional occupation to an inheritable social rank. Furthermore, feudalism's insistence that rights and obligations should rest upon the fief rather than personal status prevented it from contributing much to the formation of the nobility's corporate privileges. Essentially, its insistence that privilege, like obligation, should be imparted by land tenure and not by noble status ensured the division of the noble order by gradations of privilege.

In contrast, the corporate privileges of the nobility emerged when privilege was conferred neither by land tenure nor special title but simply by the possession of noble status. This came of the nobility's exclusive acquisition of the corporate rights of the freemen. The annexation occured in two stages. First, the knights took over the military service obligations of the freemen and their attendant rights. However, the existence of commoner knights prevented these rights from appearing as simply noble privileges. The corporate privileges of nobility were founded only with the nobility's appropriation of the rights of knighthood. This followed the nobility's appreciation of the knightly profession as the ideal noble occupation and its monopolisation of knighthood. The latter was effected either by the official belief that only nobles could become knights or by the official assumption that the provision of mounted military service ennobled. With the disappearance of the non-noble knight in the twelfth and thirteenth centuries, a body of knightly rights became closely associated with the nobility, held not personally or in return for some specific task in the original, knightly manner but hereditarily and as the corporate attribute of noble status.[12] In England, where, perhaps because of the persisting influence of Danelaw, knights did not distinguish themselves from freemen by exclusively annexing their rights, and where it was never established that only nobles could become knights, and where knighthood was allowed to acquire only the fewest hereditary rights—no more than coats of arms and the title of esquire—and was not subjected to a special hereditary obligation of military service, and where, following the central imposition of feudalism by the Normans, the peers exclusively usurped the rights of the tenants-in-chief and attached them to membership of the upper house in parliament: all this shaped a noble order whose corporate privileges were minimal and whose special privileges by the end of the fourteenth century were abundant.[13] On the other hand, in France or Flanders, where knighthood acquired hereditary privileges and obligations and was eventually captured by the nobility, or in Sweden, Poland and Hungary, where mounted military service was rewarded with an extensive range of hereditary privileges and was regarded for a time as ennobling, the corporate rights of nobility were far more evident.

(c) The rights of rulers

By definition the privileges of the nobility were the rights of subjects. Nevertheless, many, notably the immunities and bannal rights, were originally the rights of rulers.[14] Their conversion into subject rights owed much to the development of the monarchical state. Several were usurped by subjects in times of political disorder. However, the Crown's political weakness could have the opposite effect, especially when it allowed a state to fragment into autonomous principalities and subjects to be transformed into independent princes. Certainly the breakdown of the Carolingian monarchy profoundly affected the development of noble privilege in the West by causing regalian rights to be alienated to subjects, but the process was also influenced by the achievement of the Capetians in preventing the political parcelisation which in much of Germany awarded former subjects autonomous ruler status. In the first instance much depended upon the superimposition of monarchy as a political organisation upon a motley collection of bannal lordships, a development which integrated conquered chiefs within the monarchical state, especially by permitting them to retain as subjects some of their rulership privileges, and also led to the alienation of regalian rights to leading subjects as a means of raising revenue and of securing their allegiance. At a later stage the rulership privileges which were thus converted to noble rights were maintained as a noble preserve by the Crown's ability to prevent their holders from becoming completely independent rulers.[15]

(d) Landlord rights

Seigneurialism rested on the capacity of landlords to require more of their tenants than simply the payment of rent. Its roots were the rights of the Roman latifundists and also the bannal rights of rulers which were alienated to subjects and in the process became interconnected with landownership. The survival of the latifundist rights in spite of the fall of Rome, their extension east of the Rhine by Frankish imperialism and their enlargement either as a result of the demotion of free tenants to serf status or the alienation to landlords of bannal rights, especially following the collapse of central authority in tenth- and eleventh-century Western Europe and its collapse in Eastern Europe in the late middle ages, helped to create the seigneurial system. Seigneurial rights were not wholly connected with landownership. Just as important a source were the lordship rights of slave owners and the bannal rights over territories rather than tenants. However, landlordship remained a central feature of seigneurial authority, if not an all-embracing one, its importance emphasised by the frailty or absence of the seigneurial system in regions where peasant allods predominated.

(e) Rights and the development of the state

Consolidating the privileges of nobility was the institutional development of the monarchical state, notably between the twelfth and fourteenth centuries.[16] The emergence of national systems of taxation helped to create the privilege of fiscal exemption or, at least, to give it definition. The development of national systems of royal justice extended and substantiated the nobility's judicial privileges, while the rise of representative assemblies and the state's development of military resources other than those of the militia and feudal service, especially in the form of standing armies, added to, and moulded, the nobility's repertoire of rights.

Disseminating the privileges of nobility was the dynastic aggrandisement to which the monarchical state was prone. The conjunction of states under one ruling family promoted the spread of noble privilege as kings were unable to resist the demands made by some of their noble subjects for the privileges which their other nobilities enjoyed. Royal dynasticism was frequently the means by which nobilities acquired the rights of neighbouring nobilities. For example, in Lithuania, Royal Prussia, Masovia, Livonia,

Kurland and Moldavia the desire of the traditional elite to acquire the greater privileges of the Polish nobility proved irresistible when they were ruled by the same Crown. Likewise, in Poland an important step in the formation of noble privilege was King Louis of Hungary's election to the Polish throne (1370), an event which realised the desire of the Polish nobles to ape the more highly privileged Hungarian nobles. A similar conferment of privilege occurred in the Aragonese Empire of the late middle ages: the extensive privileges of the Aragonese nobles were imparted to the nobles of Sardinia, Naples and Sicily when all became subjects of the same monarchy.[17] Privileges imparted in this manner tended, however, to be a one-way process, passing only from the nobility of the state in which the ruling family based itself to the other nobilities under its allegiance. Thus the privileges of the Aragonese nobility were not acquired by the Castilian nobles after the dynastic union of the two kingdoms in the late fifteenth century; and the privileges of the Hungarian nobility were not conferred upon the Austrian nobles when Hungary became a Habsburg possession in 1526.

Essentially, noble privileges were acquired because of the readiness of princes to authorise or confirm them as the rights not just of favoured individuals but of social groups which possessed some justifying feature in common. Responsible for their creation was not only the nobility's appreciation of them but also the Crown's willingness to permit their existence. In parts, the political or constitutional weakness of the Crown allowed its hand to be forced. Elective monarchy was clearly a spawning ground for noble privilege, especially when the nobles as electors could make the enlargement of privilege a condition of the next king's election. In each case the replacement of hereditary by elective monarchy in Poland, Bohemia and Hungary in the fourteenth century was an important landmark in the history of its nobility's privileges. Thus in Bohemia the basic source of noble privilege was the extinction of the Premyslides dynasty in 1307. In the following three centuries, through the accession to the throne of a number of foreign dynasties, each of them driven to make concessions to the nobility in return for its election, the privileges and powers of the nobility were founded, extended and confirmed. This happened notably in 1310 when the Luxemburgs ascended the throne, in the fifteenth century with the election of the Jagellons and again in 1526 with the succession of the Habsburgs.[18] In Poland nearly all the privileges of the nobility were acquired between 1374 and 1574, following the termination of the Piast dynasty and as a result of the concessions which the Crown had to make to persuade the nobles to comply with its plans for the succession to the throne. The Crown also needed to concede privileges in order to enlist noble support in its struggles against native magnates and for its extensive wars against the Teutonic Order (the concessions of 1454) and the Turk (the concessions of 1496). In Poland the privileges of nobility certainly ante-dated 1374 but were then confined to certain individuals and families who had been singled out to receive royal favour. In contrast, after 1374 the noble privileges tended to be awarded as a corporate right, except in the Grand Duchy of Lithuania, where, following the union with Poland in 1385, privileges similar to those of the Polish nobles were awarded only to the princes and the boyars. It was not until the sixteenth century that these privileges were extended to the whole range of landowners who owed military service to the state.[19] On the other hand, the noble privileges in Hungary were substantially formed before the establishment of elective monarchy in 1301. They derived from King Stephen's grant of privileges to the Magyar nation at the end of the tenth century and the Golden Bull of 1222 which converted the privileges of the nation into the privileges of the nobility. The contribution made by elective monarchy to the development of privilege in Hungary was to add extensive rights of landed lordship and of parliamentary representation to the existing range of privilege.[20]

Elective monarchs were not alone in generously granting privileges to the nobility. Hereditary monarchs also dispensed them, especially when impoverishment caused them to sell regalian rights, as, for example in fourteenth-century Brandenburg or sixteenth- and seventeenth-century Castile, Sicily and Naples; or when the possession of several kingdoms or principalities by one royal dynasty led to privileges being granted in order to secure the allegiance and co-operation of subject but alien elites, as in the dynastic empires of the Hohenzollerns and the Spanish and Austrian Habsburgs; or when the Crown was driven to concede privileges in order to enlist support for its retention of the throne and to strengthen its political effectiveness, as, for example, in Sweden in the century following the establishment of hereditary monarchy in 1544. But it would be totally misleading to regard monarchy as capable of creating and extending the privileges only when its permanent constitutional or temporary political disabilities allowed the nobility to take what it wanted. The capacity of absolute monarchy to grant new privileges as well as to tolerate old ones demonstrated that basic to the Crown's creation of noble privileges was its appreciation of the nobility as not only a ruling class but also a class which deserved to be juridically distinguished. Having crushed the Bohemian nobility at the battle of White Mountain in 1620 and after successfully asserting its right to rule Bohemia by hereditary rather than elective right, the Habsburg monarchy, which now stood more powerfully within the Bohemian state than any ruling dynasty since the Premislides, respected a number of traditional noble privileges and also created new ones, notably of a seigneurial kind. The royal absolutism established in Denmark in the 1660s likewise preserved old, and created new, privileges, allowing nobles a range of reserved offices and promotional favours in its bureaucracy and army as well as upholding until the early nineteenth century some of their traditional fiscal privileges and private jurisdictional rights. In Cleves and Mark the nobility's acquisition of rights of private jurisdiction and of exemption from the payment of direct taxes derived from the willingness of the Hohenzollern dynasty to permit their introduction in the late seventeenth century, while a range of traditional noble privileges formed one of the bases upon which Prussian absolutism stood. Yet in most cases royal absolutism only shaped a body of privilege established long before, usually in times of political weakness. Quite unique was Russia, where, in an attempt to westernise the state, royal absolutism in the late eighteenth century was responsible for introducing a whole corpus of noble privileges.[21]

Monarchy's ability to tolerate the privileges of the nobility was tried only when privilege seemed to impede the efficient operation of royal government. In this respect the privileges which proved most consistently obnoxious to kings were exemption from the payment of state taxes and some of the seigneurial rights, notably high justice and labour services. However, since neither the seigneurial system nor the concept of the nobility as a juridically privileged class was naturally repugnant to monarchy, the reforms carried out under the old regime, even those of the Hohenzollerns, Habsburgs and Bourbons, had no radical effect upon the privileged character of the nobility. They only altered the number and value of the privileges enjoyed. Privileges were removed, but others were allowed to stand, usually in a devalued state. Moreover, in exchange for the quashed privileges, other privileges tended to be granted. The effective enemy of noble privilege was republicanism, both in its medieval form, the urban communes of North Italy, and its modern form, the republican states created in the twentieth century, and whose threatened establishment in the nineteenth persuaded the Crown to seek salvation by proceeding against the birthrights of the nobility.

3 *Termination and survival*

The abolition of noble privilege, like its creation, was not peculiar to the modern or medieval periods but general to both. Privileges were still being created in the nineteenth century, while the removal of privileges stretched back to at least the twelfth and thirteenth centuries. Largely responsible for their eventual disappearance was the failure of governments to substitute new privileges for the ones they took away. Responsible for their survival was the traditional incapacity of governments to terminate the system: for centuries they could only reduce its advantages, eliminate certain rights or restrict the numbers of those entitled to enjoy it. All these reforms left the privileged status of the nobility altered but intact.

By 1850 the noble privileges had largely gone, yet by 1900 only Norway had permanently abolished all of them. Twenty years later, however, several states had followed suit, the cumulative result of government actions precipitated by a succession of revolutions. Furthermore by 1920 the capacity of privileges to survive revolutions as a result of the concessions made by revolutionary governments or the restorative acts of successful counter-revolution was no longer evident. Spain in 1947 and Hungary in the 1920s provide the last examples of a recovery process which had formerly helped to preserve the nobility's privileged position, notably in France, the Prussian monarchy, the Austrian Empire and several German principalities.[22]

The interacting opposition of peasants, artisans, professionalmen and some nobles put paid to many noble privileges and most seigneurial rights in the late eighteenth and early nineteenth centuries. The total elimination of privilege, however, usually accompanied the replacement of monarchy by republicanism, a development largely of the early twentieth century. By the late twentieth century privilege endured only as an honour, except in Great Britain where the peers retained parliamentary and judicial as well as honorific privileges, perhaps because its political revolutions occurred in the seventeenth century, long before noble privilege came to be regarded as a serious social grievance, and also because in the era of continental revolution the birthright element preserved itself by avoiding unresolvable conflict with the rest of the nation. In these circumstances the noble privileges fell in number and value but were not extinguished.

The seigneurial rights had largely disappeared by 1870. However, the process of elimination was already underway in the twelfth and thirteenth centuries when rights were either abandoned by lords or confiscated by princes and communes. Over the centuries landlords liberated themselves and their tenants of dues and services essentially by discovering and exploiting alternative sources of landed income: usually leasehold rent or the profits of direct farming with wage or slave labour. Much depended upon the density of the rural population and the landlord's opportunity to incorporate the traditional peasant tenures within the demesne, and so to abolish them. Abolition of the tenures opened the way for leasing land at an economic rent. It lessened the landlord's dependence upon seigneurial dues which basically served as compensation for a rent which, fixed by custom and devalued by inflation, tended to become practically worthless. Overpopulation allowed leasehold rents to be raised through creating a surplus demand for leases, and permitted wages to be kept low by producing an excess of labour, inducing landlords to cede their seigneurial rights. Such conditions prevailed over much of Europe in the nineteenth century, but had existed in earlier centuries: for example in the thirteenth century for much of Western Europe. In these periods landlords voluntarily abandoned seigneurial rights; and as a result the seigneurial system, in so far as it resided in the payment of dues and labour services, was in serious decline in Flanders, parts of the Rhineland and Northern and Central Italy by 1300, in Hungary, Bohemia and parts of Poland sometime before the government ordered its complete abolition in the course of the nineteenth century, and in England in the thirteenth and the late sixteenth/early seventeenth centuries, although in England depopulation particularly in the late fourteenth and early fifteenth centuries also played a vital part in the removal process.

By the thirteenth century the Crown in England and France had encroached extensively on private rights of jurisdiction, particularly high and middle justice, a consequence of its attempts to annex the considerable profits made from dispensing justice in private courts. The communes of Northern Italy waged a similar onslaught in the twelfth and thirteenth centuries upon the jurisdictions of the fiefholders in the adjacent *contado*. In the following centuries political centralisation, and the administrative developments which promoted it, furthered the reduction of patrimonial justice, so much so that what the government finally abolished in Prussia, Austria, Bohemia, France and Spain had become a very limited right. Other seigneurial rights which came under government attack long before the formal abolition of the seigneurial system were private rights of taxation, a victim of the national systems of taxation which developed in the thirteenth and fourteenth centuries, and labour services, although not before the eighteenth century and, except upon royal estates, with very little effect. In fact the reforms in estate management, as with the nationalisation of jurisdiction and taxation, rarely disposed of seigneurial rights in their entirety. Government tended to confine its reforms to private jurisdiction and taxation, while the reforms of the landlords were limited to dues and services. Unless the two processes coincided, as was the case in Northern Italy in the twelfth and thirteenth centuries, either the one or the other managed to survive. Mainly responsible for the endurance of lordship rights, however, was the view that the seigneurial system was an evil because of its excesses rather than because of its existence. Until the late eighteenth century this was held in common by dissident peasants, reforming landlords and critical governments. Initially, the belief that social improvement required the complete removal of seigneurial rights was a consequence not a cause of their abolition. It resulted from the dismantling of the seigneurial system in France between 1789 and 1793. The concept of complete abolition was then conveyed to the rest of Europe by the French Revolution and the revolutionary events of 1848. The acts of abolition carried out by revolutionary movements were successful because conservative governments when back in power could not afford to undo what revolution had granted, such was their dependence upon either peasant support or the absence of peasant opposition. The abolition of the seigneurial system, then, resulted from the government's struggle for popular support, especially when the political situation was complicated by the presence of a militant peasantry bent on physical protest. In August 1789, the French National Assembly acted upon a traditional fantasy that peasant rebels were revolutionaries, gave them more than they were demanding and, in doing so, unintentionally educated the peasantry to require abolition rather than reform. Consequently, the ensuing official acts of abolition, in France and elsewhere, were a direct response to peasant demands. In several instances the government's plans for the abolition of the seigneurial system were readily complied with by landlords who could perceive advantages in its termination. One was the redemption money which governments frequently required the peasants to pay their lord for their emancipation; another was the prospect of residing on the manor free from the molestation of a tenantry enraged by seigneurial exaction.

The abolition of the noble privileges also had a very long history, especially that of the fiscal, parliamentary and judicial indemnity rights. In Northern and Central Italy the fiscal exemption of the fiefholders was terminated before the close of the thirteenth century. Prior to 1789, exemption from at least direct taxation had been confiscated in Bohemia, Aragon, Saxony and Bavaria. In England the peerage had lost all but one of its fiscal privileges by 1700. Long before the disposal of the traditional estates parliaments, many parliamentary privileges of the nobility had disappeared either because the nobility ceased to attend parliament as an estate (e.g. in Baden, Württemberg, the Palatinate, Bamberg, Trier and Ancona) or because parliaments ceased to be convened (e.g. in Denmark, Brandenburg, Bavaria, Naples, Portugal and Sardinia).

Several privileges of judicial immunity, notably trial by peerage, were also confiscated centuries before the final termination of noble privilege. On the other hand, the removal of certain categories of privilege, especially the honorific and service immunity rights, was in the interest neither of princes nor lords and therefore they stood a better chance of survival than the privileges which handicapped the Crown. Fiscal and parliamentary rights became tolerable to a government when it could render them harmless either by introducing taxes from which the nobility had no immunity or by reducing the powers of parliament. Furthermore, in contrast to the reduction or removal of seigneurial rights, the removal of the noble privileges was frequently accompanied by the creation of new privileges. Thus, fiscal rights could be replaced by parliamentary rights; the right of fiscal exemption could give way to a right of special assessment; and the right of trial by peerage could be supplanted by the right to special processes in the law. Like the estates parliaments, some of the modernised parliaments allowed nobles rights of representation which depended not upon their citizenship but upon their noble status or the possession of a noble estate. Contributing to this process of renewal was the frequently demonstrated fact that the impact of revolution upon privilege could be undone by the privileges which the nobility could extract from successful counter-revolution.

Of the noble privileges which came under attack from both the old and the new order, the parliamentary ones showed the greatest powers of endurance. By 1900 they remained strongly entrenched, while the fiscal rights and those of reserved office had mostly gone under. The preservation of the parliamentary rights owed something to their association with privileges which, in being conferred by titles of nobility or the possession of noble estates, were non-corporate, and the fact that the onslaught waged by conservative and revolutionary governments in the eighteenth and nineteenth centuries mainly focused on the privileges imparted by noble status. Under the old regime in France, Spain, Poland, Hungary and Russia, governments moved by financial considerations had taken radical action against corporate noble privilege, notably by denying it to certain categories of lesser noble. The attack continued during the revolutionary era, the noble privileges removed in this period being mainly of the corporate kind. As a result, noble privilege tended to become largely confined to the titled nobility. In this respect, the manner in which noble privilege managed to survive helped to ensure its eventual downfall. This was because the process of survival made it increasingly difficult for commoners to secure nobility, and consequently accessibility, the traditional upholder of nobility, ceased to justify the existence of noble privilege in the eyes of the commonalty. Nevertheless, buttressed by the Crown, noble privilege endured in spite of society's antipathy towards it. Basically, the permanent abolition of noble privilege stemmed from the abolition of monarchy. Only two monarchies, those of Norway and Denmark, proved capable of the act of outright abolition and only in one republic (France) did noble privilege persist. Elsewhere it survived in conjunction with monarchy, although without political authority and only as the honorific right of the entitled, except in Great Britain. Furthermore, in the monarchies of the twentieth century the enjoyment of noble privilege was radically limited by the unwillingness of governments to grant hereditary titles and by a reversion to the early medieval practice of confining hereditary entitlement to members of the royal family. For the most part, hereditary privilege became attainable only through birth. Since the failure of family lines to propagate can no longer be effectively countered by new creations, noble privilege as an hereditary right will fade away with the gradual extinction of those entitled to enjoy it.

4 Effect

The noble privileges stratified the nobility by making distinctions between types of noblemen, as well as structuring society by distinguishing nobles from commoners. Since the second effect was not undone by the first, privilege helped to give the nobility a corporate identity. Moreover, because the privileges were bestowed by central government, they encouraged the nobility to adopt a national rather than a local or regional class-consciousness. Privilege was equally important in determining the nobility's social composition. Sustained by their privileges, nobles could lose all the other marks of nobility, yet remain definably noble. On the other hand, subjects could subscribe to a noble way of life and fulfil the functions expected of the nobility, but, without the right to enjoy the noble privileges, would nonetheless lack noble status. Privilege and nobility were so interconnected that the latter was not possible without the former. The existence of the corporate privileges meant that the nobility was not simply a class of titled lords, and even ensured that it contained members whose illiteracy and poverty rendered them incapable of a ruling function and who, apart from their privileges, lacked social advantage. Because of the corporate privileges the nobility could not be a plutocracy; it only became one in the late eighteenth and early nineteenth century with their abolition. Furthermore, the generally accepted convention of transmitting the corporate privileges to all the offspring of a nobleman guaranteed a high proportion of nobles who were either poor or of modest wealth. Traditionally the nobility included both the rich and the poor, the titled and the untitled, the landed and the non-landed, men with the expected ruling function and others who unexpectedly farmed, traded and manufactured. It was a miscellaneous class, then, held together, in spite of incorporating the whole spectrum of society, by commonly shared privileges, and hierarchically organised by the privileges which only some nobles were allowed to enjoy. Its composition and class-consciousness were essentially determined by privilege since it was the only constant distinction between noble and commoner. The existence of commoners with noble privileges and of nobles with very few privileges does not erase this distinction because nobles could never be totally without privilege whereas the commoners with noble privileges were social exceptions and tended to hold them differently from the nobles.

The noble privileges differentiated the European nobility not only from the elites of the present day but also from most other elites of the past. In the sophisticated political systems of the Moghul, Ottoman and Chinese Empires and in the more primitive polities of American, African and Asian tribes, hereditary privileges were usually confined to the monarchy, and nobility tended to be found only if implanted by European influence or rule. The elites of these societies were identified not by sanctioned, hereditary rights but by actual wealth, political function and non-heritable privileges.[23]

As a source of noble power and wealth, the value of the noble privileges depended upon whether or not they conferred rights of political participation, fiscal exemption and landlordship and the degree of advantage which these rights imparted. In addition, judicial privileges could save the noble money by allowing him to start proceedings in a higher court or by protecting him from the actions of his creditors. Noble banks with their low interest and their unwillingness to foreclose, and the noble's indemnity from the billeting of royal troops likewise provided the nobility with financial assistance. The other privileges were basically important as a source of social distinction or of personal convenience.

The value of parliamentary privilege relied upon the importance of the noble chamber in parliament and the political authority of parliament. In Poland and Hungary where the nobility had controlled parliament by means of its privileges and parliament enjoyed an overbearing influence in the running of the state, parliamentary privilege had awarded nobles a great deal of power. In many cases, however, the nobility's control of parliament had depended upon its ability to enlist the support of the clerical and commoner estates. As in Sicily and England, noble control of parliament rested upon the capacity of nobles to secure membership of the non-noble chambers or to influence them by patronage and policy. Furthermore, the limited authority of a parliament could neutralise the value of noble privilege. Many parliaments traditionally lacked legislative powers; many had their rights severely attenuated by royal absolutism. And since, in the English manner, the nobility's parliamentary privileges were frequently confined to one part of the noble order, they were often of no direct value to large numbers of nobles.

The privilege of reserved office could award the nobility a monopoly of state offices or of vital administrative posts, thus ensuring that the civil and military services were noble-dominated. Sometimes it provided the nobility with a control of the executive. However, reserved office does not fully explain the nobility's long-term political ascendancy. In only a small part of Europe did the privilege ever encompass the whole political system and where it was partial, minimal or non-existent, the nobility could maintain its ruling position as effectively as in states where the privilege was all-embracing. Sustaining the nobility as a ruling class was certainly its ability to occupy public office; but this usually resulted from society's acceptance of the nobility as the divinely ordained instrument of government, the Crown's conviction that its best means of social control was the nobility, the nobility's keenness to hold public office and the Crown's readiness to ennoble commoners who achieved high public office. Reserved office could be a means of persuading a 'rising bourgeoisie' to accept the nobility's social and political superiority, especially when it permitted office-holders automatic ennoblement and so increased the access to noble status; but office-holding privileges also played a vital part in the nobility's political decline. An important source of bourgeois support for revolution was the hostility which the noble privileges of reserved office and preferential promotion incited among commoner officials.

Notably in Poland, Hungary, Russia and France north of the Loire, all nobles drew considerable material benefit from their fiscal privileges since they were corporately held and effectively protected noble wealth against the main revenue-raising devices of the government. Yet in a number of states (e.g. in Brandenburg, France south of the Loire, Bohemia) fiscal privilege was confined to the owners of noble estates. Thus only some nobles and, because their estates were a compound of noble and commoner lands, only parts of their estate benefited from it. Furthermore, the nobility's fiscal immunity often applied only to a minor part of the tax system and was therefore unable to protect its beneficiaries from a weight of taxation. In early modern Castile, Aragon and Portugal the nobility's fiscal exemption was minimised by the government's heavy reliance upon forms of taxation which made no exception for noblemen. Because of the fiscal liability which had been imposed upon most nobilities by the late eighteenth century, fiscal exemption had become, with one or two exceptions, a source of social distinction rather than a major financial advantage, and, by this time, of greater material benefit to the nobility was the aptitude of its members to evade their fiscal obligations.

Seigneurial rights were of value to nobles both as a source of income and for providing them with a ruling function. Although lordship rights were not an essential component of nobility, they did impart much of its distinctive character as a political elite, especially through allowing nobles to exercise authority in local government apart from the tenure of public office. From the early middle ages landlords relied upon non-seigneurial sources of revenue, notably derived from working the demesne with hired labour or from leasing the demesne, but the durability of the customary tenures and the resurgence of serfdom in early modern Eastern Europe, left landlords over much of Europe dependent until the revolutionary era either upon labour services for demesne farming or upon seigneurial exactions. In depending upon tax evasion rather than tax exemption, in controlling parliaments not through the noble chamber but through the non-noble chamber and with most of its privileges confined to a small proportion of the nobility, the English aristocracy was more normal than is often alleged; but highly unusual was its capacity to become independent of the seigneurial system centuries before its abolition.

Seigneurial rights provided lords with a means of tenant control, but could also weaken their authority through generating a long tradition of peasant disobedience in the form of non-co-operation, flight or revolt. Of all the noble privileges, the seigneurial rights were the most capable of provoking popular antagonism. The opposition aroused in a middle class by reserved office and parliamentary privileges eventually combined with that of a peasantry incensed by seigneurial exactions to produce a movement of political revolution whose specific target was not the upper classes and their wealth but the nobility and its rights. In this respect privilege played a crucial role in the decline and fall of the nobility.

Also of special value was the privilege which confined the acquisition of land to the nobles (as in Russia, Poland and Hungary) or allowed only nobles to acquire noble estates (as in Austria, Bohemia, Bavaria, Sweden and Denmark). For the nobility this privilege was of great political and economic importance since it awarded the class the exclusive right to enjoy the privileges stemming from landownership which could include not only seigneurial rights but also parliamentary and fiscal privileges. In practice it certainly did not prevent commoners from possessing what the law denied them, but it did restrict the commoners' ability to compete with nobles in acquiring rights of landownership. The privilege was less than a blessing for the nobility. Essentially it reduced the competition for land. This favoured the noble purchaser but disadvantaged the noble vendor. For the latter reason the nobility offered little opposition to its removal, and in Poland, Hungary and Sweden positively supported its elimination. The privilege had little effect in ensuring that a high proportion of the land should be noble-owned in the sense that nobilities without the privilege tended to own an equally large share of private land.

The importance of privilege to the nobility is seriously questioned by its ability to remain powerful, wealthy and state-favoured in spite of the devaluation and abolition of its rights. The latters' loss in the early nineteenth century did not topple the nobility as a ruling class. Throughout most of Europe the nobility enjoyed a vigorous and assertive existence into the twentieth century, dominating the parliaments which replaced the estates assemblies, occupying the leading civil and military offices and effectively evading its obligations to the state. It achieved this much not by altering its ways but by intensifying and extending the old ways to compensate for the loss of privilege. The slowness with which both state and society abandoned their traditional habit of deferring to the nobility also helped. Equality of political participation and treatment was easy to conceive after 1789 but, because of the persistence of traditional attitudes, difficult to implement. Following the loss of its fiscal privileges, the nobility in a traditional manner protected its wealth by tax evasion. Until the twentieth century the state

persisted in supporting the nobility both by doing little to curb this offence
and by failing to tax capital. Over the centuries, the state had favoured the
nobility as much by its tax policy as by its acceptance of fiscal privilege. The
readiness of governments to tax consumption and their unwillingness to tax
wealth, except in the form of income, placed the nobles at an immense
advantage over the bulk of society. This avenue of favour remained open
until blocked by the introduction of death duties and wealth taxes in the
twentieth century.

Traditionally, the nobility's political power and influence had resided not
only in the privileges of lordship, reserved office and parliamentary membership but also in the ability of nobles to secure offices of state which were not
reserved for the noble order, to obtain control over non-noble parliamentary
chambers and to dominate tenants over whom they had no seigneurial right.
Securing offices of state relied heavily upon the government's willingness to
prefer noblemen for high office; obtaining parliamentary control chiefly
relied on the willingness of clergy and commoners to seek the patronage,
leadership and representation of noblemen; and peasants who were free of
seigneurial obligations could be effectively controlled by short term, rack-
rent leases. Thus, in spite of losing its privileges of political participation and
its seigneurial authority, the nobility retained power until some of these
favouring conditions faded away. This happened as the professional politician and administrator took over the political machine. Also responsible was
the not surprising failure of peasant emancipation and industrialisation to
restore the bonds of deference which had been weakened in the closing days
of the seigneurial system. Faced by democracy and professionalism, the
noblemen either bowed out of politics or survived by substituting a professional for an aristocratic mien.

Finally, the wealth of the nobility as a landed class easily outlived the
destruction of the seigneurial system. Terminating it was not the abolition
of seigneurial right but the disposal of estates either as a result of government
compelled land reforms or as a result of sales enforced either by poverty or
by the search for more profitable investments.

Juridical privileges had only been one source of advantage for the nobility.
Relatively underprivileged nobles like the English gentry or the non-baronial
Sicilian nobles had enjoyed political benefits equal to those of nobilities with
greater privileges. In fact, the capacity of a nobility to control politics cannot
be measured in terms of its juridical privileges since no simple inverse
relationship existed between the power of the state and the extent and value
of noble privilege. In political terms, nobilities could be highly privileged and
relatively weak or underprivileged but relatively strong. The same was true
of the relationship between seigneurial rights and noble wealth: nobles with
few seigneurial rights could be immensely wealthy landlords while nobles

with many seigneurial rights could be poor. Nonetheless although nobles repeatedly demonstrated their independence of them, it was privileges which in many cases actually awarded the nobility a ruling function, much of its wealth and some legal protection against the demands of the state. Moreover, it was noble privilege which accounted for a nobility's composition, self-awareness as a class, even its very existence. The abolition of all noble privileges signified the end of a nobility, except where the public willingness to recognise the continued use of former titles allowed it an unofficial afterlife.

The ideology of revolution presented privilege as an impediment on the development of the modern state and the modern economy. But in several respects, privilege promoted modernisation. For example, fiscal privilege interconnected with the development of direct taxation. Important in the emergence of a national system of taxation was the willingness of medieval lords to allow the intrusion of royal taxes upon their domains. This was conceded in exchange for privileges, especially the right of consent and the confirmation of personal fiscal exemption. Furthermore, regular direct taxation established itself more easily and earlier in states where the privilege of fiscal immunity cushioned the nobility against its effect. Privilege could be regarded as a device whereby royal governments extended their control of the state. Acting in a long tradition, royal absolutism implanted itself not by crushing the nobility but by securing its allegiance. This was accomplished by respecting and even extending some of the nobles' privileges, as well as by incorporating the nobility as a service class within the State apparatus. Since royal absolutism not only gave the government greater authority and power but also improved the state's machinery, particularly through the creation or extension of professional bureaucracies and standing armies, noble privilege, as an important factor in its development, played a part in the process of political modernisation.

Under the old regime, the Crown provided the dynamism and initiative for the reform of the political system. The nobles complied and co-operated with these changes to some extent because of the Crown's abiding respect for their right to be juridically privileged. Nobles had a more positive part to play in the development of representative systems of government. This also owed something to noble privilege. Parliaments originally developed in conjunction with the establishment of national systems of taxation and out of respect for noble rights. To override the nobility's fiscal immunity or the noble's sole right to tax his dependants, the principle of parliamentary representation became firmly and widely established. Because of its appreciation of parliament, a consequence of the system of privilege, and its capacity to resist the government, either in parliament or by armed revolt, the nobility helped to uphold the idea that the authority of the state should rest upon the consent of subjects as well as upon the divinity of the king, and that subjects as well as governments should have rights. Furthermore, implicit in the privileges of nobility were limitations on the authority of the state, the idea of consultation between ruler and ruled and the existence of a contract which, if breached either by king or subject, justified punitive action against the offender. As the traditional founder and protector of this pluralistic polity, the nobility contributed something to the development of democracy, even though their social values gave them no sympathy with it and their contribution to its realisation was little more than a grudging compliance with popular demand.

In encouraging nobles both to permit and to resist the growth of the state, their privileges contributed to its modernisation. Yet basic to the modernising process was the elimination of noble privilege. This was accomplished either by revolutionary governments or by traditional governments seeking to counter the threat of revolution. Central to the European revolutions of the late eighteenth and early nineteenth centuries was the issue of juridical privilege, enshrined in the demand for *égalité*. The attack on the nobility was a consequence of the popular hostility to its privileges just as the attack on monarchy followed the Crown's inability to disassociate itself from the noble order by disposing of these rights. In this sense, the role of privilege in the modernisation of the state was to provoke revolution and to mould its character by causing injustice to be defined as a discrepancy of juridical right rather than of wealth.

Both seigneurial rights and fiscal exemption have been regarded as sources of economic retardation. Yet there was no leap forward following their abolition. The farming community was oppressed and deprived for several reasons, not simply because nobles failed to pay certain taxes and imposed seigneurial exactions. The weight of taxation which oppressed the peasantry reflected upon the primitive nature of government finance, while indirect taxation reached a size capable of harming the economy not because of the nobility's immunity from direct taxation, as it has been alleged, but because it was a convenient means of bridging the gap between a government's income and expenditure. Seigneurial rights led to peasant exploitation but, by fixing rents, also allowed peasants the opportunity to accumulate capital. Moreover, the oppressiveness of seigneurial exactions often accompanied the domination of agriculture by direct landlord cultivation. In these circumstances, farming in general could be served rather than impeded by the seigneurial system. In fact, the seigneurial system could form a vital part of capitalist enterprises, both industrial and agrarian.

Noble privilege was central to the concept of the estates society. The estates society was essentially an organic political organisation based on the belief that there was a natural ruling class whose membership was determined not simply by performance or possessions but by an inherent quality expressed through birth or royal sanction. The natural ruling class was complemented by a natural ruled class. Upholding the system was the ability of the whole society to believe in it. By making distinctions between the political rights of nobles and commoners, and by allowing noble rights to be conferred by birth, noble privilege gave a specific form to the estates society. By virtue of its privileged nobility, the estates society differed from the modern class society, essentially an economic structure whose rights are not socially divisive but protect the citizen from the actions of the state, and whose elites are only sustained by the informal advantages conferred by the possession of wealth and power. To what degree did privilege impede the development of modern society? Class relations, with a social evaluation dependent upon wealth, developed not as a result of the decline and fall of the estates society but traditionally existed within its living body. Their development was neither discouraged nor retarded by the existence of privilege. Moreover, seigneurial rights eventually undermined the estates society by generating friction between noble and peasant and played a vital role in demolishing it by allowing massive popular support for the repudiation of nobility as the one and only ruling class. By becoming a source of social antagonism the privileges of nobility ensured that the beliefs of the estates society should be rejected in the first bout of revolution; class only became a target in later bouts. Privilege, however, had exerted a highly conservative influence on the mentality of the bourgeoisie. The broad base given to the nobility by privileges which were imparted by the possession of noble status, as opposed to titles of nobility, and the generosity of the Crown in granting noble status to members of the bourgeoisie had made nobility acceptable, through its accessibility, to the economically dominant element within the commonalty. Only with the removal of noble privilege was the bourgeoisie liberated from its noble orientation. The redefinition of the noble order caused by the loss of the corporately-held privileges, ensured that the work of revolution would be consolidated by the formation of a new elite consisting predominantly of a bourgeoisie freed of its traditional social aspirations, equipped with a sense of social superiority which formerly only the nobility had emitted and capable of abandoning the idea that there was a naturally ordained social order higher than itself. This change in the bourgeoisie's outlook did not necessarily express a relentless antagonism to the nobility. Allied by the fear of democracy and the licence which both thought it would give to the propertyless masses, nobles and bourgeois in the late nineteenth century were capable of reaching a mutually appreciative *modus vivendi* which reflected something of the bourgeoisie's traditional respect for the nobility. Moreover, the bourgeoisie's change in attitude towards the nobility did not completely break its traditional habit of noble imitation. Among the bourgeoisie there persisted the customary inclination of putting wealth, in the noble manner, to non-productive uses such as the acquisition of property and the purchase of other marks of elite status. Just as class relations thrived within the corpus of the estates society, the preoccupations of the estates society outlived the demolition of noble privilege.

II

Fiscal privilege

The nobles were fiscally privileged not simply because of the opportunities available to them for evading their obligation to pay taxes and not only because of the prevalence of taxes which, in applying to consumption or income rather than to capital, fell lightly upon noble wealth.

Essentially, their fiscal privilege was a collection of rights, all of them sanctioned by the government and most of them the special possession of the noble order. It included fiscal exemption; the right to tax or to pocket state taxes; the right to a more favourable tax assessment than the commonalty; the right of consent to the levy of taxes granted by parliament; and the right to collect and apportion the taxes paid by their tenants to the state. Of medieval origin, fiscal privileges continued to be created for the nobility until the nineteenth century. The long process of creation was accompanied by one of abolition; although the privileges were for the most part eliminated in the nineteenth century, their demolition extended well into the middle ages. Fiscal privilege was finally terminated because the process of elimination ceased to be accompanied by a process of recreation.

1 Fiscal exemption

Exemption from the payment of taxes served over the centuries as a chief distinguishing mark of nobility. Yet it was never enjoyed by all the European nobilities. Moreover, it tended to appertain, especially with regard to direct taxation, to no more than a fraction of a nobility's membership and generally it applied only to certain taxes, not the whole revenue system. Anomalously, in some states privileges of fiscal exemption which, although noble, were denied to certain elements of the nobility could be enjoyed by non-nobles, both lay and clerical. In fact, large numbers of commoners legitimately enjoyed fiscal exemption, in spite of its close association with the nobility: as owners of noble estates; as government officials; as members of privileged occupations such as doctors and lawyers or of privileged corporations, such

as universities or the Inquisition; as the inhabitants of privileged town-ships
and provinces; as specially honoured individuals; as the tenants of tax-free
nobles; or simply on grounds of poverty. By these means, nobles could
acquire a fiscal right which their nobility did not qualify them to enjoy.[1]

The nobilities which never possessed fiscal exemption, or enjoyed the
privilege not as a traditional right but only for a very limited period, were in
a small minority. The Tuscan nobles lost their privilege in the mid-thirteenth
century. The Venetian, and possibly the Silesian, nobles never enjoyed the
privilege, while those of East Prussia and the British Isles only possessed it
briefly and very restrictedly.[2] Elsewhere it prevailed, but did not usually free
the nobles from making some financial contribution to the government. In
spite of the widespread rights of fiscal immunity, most nobilities remained
liable to state taxation and a variety of other government exactions in the
form of loans, feudal dues, the commutation of feudal services and payments
for the purchase of titles or offices of state.

Among the nobilities most extensively exempted from state taxation were
those of Brandenburg and Hungary. Established in 1281, the fiscal immunity
of the former was probably at its greatest in the late seventeenth century
after the Recess of 1653 had reformed the tax system but had carefully
respected the nobility's traditional rights, allowing them exemption from the
land tax and from most customs dues. Moreover, the government's decisions
in 1667 and 1680 to restrict the operation of the general excise to the towns
permitted the nobility's traditional immunity from taxes on goods purchased
for home consumption to survive. Protected in this way by royal absolutism,
the nobility for a time legitimately enjoyed a freedom from much of the fiscal
system. The substance of its fiscal immunity only went after 1799 when the
nobility was subjected to customs dues on all its exports and on its impor-
tation of luxury articles, and after 1820 when it was made liable to a
graduated income tax as well as a tax on consumption.[3] Yet prior to these
measures, the Brandenburg nobility was not completely free of fiscal obligations. Since its immunity from direct taxation was traditionally conferred
by the ownership of a legally defined noble estate, many nobles had lacked
the privilege. As for the owners of noble estates, even when under obligation
to provide military service, which still persisted in the late seventeenth
century, they were nonetheless made liable to state taxation: for example, in
1569 the government introduced a levy on the export of all corn, a due which
would have fallen heavily on the nobles as corn producers dependent on
foreign sales, if they had not managed to evade its payment; the general
excise established in the late seventeenth century affected the nobles if they
bought from the towns; and in 1717 an annual tax was imposed upon them
in commutation of their military service.[4]

The fiscal immunity of the Hungarian nobles likewise encompassed direct and indirect taxation, but a large section of the nobility lost it long before its abolition. From 1222, when fiscal exemption was conferred as a noble right rather than a right of the Magyar nation, until 1849 when it was terminated, the fiscally exempt nobles contributed to the state revenue only by means of voluntary contributions in time of war—for example, in 1741 and in the following wars of the eighteenth century—and also from what the Crown could extract by manipulating its regalian monopoly to sell salt. Unlike the Brandenburg nobles, the Hungarian nobility was never made to commute its obligation of military service to the state for a sum of money; nor was it under obligation to pay the Crown feudal dues. On the other hand, from the fifteenth century, it had to pay county taxes, although many nobles managed to escape this obligation in the seventeenth century and remained free of it until 1847.[5]

The other nobilities tended to enjoy less extensive rights of fiscal immunity, largely because exemption at any one time was either confined to indirect or to direct taxation or restricted to a small corner of the fiscal system. Over a large part of Europe, fiscal exemption left the nobility exposed to a broad range of taxes and frequently served less as a protection against taxation than a mark of social status. Notably liable to the payment of state taxes were nobilities whose immunity was confined to indirect taxation. In East Prussia the nobility's fiscal exemption safeguarded it from the excise established in 1655 and the earlier excise on beer. Yet the immunity only covered what was bought or made for personal consumption. With these exceptions, the Hohenzollerns maintained in East Prussia the traditional practice of the Teutonic Order, the former owners of the duchy, requiring much the same fiscal liability of the nobles as of the commons. As a result, over a very long period this nobility was liable to a weight of direct taxation from which it found protection not in privilege but in evasion.[6] In England the peerage came to possess the right to buy a certain amount of wine duty free for home consumption. Otherwise, its liability, apart from the early medieval danegeld, was no different from that of the rest of society.[7] In Poland, the nobility had acquired exemption from the salt tax by 1454, from the state tolls and customs by 1496 and from the tax on alcoholic drinks by 1500. However, much of this exemption only applied to goods bought for the noble's own use or directly produced by him. Moreover, the nobility remained subjected to the land tax until relieved of it in 1629 and had become liable to the poll tax by the close of the seventeenth century and to a general income tax by the late eighteenth century. In addition, their fiscal liability extended to the *quarta*, the tax on the income from royal estates, and a chimney tax.[8] In Bavaria exemption from indirect taxation replaced exemption from direct taxation in the course of the sixteenth century. Since direct taxes continued to be levied and the nobility's immunity failed to cover the whole range of indirect taxes, the Bavarian nobles attained a high degree of fiscal liability long before the abolition of the privilege in 1749.[9] The nobles of Upper and Lower Austria and Tyrol likewise enjoyed a minimal fiscal exemption. Their freedom merely applied to the payment of state toll and customs dues on provisions bought for home consumption. Between the fifteenth and seventeenth centuries several taxes fell upon them: excises on the sale of alcoholic drinks as well as direct taxes, both regular (*Landsteuer* and *Haussteuer*) and irregular (*Türkensteuer* and *Kopfsteuer*). In not allowing noble exemption, the *Kontribution* which the Habsburgs established as their main direct tax in 1749 followed in a long tradition. Liability, however, did not necessarily entail payment. This was notoriously the case with the *Haussteuer* whose apportionment and collection was a seigneurial right, the manipulation of which allowed landlords to make a profit from its levy.[10] In Poland a similar collecting right enabled the nobles to evade payment of the general income tax introduced in the early eighteenth century by Augustus II.[11]

In several states where the nobles' immunity was confined to direct taxation, the privileged became highly exposed to the fiscal system when indirect taxes, especially excises, developed as a major source of government revenue. In Castile, for example, the nobility's exemption was limited to the *servicio ordinario y extraordinario*, a hearth tax which, having originated as an extraordinary levy dependent on consent, had become by the late fifteenth century an almost annual imposition, and to the *moneda forera*, a regular, arbitrary levy exactable every seven years.[12] Although the privilege of exemption survived until the abolition of the *servicio* in 1795, its value to the nobility was reduced from the fifteenth century onwards by the government's heavy reliance upon indirect taxes, especially the *alcabala* and the *millones*, from which the nobility could claim no immunity, and by the freezing in the late sixteenth century of the revenue levied from direct taxation. By the late eighteenth century, the *servicio* contributed no more than $2\frac{1}{2}\%$ of the annual revenue raised in Castile. Thus, in eventually excusing it from only a very small part of the tax system, the fiscal immunities of the Castilian nobility acquired an essentially honorific value. Responsible for the Castilian nobles' fiscal liability, however, was not just the preponderance of indirect taxes but also the introduction in the early seventeenth century of direct taxes which fell specifically upon the nobility: the *derecho de lanzas* and the *milicias*, both of them commutations of military service, the former applying to the grandees and *títulos*, the latter to the rest of the nobility, and the *medias anatos*, a tax paid by titled nobles upon succeeding to their patrimony and by officials upon entering office.[13] In Portugal the nobility's fiscal exemption applied only to the *subsidio*, an extraordinary direct tax requiring parliamentary consent.

From the late fourteenth century excises (*sisas*) were levied on the whole of Portuguese society. By the sixteenth century they provided the bulk of the government's revenue and in the course of the seventeenth century the *subsidio* and the *cortes*, the parliamentary assembly whose principal function was to grant it, fell into abeyance. As a result, the nobles retained a fiscal privilege of no material value.[14] The same was true of Catalonia, Aragon and Valencia, the three provinces of the Crown of Aragon where, following the union with Castile in the late fifteenth century, indirect taxation replaced direct taxation as the means by which the limited tax demands of the Crown were met and therefore in practice the nobility's exemption, which related only to direct taxation, allowed them no immunity. Its elimination prevented it from regaining value when direct taxation was restored in the early eighteenth century.[15]

In Lombardy the nobility also acquired an extensive liability long before the abolition of its fiscal immunity in the late eighteenth century, again because the privilege was confined to direct taxation and the government became heavily reliant upon indirect taxes.[16] The Bohemian nobles suffered a similar fate, enjoying immunity from the *Haussteuer* on their demesnes until the reorganisation of direct taxation in 1749, but subjected to the rest of the fiscal system which included a regular direct tax, the *Landsteuer*, duties on alcoholic drinks, salt and tobacco and irregular direct taxes such as the *Türkensteuer* and *Kopfsteuer*.[17] The Russian nobility was likewise blessed with an immunity from direct taxation, at least from the sixteenth century until 1887. In their case, exemption applied to all direct taxation, except for the short-lived land tax of 1812 and the levy briefly imposed by Tsar Paul I (1796-1801), but not to indirect taxation which furnished the government with much of its revenue.[18]

Several nobilities enjoyed a simultaneous exemption from direct and indirect taxes, yet suffered, nonetheless, a heavy fiscal liability. In Sweden, for example, nobles were traditionally exempted from the land tax, from the customs dues on the export of their own and their peasants' farm produce and from the *régale*, a tax on the iron mined on noble estates. Exemption from the land tax was also allowed their tenants.[19] However, although retaining the privilege until the first decade of the twentieth century, the Swedish nobles were liable to a weight of taxation from the seventeenth century onwards. Their exemption from the traditional customs dues was confirmed in 1612, but in 1622 a new customs duty was created—the Little Toll—which fell indescriminately upon the whole community. Then, in 1644 the nobles renounced their immunity from the traditional customs dues. In addition, a great deal of direct taxation included the Swedish nobility. Apart from the ordinary revenue which was levied by prerogative right and admitted the noble privilege of exemption, there were the extraordinary revenues which were irregularly exacted, required the consent of the realm and, but for the poll tax introduced in the early seventeenth century, affected noble and commoner alike. From the early years of the seventeenth century, the government grew more reliant upon the second category of revenue which included personal contributions, taxes on officers' and officials' pay and taxes on servants.[20] Closely related in character was the history of fiscal privilege in Denmark. The Danish nobility retained the privilege of fiscal exemption until the nineteenth century, but became subjected to a large number of indirect and direct taxes following the establishment of royal absolutism in the 1660s. The latter introduced excises along Dutch lines which allowed no immunity for the nobles. It also imposed a new land tax which first eliminated the exemption previously enjoyed by the nobility and their tenants and then readmitted the privilege in 1671, although in a much restricted form, by allowing the nobles exemption from the new land tax on the income of their demesne lands. As they were held responsible for collecting the land tax from their tenants, the nobles became liable to pay the difference in cases of default.[21]

From the fourteenth century until the Revolution, the French nobles enjoyed exemption from both direct and indirect taxes, yet the privilege applied only to the *taille* and its forerunners, and also to the *subsistances* and *étapes* taxes, as well as to a small part of the indirect tax system, chiefly the *huitième*, a tax on the retail sale of wine and the *gros*, a tax on the wholesale of wine. If the wine was home-grown, noblemen could sell it free of these two taxes. They were also excused the payment of the *huitième* on wine which they bought in quantity for their own consumption. In certain provinces nobles had the right to purchase a range of duty free provisions for the home.[22] On the other hand, many taxes developed over the centuries to which the nobility were as liable as the commonalty. This was true of several subsidies levied in the fourteenth century, notably those of 1347, 1348 and 1356, and the *capitation* (1695), the *dixième* (1710) and the *vingtième* (1750). In addition, several exactions fell particularly on the nobles: for example, the scutages imposed in the thirteenth and fourteenth centuries and again in the sixteenth and seventeenth centuries, the feudal dues owed by fiefholders to the Crown and other nobles and the *taxes d'office* raised in the *pays d'élection* in the mid-seventeenth century. As office-holders the nobility was also subjected to the *paulette* from 1604, an annual tax which guaranteed the hereditary ownership of office.[23] Furthermore, by the eighteenth century many indirect taxes awarded no right of exemption to the nobility. These included the *sous pour livre* (surtaxes on the retail trade), the *augmentation* (a surtax on the wholesale wine trade), the royal *octroi* on livestock, the *gabelle* and the *douanes*.[24] Moreover, the nobles of the *taille réelle* regions were heavily exposed to direct taxation since only about one quarter of their landed possessions qualified for exemption as noble estates.[25] In the regions of the *taille personnelle* the regulations of 1634 and 1667 which restricted the noble's right of immunity to a portion of his income—that deriving from one house and its estate, the estate being defined as manageable with no more than four ploughs—rendered the nobility taillable, while the *chambre des comptes* could require the newly ennobled to pay compensation for the taxes lost by their acquisition of fiscal exemption.[26] The government could also tap noble wealth by non-fiscal means: by reducing the fees of office (*gages*), by devaluing state bonds (*rentes*), by the sale of office, by the demand for loans as well as by the revocation and reissue of *lettres d'enoblissement*. What protected the French nobles from the revenue demands of the state was not the extent of their fiscal exemption, but the fact that over the centuries the direct levies from which they enjoyed exemption provided the government with the bulk of its tax revenues.[27]

Like most other German principalities, Saxony allowed its nobility immunity from both indirect and direct taxes. Yet the exemption from indirect taxation was typically restricted to the sale of home-grown produce and the purchase of goods for home consumption, while exemption from direct taxation was confined to the fiefholders who were, nonetheless, liable to the land tax on their estates which did not form a recognised part of the fief and were expected, as in 1529, 1541-2 and 1557, to pay tax on all their estates in time of emergency. They were also capable of making voluntary contributions to the government, as in 1622 when they acquitted the elector's debts. Furthermore, they continued to fulfil their traditional military obligations, the prime reason for their fiscal exemptions, raising, for example, two companies of cavalry in 1684 and paying scutage in 1639 and 1659. Exemption in Saxony was virtually ended in 1705 when a general excise was extended to the countryside and in 1763 when a poll tax was levied on the whole community. But these reforms only increased the nobility's fiscal liability; they did not create it.[28]

Exempted from the payment of both direct and indirect taxes, the Sicilian nobility was another example of immunity co-existing with liability. Its fiscal exemption, largely the result of a system of parliamentary taxation first introduced in the fifteenth century and finally ended in the early nineteenth century, was restricted to the fiefholders and was only partial: of the eighteen taxes in operation in the 1780s, the accumulation of the previous three centuries, five fell upon the whole community. In addition, both Habsburg and Bourbon tapped the wealth of the Sicilian nobility through feudal dues, scutage and the sale of offices, titles, fiefs and regalian rights. A roughly similar system operated in the kingdom of Naples, although the degree of exemption from direct taxation was broader since immunity from the capitation tax was not confined to the fiefholders, but was enjoyed by the nobles as a class. In Naples only exemption from the land tax was an exclusive fiefholder's right.[29]

Although the mark of the noble order, the rights of fiscal exemption were not always equally enjoyed by every member of a nobility. In many states a distinction existed between the nobles entitled to enjoy all the nobility's privileges of exemption and the nobles with the right to enjoy only some of them. The outstanding arbiter was the ownership of an estate legitimately defined as noble either because of its obligation to provide military service or because of its rights of patrimonial jurisdiction. Further distinctions were created within the noble order by the government's policy of retaining fiscal exemption while reducing the numbers of nobles with the right to enjoy it.

Whereas in Northern and Central France exemption from the taille rested upon noble status, in the south—particularly in Languedoc, Provence, Dauphiné, the *pays* of Bigorre and Roussillon, the *élections* of Agen and Condom, the *généralités* of Auch and Montauban—it was confined to the owners of noble estates.[30] Elsewhere in Europe exemption from direct taxation tended to follow either of these practices. In the Kingdom of Naples it followed both. In France the presence of nobles without noble estates in the Midi meant the existence of nobles who paid the *taille*. Nobles could be as liable to direct taxation as commoners in most of the German principalities, Bohemia, Sweden, Denmark, Sicily and Piedmont where fiscal exemption was likewise conferred not by noble status but by the ownership of a noble estate. In some of these states the rights of exemption were more restricted than in others. For example, in Sicily, Saxony and Piedmont it was confined to the fiefholders, while in Brandenburg, Bohemia, the south of France, Sweden and Denmark it was restricted to estates which had acquired over the centuries a noble definition. In the duchies of Jülich and Berg the government imposed a severe restriction in the late sixteenth century when it confined the nobles' exemption from direct taxation to one fief per noble family. In none of these instances was a nobleman's ownership of land a sufficient qualification for exemption. In other words, exemption was not simply a consequence of nobility. Essentially it was a right attached to certain forms of property. Normally this type of immunity appertained to direct taxation. In contrast, exemption from indirect taxes was usually a corporate right. As a result, a noble's liability to direct taxation could be compensated with an exemption from indirect taxation. Rather than being with or without exemption, the members of these nobilities tended to be unequally exempt, some enjoying immunity from a greater range of taxes than others.[31]

Immunity from direct taxation was not often imparted simply by noble status. In addition to parts of Northern and Central France, the privilege took this corporate form in Castile, Portugal, Poland, Hungary, Naples, and Russia.[32] In several of these states, the government sought to curtail the noble's fiscal immunity long before the final abolition of the privilege, not only by introducing taxes to which it did not apply, but also by reducing the number of nobles in possession of the right. This was done in seventeenth-century France, eighteenth-century Castile, post-partitioned Poland and eighteenth and nineteenth-century Russia by detecting spurious noblemen and dismissing them from the noble order or by denobling sections of the nobility. The effect was to reduce the size of the nobility.[33] On the other hand, in Hungary the government's policy was to deprive certain parts of the nobility of some of their privileges. This created a class of noblemen distinguished from the rest of the order by their lack, or limited possession, of fiscal exemption. The Hungarian nobility may have been fiscally overprivileged, but a large section of it lost the right to enjoy the immunities in full centuries before their total abolition in the mid-nineteenth century. In 1720 a nobility which composed about 5% of the population formed 3.6% of the taxpayers and the imperfect census of 1754–5 recorded that, of the 32,000 families registered as noble, 14,000 fell into the taxable category of the population. They were the minor nobles with very small estates or no estates at all. This sizeable group had been subjected to state taxes in the sixteenth century, although in 1723 it was relieved of them as a permanent obligation and was not finally subjected to them on a regular basis until 1836. The same group had also failed to secure exemption from the payment of county taxes which Matthew Corvinus in the late fifteenth century had imposed exclusively upon the noble order and from which the high and middle nobles had gained exemption by the eighteenth century. Thus, when the Hungarian nobility's immunity from paying county and state taxes was abolished between 1847 and 1849, only the upper and middling nobility was seriously affected, the numerous remainder having lost their fiscal immunity long before.[34]

The privilege of fiscal exemption was never restricted solely to the nobility. Nor was the clergy the only non-noble element to possess the right. Collectively or individually, it was widely enjoyed by the commonalty, although not as an order. When the privilege interconnected with landownership, commoners attained it simply by purchasing a noble estate. It is true that for a time in Bohemia, Brandenburg, Denmark and Sweden this was forestalled by a law forbidding commoners to own noble estates, but only in Bohemia did this law outlive the fiscal exemption imparted by landownership. In the other states, the removal of the law long preceded the abolition of the fiscal privilege: as a result, commoners could acquire fiscal exemption through the purchase of land in Brandenburg from 1807 to 1861, in Denmark from 1660 to 1818 and in Sweden from 1810 to 1892.[35]

Elsewhere, in the France of the *taille réelle* and in parts of Italy, notably Sicily and Naples—areas where noble estates awarded fiscal exemption but not noble status and their ownership was not legally restricted in the law to noblemen—commoners over several centuries enjoyed fiscal exemption as a perquisite of landownership. In France, commoners came to enjoy the privilege by this means in greater numbers after the *Ordonnance de Blois* of 1579 had outlawed the possibility, which had legitimately existed since 1275, of securing noble status simply by owning a fief, and thereafter allowed commoners to enjoy its privileges in return for the payment of the *franc-fief*.[36] In other states, commoners with tax-exempting estates were not subjected to special fiscal demands but only paid the various feudal dues and scutages to which these estates were normally subjected.

Commoners also acquired fiscal immunity through the exemption of whole townships from the payment of taxes. In France, this practice originated in the closing stages of the Hundred Years War. The Crown dispensed the privilege so generously that as a result, by the eighteenth century, possibly 4% of the non-noble population enjoyed exemption from the *taille*—over twice the number of subjects enjoying the privilege by right of their nobility or the ownership of a noble estate. Urban exemption applied also to the *aides*, certain townships in the *pays d'aides* enjoying the noble and clerical immunity from the *gros* and the *huitième*.[37] Similarly in Castile several were granted fiscal exemption, mainly in the fifteenth century and notably in the regions bordering Portugal and Granada. Some of these townships enjoyed immunities in excess of those of the nobility, having the right of exemption from the *alcabala* as well as from the *servicio*, just as in France the *villes franches* acquired a greater fiscal immunity than the nobility when they were exempted from the *vingtième* in the mid-eighteenth century.[38] From the late middle ages some degree of fiscal exemption was also the right of residents in the huge cities of Naples and Palermo. In sixteenth- and seventeenth-century Poland the nobility's immunity from tolls was shared by the citizens of Warsaw, Włocławek and Brześć Kujawski. In addition to privileged townships, the Spanish and French monarchies possessed privileged provinces: for example, in Spain natives of Viscaya enjoyed freedom from royal taxes; in France the *pays francs* did not pay the *gabelle*, and the *pays d'exempts* did not pay the *aides*, the two areas roughly coinciding, while the Boulonnais, the *élection* of Bordeaux and several *pays* on the Pyrenean border (Foix, Nébouzan and Labourd) were exempted from the payment of the *taille*.[39]

Fiscal exemption was imparted by certain occupations, notably in the public administration and military service. In France, it became the perquisite of certain officials from the fourteenth century onwards. By the late seventeenth century the king's household servants, the members of the sovereign courts, royal secretaries, *élus*, the officials of the bailiwick and *élection* were all free of the *taille*.[40] In Prussia and Russia, absolute monarchy conferred some fiscal immunity upon its commoner officials and officers in the course of the eighteenth and nineteenth centuries.[41] In several countries fiscal immunity was enjoyed by the officials and servants of the nobility.[42] In parts of medieval Europe, notably in Sweden, Castile, Portugal, Poland and Hungary, it was frequently granted to subjects who merely provided mounted service for the king or the commune. Many of the recipients became ennobled but not always immediately and so formed, for a time, a class of privileged, commoner knights.[43] In certain countries, fiscal immunity was acquired by the legal and medical professions: in late medieval Portugal and Piedmont by the lawyers, by medical doctors in the Crown of Aragon after 1626 and by notaries in eighteenth-century Naples.[44] Fiscal immunity also accompanied lay membership of the Inquisition. As familiars, commoners secured freedom from state taxes in sixteenth- and seventeenth-century Portugal and Sicily. Like residence in Palermo, service as a familiar allowed Sicilian nobles to acquire or to extend their fiscal exemption. Furthermore, in both Castile and France the graduates and members of certain universities were exempted from *servicio* or *taille*. In 1832 the Russian government created an order of 'honoured citizens' for lesser state officials, meritorious writers, academics and businessmen which was exempted from the poll tax.[45]

Reviving a traditional practice, the Swedish Crown in the seventeenth century exempted from the land tax Swedish and Finnish peasants who agreed to furnish it with properly equipped cavalry. In this way, 10% of the Finnish peasantry came to be fiscally privileged. By making this concession, the Crown continued the practice which had originally established the privilege of fiscal exemption in Sweden. However, whereas the noble privilege had become the hereditary right of estates whose owners formerly, but no longer necessarily, provided the king with military service, the privilege granted to the peasantry by Gustavus Adolphus and Charles XI was a personal, uninheritable right strictly conditional upon the provision of cavalry. For this reason the fiscal exemption enjoyed by Swedish and Finnish peasants in the seventeenth century differed in kind from that of the Swedish nobility.[46]

In most cases the fiscal immunities of commoners were quite distinct from those of the nobility. They were never a corporate right of the commonalty. Moreover, except for what he acquired through the ownership of a noble estate, the commoner normally possessed fiscal exemption as a personal right; in contrast, the noble normally held it by birthright. The commoner's fiscal exemption usually depended upon his personal fulfilment of specific requirements: for example, residence in certain towns, or the actual performance of certain services, or the achievement of special qualifications. Originally the nobility's right to enjoy fiscal exemption was saddled with similar personal requirements, but outlived them. Except for the nobles who secured tax rights by non-noble means, the nobility whose fiscal exemption most closely resembled that of the commonalty was the personal nobles of France

and Russia.[47] In neither case was the right hereditary; but both differed from
the privileged commoner in possessing a greater range of privileges. Whereas
the noble's fiscal privileges formed a small part of the privileges in his
possession, the commoner's fiscal privileges tended to exist either in isolation
or accompanied by only one or two other noble rights. Finally, although
nobles were frequently immune to certain indirect taxes, this particular
immunity is rarely found among the fiscal privileges of the commonalty.
However, in certain states this distinction was reversed: in Castile the nobility
was liable to all state indirect taxes, but both the clergy and the inhabitants
of certain towns were exempt from the *alcabala*; similarly in France the
gabelle allowed exemption, but not to the nobles *per se*.[48]

Nevertheless, certain groups of commoners did enjoy their fiscal exemption in the noble manner. For instance, the noble privileges allowed university
doctors in Provence were transmissible to their children. The privileges of
'honoured citizens' in nineteenth-century Russia could be conferred on an
hereditary as well as a personal basis.[49] Many commoners with privileges
akin to those of the nobility were found in the Iberian peninsula where, in
the course of the Reconquest, commoners as well as nobles had been awarded
fiscal exemption in return for providing mounted military service. In Catalonia they were termed *ciutatans honrats*, in Valencia *ciudadonos honrados*,
in Castile *caballeros villanos* and in Portugal *cavaleiros-vilãos*. By acquiring
an hereditary right to their privileges and extending their range, these commoner knights came to hold privileges in a manner which closely resembled
that of the nobility. Eventually they disappeared either through elevation
into the nobility or demotion into the unprivileged commonalty. But this
process took time. In Castile, the *caballeros villanos* were assimilated with
the nobility in the fourteenth and fifteenth centuries. The remaining commoner knights—*caballeros de cuantia* which Phillip II had sought to revive
in 1562—were suppressed by royal edict in 1619. In Catalonia and Valencia
the commoners with hereditary privileges survived until the government
conferred nobility on some of them and deprivileged the remainder in the
course of the eighteenth century.[50]

Very similar were the *włodyki* of Poland who disappeared in the fifteenth
century either through inclusion in the nobility or demotion into the unprivileged commonalty, and a group of semi-privileged vassals who survived on
the royal estates in Great Poland until the eighteenth century. Lithuania
possessed a class of commoner knights, the *putni*, which merged with the
nobility in the fifteenth and sixteenth centuries. These groups held fiscal
privileges in return for mounted military service. In the course of time they
secured an hereditary hold of the privileges and a loosening of their military
obligations. Hungary, another borderland, possessed similarly privileged
military classes but, as noble status was more easily obtained, the commoner

knight stood less chance of survival. In all these instances, some distinction remained between the commoner and noble knight. The commoner knight's privileges continued to be regarded as basically conditional upon service, whereas the noble came to be seen as privileged by natural right.[51]

Finally, in Sweden and Denmark not only the noble landowners but also their tenants were free from the traditional land tax: until the late seventeenth century in Denmark and the late nineteenth century in Sweden. Since the tenants of the Crown and church possessed the same exemption and only the freeholders were liable, at least half the peasantry in Sweden enjoyed some fiscal immunity. Elsewhere, for example in medieval France and Germany, feudal lords had claimed exemption from state taxes for their tenantry, on the grounds that the latter's rightful duty was to pay taxes to them, but this claim fell victim to the establishment of national systems of taxation. From the thirteenth and fourteenth centuries the Crown was able to tax the dependants of the tenant-in-chief principally in return for respecting his fiscal exemption, allowing him to control royal taxation through the right of parliamentary consent and leaving him with the responsibility for its local allocation and collection. After royal absolutism had terminated the privilege of tenant exemption in Denmark in the 1660s, Sweden, a state with no feudal tradition, remained the outstanding practitioner of this feudal ideal.[52]

Fiscal exemption was not simply a noble right. It was often a clerical, and occasionally an urban and provincial, right. In both England and Scotland fiscal exemption from direct taxation was unconnected with nobility. In Scotland it was the perquisite of certain offices of state, corporations and tenures; in England it was the privilege of the inhabitants of regions with a special obligation of defence, notably the Cinque Ports and, prior to the union of 1603, the palatinates of Durham and Chester and the northern borders.[53] In many instances fiscal exemption was secured not through the acquisition of noble privilege, but as a concessionary reward for special service. Nonetheless it remained closely associated with the nobility: it was frequently granted to commoners in conjunction with other noble privileges;[54] and its acquisition was seen not simply as a financial advantage, but also as a gain in social status. Fiscal exemption was a major part of the trappings of nobility, and commoners sought to acquire it in compensation for their failure to attain ennoblement.

2 Private taxation

A second category of fiscal privilege was the nobles' rights either to levy their own private taxes or to annex royal taxes for their own benefit. These rights were never the corporate possession of a nobility. Only those who qualified as tenants-in-chief, seigneurs or recipients of a grant of regality lawfully enjoyed them. Landlordship was the basis of the first two qualifications, but not necessarily of the third. The tax rights conferred by grants of regality and tenancy-in-chief predominantly belonged to the higher nobility. Only seigneurial right made private taxation readily available to the lesser nobility. Like fiscal exemption, these rights could be exercised by commoners, authorised to hold them by royal grant or by the ownership of a privileged estate.

Royal taxes fell legitimately into private hands in three ways: through their direct assignment to subjects as a payment for service, for this was a primitive means of meeting the salaries of officers and officials as well as a way of repaying financiers who advanced money to the government;[55] through tax farming, a main device for collecting indirect taxes until the nineteenth century;[56] and by a permanent alienation of regalian right which allowed the recipient's family the perpetual authority to collect royal taxes for its own benefit or to replace them with its own private taxes. All three forms of alienation placed royal taxes in noble hands, but none of these rights was exercised on account of either nobility or ownership of a noble estate; all were simply held by men whose families or persons had been specially favoured by the Crown. They were privileges which nobles could attain rather than noble privileges. However, the third form of alienation was particularly noble because it tended to be confined to noblemen and was held by right of inheritance.

In the mid-fifteenth century the dukes of Brittany, Burgundy, Bourbon, Anjou and Orléans, among other French nobles, held the regalian right to enjoy public taxes collected in their territories. This resulted from the Crown's policy of securing the loyalty and co-operation of powerful subjects by awarding them royal tax revenues. By the late fifteenth century this form of royal patronage had ceased to be dispensed in France and by the mid-sixteenth century the Crown had reclaimed the alienations.[57] In Medieval Castile, Navarre and Aragon the Crown from the twelfth century onwards granted to subjects the right to pocket royal taxes; in sixteenth and seventeenth century Castile, the Crown's policy of alienation continued with the granting of *señoríos*, which conferred the right to collect the *alcabala*, and the awarding of *juros*, annuities paid by the direct assignment of royal taxes. Similarly, in both Naples and Sicily, royal patronage conferred tax revenues upon favoured subjects in both the late medieval and early modern periods. In all three cases reclamation was not complete until the early nineteenth century.[58]

In a number of states the alienation of regalian right conferred upon subjects the right to levy their own taxes. Between 1300 and 1536 the marcher lords in Wales were freed from the Crown's fiscal demands and privileged to exact their own taxes; so were the holders of county franchises in late sixteenth- and early seventeenth-century Sweden. The fiscal independence of the marcher lordships was ended by Henry VIII; that of the Swedish franchises by Charles XI in the 1680s. In medieval Portugal, certain members of the nobility received by royal grant immunity from royal taxation accompanied by the right to exact their own tolls and *octrois*, preserving them until 1821.[59] Such hereditary rights to annex royal taxes or to levy alternative taxes certainly lacked the staying power or the geographical spread of most of the other fiscal privileges, but where they survived they endured for almost as long.

The nobility's receipt of taxes by feudal right centred upon the aid; its receipt of taxes by seigneurial right centred upon tallage. The aid was an exaction which for specific purposes such as his ransom or the marriage of his daughter, the tenant-in-chief could make of his military tenants, who were usually nobles; tallage was a levy which the landlord could impose on his free and unfree peasants. Tallage was much less conditional than the aid and could be regularly exacted. The basis of the aid was feudal obligation; that of tallage, bannal right. The aid disappeared either because the Crown monopolised the right or because it became merged with tallage. In the modern period the aid paradoxically and exceptionally lingered on in Hungary, a state without a feudal tradition, essentially as a seigneurial due which was officially santioned in 1548, the peasantry having the responsibility of paying their lord's ransom and of meeting his wedding expenses, until relieved of it by the urbarial regulations of Maria Theresa. Tallages likewise failed for the most part to outlive the middle ages. Originating in the eleventh and twelfth centuries, they either came to be forbidden, as in France where the ordinance of 1439 terminated the subject's right to levy *tailles* on freemen, or merged with the rent. Tallages, however, were long outlived by seigneurial indirect taxes. These appeared in the West in the twelfth century and survived the threats of royal absolutism but not of revolution.[60] A final source of private taxation, first found in the tenth century, was the arbitrary fiscal demands (chevage) which lords were entitled to make of their serfs.[61] This tax escaped the restrictions or prohibitions placed upon feudal and seigneurial taxes because the legislation responsible for them was confined to the rights of freemen. In the West chevage died with the demise of serfdom; in the East it failed to accompany the resurgence of serfdom in the early modern period, excluded by the Crown's wish to retain for itself the right of direct taxation. This consideration had not featured in the West since national systems of taxation had not existed when the seigneurial practice of taxing serfs was first developed.

3 The remaining rights

A third category of noble privilege included rights of special assessment, collection and consent. Forming a part of the concessionary process whereby the state encroached upon the nobility's fiscal immunities, these palliative rights were well established by 1500 and still emerging in the eighteenth and nineteenth centuries.

Cushioning the nobility's loss of fiscal exemption was the right of nobles to be more lightly assessed for tax purposes than commoners. In France, special assessment was a device to persuade the nobles to cede their privilege of fiscal exemption. Thus in Languedoc the nobility was offered a lower assessment of the hearth tax than the commonalty in 1337. The offer was affirmed in 1338 and in 1340, but became unnecessary when, in the course of the fourteenth century, the nobility firmly established its exemption from the payment of direct taxes. In the seventeenth century the Swedish nobles received a special assessment privilege in return for the loss of fiscal exemption. Since 1485 the nobles had enjoyed immunity from the *régale* on the iron ore which their estates produced. By the close of the seventeenth century, this exemption had been replaced with the right to pay duty of one-thirtieth of the output, instead of the one-tenth required of iron mined on the lands of commoners. In 1749 the Habsburgs gave a special assessment privilege to the Bohemian nobles, again in compensation for the loss of fiscal exemption: noble demesnes were taxed less severely than the peasant tenures because the owners were allowed tax relief to cover the cost of their demesne operations while the peasantry was taxed on the gross annual income of its farms. The Bohemian nobles were also allowed to pay tax at a lower rate than the commonalty. Having survived the onslaught mounted by Joseph II in 1789, special assessment lasted in Bohemia until 1867, subjected to an amendment made on the request of the nobility in the Land Tax Patent of 1792: an example of nobles taking the initiative to reduce the privileges of their order. This amendment equalised the rate at which noble and commoner lands were taxed. A differential rate of assessment between noble and commoner estates was introduced in Denmark in 1818, yet again following the removal of the right of fiscal exemption, and lasted until 1849. This permitted the owners of noble estates to pay tax at a rate 25% lighter than the owners of non-privileged lands. A similar concession was awarded the Russian nobles after the elimination of their immunity from personal taxation in 1887. By 1900 and until 1917 the tax rate on noble estates was roughly half that on peasant lands. Except for Sweden, in all these cases the exemption replaced by special assessment applied to direct taxation.[62]

Yet the right of special assessment was not always created by the elimination of fiscal exemption. Certain nobilities acquired it for other reasons.

In Poland, it was a longstanding equivalent of fiscal exemption and amounted to much the same thing. When it was abolished in 1629, fiscal immunity was put in its place. The Privilege of Kassa of 1374 ensured that the nobles paid towards the ordinary land tax no more than two *groschen* per hide on their demesne lands. For the imposition of a heavier burden of tax, their consent was required. In Venice, the only noble fiscal privilege ever attained was the right not to declare income from wages or public bonds when assessed for the *decima*, an income tax introduced in 1463. In Upper and Lower Austria nobles enjoyed special assessment in relation to the *Türkensteuer* from 1530 and to the *Kontribution* from 1749, having, in the Bohemian manner, the right to claim tax relief for the cost of operating their demesnes. This privilege did not replace the nobility's right of fiscal immunity but was simply added to it. Following their annexation by the Hohenzollerns, the nobilities of Silesia and West Prussia, neither of which had ever enjoyed fiscal immunity, were also awarded special assessment rights: both were taxed at a more favourable rate than the commonalty. In the seventeenth century the ruler of Hesse allowed the nobles to add special assessment to their privilege of exemption. While remaining exempt from the regular direct taxes, they were authorised to contribute to the extraordinary levies at one half the rate of the townsmen. In the sixteenth century the nobles of Albertine Saxony likewise acquired the right of special assessment while retaining the traditional right of exemption.[63] However, in all these cases, the conferment of special assessment was a response to the nobility's increasing fiscal liability and resulted either from the denial, abolition or curtailment of fiscal exemption or, as in the Hohenzollern and Habsburg monarchies, from the radical alteration of the fiscal system brought about by the replacement of taxes traditionally regarded as extraordinary and granted for one year by taxes conceived as ordinary and granted for several years at a time.

Like fiscal exemption, the nobility's privilege of special assessment was attainable by the commonalty, especially through landownership. Where the privilege was linked to the ownership of a noble estate, commoners could acquire it by an act of purchase unless noble estates were confined to the nobility as, for example, in Austria, Bohemia and Sweden. However, this restriction was abolished some time before the termination of the special assessment right.[64] Because special assessment was frequently conferred by the possession of a noble estate, many nobles were denied the right. Only in Russia and Poland was the privilege the natural right of all nobles.

Much more widely enjoyed by the European nobilities was the privilege of fiscal consent. This right mainly co-existed with fiscal exemption; only in a few cases was it a palliative for the elimination of fiscal immunity or a compensation for the latter's absence. Like fiscal exemption, it was originally a device for persuading nobles to accept the development of national systems of taxation. The obstacle to be overcome was the nobles' own rights of taxation which stood to suffer if the Crown made fiscal demands of their dependants. In parts of Germany a further problem to which consent was a solution stemmed from the ruler's alienation to subjects of his right of taxation; consent was the means whereby he reclaimed it.[65] In a substantial number of states—for example in France, the Crown of Aragon, Hungary, Sicily, Naples, Bohemia and the German principalities—the nobles enjoyed both fiscal exemption from, and the right of consent to, the same tax.[66] On the other hand, in a small number of states, the nobles' right of consent was closely connected with the absence of fiscal exemption: for example, in Upper and Lower Austria, England and Scotland where exemption from direct taxation did not exist, and in Poland and Sweden where state taxation initially developed as an ordinary levy arbitrarily imposed by the Crown and where parliamentary taxation developed in the course of time as an addition to the ordinary levies. In this bipartite system, noble exemption or, in Poland's case, special assessment was originally confined to the non-parliamentary taxation and consent was a consequence of the nobility's fiscal liability.[67]

The nobility's privilege of fiscal consent interconnected with the history of estate assemblies which, in the early stages, developed predominantly as tax-granting bodies. Before the nineteenth century they usually contained one or two noble chambers.[68] In possessing a traditional parliament which did not represent the nobility as an order, Castile was exceptional, and Russian representative assemblies were unique in lacking, prior to the twentieth century, tax-granting powers. Elsewhere the force of royal absolutism succeeded, notably in the seventeenth and eighteenth centuries, in minimising the value of the consent privilege without necessarily eradicating it: only in parts of Northern and Central France, Piedmont, Denmark, Portugal, Naples, Sardinia and the Crown of Aragon did it disappear, the result of the total elimination of parliament. In the Prussian monarchy, parts of France, Sicily, Poland, Bohemia, Hungary, Sweden, most of the German principalities and the territories of the Austrian Habsburgs, the nobility's right of consent survived until the revolutionary era—in Bavaria and Brandenburg in spite of the demise of the diet—although in most cases gelded of its original powers. And the preservation of noble privilege in democratic parliaments extended its life into the twentieth century. Quite exceptional was the history of the English house of lords which maintained the noble estate in a parliamentary assembly, but completely bereft from the late seventeenth century of its traditional right of fiscal consent. In the English parliament finance bills came to be enacted with the sole consent of Crown and Commons. From 1678 onwards bills of supply began: 'We, your

Majesty's most faithful Commons, have given and granted to your Majesty . . .'.[69]

Like the other fiscal rights so far examined, the noble privilege of consent was not enjoyed by all of noble status. Its enjoyment could depend upon special qualifications such as the ownership of a noble estate, the antiquity of a lineage or the possession of a title. Furthermore in states where fiscal consent was a corporate right of the nobility (Hungary, Poland, parts of France, Sweden and the Crown of Aragon), the right did not always entitle actual membership of the tax-granting body: for most Hungarian and Polish nobles it was only a right of deputation.

In states where parliamentary representation in the noble estate was restricted to specially qualified nobles, the rest of the nobility could, at least, exercise the fiscal consent of the other estates either by electing members, or by being elected to the third estate or, by gaining access to the first estate as clerics. Unlike fiscal exemption or special assessment, fiscal consent was frequently the corporate right of the non-nobles and exercised in their own parliamentary chambers. The consent right of the commons differed from that of the nobility in always resting upon election and in being restricted to a minority of that order. Often, as in Sicily, Naples, the Austrian territories, Poland, Bohemia and Hungary, the consent rights of the third estate belonged only to the residents of royal townships; the remainder were regarded as the subjects of lords and, therefore, represented without the right of election by their lords in the noble chamber. Rarely was the peasantry represented by their own estate. On the other hand, only in a handful of parliaments was the right of fiscal consent totally confined to the nobility. This had happened in Poland by 1600 and in Brandenburg by the late seventeenth century. It was also the case in Hungary although non-nobles could gain parliamentary membership through being temporarily defined as noble. The nobles' right of fiscal consent was further distinguished by the authority which the constitution conferred upon it. In some parliaments—those of East Prussia, Catalonia and Sicily—the decision of the noble order could not be ignored because of the principle that all the orders should be in agreement. However, this procedure left the orders equally privileged. Elsewhere, a parliamentary vote of supplies could be heavily influenced by the nobility because the constitution permitted an excess of noble over commoner members, or an excess of noble over commoner chambers and allowed matters to be decided by a majority vote of the membership or of the chambers; or it penalised the commoner membership by allowing the nobles head votes and the non-nobles only a collective vote. Notably in Naples, Bohemia, Austria, Poland, Hungary the nobles' fiscal rights were clearly distinguishable from those of the commonalty because through privilege alone the nobility could determine parliamentary decisions.

To make systems of national taxation acceptable to them, nobles were awarded not only fiscal exemption and consent, but also the right to collect for the government's use the taxes which the Crown exacted of their tenants and other dependants. The practice had Roman origins: a precedent was the *dominus fundi's* responsibility for collecting his tenants' taxes. It was then revived in the thirteenth and fourteenth centuries along with the idea of national taxation. Like fiscal consent, it was granted to landlords in exchange for the imposition of royal taxes. It was also an easy solution to the problem of administering these taxes locally. In time the right became associated with absolute monarchy. As a means of persuading the nobility to accept the bureaucratisation of the state, the latter's administrative authority was made to stop at the boundaries of the nobles' estates. Thus in the late eighteenth century landlords collected the royal taxes owed by their tenantry not only in the administratively primitive and noble-dominated states of Poland and Hungary, but also in the Crown-dominated, bureaucratic states of Prussia, Austria, Bohemia, Russia and Denmark.[70]

Special assessment and the right of consent provided compensation for the nobility's fiscal liability. So did the noble privilege of exemption from the normal machinery of assessment. The English peerage was fiscally privileged in this respect. From 1523 until the establishment of the land tax in 1692, the assessment of its wealth for the subsidy and the collection of its contributions were in the hands of special commissioners working under the direction of the Lord Chancellor and the Lord Treasurer. This arrangement freed the peerage from the system of assessment and collection to which the rest of society was subjected. Related was the Sicilian fiefholders' right of exclusion from the tax censuses carried out between the mid-fifteenth and early nineteenth centuries. In Sicily commoners could also attain this right, as owners of fiefs and as residents of Palermo.

In England the privilege of special commissioners was closed to commoners and, since it was restricted to the peerage and enjoyed not even by peerage families but only by the holder of the title, to most of the aristocracy as well. Unlike the right of special assessment, this privilege was not usually awarded in compensation for the loss of other fiscal privileges. Essentially it belonged to nobilities with a longstanding liability to a wide range of direct taxation. For this reason, its practice was limited by the prevalence of fiscal exemption. Moreover, because it radically opposed state control, it became inadmissible in the late modern period as an anodyne which governments could grant to nobles deprived of their fiscal immunities. The Russian government in 1812 breached noble immunity by introducing a tax on landed income and allowed the noble landowner, in compensation, the special right to submit a self-compiled assessment of his wealth. But this was the exception.[71]

4 Origins of fiscal exemption

Fiscal exemption first became widely enjoyed as a noble privilege between the twelfth and the fourteenth centuries. By the end of the twelfth century the Castilian nobility had obtained exemption from the *servicio ordinario y extraordinario*. In the twelfth and thirteenth centuries, the nobilities of Portugal, the Crown of Aragon and of Northern Italy acquired an equivalent privilege, which the North Italian nobles lost in the same period. In the thirteenth and fourteenth centuries, the French nobility secured exemption from the hearth taxes (*fouages*) which in the fifteenth century crystallised as the *taille*. In Hungary fiscal exemption was confined to the nobility in 1222 rather than to the Magyar nation. In Brandenburg the exemption of noble estates from the land tax first appeared in 1281. In the same year fiscal exemption was introduced to Sweden; by 1396 it was fully established as a noble right. The process of creation was also extensive in the fifteenth century when the nobilities of Poland, Bavaria, Saxony, Austria, Sicily and Naples acquired some form of fiscal immunity.[72]

Mainly responsible for establishing the privilege was the creation and extension of a royal tax system which comprehended the realm rather than merely the king's domain. This ended the exclusive reliance of governments upon the feudal-seigneurial methods of raising revenue which had predominated after the collapse, in the sixth and seventh centuries, of the fiscal system founded by the Romans.[73] Fiscal exemption was one of the means by which noble consent was secured for this major increase in the power of the state. Also contributing importantly to the development of the privilege was the mounted military service expected of the nobility, a service which was usually presented as the privilege's main justification.

However, the privilege of fiscal exemption continued to be granted to the nobility long after the creation of national tax systems and long after military developments had rendered the heavily armoured knight redundant and had placed priority on the employment of paid professional troops. In times when the government had greater need of the nobles' taxes than their personal military service, it remained, nonetheless, capable of awarding them fiscal immunities. Some of these grants of exemption were merely a restoration of lost privileges, as in Mark and Cleves where in the 1660s the nobility was excused the payment of most taxes, and as in Denmark where the government restored a measure of exemption from the land tax to the nobility in 1671.[74] Other grants of immunity represented the extension of an existing privilege, accompanying the introduction of new taxes, especially excises, customs and tolls, as in fifteenth-century Brandenburg, sixteenth-century Bavaria and Poland, seventeenth-century Jülich and Berg and eighteenth-century Saxony. In Poland, noble exemption was admitted to a

traditional levy, the land tax, in 1629.[75] Other grants of exemption marked
a complete innovation: for example, in East Prussia when the nobles in the
seventeenth century were allowed exemption from excises on goods purchased for their own personal consumption, and in Bohemia when the
nobility was granted exemption from the *Haussteuer* in 1567.[76] In none of
these instances could a special military service be convincingly offered as the
justification for the granted privilege. Mainly responsible was, on the one
hand, a noble demand for fiscal immunity inspired either by a tradition of
exemption or by the coveted privileges of neighbouring nobilities, and, on
the other, the strength of the nobility in its relations with the Crown. The
same factors had operated in the middle ages. Fiscal exemption, then, was
not a simple concomitant of military obligation. It was something enforced
by the Crown's dependence upon its nobility, a dependence principally
stemming from the nobility's role in granting parliamentary supplies, serving
as the instrument of local government and providing troops and leadership
for the king's wars.

In spite of the close connection between the fief and fiscal exemption, the
importance of military obligation can be easily exaggerated, even when
explaining the medieval origins of fiscal exemption. After all, feudal regimes
in Sicily, Naples and England managed to do without the privilege for
centuries; and, when eventually granted to the tenants-in-chief of Naples in
1443, it followed the government's decision to relieve the barons of their
military obligations to the Crown. Furthermore, tax exemption in Brandenburg and Pomerania was not restricted to military fiefs, but also applied to
estates without military obligations attached. In France, the fiscal exemption
enjoyed north of the Loire was the right of those with noble status and not,
as was to be expected of a region with a long feudal tradition, the right of
those with military tenures.[77] A simpler connection between military obligation and fiscal immunity is evident in states which were largely untouched
or only lightly affected by the feudal system: for example, in Hungary,
Sweden, Portugal and Castile. Yet in these instances fiscal exemption was
the cause, not the consequence, of the military obligation. Initially in these
states the military service which conferred fiscal exemption was not an
obligation: anyone providing cavalry service qualified for the privilege. Only
in the course of time was a military obligation imposed upon all those
entitled to enjoy fiscal exemption. Thus, the formation of fiscal exemption
began with the subject's offer of military service and was only completed
when the state imposed upon him and his descendants an obligation to
provide future military service. In this way fiscal exemption ceased to be
simply a reward for military service and became the reason for a military
obligation, the existence of the latter allowing the fiscal privilege to be
enjoyed as a hereditary right.[78]

In France the emergence of fiscal exemption coincided with the failure of feudalism to provide the Crown with sufficient resources for its military purposes. To furnish the means for waging war with paid troops, the French Crown in the late thirteenth and early fourteenth centuries ended the Frankish practice of financing government with the king's seigneurial and feudal income and developed instead a national system of taxation. This was done by commuting for a money payment the militia service expected of every able-bodied freeman. The Crown's attempt to make the nobility contribute to this fiscal system failed. The nobility's case was that, even if it commuted a money payment for militia service, there remained its feudal military and fiscal obligations as well as the military requirements of knighthood, an occupation annexed by the nobility and still central to its character. Because the tax system developed out of militia service, the nobility could reasonably claim tax exemption from it, in return for the continuation of the feudal military obligation—fulfilled by actual service or by the payment of scutage—and the maintenance of the tradition that knightly families owed a special military service.[79] Basically, however, the French nobility's fiscal immunity was not secured by the strength of its case: in the fourteenth century the Crown succeeded in levying direct taxes on the whole community. Nor did the French nobility establish its fiscal immunity because of the Crown's reliance upon its obligation of military service. By the late thirteenth century the Crown preferred other means of raising armies. In the long run, the nobility secured its fiscal exemption because the Crown was too weak to have its own way, especially in its plan to transform the feudal aid into a national tax. This was thwarted partly by the opposition of nobles who were not under feudal obligation to the Crown, and partly by vassals of the Crown who felt that the feudal dues paid by their own vassals should rightfully come to them.[80]

In contrast, the nobility's fiscal liability in feudal Naples, Sicily and England came of the Crown's success in basing a national system of taxation upon the feudal aid. Furthermore, since the establishment of feudalism in England, Naples and Sicily followed an act of conquest and was imposed by the Crown, the royal government had a greater control over feudal rights than the French monarchy possessed north of the Loire where feudalism was not simply the Crown's creation, but the result of a natural development reaching back to the eighth century.[81] The Midi was different. There feudalism developed much later—in the twelfth and thirteenth centuries—and was to a much greater degree created by the government, a fact which helps to explain why the nobility's fiscal exemption in this region was more limited than that enjoyed elsewhere in France.[82] Undoubtedly upholding the distinction between north and south was the fact that north of the Loire the *taille* became a tax on movables while in the Midi it became a land tax. Generally land taxes and property rights of exemption tended to go together, whereas personal rights of exemption usually accompanied other forms of direct taxation. The traditional distinction between noble and *roturier* estates gave the Crown the opportunity in the Midi to curtail the amount of fiscal exemption available to the nobility, an opportunity which it seized in the course of the fifteenth century, by insisting that exemption from the *taille* should be confined to noble estates.[83] Elsewhere in the kingdom the nature of direct taxation and fiscal exemption provided fewer openings for the curtailment of fiscal privilege and left the Crown with the enforcement of derogation laws and the employment of commissions to examine claims to nobility as its basic means of keeping fiscal exemption in check. In view of the nature and development of fiscal exemption in France, explaining the privilege simply in terms of the feudal system and its obligations is bound to be inadequate.

In spite of these qualifications, however, military obligation remains central to the genesis and maintenance of fiscal exemption. Of less importance in upholding the privilege was actual military service. In several states exemption became dependent upon the payment of scutage, a commutation of military service. Moreover, in the course of time, governments called upon the military obligation as an excuse for imposing scutage rather than as a means of manning the royal army. Military obligation thus became a pretext for taxing the nobility as well as remaining a prime justification for its fiscal immunity.[84]

In accounting for the origin of the nobility's other fiscal privileges, its military obligation seems much less important. Some private taxes were levied by fiefholders to equip them with sufficient means for exercising their military obligations; but not all private taxes had a military purpose. In resulting from the Crown's alienation of its regalian rights or the nobility's acquisition of seigneurial rights, many had nothing to do with military service.[85] The rights of special assessment, fiscal consent, tax collection and exemption from the normal machinery of assessment also had few military associations. The right of special assessment was normally granted as a consolation for the nobility's increasing fiscal liability. Frequently it was a replacement for fiscal exemption, created as a result of the latter's abolition. Exemption from the normal assessment machinery was another means of enlisting noble co-operation for the development of a fiscal system which fell upon the whole community. It had the same palliative purpose as the right of consent to taxation and as the right of nobles to collect for the government the taxes of their tenantry. Essentially, this body of privilege was granted to the nobility as a means of giving it a reason for accepting and promoting state control.[86]

5 *Survival and abolition of fiscal privilege*

Fiscal privilege underwent a long process of renewal and recreation. For fiscal exemption and private taxation, the process continued until the seventeenth century; while the other privileges were still being founded in the eighteenth and nineteenth centuries.[87] Likewise, with the abolition of fiscal privilege: the nineteenth and twentieth centuries may have seen its termination, but the process of elimination began long before. A great deal of fiscal privilege was removed in the middle ages. This included private rights to levy taxes, the result of either the Crown's policy of centralisation as in England and France, or as in Germany, the private tax owner's success in securing independent princely status. In the middle ages the privilege of fiscal exemption also came under attack. For example, the fiscal immunities of many of the fiefholders of Northern and Central Italy were destroyed by the urban communes well before the close of the thirteenth century, while in much of Northern and Central France the right of fiscal consent came to be eliminated in the fifteenth century.[88]

The process of abolition continued in the early modern period, principally at the hands of royal governments hard pressed by indebtedness and occasionally encouraged to respond to the anti-noble complaints of the commonalty. The nobility's exemption from direct taxation was ceded in Bavaria in 1526 and in the duchies of Mark and Cleves in 1557. In 1644 the Swedish nobility lost its exemption from the traditional customs dues, as did the Norwegian nobility in 1646. In the early 1660s the Danish nobility lost its exemption from the land tax, although it was compensated with another exemption in 1671. A mass of fiscal privilege was eliminated in the eighteenth century prior to the French Revolution. The traditional fiscal exemptions of the Saxon nobility had gone by 1763; those of the Bavarian nobility by 1749. At this time the nobility's exemption from direct taxation was also eliminated in Bohemia and Poland. In the late eighteenth century the Austrian Habsburgs removed the privilege in Lombardy and Galicia. In the Crown of Aragon, the Bourbons introduced a system of direct taxation in 1716 and 1718 which allowed the nobility no fiscal exemption. After the termination of the Turkish war in 1718, the Habsburgs sought to deprive the Hungarian nobility of their fiscal exemption and also in the early eighteenth century the Hohenzollerns tried to make the Brandenburg nobility pay the land tax, but in each case without success.[89] Accompanying the onslaught against fiscal exemption was an attack on the privilege of consent. In a number of countries the privilege disappeared as diets in the course of the sixteenth and seventeenth centuries ceased to meet.[90]

Nevertheless, in many of these instances the fiscal privileges of the nobility were not entirely wiped out. Before the French Revolution the medieval

Italian communes proved to be much more rigorous in totally eliminating fiscal privilege than the princes who proceeded against it. In spite of their anti-noble actions, the princes showed a remarkable capacity to preserve the nobility as a fiscally privileged class, either failing to confiscate all its tax privileges or awarding further privileges to replace the abolished ones. Thus, in the middle ages the right to tax was replaced by the right of exemption from, and by the right of consent to, royal taxes. In the modern period the right of exemption was frequently replaced by the right of special assessment. Alternatively, the process of abolition could leave traditional fiscal rights intact. From the government's point of view the fiscal privileges were permissible because of its success in limiting their number and scope. The ability acquired by the Crown to tax the subjects of the nobility rendered the fiscal exemption of the noble order a tolerable concession; the abolition of fiscal exemption allowed the Crown to accept the privilege of special assessment; and the compliancy of the diets, notably in the Austrian and Bohemian territories and in the Prussian monarchy in the eighteenth century and earlier in France, ensured the survival of the right of fiscal consent. Furthermore, governments could allow the traditional fiscal privileges to stand when, in spite of their existence, the nobility could be appropriately taxed. Monarchs permitted fiscal privilege to endure so long as it did not shelter the wealth of the nation from their revenue demands, or threaten the security of the state by causing an overtaxed commonalty to revolt. Fiscal privilege was completely eliminated in certain states prior to the French Revolution—for example in the Crown of Aragon in the early eighteenth century and in parts of Northern Italy in the middle ages—but in much of Europe it survived in some form or other, although much reduced in value.

Since fiscal privilege outlived the performance of the military services that were its original justification, the eventual loss of fiscal privilege was not simply caused by the nobility's failure to keep its part of the original bargain. Nor did the survival of fiscal privilege result from the absence of popular resentment. Popular opposition to fiscal privilege had a very long history and can be found, for example, in thirteenth-century Lombardy and Tuscany, fifteenth-century Spain, in the sixteenth-century Low Countries, sixteenth-century Dauphiné, and in the early modern period in both the German principalities and Sweden.[91] Fiscal privilege eventually disappeared partly because there developed a popular capacity to conceive its total abolition, a consequence of the French Revolution and its imparted belief that noble privilege was evil, and partly because of the effectiveness acquired by popular resentment in the sixty years after 1790. The latter was due to the Crown's readiness to respond to popular opinion by disposing of many noble privileges. It was also due to the willingness of the nobility and those commoners who shared the same fiscal privileges to yield them in order to avert revolution or to attract popular support for the cause of counter-revolution. The French Revolution's decisive eviction of fiscal privilege in 1789, an event long prepared by the ineffectual, fiscal policies of royal absolutism, was a turning point because in the next sixty years, and prodded into further action by the revolutions of 1848, other regimes followed suit. Now that popular revolution, a long-held fear of kings, princes, nobles and clerics, had happened, kings proceeded against fiscal privilege with a new radicalism, sweeping it away rather than being content to replace old privileges with new ones or merely to reduce their range, and acting not principally to make money as in the past, but to distract popular support from revolutionary causes. With everything to lose if monarchy was to sink, the nobility became doubly compliant—unless involved in nationalist movements against imperial monarchy as in Poland and Hungary—hoping to acquire power in place of privilege through the development of an English-type polity. In Poland and Hungary nobles also acquired a readiness to cede privileges in order to enlist popular support for their war against the imperial crown and to safeguard against jacqueries.[92] In these circumstances fiscal privileges found few defenders. Devalued over the centuries by the introduction of counterbalancing liabilities and reduced in extent by the limitations placed on them, the surviving privileges could now be terminated. After 1850 fiscal exemption persisted only in the Prussian monarchy, but not after 1861, and in Sweden, but not after 1904, and in Russia, but not after 1887. Otherwise fiscal privilege lingered on only as a special assessment in Russia until 1917 and as a right of fiscal consent in states where the traditional estates parliament managed to survive (in Sweden until 1865 and in Mecklenburg until 1918) or where the parliamentary reforms of the nineteenth century allowed the nobility to retain parliamentary privileges.[93]

6 Value to the nobility

In comparison with the commonalty, the nobility over the centuries was grossly undertaxed. For the most part, this did not simply result from its privilege of fiscal exemption. Undertaxation was enjoyed by nobilities such as the English and the East Prussian whose fiscal immunity was minimal and, as in Spain, it continued to benefit the nobles long after their fiscal exemption had gone.[94] Moreover, because privilege was sometimes a poorer safeguard than evasion against the payment of taxes, fiscally exempt nobilities could contribute as much of their income to the treasury as those with no immunity. Basically, the value of fiscal exemption to the nobility depended upon whether the taxes to which it applied were regular; whether they provided the government with the bulk of its revenue; and whether the government could tap noble wealth effectively in spite of the privilege.

In 1750 the French nobles still enjoyed exemption from the *taille* whereas the English aristocrats were subjected to a regular land tax. Nevertheless, little difference probably existed between the proportion of wealth which each contributed to the state. Under 20% of total income, neither contribution was onerous. Until the last decade of the seventeenth century, the English aristocracy had been protected from a heavy weight of taxation by the traditional insistence that direct taxation should be irregular and levied only with parliamentary consent. Making the aristocracy's tax burden even lighter were the fiscal privileges of the peerage, especially exemption from the normal assessment machinery, and the fact that the local administration of direct taxes, except for those of the peerage, lay in the hands of the gentry rather than an independent bureaucracy. When the government reformed the fiscal system in the late seventeenth century, introducing regular direct taxation and completely eliminating the peers' fiscal privileges of consent and assessment, it continued to protect aristocratic interests by relying heavily upon indirect taxes—in 1786 the latter contributed £12.3 out of a total fiscal revenue of £15.1 million—and also by failing to revise the official assessments of landed wealth upon which the land tax was based. This failure reduced the fiscal liability of the aristocracy as, in the course of time, the original assessments were devalued by inflation. Also helpful to the aristocracy was the availability, in the absence of an efficient and extensive provincial bureaucracy, of ample opportunities for tax evasion.[95]

While the English aristocracy had not needed fiscal immunity to protect itself from heavy taxation, having other means of self-protection, the French nobles badly needed it because they lacked equivalent safeguards against the government's greed. In the fifteenth and sixteenth centuries, a system of regular direct taxation developed which provided the government with the bulk of its tax revenue. Representative assemblies could provide little shelter since they soon lapsed in much of the country and the survivors lacked the capacity of the English parliament to restrain the government's fiscal policy. The *parlements* also offered little protection. Furthermore, although a range of indirect taxes developed from the mid-fourteenth century and direct taxes were eventually introduced which made no exception for the nobles, the *taille*, from which the nobles were protected by the privilege of exemption, remained for the government its main tax until the Revolution, the collection, like that of the other direct taxes, administered by a reasonably efficient and objective bureaucracy and the chances of evasion thereby curtailed. As there were fewer restraints in France upon the government's demands for taxes than in England, it is likely that, without fiscal exemption, the burden of tax falling upon the French nobles would have been much greater.[96]

Fiscal immunity became of much greater value to the European nobility with the development of regular direct taxation. At the start of the fifteenth century very few states possessed it. By this time fiscal exemption from direct taxation normally protected nobles only from taxes which were regarded as sources of extraordinary supply and whose levy was irregular. However, between 1400 and 1700, direct taxation was widely established as a means of raising ordinary revenue and therefore became regularly exacted. With this transformation, the value of fiscal exemption was greatly enhanced.[97] Countering this gain was the government's use of taxes, notably forms of indirect taxation, which permitted the nobility much less immunity than the traditional direct taxes. A heavy reliance upon indirect taxation first developed in parts of Italy in the thirteenth and fourteenth centuries and in the monarchies of Castile, Aragon and Portugal in the fourteenth and fifteenth centuries. Inspired in its later stages by Dutch example, a further wave of dependency occurred in the sixteenth and seventeenth centuries, affecting England, Austria, Bohemia, many of the German principalities, Sweden and Denmark.[98] Indirect taxation could work both against and in the noble interest. On the one hand it could devalue the privilege of fiscal exemption. In Castile the *servicio ordinario y extraordinario*, a direct tax from which all nobles were exempt, became a regular tax in the fifteenth century. But since the government came to rely upon a range of indirect taxes to which the nobles were liable, the nobility's privilege of fiscal exemption was rendered essentially honorific, their wealth protected from the state not by fiscal privilege but by the nature of the fiscal system, especially its opportunities for tax evasion and its tendency to favour the rich by taxing consumption rather than income or wealth.[99] The government's dependence upon indirect taxation had an even more dramatic effect in the Crown of Aragon under the Habsburgs. There the taxes paid to the government were levied as indirect taxes, and in consequence the nobles traditional fiscal exemption which was restricted to direct taxation became of no financial value whatsoever.[100] On the other hand, these indirect taxes were in themselves a source of noble undertaxation because their intrinsic nature tended to favour the wealthy. Appreciating the value of indirect taxation, the Sicilian nobles from the fifteenth to the nineteenth centuries arranged that taxes should be levied locally as indirect taxes on food and drink even when granted as direct taxes by the Sicilian parliament.[101] Irrespective of exemption, the growth of indirect taxation produced a fiscal system which was extremely favourable to the interests of the nobility.

Fiscal exemption, of course, could apply to indirect as well as direct taxation. When it did so, it conferred upon the nobility benefits which were commercial as well as fiscal. Not only did it allow tax avoidance, but it also gave the nobles a commercial advantage over non-nobles. Nobles in Hungary, Poland, Brandenburg, Pomerania, Sweden, Holstein, Bavaria and France in the early modern period were encouraged to become merchants and entrepreneurs because of the competitiveness awarded them as a class by their customs and excise immunities. However, in some of these cases, especially Holstein, the German principalities and France, the commercial advantage was gained by unlawfully extending a privilege which, to prevent commercial exploitation, had been confined to goods produced or consumed at home. In this respect, commercial advantage sprang from the misuse rather than simply the use of fiscal privilege.[102]

The value of fiscal exemption to the nobility also depended upon the existence and extensiveness of direct taxes which did not admit the privilege. Devaluing fiscal exemption was the government's reliance upon direct taxes which either confined exemption to an element within the nobility or allowed the nobility no immunity whatsoever. The practice of restricting fiscal exemption to noble estates meant a partial liability to the land tax for the nobles of Sweden, France, Brandenburg and a number of German principalities. Furthermore, in several instances, the nobility became subject to a weight of taxation long before the elimination of its privilege of exemption, through the imposition of direct taxes which did not allow immunity: in Sweden and Denmark as a result of the financial reforms of the seventeenth century, in France with the introduction of the *capitation* and the *vingtième*, in Brandenburg when an income tax was introduced in the early nineteenth century. Yet all these taxes which denied the nobility the protection of immunity were essentially exactions upon income. Accompanying the growth in the nobility's fiscal liability was the preservation of a fiscal system favourable to noblemen because it did not tax capital.

Finally, the value of fiscal exemption as a safeguard for the nobility against the financial demands of the state depended upon the government's alternative means of gaining access to noble wealth. Noble wealth, for example, could be tapped by the government's exploitation of the Crown's feudal rights; or by the sale of government stock, offices of state, titles of nobility or confirmations of noble status and regalian rights; or by the arbitrary reduction of fees and pensions. The French monarchy in the seventeenth and eighteenth centuries provided an outstanding, but not a unique, example of how revenue could be extracted from the nobility in these three ways. By the eighteenth century the sale of government bonds was well established in Europe; in the sixteenth and seventeenth centuries, the sale of titles and regalian rights developed on a massive scale in Sicily, Naples, Spain and Portugal. The exploitation of feudal rights was a medieval device for extracting wealth from the nobility. It was abandoned in England in the 1660s but several European governments continued to practise it until the revolutionary era.[103]

As for the value of the other fiscal privileges, the right of special assessment was subjected to roughly the same conditions as fiscal exemption, although, by its very nature, it was bound to be less valuable. Its value partly rested upon the degree of concession it permitted the nobility. In Poland, the advantage conferred by special assessment almost equalled that of fiscal exemption. In Sweden, Hesse and Russia, the privilege awarded a rate of assessment which was half that of the commonalty. In Denmark the difference in the rate of assessment was one quarter. In Venice the right of nobles not to declare income from wages was of little use, but the attendant right not to declare their income from public bonds was of great material benefit in causing the *decima* (an income tax) to fall less heavily upon them than upon the rest of the community. As with the privilege of fiscal exemption, the value of special assessment depended upon whether it was the only fiscal safeguard enjoyed by the nobility, and upon the importance of the tax to which it applied within the government's revenue system. Since it was, in most cases, an alternative to exemption and applied to a tax which was a main source of revenue, the privilege was usually of tremendous importance for its beneficiaries.

Of the remaining palliative privileges, the right of immunity from the normal assessment machinery seemed partly responsible for the nobility's undertaxation in England and Sicily, and the right of tax collection was of benefit to nobles who could profit from collecting more than the government required. However, as the landlord was expected to provide the difference between the amount assessed and collected, the privilege could also place him at a financial loss. Further advantages of this privilege were the control which it gave the noble landlord over his tenantry and its effectiveness in preventing government officials from interfering in the affairs of his estate. As a form of tenant control, however, it was but one of several rights, all serving the same purpose; serfdom rights, judicial rights and the authority to determine tenancy likewise assured the compliancy of the tenant. The collecting right was closely associated with societies which serfdom had placed firmly under the landlord's thumb. In this respect it probably did not give him much additional power over his tenantry since, quite apart from the collecting right, that control was already sufficient. Furthermore, the tax collecting right was but one of several rights protecting the noble estate from the inroads of bureaucracy. Helping to keep the state at bay were also the landlord's rights to dispense justice and to administer the military obligations which the state required of the tenantry.[104]

The value of the nobility's right of fiscal consent depended upon the government's ability to call upon revenues which did not need parliamentary authorisation. It also depended upon parliament's capacity to query effectively the government's tax demands and the degree to which the nobility's parliamentary privileges could determine parliamentary decisions.[105] In Denmark, Sicily, Hungary, Portugal, Brandenburg and France, for example, only a small part of the government's revenue in the early modern period relied upon parliamentary consent. As a result, the privilege stood little chance of dominating the government. Moreover, in several states, notably France throughout the early modern period and the territories of the Austrian Habsburgs and the Hohenzollerns from the late seventeenth century, the privilege of consent was neutralised by the Crown's ability to render representative assemblies as compliant as rubber stamps. Although in Poland, Hungary, Bohemia, Austria and Naples, privilege alone allowed the nobles to control parliamentary decisions, in many cases noble privilege did not offer as much. Instead, the nobles gained control through directing the other parliamentary estates either by outside influence or internally by obtaining membership of them. In this respect, the English aristocracy's control of parliament through its domination of the house of commons was not untypical.

Finally, regalian and seigneurial rights of private taxation were of undoubted benefit to their owners but were devalued by the emergence of national systems of taxation. Before this happened, in parts of twelfth-century Western Europe, for example, they could compose, in conjunction with the profits of justice, a larger source of noble income than that derived from dues, rents and direct farming. On the other hand, while private rights of direct taxation became unimportant to the nobility in the course of the late medieval and early modern period, rights of private indirect taxation in the form of tolls and *octrois* remained a significant if supplementary source of noble income until the abolition of the seigneurial system.[106]

To be fully evaluated, fiscal privilege needs to be measured against the other factors responsible for the nobility's undertaxation. Nobles could enjoy enormous tax benefits even though their fiscal privileges were few or non-existent. A lack of fiscal privilege did not automatically mean a heavy fiscal liability. Where direct taxation was a land tax and exemption from it was limited to the owners of noble estates, landless nobles paid no direct taxes; and nobles with a high proportion of non-noble lands could be heavily taxed. Furthermore, in reaction to the government's increasing capacity in the early modern period to tax the wealth of the nobles in spite of their privileges, the fiscally privileged nobilities, in the manner of the fiscally unprivileged or underprivileged nobilities, tended to resort to tax evasion as the most effective means of protecting their wealth against the demands of the state.

Governments favoured the nobility by tolerating their fiscal evasions and also by preferring to use taxes which fell lightly on noble wealth. For preserving the nobility as an undertaxed group, the government's avoidance of certain forms of direct taxation was at least as important as its acceptance of fiscal privilege. Heavily favouring the nobility was a general failure to impose direct taxes on wealth as opposed to income. Taxes on capital, such as death duties or wealth taxes, were, with a few exceptions, the preserve of the twentieth century. Also important to the nobility was the tendency of governments to rely on certain forms of indirect taxation, notably sales taxes, levied on consumption. Quite apart from their privileges, the nobles enjoyed profitable fiscal advantages. For this reason, their long-term under-taxation cannot be wholly explained in juridical terms.

The nobility's fiscal privileges imparted more than material benefits. Even when their financial return was minimal, they could be highly valued as a means of noble definition. In certain states, notably that of Castile, the identity of the noble, especially the lesser noble, relied upon the possession of fiscal immunity. However, noble definition was conferred only by the fiscal privileges which were corporately held. Many were not. For instance, rights of private taxation were confined to the owners of seigneurial, feudal or regalian rights. The tax collecting privilege only went with the ownership of a noble estate. In several states, the nobility's right of parliamentary consent to taxation was restricted to the noble landlords or nobles who qualified by virtue of additional attributes to their noble status such as title or lineage (for example, in the Austrian territories, Bohemia, the German principalities, Naples, Sicily and parts of France). Exemption from direct taxation was frequently the sole right of the owners of privileged estates (for example, in Sweden, the Midi, Prussia, Sicily and Naples). Only when fiscal privilege was the automatic right of those with noble status can it be regarded as a crucial means of noble identification. Otherwise it distinguished not noble from commoner, but noble from noble. However, the value of corporate fiscal privileges as a means of noble definition, can be easily exaggerated. When fiscal privilege was a corporate right, as for example in Spain, France, Poland, Russia, Hungary, it was not the only right of those with noble status. It was part of a parcel of privileges, honorific, judicial and political, all of them declarations of nobility. In this respect, nobles could lose their fiscal privileges and remain nonetheless definably noble.

7 Effect

To what extent did the nobility's fiscal privileges affect the economy and society? Fiscal privilege has been presented as a source of economic back-wardness because (1) fiscal immunity caused the weight of direct taxation to fall heavily upon the peasantry and so contributed to the decline or stagnation of agriculture; (2) it compelled governments, as a means of sidetracking fiscal exemption, to rely upon forms of indirect taxation which handicapped economic growth; (3) it forced governments to sell offices and honours which encouraged wealth to be invested unproductively in the acquisition of social status and (4) the nobility's exemption form indirect taxes was responsible for the decline of an independent bourgeoisie.[107] Yet peasants were not liberated from hardship by the removal of tax privileges; and the inclination of the bourgeoisie and nobility to waste their wealth on the acquisition or enlargement of social status existed in its own right, not simply as a consequence of government sales. Underlining the limited impact of fiscal privilege is the minor importance of its elimination in the long-term development of the economy.

That the peasants could be hard-pressed by state taxation is attested by the long history of anti-fiscal popular revolts; but the popular revolts against seigneurial exactions show that taxation was not the only source of their exploitation. In most cases, seigneurial dues, clerical tithes and government taxes combined to oppress the peasantry, tithes and dues imposing in the modern period the greater burden in Eastern Europe and taxes, the greater burden in much of Western Europe.[108] Moreover, there is no clear proof that the tax burden of the peasantry was simply caused by fiscal exemption. Basically it resulted from a natural clash between the sophisticated needs of the state and the intrinsic backwardness of the agrarian economy. It also sprang from the primitive nature of government finance and its inability to cope when, in the early modern period, inflation, war and the introduction of extensive professional bureaucracies and standing armies led to a massive escalation in the cost of government. Fiscal exemption was not normally at the root of the problem since it was usually enjoyed only by a small number of subjects, and governments could counteract its effect by developing taxes without immunity or by drawing revenues from non-fiscal sources. For example, in eighteenth-century Brandenburg and Hungary the nobility's almost comprehensive exemption from the payment of taxes, was countered by the fact that taxation furnished the government with no more than half of its income: the remainder was drawn from the royal estates and regalian rights.[109] A greater cause of peasant hardship than fiscal exemption was the general tendency of governments to impose direct taxes upon communities rather than upon individuals, leaving the individual's share to be determined by the community or its overlord.[110] In times of high mortality and large-scale migration, the effect could be disastrous. Only where there were large numbers of tax-exempted nobles or large numbers of tax-exempted commoners and where general taxes failed to replace 'exemption' taxes as the major source of government revenue, could peasant impoverishment owe something to fiscal immunity. With the *taille* dominant and apportioned according to community and with large numbers of commoners as well as the nobles enjoying the right of fiscal exemption, this was perhaps the case in parts of seventeenth- and eighteenth-century France.[111]

Governments introduced further taxes to counteract the fiscal exemption which safeguarded the nobility from the traditional taxes. This explains the supplementary direct taxes introduced in Spain, Sweden, France and Southern Italy between the sixteenth and the eighteenth centuries, but not the introduction of most indirect taxes. Their adoption seemed a natural step for governments to take in the search for further funds and occurred in countries such as England, Tuscany and East Prussia where fiscal exemption was of no consideration as well as in states where fiscal exemption mattered. If indirect taxes were introduced to counter privilege, that privilege was the right of fiscal consent, a right shared by noble and commoner. Thus in the German principalities it developed to reduce the ruler's dependence upon diets which were using their right of granting supplies to extend their powers. In France and Spain indirect taxes such as the *gabelle* and the *alcabala* became permanent, levied without regular parliamentary consent, and free of subject interference. Castile was, perhaps, the exception since the *millones* was introduced in the 1590s following the government's failure to supplement the *alcabala* with a series of direct taxes whose yield had been limited, notably in the northern provinces, by a glut of fiscally exempt subjects. Yet, even in this case, it is doubtful that the spectacular economic decline of early seventeenth-century Castile resulted from the fiscal immunity of the nobles.[112] If this economic decline had a fiscal cause, it was the weight of taxation which fell upon Castile because of the Crown's difficulty in levying taxes in Navarre, the Basque provinces, Catalonia, Valencia and Aragon.[113]

A further possible source of economic backwardness was the way certain governments—notably those of France and Habsburg Spain, Naples and Sicily in the sixteenth and seventeenth centuries—encouraged subjects to invest their capital in the court by selling to them offices of state, noble titles and regalian rights.[114] The capital of both bourgeois and noble was quite clearly diverted into unproductive channels by the attractive wares of the court; but there is no good reason to believe that, if they had not been sold, more capital would have been put to productive uses. Laws and customs of derogation, as well as the traditional lure of landownership, would probably have caused the same diversion of capital. Responsible for the waste of capital was the structure and mentality of societies which emphasised the superiority of the noble way of life.[115] Moreover, it is far from certain that the use of these expedients was forced upon governments by the existence of fiscal privilege. After all, the sale of office, titles and regalities extended the range of wealth protected by fiscal immunity. Essentially they were further straws for poverty-stricken governments to clutch at, adopted because of the fiscal system's incapacity to satisfy the government's needs.

Although the nobility's commercial impulses could flourish without the aid of fiscal immunity,[116] this privilege may have encouraged certain nobilities to trade especially if it relieved them of tolls and customs; and in some of these instances, notably Poland, Livonia, Holstein, Brandenburg and Hun-

gary in the early modern period, their commercial activities seemed to have
had effect upon the character of the native bourgeoisie. The latter did not
wither away but certainly lost its former social independence and tended to
survive as the factors and agents of nobles rather than as a social group with
its own rights and attitudes. Yet this change in character cannot simply be
explained by the nobility's exploitation of its fiscal privileges. In Sweden and
Denmark, the nobility's exemption from customs dues only produced noble
profit. The bourgeoisie was unaffected. In Eastern Europe, the decline of the
bourgeoisie resulted from its traditional weakness as a social group. This
was true even of the Hanse towns which had flourished in the late middle
ages but only under the aegis of the Teutonic Order. Also responsible was
the profitability of primary production, notably cereals, timber and forest
products, the competitiveness of foreign manufactures and the intrusion of
foreign merchants. The economy of much of Eastern Europe in the sixteenth
and seventeenth centuries became a plantation economy serviced by jews,
foreigners and the agents of the nobility. The nobles contributed to this
development as an entrepreneurial class involved both in production and
marketing and as a dominant political elite bent on avoiding mercantilism
and favouring foreign traders. Its commercial involvement probably sprang
as much from its farming activities as from the trading advantages imparted
by its tax privileges. Furthermore, economic backwardness was not pre-
determined by the fading away of an independent bourgeoisie. In the circumstances of the time there is no reason to believe that the entrepreneurial
activities of an independent bourgeoisie would have been more economically
progressive than those of the nobility: the merchants of Danzig who preserved their medieval independence in the early modern period had the same
commercial outlook as the noble-dominated bourgeoisie. The course taken
by the economy was determined in the short term by war. In the long term
its course was directed by the competitiveness of native corn, timber and
cattle in foreign markets and the competitiveness of foreign manufactures in
native markets, as well as by the development of serfdom as the main
instrument of production. Essentially it was controlled by the demand and
supply of the more advanced economies of Western Europe.[117]

Much more decisive than the economic and social consequences of fiscal
privilege was its effect upon the modernisation of the state. The establishment
of systems of regular direct taxation owed much to noble privilege, especially
since their early development rested upon the nobility's readiness to accept
them. Protected from what they were required to grant by fiscal immunity,
and moved by the government's willingness to respect their right of fiscal
consent, nobilities complied with the wishes of the Crown. Eventually it
became clear, as in early seventeenth-century France, that regular direct
taxation could materially harm the nobles, in spite of their immunity, in

rendering their tenantry less capable of paying rents and seigneurial dues, but this drawback was not initially evident.[118] Notably in England regular direct taxation was belatedly introduced; until the 1690s direct taxation continued to be regarded as a source of extraordinary supply rather than of ordinary revenue, perhaps because the aristocracy was subjected to it.[119] Closely involved with direct taxation was the development of representative assemblies most of whose powers before the nineteenth century stemmed from their right to grant taxes.[120] Since the regular levy of direct taxes led to regular sessions of parliament, the willingness of the nobles to consent to regular direct taxation converted parliaments from bodies which were only summoned in response to a crisis to assemblies with a role in the normal running of the state.

The modern state's acquisition of an extensive, state-controlled bureaucracy and standing army was a further repercussion of the nobility's fiscal privilege. Royal absolutism, which first developed this apparatus, established itself not only by over-riding noble interests but also by respecting noble rights.[121] Central to the establishment of royal absolutism in France, Prussia and Russia was the preservation or creation of noble privileges, particularly fiscal exemption. Even in Bohemia where immunity from direct taxation was confiscated in 1749, other fiscal privileges, notably special assessment and parliamentary consent, survived for another century. In Cleves and Mark, the Hohenzollerns granted exemption from direct taxation to the nobles as part of the process whereby royal absolutism was imposed.[122] The establishment of royal absolutism is partially explicable in what it had to offer the nobility as well as in its capacity to quell their resistance. Opportunities for employment in the service of the state was an advantage which the nobility was slow to seize. More immediately attractive was the government's toleration of privileges which served as a mark of distinction and as a shield against the demands of the state. Notably in England where the fiscal privileges were exiguous and confined to the peerage, and where the Crown in the process of asserting itself allowed the existing privileges to be reduced even further, royal absolutism failed and the state remained bureaucratically primitive until the nineteenth century.[123]

Finally, the durability of fiscal privilege and the popular hostility it could arouse, notably in the period 1789–1850, influenced the downfall of the old regime. Yet it could not be said that the old regime fell because noble privilege prevented the government from taxing noble wealth. When it came under revolutionary attack, fiscal privilege was of limited financial value, tending to confer honorific rather than material benefits: this was so in France by 1789, Prussia, Austria, Bohemia and Denmark by 1848 and Russia by 1917. Revolution did not occur because royal governments had failed to solve the problems which fiscal privilege created. Thanks to royal absolutism, fiscal exemption was overridden if not destroyed, and the right of consent was rendered impotent. Nevertheless, fiscal privilege helped to determine the character of revolution. For the revolutionaries of the late eighteenth and early nineteenth centuries, equality, one of the leading principles of revolution, signified not the inequality of wealth but the legal inequalities symbolised by the privileges of fiscal exemption and consent. Revolution was, therefore, initially waged on an issue of injustice which concerned not rich and poor, but noble and commoner. Focused in this way on the lesser evil of juridical distinction, revolution was able to tolerate the greater evil created by the discrepancy of wealth. In helping the revolutionaries to define injustice, fiscal privileges, along with seigneurial rights, played a main role in ensuring that, prior to the twentieth century, the overthrow of the old order upheld more than it tore down.

III

Judicial, service and seigneurial indemnities

The nobility's indemnity privileges protected it not only from taxation but also from the service obligations required of subjects by the state and from the judicial procedures and penalties to which the state normally subjected the laity. In addition, they offered shelter from the seigneurial system: the noble tenants of seigneurs were usually exempt from services and dues and immune to private jurisdiction.

In Western Europe indemnities of this sort formed some of the earliest noble privileges. Most nobilities enjoyed them. Predominantly they were conferred by noble status rather than by landownership, lineage or rank. When held corporately, the indemnity privileges were crucially important as a public declaration of a subject's noble identity. They helped to give nobles of differing fortunes a sense of belonging to the same order. However, like most other noble privileges, they were widely enjoyed by commoners, predictably by those with noble functions such as commoner knights and royal officials, but also by merchants, artisans and professionalmen.

Their value to the nobility depended upon the degree to which the state and the seigneur were prepared to respect them, and upon the nobles' capacity to evade governmental and seigneurial demands. For example, the indemnity privileges granted to the Russian nobles by the charter of 1785 were often ignored by the bureaucracy in its treatment of the nobility; and in parts of eighteenth-century Hungary landlords ignored the immunity of their noble tenants from seigneurial exaction.[1] Moreover, the early dissolution of their judicial privileges did not subject the Sicilian nobles to less lenient treatment in the law than the nobilities which preserved their judicial rights.[2] The abolition of indemnity privileges in the late eighteenth and early nineteenth centuries did not necessarily produce a judicial machinery capable of dispensing to nobles and commoners an equality of treatment; nor did it immediately make the state impartial in exacting service obligations of its citizenry. Noble favouritism outlived noble privilege.

1 *Judicial privileges*

They were not just immunities. Long preceding the development of judicial indemnity was the custom of *wergild* which laid down fines appropriate to the status of the victim.[3] Furthermore, in medieval Castile the courts systematically imposed heavier fines for damage to noble than to commoner property. In several states nobles were protected against the verbal abuse of commoners by special provisions in the law. Thus, in sixteenth-century Lithuania commoners convicted of defaming nobles lost their tongue, while in England the privilege of *scandalum magnatum* allowed peers in the early modern period to take special action against the rest of society for slander.[4] As a replacement for the duel, courts of chivalry developed in England and France to enable nobles to settle their affairs of honour.[5] Besides the more extensive and durable body of judicial privilege which relieved nobles of the normal legal processes and penalties, a body of judicial privilege existed, then, designed to protect them against the physical and verbal malevolence of commoners and other nobles.

The judicial indemnities not only safeguarded nobles from the normal court procedures but also awarded them the use of procedures closed to commoners. In addition, they excused nobles of certain punishments and reserved others exclusively for nobles. For example, before 1768 Polish nobles were excused the death sentence for murdering a peasant and paid a fine instead. Moreover, if a band of Lithuanian nobles murdered a noble only the actual murderer was liable to execution, whereas if a band of commoners committed the same offence all could be sentenced to death.[6] Normally, however, privilege only liberated the noble from certain forms of capital punishment. In France and Spain hanging was regarded as ignoble and the mode of execution thought suitable for nobles was decapitation.[7] In this respect, the French revolutionaries' use of the guillotine in the 1790s showed consideration for both humanity and a traditional noble right. On the other hand, in using it to execute noble and commoner alike, they ended its exclusiveness and also scorned the commoner's traditional right, the obverse of the noble privilege, to be spared decapitation. Breaking on the wheel was another sentence which the noble privilege confined to the commonalty. When authorised by Pombal as a proper punishment for nobles in 1758, it was regarded as a massive insult by the Portuguese nobility.[8] The convention prevailed, sometimes but not always enshrined in the law, that, whereas nobles and commoners were equally liable to the sentence of death, its form should differ. A similar convention applied to corporal punishment. Catherine II's Charter to the Nobility awarded the Russian nobility a total immunity from corporal punishment.[9] The privilege, however, was not often so generous. For example, in Poland, nobles could be sentenced to the same corporal punishment as commoners but enjoyed the special right to be flogged on a carpet. In France the penalty from which the nobility was exempted was specifically flogging; in Spain it was flogging, galley service and torture.[10] Except in Poland, the nobility's indemnity from corporal punishment certainly seemed more protective than it was from capital punishment, but the practice in both cases similarly forbad not the penalty but some of its forms. Indemnity privileges also allowed nobles either to avoid imprisonment or to receive a different prison sentence from commoners. In Spain, England and Denmark nobles could not be imprisoned for civil offences.[11] In Bohemia the right of nobles to receive a different prison sentence from commoners survived Joseph II's onslaught upon noble privilege, thanks to the concessions extracted from his successor, Leopold II.[12] In seventeenth-century Spain imprisoned nobles were privileged to be segregated from imprisoned commoners.[13] Another indemnity privilege forbad the confiscation of noble property. In Castile, for example, creditors could not legally redeem bad debts by seizing the possessions of noble debtors.[14] However, the nobility's chances of securing complete indemnity against sequestration was strongly countered by the ruler's right to confiscate the property of all subjects convicted of felony and treason. Although this prerogative could often be circumvented by legal devices such as entailment, rarely was it breached by noble privilege. The Swedish nobility's right to transfer forfeited estates to the next of kin rather than to the Crown was most unusual.[15]

The penal indemnities did not necessarily entitle the nobles to be more lightly punished than commoners. Loyseau observed of the French nobility that while its corporal punishments were lighter its fines were more severe; and for especially ignoble crimes such as theft, perjury and fraud, nobles were thought to deserve a harsher sentence.[16]

The penal privileges were usually accompanied by privileges of judicial procedure. The duel gave the nobles an exclusive right of redress outside the courts through trial by battle until it was outlawed in the course of the seventeenth and eighteenth centuries.[17] In the courts nobles enjoyed several procedural rights. Sometimes they were freed from the jurisdiction of the lower courts and were allowed to use courts of appeal as courts of first instance. In seventeenth- and eighteenth-century France, the nobility was privileged to go direct to the higher courts of royal justice. In criminal matters they had immediate access to the *parlements*; in civil matters their exemption from appearing before the courts of the *prevôts des marechaux* gave them immediate access to the bailiwick and seneschal courts. By the sixteenth century a similar system operated in Spain, although it was confined to criminal matters. In the first instance nobles could only be tried by the *audiencias* or special *alcaldes de Corte* and the sentences passed upon them required confirmation by the Council of Castile. Similar privileges developed in the territories of the Austrian Habsburgs and the Hohenzollerns. In the late eighteenth century the Austrian and Bohemian nobles were awarded the special right to have their civil actions tried before the *Landrecht* court and their crimes judged by the magistrates of the *Provinzhauptstadt*. In Brandenburg the junkers by the late seventeenth century were indemnified from the jurisdiction of the lower courts.[18] Before 1789 the procedural privilege was well established; by 1850 it had largely gone.

At the root of the procedural privilege was the nobles' right of direct access to the king's justice and the alternative right to be tried by their peers. In matters of felony and treason the latter tended initially to be substituted for the former, essentially as a safeguard against the partiality of judgment likely to stem from the king's right to forfeit the property of the convicted.[19] Eventually, the Crown redressed the balance in its favour by substituting for trial by peerage the privilege of special access to a court manned by royal judges. This development had occurred in France by the end of the thirteenth century, in Castile by 1500 and in Bohemia and Austria by the late eighteenth century.[20] In the German principalities trial by peerage did not develop. In Germany it operated only at the imperial level for the exclusive benefit of the immediate nobility.[21] In the principalities procedural privilege arose not from a debasement of trial by peerage but from the Crown's alienation of regalian rights and the nobility's preservation of the freeman's right to be tried in public rather than private tribunals. For this reason the right of special procedure was evident in Brandenburg where the lower public tribunals had been extensively alienated to subjects in the late middle ages, but not in Saxony where the ruler managed to retain them in his possession.[22]

Elsewhere trial by peerage persisted as the principal means of judging noble crimes. In England the right survived until 1949. Essentially it exempted the peers from trial by a common jury for felony and treason. The right to enjoy benefit of clergy was added in the reign of Edward VI. Except in civil matters, the two rights enabled the peers to escape entirely from the machinery of the common law.[23] Trial by peerage was frequently found in Eastern and Northern Europe. In Sweden it was restricted, as in England, to major crimes but did not exclude so completely the rest of the legal system since by 1614 the case had to be opened in the appropriate local tribunal (*häradsrätt*). Nor was the privilege so long-lived. Upheld in 1614 when the *hovrätt*, a bench of noble judges, was erected as both a high court of appeal and a special court to try the capital offences committed by noblemen, trial by peerage was terminated when Gustavus III established in 1789 a new high court of appeal whose membership was not limited to the nobility.[24] In Poland trial by peerage was institutionalised with the establishment of the Crown Tribunal for the Kingdom of Poland in 1578 and a similar court for the Duchy of Lithuania in 1581. They lasted until the partition. Both were staffed by elected nobles and tried all cases in which nobles were a party as well as appeals from the lower courts. In Poland the means of trial for nobles, accusatory rather than inquisitorial, differed from the one used for commoners.[25] Similarly in Hungary the *Tabula Regia* acted as a trial-by-peerage court of first instance for nobles and a court of appeal for commoners. It lasted from the late middle ages until 1848. In Bohemia and Austria, trial by peerage lasted until 1783 when Joseph II deprived the nobility of its monopoly of office in the central courts of justice.[26] In all these cases trial by peerage had survived interlocked with an appellate court whose membership was exclusively noble. In imitation, article fifty-eight of the 1785 Charter to the Russian Nobility awarded the Superior Land Court of each province, a body of judges elected by and from the provincial nobility, jurisdiction over 'all civil and criminal matters, complaints and litigations lodged either by or against a nobleman and involving his estate, his privileges, his rights, his honour, or a disputed will or inheritance', and prevented a noble from being deprived of his property or life without trial by peerage.[27] This collection of rights endured until 1917.

The nobility's indemnity also extended to other court, and some police, procedures. Before 1848, for example, a nobleman's word was sufficient in Bohemia and Austria; he did not need, like a commoner, to testify under oath. The English peerage was likewise privileged. In addition it was immune to various writs enforcing appearance in court. In Spain torture could not be used to extort evidence from noblemen, unless their crime was treason.[28] In Poland and Hungary, nobles possessed an inviolability of person and household until proved guilty. The right was established in Poland by 1433 and in Hungary by 1222. In preventing apprehension before trial, this privilege was somewhat different from the Englishman's right of habeas corpus which forbad imprisonment without trial. Besides enjoying freedom from arrest prior to conviction, Hungarian and Polish nobles could deny public officials entry to their households until found guilty. Furthermore, in neither case could commoners bring actions and evidence against nobles in court. In Poland these rights were a victim of the partition. In Hungary they were retained until 1848.[29]

Of the European nobilities, those of Poland and Lithuania possessed the most extensive judicial privileges, enjoying immunity from the death penalty for the murder of commoners, trial by peerage in civil and criminal matters, personal and household inviolability, and freedom from the actions or evidence directly brought by commoners. Although lacking the penal immunities of the Poles, the Hungarian nobles were also highly privileged in judicial matters; so was the English peerage with exemption from arrest in civil actions and a special jurisdiction free of government control to try its crimes.

Less advantaged by judicial privileges were the nobilities of Spain and France. Nonetheless, both enjoyed exemption from certain forms of capital and corporal punishment and possessed procedural indemnities which relieved them of the jurisdiction of the lower courts.[30] Notably short of judicial privilege were the nobilities of Italy, not only the commune-dominated nobles of the north but also the feudal-based nobilities of Naples and Sicily. They certainly did not lack legal advantages, but these were mostly attained by influence and patronage, unless they enjoyed the judicial privileges of corporations such as townships and the Inquisition. As lay familiars of the Inquisition, for example, Sicilian nobles acquired indemnity from the ordinary courts.[31]

The nobility's judicial indemnities derived from the freeman's basic right to be judged in a different manner from the slave, notably with access to a public, as opposed to a private, tribunal and, in the early Germanic societies, with the right of trial by his peers. A second important source was the right of military vassals to receive special judicial treatment from their overlord.

Yet the fact that the privileges which eventually emerged were confined to freemen with the status of nobility and not to fiefholding nobles suggests the significance of other influences. Of supreme importance was the medieval tendency of public tribunals to fall into private hands. This happened in France in the eleventh and twelfth centuries and in Brandenburg and other German states in the fourteenth and fifteenth centuries. As a result, the right of public tribunal, formerly the right of all freemen, became the exclusive right of the nobility whose privileges protected them from subjection to private justice.[32] A further important factor was the association established between the profession of knight and the right to enjoy a special jurisdiction. In early medieval France, Castile, Poland and Sweden, for example, commoners providing mounted military service had access to special courts. The eventual incorporation of knighthood within the nobility was a further means by which the judicial indemnities of freemen commoners were transmuted into exclusive noble rights.[33] Generally, the nobility's judicial indemnities took form in response to its desire for corporate rights rather than for rights confined to individual families or specific types of noble. Also responsible was the revival of public justice in Western Europe in the twelfth and thirteenth centuries since its effective extension involved granting to noblemen degrees of immunity from its operation.[34] In Eastern Europe a more important factor was the constitutional and political weakness of the Crown which was promoted in the fourteenth century by the substitution of elective for hereditary monarchy. As a result of the dynastic interconnexion of the Polish and Hungarian monarchies and the inclination of the two nobilities to imitate each other, nobles in Poland and Hungary were able to add to their corporate privileges spectacular rights of judicial immunity, especially in the fifteenth and sixteenth centuries when the Crown was obliged to comply with their demands in order to secure or retain their allegiance and to enlist their military support in wars against the Turk.

The nobility's judicial privileges had fully crystallised by 1600. After this date important additions were made only in Russia where trial by peerage and penal exemptions were awarded in 1785 as part of the government's attempt to modernise the state by westernising its ruling class. In this case the judicial privileges were not extorted from the Crown by an overpowerful nobility; in all likelihood they came of the Crown's attempt to strengthen a puny nobility so that it could serve as a buttress against popular revolution. They were a direct consequence of Pugachev's revolt and the fears which it instilled in the government's mind.[35] Otherwise new privileges only emerged in exchange for the removal of old ones. The tendency of absolute monarchy to favour judicial privileges not so much extended as preserved and modified them. The exception was trial by peerage to which strong monarchy was traditionally hostile: for example, in thirteenth-century France and in eighteenth-century Sweden, Austria and Bohemia.[36] Significantly, trial by peerage survived longest in England and Hungary where royal absolutism was effectively resisted. Apart from trial by peerage, the abolition of the judicial indemnity privileges mostly came of revolutionary events and accompanied the removal of other corporately held rights; occurring in France in 1789, Prussia in 1807, the Habsburg lands in 1848 and Russia in 1917. They showed the greatest capacity to survive in England, a state which experienced its political revolutions long before noble privilege came to be regarded as an impediment on the workings of a well-run state.[37] On the other hand a number of judicial privileges could be undone without formal abolition, usually when rendered meaningless as specific noble privileges through being awarded to the commonalty. This happened to the Polish privilege of personal inviolability when it was extended in 1791 to burghers and jews. The Russian nobility's immunity to corporal punishment could no longer count as a noble privilege when it was granted to townsmen in 1863 and to peasants in 1904; the English peerage's right of freedom from imprisonment for debt was extinguished as a noble privilege when granted to the whole community in 1869.[38]

2 Indemnity from state service

Noble privileges not only assumed that nobles owed duties to the state but also indemnified them from certain civil and military obligations. What the state required was not services from the nobles and taxes from the commoners but services from both, the duties of the one differing markedly from the other. Like the judicial privileges, the indemnities from state service usually belonged to every member of the nobility.

The civil services from which nobles were exempted mainly involved communications: the upkeep of roads in France and Denmark; haulage in Denmark and Sweden; postal services in Sweden. Indemnities of this nature, however, were uncommon, simply because the state rarely exacted this type of obligation. The privilege lasted in Denmark until 1849 and in Sweden until 1878. In Western Europe the subject's obligation to provide the ruler with civil services had existed as bannal rights in the early middle ages but their alienation to subjects had transformed them into a seigneurial exaction. In France the *corvée des routes* was only introduced in the early eighteenth century. It survived, usually as a commutation of money, until the Revolution. The noble's immunity from it must have been one of the final privileges created in France under the old regime.[39]

Nobles could also be exempted from some of the tasks of local government. But this was even rarer than the communications indemnity: exceptionally, the English peerage was excused the obligation to serve on juries and to act as sheriff.[40] The nobility's essential function in local government ruled that this type of indemnity should not be a corporate right. In England the indemnity was feasible because the peers formed no more than 1% of the aristocracy and therefore it could not seriously affect the manning of local government.

Much more common was the nobility's indemnity from military duties. Noble households were often immune to the billeting of royal troops. When this right was finally awarded the Russian nobility in the Charter of 1785, the nobles of at least Hungary, France, Spain and Prussia had long enjoyed it. In Spain the privilege was eventually diluted into the right to charge royal troops for their stay rather than to prohibit their compulsory residence; in eighteenth-century Hungary several groups of minor nobles were forced to quarter soldiers in their houses as well as to pay taxes, and, with the emergence of garrisons, the privilege could become an exemption from the taxes levied in commutation of the billeting obligation. Yet, in some form or other, the privilege lasted until the early nineteenth century, if not beyond 1848.[41]

The nobility also came to be indemnified from obligations of personal military service, especially those required of the commonalty. The nobles usually had a traditional duty to provide a special military service, but tended to enjoy exemption from all other compulsory military services to the state. This could mean exemption from militia service. In England the peers were not required to attend county musters; in Spain the nobles were privileged not to serve in the militia which developed in the late sixteenth century and, similarly, the French nobles were excused the militia service established in France in 1688. Military indemnity also conferred freedom from pressganging and conscription. Conscription was a comparatively late development, created in conjunction with the establishment of standing armies or militias. It became widespread in the course of the seventeenth and eighteenth centuries. It was found, for example, in Sweden, Bohemia, Austria, Prussia, Russia, France and Denmark. In most of these cases the nobility enjoyed immunity from it, but not after 1848 except in Russia where the privilege lived on until 1874.[42]

Responsible for the nobility's military indemnities were its special military obligations. But the latter only determined the origin of the privilege, not its survival. By 1700 they had largely gone, yet the military indemnity privileges endured, their real value enhanced enormously by the rise of standing armies, the recruitment and quartering of which had intensified the military demands made of subjects by the state. Because the privilege outlived the performance of the obligation, by the mid-eighteenth century the majority of nobilities were free from compulsory military service.

The degree of military indemnity enjoyed by a nobility depended upon the limitations it was able to impose upon its original obligations. For example by the start of the eighteenth century the Hungarian nobles, one of the few to retain a military obligation, had confined its service to the *insurrectio*, had limited the function of the *insurrectio* to the defence of the realm and had deprived the Crown of the right to summon the general *insurrectio* without the permission of the diet. Then, contrary to developments elsewhere, and directly in response to the introduction of a standing army in 1715 and the need to preserve its threatened fiscal immunities, they agreed to increase their military obligation by maintaining a *posse comitatus*. This concession was sugared by the act of 1723 which reduced the penalty for the evasion of military duty, substituting arbitrary imprisonment for loss of life and property.[43] In the West, the feudal military obligation was soon limited in the nobles' favour. By 1050 the vassals of France were relieved from serving for more than forty days without pay. By the mid-twelfth century the nobilities of England and Germany enjoyed similar indemnities. By the end of the tenth century the Castilian nobles owed no military obligation to the Crown unless it was in return for a benefice of land or money. In Sweden the nobility was freed by the sixteenth century of the obligation of personal military service. Instead they were merely required to furnish the king with properly equipped cavalry. As the estates and status of the nobility secured immunity from confiscation for the non-fulfilment of the traditional military duties or for the non-payment of the taxes to which these obligations were commuted, nobles came to be emancipated in practice from their service requirement even where governments continued to expect its fulfilment.[44]

The military indemnities followed a simple and regular pattern, relieving all nobles of the obligation to serve the government in the manner required of commoners and ensuring that their special military duties were extremely limited. Exceptions to this pattern are found in England and Sweden. In England military indemnity was the preserve of the peerage; it was not a corporately held right. In Sweden, the nobles' indemnity from personal military service, like their privilege of fiscal exemption, immunised not only themselves but also their tenants. From 1569 freedom from the national system of conscription applied both to the nobles and to tenants living within a mile of the manor house.[45]

Like the judicial privileges, the service indemnities had their beginnings in the social systems of the early middle ages, owing much to the belief then current that the nobility, either because of enfeoffment or knighthood, had a special military function for which it deserved some relief. Later they were extended in meaning as the state ceased to depend upon troops raised by nobles and instead established standing armies partially manned by conscripted or impressed subjects. Thus, while the strengthening of the state under royal absolutism generally diminished the worth of the judicial privileges, it enlarged the importance of the service indemnity. The nobility did not achieve its service indemnity by exploiting the political weaknesses of the Crown, except in the sense that a nobility's hold on the Crown helped to reduce the original military obligation. Originally, the basic rights of immunity—from militia service and billeting—were the natural complement of the noble's special military obligations. Nor was the indemnity's capacity to outlive the obligation's fulfilment necessarily the result of royal weakness. Sustaining the nobility's military immunity was the Crown's fervent belief in a privileged nobility and its ability to tolerate this particular privilege. The latter was encouraged by the willingness of nobles to follow military careers without compulsion and the consequent failure of the privilege to inconvenience the government. Similar factors upheld the other indemnities. Absolute monarchy created service indemnities in eighteenth-century Russia and seventeenth- and eighteenth-century France, and generally took care that its military innovations did not breach the traditional indemnities. Before the revolutionary era the service indemnities were questioned less persistently by governments than the fiscal privileges, the privileges of political participation and seigneurial rights.

The indemnity privileges did not incite much popular opposition. They seemed to lack the social abrasiveness of fiscal exemption, seigneurial exactions or reserved office. The *corvée* and militia service both provoked popular disapproval in France but the grievance related to the obligation rather than the noble's immunity. The indemnity privileges certainly disappeared as a result of revolutionary pressures, but did so because they were part of a condemned corpus of noble privilege rather than a special source of social friction.

3 Seigneurial indemnity

Indemnity rights also safeguarded nobles from the private demands of the seigneur. Throughout the history of the French seigneurial system, nobles who rented peasant tenures were legally exempt from labour services, the banalities of oven, mill and wine press, private taxes and patrimonial justice. In Hungary, nobles working serf holdings were free of the dues and services associated with serfdom.[46] Instead, the noble paid for his tenure with a simple rent. Invariably this immunity was the right of a whole nobility, although, as the tenants of peasant holdings, only a minority of nobles were in the position to benefit from it.

The privilege originated in the close association maintained between free and noble status and the reduction of the peasantry and their tenures to a state of serfdom. Freedom from seigneurial exactions in eleventh- and twelfth-century Western Europe went hand in hand with the right to carry weapons. Yet again, a noble privilege was created because the rights of the freeman became conditional upon knighthood and knighthood and nobility merged to form one estate.[47] Limiting the nobility's enjoyment of this privilege was the government's practice of relegating to the commonalty the nobles who worked peasant holdings, a process evident in eighteenth- and nineteenth-century Poland and Russia. Generally, however, the privilege was terminated only by the abolition of the seigneurial system. Although frequently found, its actual enjoyment depended upon the degree to which nobles occupied peasant tenures. In seventeenth- and eighteenth-century Hungary, Poland and Russia, states where the poverty and populousness of the nobility ensured that large numbers of them worked rented smallholdings, the privilege was widely enjoyed.[48] Elsewhere the inclination of noble tenants either to rent demesnes or to hold tenancies of the Crown limited its existence.

4 Value and effect

Usually the indemnity privileges were the right of the whole nobility. The possession of noble status was a sufficient qualification for their enjoyment. The outstanding exception is the indemnity privileges of the English aristocracy which were closed to the gentry and baronetcy. As the possession of every member of a nobility, the indemnity privileges were an important source of noble identity, especially for nobles without estates and incapable of living nobly. Yet commoners also possessed many of these privileges. For this reason they failed to draw a neat line between nobility and commonalty. By the late eighteenth century, royal officials of commoner status enjoyed judicial indemnities in France and Prussia.[49] In the middle ages they had been widely acquired by commoner knights.[50] Commoners not only obtained them by performing a noble function. The citizens of royal free boroughs in Hungary received both the privileges of freedom from arrest before conviction and the right of trial by a panel of their own peers.[51] In Poland the privilege of personal inviolability was granted to burghers in 1791, while in Spain a royal decree of 1786, which prevented creditors from sequestrating the tools of artisans in payment for debt, reflected the right preventing creditors from seizing the possessions of indebted nobles.[52] Exemption from state services was another noble privilege widely held by commoners. In France immunity from militia service and from the *corvée des routes* was as widespread as the tax privileges among the commonalty, having been granted to the inhabitants of the *villes franches*.[53] In 1773 exemption from militia service was conceded to the wholesale merchants of Spain. In the 1770s and 1780s it was frequently conferred upon Spanish artisans.[54] The Austrian nobility's exemption from personal military service came to be shared by the *honoratiores*, a privileged group of commoners drawn from the professions and the state services and mostly composed of graduates in law, medicine and philosophy.[55] Yet profound differences existed between the nobles' and the commoners' enjoyment of these privileges. Most commoners were awarded only certain indemnities, not the complete range that was available to the nobles. Moreover, commoners normally held their privileges not by inheritable right like the nobles but because they held public office, inhabited certain towns or followed certain occupations. And they held them not as the natural right of a class but because of a special concession made by the Crown. Although widely distributed among the commonalty, the indemnity privileges remained, nonetheless, badges of nobility; and, in acquiring them, commoners were thought to have assumed some of the trappings of that order.

What was their value, apart from being declarations of nobility? The judicial privileges did not exempt the nobles from trial and punishment, and they did not guarantee that the guilty escaped scot free or lightly penalised. Only in Poland were nobles legally excused the death sentence. Nevertheless, the nobility's widely enjoyed freedom from corporal punishment was a clear advantage to its members, as was its exemption from imprisonment for civil offences such as unpaid debts. In allowing scope for incorrigible indebtedness, the latter privilege greatly extended the financial resources at the nobility's disposal. On the other hand, there is no strong evidence to suggest that trial by peerage, or the right to avoid the lower courts, or the freedom from testifying under oath, or even freedom from arrest until proved guilty, conferred more than an honorific benefit. In all likelihood, the inviolability of the noble household prior to conviction limited the capacity of courts to find nobles guilty, but this privilege was confined to Hungary and Poland.

Of greater practical benefit to nobles than any of the judicial indemnities was the deferential attitude of the courts and the commoner's disinclination to take action against nobles because the latters' power and influence ruled out a favourable settlement. Social inequality in the administration of the law was not simply due to noble privilege. Nobles had more to gain as men of power and influence than as men of privilege. The purpose and effect of judicial privilege was to impart a distinction, not an inequality, of treatment. In this respect it differed in kind from the fiscal and service indemnities. The capacity of a nobleman to escape the law lay in his resources and his resourcefulness, not in his inherited rights. Judicial privileges, arguably, were of greater importance for poor nobles than for nobles with the material means of swaying the courts in their favour, yet alone they could confer little advantage in the law.

Except as a means of social distinction, noble indemnity from the state's civil obligations was of little value. Of much greater practical benefit to the nobility was its indemnity from military obligation, although its freedom from having royal troops quartered in its households would only have been a gain in frontier districts where troops were likely to be stationed. Moreover, the benefits of indemnity from the compulsory military service required of commoners only followed the decay of the special military service required of the nobility and the development in the early modern period of militias and standing armies manned by conscripts or pressed men. By the time of their abolition, privileges of this nature were of great value especially for the smaller nobles who would have lacked the means to evade national military service if an absence of privilege had made them liable.

The value of seigneurial indemnity depended upon the extent to which nobles held tenures subjected to seigneurial exactions and the weight of the seigneurial exactions relative to the fee owed by the nobles as an alternative payment. Just as the incorporation of tenures into the demesne and the consequent replacement of seigneurial exactions by an economic rent did not necessarily alleviate the tenants' lot, the fee owed by a noble tenant to a seigneur was not always lighter than the dues and services demanded of a peasant tenant. The advantages which nobles gained from the privilege were not so much economic as the personal convenience of being freed from seigneurial services and the honorific distinction of being treated differently from a peasantry whose way of life closely resembled their own. The value of this indemnity also relied upon the willingness of seigneurs to respect it. In the late eighteenth century the landlords of the Upper Tisza region in Hungary were not averse to subjecting their noble tenants to the same exactions as their serfs.[56] Noble tenants had little protection against their landlords since their right of public tribunal entitled them only to have their suits adjudicated by the landlord class who formed the magistracy of the royal courts. However, it was in the landlord's interest not to alienate a section of the tenantry which had good cause to ally with him against the serfs.

In assessing the value of the indemnity privileges a distinction needs to be made between types of nobility since the main beneficiaries were the minor nobles who lacked titles, estates, wealth and way of life to distinguish them from the commonalty and lacked the power and influence to bend the law in their own favour. Furthermore, the value of these privileges as indicators of noble status depended upon how many other corporately held privileges there were. As one of the first corporate privileges to be created in Western Europe, indemnity rights were of tremendous importance to the nobility in its very early stages.[57] In the final stages of its development they were of less importance, tending to fade away earlier than other corporate rights such as coats of arms and lesser titles. In the intervening period the indemnity privileges, along with the other corporate rights, upheld and publicly declared the noble identity of subjects who were otherwise unrecognisable as noblemen and so helped to determine the character of the nobility as a highly variegated class with a membership encompassing the whole range of society.

Privilege only represented the inequality which could be erased by a change in the law. For this reason the removal of the indemnity privileges did not have much practical effect. Less easily excised were the unofficial and informal inequalities which resided in the practical opportunities for the rich and the powerful to have their own way at the rest of society's expense.

IV

Rights of political participation

Nobles fulfilled a ruling function not only as the proprietors of public offices and seigneuries or because governments selected them to hold offices of state, but also because they possessed certain privileges of political participation. These privileges stemmed from (1) the practice in most European states of giving nobles exclusive access to some public offices and preferential promotion to others; and (2) the nobility's rights to attend, or to elect deputies to, parliamentary assemblies. Privileges as well as practical necessity obliged the Crown to employ noblemen in the government: reservation of office gave the nobility an inevitable role in the state's military and civil services, while parliamentary membership could award the right to participate in the grant and administration of taxes, the enactment and repeal of laws, the formulation of foreign and domestic policy, the appointment and dismissal of royal officials and even the creation of nobles and kings. Yet, although officially recognised as a noble right, the privileges of political participation were rarely available to every member of a nobility. Traditionally, parliamentary membership was often restricted to nobles who owned noble estates, possessed titles of higher nobility or belonged to families of ancient lineage. Many reserved offices were confined to members of the titled or old nobility. Not surprisingly, these political participation privileges were mostly inaccessible to commoners. For the nobility the battering which parliamentary privileges sustained under absolute monarchy was alleviated by the Crown's respect for reserved office and its willingness to tolerate both the estates structure of representative assemblies and the nobles' right to represent in parliament their tenantry. Extending the life of the political participation rights was the capacity of noble parliamentary privileges to survive revolution and to co-exist with democratically elected assemblies, although not beyond 1918, except in Great Britain and Hungary.

1 *Office-holding privileges*

Upheld by custom or law, the nobilities of most European states enjoyed special rights in the tenure of public office. These rights either gave the nobility precedence over commoners in official appointments and promotions, or confined offices to the nobility. With the seigneurial rights, the office-holding privileges eventually became the most effective of the privileges in rousing popular hatred of the noble order. Whereas in the period 1789–1850 the grievance against seigneurial rights provided revolution with the bulk of its following by turning the peasants into revolutionaries, the office-holding privileges provided revolution with its leadership and ideology by inciting against the old regime an opposition of nobles and professional men.

The original sources of reserved office were the close association established between knighthood and nobility which rendered military commands a noble preserve, the privilege of trial by peerage which necessitated a noble membership of certain judicial tribunals, and the esteem of the royal court which made it essential for the Crown to confine certain of the leading court offices to high ranking noblemen. But eventually the privilege came to infiltrate the whole political administration, partly on the insistence of nobles who saw themselves threatened by the *parvenu*, but also because of monarchy's belief that, under the Crown's direction, nobles should rule and commoners should be ruled. Of all the noble privileges, the office-holding ones were the most strongly supported by absolute monarchy which blatantly declared its belief in a noble ruling class by making them a crucial part of its bureaucracy and army.[1] In this way it provided the nobility with cause for accepting its measures of political modernisation.

Between 1660 and 1809, the absolute monarchy of Denmark possessed a range of offices which only noblemen could hold. The central administration consisted of a system of colleges each staffed by a president and a specific number of assessors. While demolishing the privileges of political participation vested in the nobility's membership of the *rigsdag* (parliament) and the rigsraad (council), royal absolutism made half the offices in each college a noble preserve. Not only were offices reserved exclusively for noblemen, but in those accessible to commoners, the nobles were preferred both in appointment and promotion. Royal absolutism did not introduce office-holding privileges to Denmark. They had previously existed in the *rigsraad*. Essentially it transferred them from the executive to the administration where they survived in the form of reserved office until 1809. Then the Crown replaced the nobility's exclusive right of appointment by a less extreme right of presentation which assured noble candidates of serious consideration, but allowed commoners the right to apply for the same posts. This modification lasted until 1849.[2]

Similarly in France, Russia and the monarchies of the Austrian Habsburgs and Hohenzollerns, the absolutist machinery of government contained a wide range of offices reserved for noblemen. This was partly because certain offices of state automatically conferred noble status upon their holders, a practice which in France had its roots deep in the middle ages. Traditionally, leading Crown officials such as councillors of state, masters of requests and secretaries of state were entitled to noble status by virtue of their office. However, since these officials tended to be selected from the nobility, ennoblement rarely resulted from their tenure. Then in the course of the fifteenth century the offices of king's sergeant-at-arms, *secrétaire du roi* and mayor of a *ville franche* also acquired the right of automatic ennoblement.[3] But the practice was only fully developed in the seventeenth and early eighteenth centuries when the government became heavily dependent on the sale of offices to raise revenue and attached noble status to many of them in order to enhance their market value. To the increase in the number of ennobling offices, Louis XIV made an outstanding contribution, awarding ennoblement to the judges of some of the sovereign courts, notably the *grand conseil*, the *parlements* and the *chambres des comptes*, and to municipal magistrates.[4] Office could confer either hereditary or personal nobility. By 1720 hereditary nobility was the right of all judges in the sovereign courts, many of whom could secure office by an act of purchase. Finally in 1750 the Crown allowed hereditary nobility to all *officiers généraux* in the army. Between 1700 and 1788 4,000 ennobling offices existed—1,200 of them imparting personal nobility which converted to hereditary nobility if held for two generations—although the acquisition of about half of these offices by the nobility denied them an ennobling effect.[5] In Russia ennoblement by office was introduced on a massive scale in 1722. Peter the Great's table of ranks graded public offices into fourteen categories. The civil offices in the first eight categories and the military offices in all fourteen categories awarded their holders hereditary nobility while the rest conferred personal nobility. Subject to modifications, especially in 1845 when hereditary ennoblement was confined to the first five ranks for civil offices and to the first eight ranks for military offices, the system survived until 1917.[6]

Yet in both France and Russia ennobling office was only one aspect of the nobility's office-holding privileges. A range of privilege was also confined to noblemen-born. Peter the Great and his successors sought to reserve certain high-ranking posts in the army and the administration for men of noble extraction and only failed because of the scarcity of suitable candidates. In this respect Peter continued a feature of the *méstnichestvo* system which, from the end of the fifteenth century to its abolition in 1682, had confined certain offices to the sons of the long-established nobility, the princes and the boyars, to the extent that 93% of those holding office in the first four ranks in 1730 came of families which had commanded high office in the Muscovite period.[7] Furthermore, in imitation of the Prussian *Landrat*, the provincial marshal and district marshal from 1785, the peace arbitrator from 1861 and the land commandant from 1889 came to be elected by, and from, the local nobility.[8] However, in Russia preferential promotion was a more prominent office-holding privilege than reserved office. Peter had considered withholding noble status from the sons of nobles until like commoners they earned it by achieving office in the eighth rank, but in practice he went no further than to insist that they be educated and that they enter the service of the state, working their way up from the bottom in the table of ranks.[9] By the end of the eighteenth century the sons of nobles had escaped most of these requirements and now possessed privileges within the table of ranks which clearly distinguished them from the sons of commoners. As noblemen-born they came to qualify for the court titles of *Kammmerjunker* and *Kammerherr* which automatically conferred the right to start a service career in either the fifth or fourth ranks. Nobles were also freed of the obligation of commoners-born to wait twelve years before proceeding from the ninth to the eighth rank in the civil service. And only nobles by birth were allowed to transfer from the civil to the military service.[10] In 1765 it was decreed that, in the matter of promotion, those of noble birth should have precedence over men born as commoners.[11]

Under pressure of military defeat, these privileges came to be seriously questioned: first during the Napoleonic Wars by Speransky, then after the Crimean War when Russia's defeat stimulated the army reforms of Milyutin. But Speransky's work was erased upon his fall in 1812 and the Milyutin reforms were undone by Alexander III who announced in 1885 that he wanted 'the Russian nobles to preserve a dominant place in the military leadership'. The office-holding privileges also outlived the country's defeat in the Russo-Japanese War and the doubts which it cast upon their usefulness, and were only terminated by the Revolution of 1917.[12] Complementing the Russian nobility's office-holding privileges was the legal exclusion of large sections of society from holding office within the table of ranks. Various governmental measures to exclude commoners culminated in Catherine II's ban on all poll taxpayers from holding public office. This meant that, apart from the hereditary nobility, the only source of recruitment for office-holders was the children of the clergy and of officials whose rank had entitled them to personal nobility.[13]

In absolutist France the privilege took the form of reserved office rather than preferential promotion. Besides the offices which conferred nobility, there were a large number restricted to the offspring of noblemen. The two expanded together, the latter a reaction to the former. Because the qualification of tenure could be several degrees of nobility, the privilege of reserved office was often an impediment upon the recently ennobled as well as upon commoners. The expansion in the number of offices reserved to the noble-born was partly a retrenchment of the established nobility, generated by the rising tide of *anoblis* resulting from the sale of ennobling offices and clearly evident in the insistence of *parlements* and of noble chambers in the provincial diets that their members should possess more than one generation of nobility. But some responsibility for the expansion of reserved offices also lay with the government. At court and in the army and navy there developed an extensive range of offices reserved for those of noble birth and, therefore, with a more limited sales possibility than offices available to *anoblis* and commoners. Their existence suggests that the system of reserved office owed something to the Crown's belief in the efficacy of the noble background, a belief the government upheld in spite of its need to regard office as a marketable commodity and to encourage professionalisation in the civil and military services for the sake of efficiency. The same belief was also reflected in the Crown's attempts to limit the amount of automatic ennoblement by office in the late eighteenth century.[14]

In the absolutist monarchies of the Austrian Habsburgs and the Hohen-zollerns, noble office-holding privileges were also entrenched in the government machinery and remained so until the early nineteenth century. Yet ennobling offices were much less common. One could secure hereditary nobility by thirty years of service as a commissioned officer in the Austrian army from 1757, and in the Prussian monarchy by the early eighteenth century the rank of minister of state automatically ennobled the recipient and in the late nineteenth century so did the office of general if held for more than one year. However, compared with Russia and France, the bureaucracies of the Habsburgs and Hohenzollerns seemed remarkably free of the practice, and none of the ennobling offices could be bought.[15] In the Prussian monarchy, the office-holding privilege mainly took the form of reserved office. This was sanctioned in 1769 by a decree which upheld the custom of confining the office of *Landrat* to the nobility, and by the legal code of 1794 which reserved to the nobility the important offices of state. In addition, office-holding privileges in the Prussian monarchy included a salary differential in favour of the nobility, a promotional precedence which allowed noble officers and officials the right to override the seniority of commoners, easy access for the sons of nobles to the lower service grades and a dispensation from the examination requirements for state service which came into force in the 1770s.[16] The Austrian Habsburgs allowed offices to be reserved for noblemen in the bureaucratised territories of Bohemia and Austria where the Crown's control of the system gave it a choice of policy as well as in Hungary where the power of the nobility left the Crown no other option than to preserve tradition. The bureaucratic circle and provincial administration which developed in the course of the eighteenth century, reserved the highest offices for noblemen, as did the imperial administration, initially established in the sixteenth century by Ferdinand I. Except in Hungary, the reserved offices of the Austrian Habsburgs tended to be confined to the higher nobility.[17]

In the Prussian monarchy the privilege was removed from the civil service in 1807 and from the army in 1808, a consequence of the impact of the French Revolution and a programme of reform enforced by military defeat at the hands of the French. In the words of Hardenberg, the government's aim was that 'every position in the state ... shall be open not to this or that caste-like group, but to all social elements possessing merit and capacity'. In this respect the government declared a wish to abolish not only the recently established legal sanction, but also the traditional practice of preferring nobles to hold office.[18] In the Habsburg territories of Bohemia and Austria, the privilege, having been challenged by the government of Joseph II, finally lost its legal authority as a result of the reforms compelled by the revolutionary events of 1848.[19] What survived until the termination of the Habsburg and Hohenzollern dynasties in 1918 was the traditional practice of ennobling commoners who achieved high office and of showing a strong preference for noblemen-born in civil and military appointments. The preference for nobles remained so blatant in Prussia that between 1871 and 1918 the offices of colonel general and field marshal went, with one exception, exclusively to men of noble birth.[20]

Absolute monarchy strongly inclined to regard the nobility of birth as the core of its ruling class and, therefore, to allow their office-holding the protection of privilege. This was evident in Louis XIV's plan of 1683 to appoint only nobles as officers in his new navy, in the policy of Gustavus III of Sweden who in 1785 planned to make all commissioned ranks in the army a noble preserve; and in the policy of Philip V of Spain who justified the regiments he established in 1704 with the words: 'these regiments are to serve as a school to the nobility of my realms ... I order them to receive in each company up to ten cadets, nobles and gentlemen, who are to be distinguished from the others in both dress and salary'.[21] A training for public office through government-sponsored, exclusively noble academies became a corollary of the nobility's office-holding privilege, and another expression of absolute monarchy's positive belief in a noble ruling class. By the late eighteenth century, noble academies had been established by the governments of Prussia, Russia, France and Austria.[22]

While absolute monarchy could occasionally take severe action against the nobility's office-holding privileges, before the nineteenth century it tended to proceed only against those which imparted executive authority.[23] In Denmark, Sweden and Russia a council developed in the middle ages staffed by members of the high nobility who attended by personal right. In Bohemia, the council's membership became diet-elected and represented the *Ritter-stand* as well as the *Herrenstand*. All these councils possessed authority to direct government policy either through their right to advise the king or through their right of consent to government decisions. In Denmark by 1665, in Sweden by 1789, in Russia by 1711, in Bohemia between 1749 and 1782, the privilege fell a victim of the Crown. In contrast, if the privilege applied to essentially administrative offices, royal absolutism proved remarkably capable of tolerating it. Quite exceptional were the restrictions imposed upon the privilege in Sweden by Gustavus III and in Bohemia-Austria by Joseph II and the Austrian Habsburg's total destruction of the traditional reserved offices in Lombardy and Tuscany in the late eighteenth century. The latter was a consequence of the Crown's need to replace the traditional civic administration by a modern professional bureaucracy rather than of animus against noble privilege.[24] Only revolution caused a change in absolute mon-archy's attitude. By 1810 reserved office had been abolished in Denmark and Prussia.[25] However, substituted for a legal requirement was a government preference. This tended to preserve the nobility as the ruling class until the rapid expansion of the civil service and army in the course of the nineteenth century enforced the employment of commoners-born in large numbers as officials and officers and radically reduced the proportion of noble-born in the state services.

The office-holding privileges which absolute monarchy permitted the no-bility are surprising but not spectacular, and significant because of the light they throw on the conservatism of governments whose control of the state did not oblige them to show too much respect for tradition, and because of the way they enlisted noble support for a radical strengthening of central government. On the other hand, it is not surprising that the more spectacular instances of the privilege should be found in states where the minimal powers of the Crown allowed the nobility a free rein. In extent, there was nothing to equal the Polish nobility which from 1374 to 1791 held the right to mono-polise all public offices.[26] Nearest to it was Hungary where non-nobles only acquired a general right to hold public office in 1843. Earlier the Crown's attempts to break the nobility's monopoly of office-holding had mainly failed; in 1723 it was driven to uphold the tradition that only nobles could be elected to office by the county assemblies while in central government, the Crown's efforts in the late eighteenth century only succeeded in giving commoners an unrestricted entry in the *Kammer*. In the Chancellery and *Consilium Locumtenentiale*, the Crown was forced by the Hungarian diet to deny commoners entry to offices above the level of secretary. Otherwise, from the mid-fourteenth to the mid-nineteenth centuries, public office re-mained a noble preserve.[27] As in Poland, abolition in Hungary was a concession initiated by the nobility in a bid to maintain popular support against the oppressiveness of royal absolutism.

Prior to the imposition of royal absolutism, an extensive range of offices became reserved for noblemen in Prussia, Pomerania, Brandenburg and Bohemia, essentially because of the pressure which noble-dominated diets could exert on the Crown. Thus in East Prussia in the 1540s it was agreed that the four *Oberräte*, the *Haupleute*, the *Landräte* and the *Hofgerichtsräte* should be chosen only from the nobility, while in the seventeenth century noblemen were awarded two-thirds of the seats in the high court of justice, as well as the position of president.[28] In Brandenburg the government decreed in 1610 that all offices were to be held by noblemen; in 1560 only nobles in Pomerania were given the right to serve as *Landräte*.[29] In these three cases, the motive for establishing the privilege was to prevent the Crown from circumventing the noble estate by relying upon commoners and foreigners. For this reason, the offices in question were confined to native noblemen. In Bohemia, the Council of State Officials was restricted to the nobility in 1564, and remained so until the offices were either abolished or left unfilled by Joseph II. Likewise, the captains in charge of the twelve circles were of necessity noblemen. The powers of both circle captains and Council of State Officials were altered and the right of appointment was transferred from parliament to the Crown but their noble reservation persisted.[30]

Similarly in Sweden, the degree of office-holding privilege enjoyed by the nobility was in inverse proportion to the power of the Crown. From the fifteenth to the eighteenth centuries the Swedish nobles exploited first elective monarchy and after the conversion to hereditary monarchy in 1544, royal minorities, in order to assert and achieve the right to monopolise the more important offices of state. The demands made by the nobility in the Recess of Kalmar (1483) and in the *Postulata Nobilium* (1594) that a noble should not find himself under the command of a commoner in a public office was upheld by the privileges granted in 1612 and in 1723. Thus in 1612 all the leading offices in the central administration were declared the exclusive province of the nobility, as were the leading offices of local government. The only important office not given wholly to the noble estate was that of *häradshörding* (sheriff), but even here the Crown agreed to prefer noblemen for the post. The monopoly embraced military as well as civil offices. This was so extensive that Oxenstierna in the mid-seventeenth century estimated that a total of 800 offices, the majority of them military, were reserved to the nobility.[31] After a retraction of the privilege in 1650, in response to the opposition of the two commoner estates in the *riksdag*, the monopoly of office was re-established and extended in 1723 following the noble revolution of 1720. In spite of the bitter opposition of the commoner estates, the public offices, which a decade earlier had been graded into forty different categories, were declared noble between the first and eleventh grades in the Russian manner. This meant either that nobles received the posts in the grades confined to the nobility, or that commoners were ennobled by receiving them. However, with so much achieved after centuries of effort, the nobility's monopoly of important offices quickly withered, largely because of the Crown's need to appoint men of ability to high office and the nobility's unwillingness to see the noble order inflated by too much ennoblement. Without legislative alteration, the monopoly had ceased to work by 1770 except in relation to the membership of the *riksråd*, and then was curtailed by Gustavus III who after 1789 was constrained by his quarrel with the nobility to ally with the commonalty. The pressures of this alliance caused him to order that only the very highest offices should be noble-held, while appointment to the remainder should rest on merit alone. Furthermore, his differences with the nobility caused him to turn the *riksråd* into a cabinet staffed not by high nobles but secretaries of state. Nonetheless, a vestige of privilege remained: until 1848 half the High Court judges needed to be noble; while throughout the nineteenth century the higher offices, especially the provincial governorships and the governorship of Stockholm, tended to be awarded to the nobility although legally open to commoners.[32]

The nobility's office-holding privileges comprehended municipal as well as state offices. This was so, for example, in France, Sicily and Spain; in France, because municipal offices from the fifteenth to the eighteenth centuries could confer nobility; in Spain, because the medieval practice of excluding nobles from municipal office was upturned in the course of the sixteenth and early seventeenth centuries when the membership of certain town councils became legally confined to noblemen; in Sicily because in the sixteenth century the candidates for elected office in towns such as Messina, Catania, Calagirone, Lentini and Syracuse had to be noble.[33] Similar office-holding privileges were found in the city states and principalities of Northern Italy, notably in Venice, Genoa, Lombardy and Tuscany where the exclusive right to hold a range of municipal offices gave nobilities privileges which in extent were second only to those of Hungary and Poland. These privileges were secured because patrician status in Genoa, Venice, Florence and Milan became hereditary and ennobling and because for centuries many of the civic officials could only be selected from the patrician class. The privileges developed in Venice after 1297 when membership of the great council was made hereditary; in Genoa initially between 1150 and 1250 and again in the sixteenth century after popular opposition in the fourteenth century had excluded noblemen from public office; in the Florentine Republic by the fifteenth century when the right of membership of the three civic councils, the *tre maggiori*, was regarded as ennobling; and in Milan by 1600.[34] In each case the system was confirmed by establishing an official record of the noble patriciate: in 1506 the Golden Books were established in Venice; in 1577 the Genoese made a similar record in their *Libro d'Oro*, and in the same century the *Congregazione degli Ordini* was set up in Milan to adjudicate on the right of patrician membership. Finally in Florence the *Libri di Ordo* were introduced in 1750.[35] In none of these instances was office-holding rendered the exclusive right of the patrician nobility, but the system ensured that a large number of important offices were confined to a minute proportion of the population and could only be held by men of commoner birth, or by nobles from non-patrician backgrounds, if they managed to acquire patrician status first.[36] Although civic in character and origin, these reserved offices were not simply restricted to municipal affairs. Because each of these cities in the middle ages came to dominate a state, they also imparted a political function.

The city states of Genoa and Venice preserved this system of reserved office until the close of the eighteenth century, largely because of their capacity to remain independent republics and to prevent, or overcome, popular opposition to the traditional oligarchic rule. In Lombardy and Tuscany, it survived on the sufferance of princes who, until the late eighteenth century, were prepared to rely heavily upon a form of government originally designed for a city to administer a principality. In Tuscany the Medici had introduced a state bureaucracy but as no more than a supplement to the civic administration of the Florentines. Only with the termination of Medici rule in the 1730s were the office-holding privileges of the noble patricians seriously challenged and only with the dissolution of the republican magistracies in 1784, and the completion of a centralised bureaucratic administration in 1789, were they destroyed. In Lombardy, in spite of a history of princely rule reaching back to the fourteenth century, the civic administration with its patrician privileges remained the basic means of administering the duchy of Milan until the establishment of a new state administration in 1749. The old municipal system was finally abolished in 1786.[37] By the end of the century the traditional civic forms of state government had gone in North Italy, replaced, or in the process of being replaced, by bureaucratic state systems which allowed advantages to the nobility but not on the traditional scale.

Like the nobility's fiscal privileges and its right of parliamentary membership, its office-holding privileges were not equally available to the whole noble estate. Differentiation, however, tended not to be achieved in the same way. Landownership was a less decisive qualification for the office-holding privileges. Essentially the privilege was a status rather than a property right, in spite of the early feudal practice of reserving to tenants-in-chief a right of summons to the king's council. This latter practice became the basis of parliamentary membership rather than of reserved office. Mainly responsible for excluding noblemen from the office-holding privileges was the reservation of offices to nobles with a title, or a noble lineage, or patrician status. In Castile, for example, before the Crown challenged their traditional position in the period of French domination from 1701–15, the grandees were specially privileged within the nobility to hold high positions at court, in the army and the administration.[38] Similarly in sixteenth-century Bohemia, certain offices were confined to the *Herrenstand*, a restriction partially removed by the land ordinance of 1627 which admitted the *Ritterstand* to some of them. However, under the influence of Habsburg absolutism, the *Herrenstand* in both Bohemia and Austria enjoyed advantages over the *Ritterstand*, and both of them enjoyed advantages over the *Edlerstand* in the tenure of office. In the late eighteenth and early nineteenth centuries, the titled nobles had not only precedence in appointments to high office, but also exclusive access to the presidencies of the *Hofstellen* (central councils) and *Gubernia* (provincial councils), while high office (the circle captaincy) in the district administration was reserved for either them or the knights.[39] In Russia the *méstnichestvo* system had closely connected the right of office-holding with high noble rank.[40] Predominant in France was the qualification of noble lineage. Traditionally, and to an increasing extent in the seventeenth and eighteenth centuries, a range of court, administrative, ecclesiastical and military offices were reserved for men with noble forbears. Admission to the office of lieutenant required four degrees of nobility. A similar qualification was necessary for nobles holding offices close to the king's person in the royal household; a noble lineage of two centuries' duration was required to hold the office of page in the royal household. Moreover, increasingly in the seventeenth and eighteenth centuries, the *parlements* insisted that their councillors should be of noble birth.[41] In both the Venetian Republic and Lombardy, the dominance of the state by a civic government, and the reservation of major civic offices for the patrician nobility of Venice and Milan meant that the nobility of feudal origin, and in Lombardy the creations of the dukes of Milan and the Habsburgs, were excluded from holding important offices unless they could secure patrician status. In Venice patrician status was extremely difficult to obtain because of the government's unwillingness to admit new members to the great council. Since patrician status was almost completely closed to newcomers from 1381 to the mid-seventeenth century, and thereafter promotions were made sparingly, most noble families on the Venetian mainland were excluded from the major offices of state, simply because they had only become subjects of the Venetian Republic after the congealment of the patricians' membership in the fourteenth century. In Lombardy patrician status was more easily obtained, but, by the early eighteenth century, admission to the patriciate had become subject to two severe qualifications. One required prior possession of noble status and thus

gave nobles an advantage over commoners. The other insisted upon a century's residence in the duchy. This favoured the nobility of feudal origin but
made difficulties for some of the Habsburg creations. In Florence, the feudal
nobles were for a time excluded from holding municipal office. However,
this tradition was terminated in 1622 and, because of the ease with which
patrician status could be obtained, nobles of non-patrician origin were able
to insert themselves into the reserved civic offices. In the Genoese Republic,
the relative inability of the city to control the rest of the state left a proportion
of the Ligurian feudal nobility ruling their estates as independent princes and
completely divorced from the system of reserved office which centred upon
the municipality.[42] Like the fiscal and parliamentary privileges which became
similarly confined to parts of a nobility, the distribution of office-holding
rights provided revolution with the sympathy and support of nobles.

The nobility's ruling function cannot be said to have depended heavily
upon its office-holding privileges. In countries such as England and Sicily
where these privileges were very limited, the nobility still dominated the
tenure of public office; and in states where reserved office was extensive but
not all-embracing, as in absolutist France, the nobility was predominant
throughout the system, holding not only ennobling and reserved offices, but
also most of the ministerial and *commissaire* posts, which were not restricted
by noble privilege.[43] Nor could it be said that the decline of the nobility as a
ruling class was caused by the removal of its office-holding privileges. In
most cases the nobility continued to dominate public office long after this
event. The nobility survived over the centuries as the core of the ruling class
for other reasons. One was its willingness to hold office and the readiness of
the commonalty to let it do so. Another was the close association between
ennoblement and public service, the former serving as the main reward for
the latter. Yet another was monarchy's inability to conceive or create a
government system which denied the nobility a prominent participatory role.

The essential social value of reserved office was the more limited one of
making it easier for certain nobles to become officials and officers. This was
at the expense not only of the commonalty, but also of other noblemen.
Ennoblement by office ensured the appearance of a noble domination of
government in Russia and France, but was of greater direct benefit to men of
commoner than noble extraction. Indirectly, however, it was of value to the
nobility in diffusing popular opposition by allowing commoners to raise
themselves into the noble estate, although this effect was probably countered
by the confinement of reserved offices and preferential promotion to the
nobles-born or to those with several degrees of nobility. In the late eighteenth
and early nineteenth centuries, the office-holding privileges tended to undermine rather than to uphold the noble estate. In provoking among the middle
classes and the nobles anti-aristocratic sentiments which, as a result of the

French Revolution, became marmorealised in the meritocratic ideology of 'careers open to talents', the office-holding privileges played a crucial part in the nobility's decline.

Nevertheless, reserved office and preferential promotion were sometimes important in giving noblemen either a control of the executive or enormous influence within the administration. This was certainly the case in Hungary, Poland and in the civic states of Northern Italy where the commonalty was for the most part excluded from the means of government by the nobility's office-holding privileges. It was also true of certain states where these privileges protected only a limited number of offices. Although the value of reserved office was severely reduced in the modern period as monarchs and their personally selected advisers monopolised the executive, for a time it allowed some nobilities to determine policy or, at least, to regulate the actions of the Crown. In the course of the sixteenth century the Council of State Officials of Bohemia became in law a noble preserve and endowed with remarkable government powers. For example, a letter of majesty in 1508 permitted it to carry on the government in the king's absence; the diet of 1606 gave it the authority to muster the country's military resources and to negotiate for assistance with neighbouring states. The Crown also conceded to it a right of consultation over the imposition of those state tariffs and tolls which traditionally belonged to the royal prerogative. In addition, the State Officials acquired some independence of the Crown, especially when it was enacted in 1526 that they could not be dismissed from office by the king alone, and in 1547 that the king could not make appointments to these offices without first consulting the diet. These gains, however, were almost completely erased in the course of the seventeenth and eighteenth centuries. The land ordinance of 1627 converted them into 'chief royal officials', beholden only to the Crown and appointed for no longer than five years' duration. Maria Theresa excluded them from politics, confining their work to judicial matters, and Joseph II suppressed their judicial role. Divorced from public affairs, the offices were either abolished by Joseph II or left unoccupied. The anti-josephine reaction which followed his death failed to revivify their function and authority.[44]

The councils with executive authority and an exclusive noble membership in late medieval and early modern Denmark and Sweden were likewise squeezed of authority in the course of time and eventually crushed by the Crown. In Sweden, the *riksråd* originally was an assembly of noblemen whose status within the nobility was defined by their right of *riksråd* membership and whose responsibility, like that of the State Officials of Bohemia, was to the community of the realm, although their appointment initially lay with the Crown. Authorised by the land law of 1350, its task was to ensure that the king honoured his coronation pledges and to organise his deposition if he did not. While the monarchy remained elective, another function was to determine the successor to the throne. In the late fourteenth and fifteenth centuries, especially during the period of the union of Kalmar, the *riksråd's* powers increased enormously, particularly because of its control of royal patronage, and then contracted dramatically in the sixteenth century following the restoration of the national monarchy and the Vasas' success in 1544 of establishing their hereditary possession of the crown. In the course of the seventeenth and eighteenth centuries, the *riksdag* annexed its role as regulator of the constitution and the *riksråd* became a body of councillors whose task was to oversee the administration and advise the king. Its political transformation was completed in the late seventeenth century by Charles XI and was not undone by the noble revolt which established a system of parliamentary government between 1720 and 1771. Throughout this time, the *riksråd* remained a noble preserve, only ceasing to be after 1789 when Gustavus III converted it into a cabinet staffed by secretaries of state.[45] The Danish *rigsraad* was similar in character and early history, but the decline of its powers was less protracted. Although the Crown was still confirming and extending its powers as late as 1648, the *rigsraad* was exposed to general blame for the country's military defeats in the early seventeenth century and was eliminated, along with the *rigsdag*, in the 1660s.[46] The privilege of reserved office also conferred executive power upon the patrician nobility in Venice and Genoa until 1797 and in Florence until the termination of the republic in 1532. In each case, the noble patriciate controlled both the administration and government policy through exclusive rights of election to, and tenure of, public office.[47]

Of the administrative offices reserved for noblemen, the most powerful were at the centres of government and tended to be confined to the higher nobility. Subject to the overriding authority of the Crown, such offices gave their occupants a remarkable control of the bureaucracy in Habsburg Spain in the sixteenth and seventeenth centuries and in Habsburg Austria and Bohemia in the eighteenth and nineteenth centuries. In the latter instance, the power conferred increased significantly in the early nineteenth century as the presidents of the central and provincial councils became less answerable than formerly to their conciliar colleagues.[48] Furthermore, at the circle level in Prussia and Austria and at both the provincial and district level in Russia there were offices of considerable influence, all of them reserved for nobles but not for the higher nobility. Under Habsburg rule the circle captain in Bohemia ceased to be a diet official and became a royal appointment whereas in Austria he developed simply as a bureaucrat. His task was to run local government. The reservation of the office by Maria Theresa for members of the *Herren-* and *Ritterstand* meant that at the imperial, provincial and local levels the bureaucracy of the Habsburg monarchy was commanded by titled or knightly officials. In the Prussian monarchy the local administration in the rural areas was controlled by the *Landrat* who, in the absence of a professional bureaucracy at the circle level, combined the functions of police chief, collector of taxes, military administrator and judicial supervisor. His appointment depended upon nomination by the *Kreistage*, the local assemblies of junkers who until 1807 were constrained by the law to select one of their own class for the post. In nineteenth-century Russia the provincial marshal, another reserved office elected by a noble assembly, was second in importance to the provincial governor in the provincial administration.[49]

2 Parliamentary privileges

Prior to the parliamentary reforms of the nineteenth century, local diets functioned alongside national and provincial diets in a number of states. Outside France,[50] the local diets were rarely assemblies of more than one estate. Many of them were exclusively noble, as in Hungary, Poland, Brandenburg, Pomerania, Hesse-Cassel, Bohemia and Russia, or essentially noble as in Saxony, where the only non-nobles with right of attendance were the commoners who owned fiefs, and East Prussia, where the noble-dominated *Amt* assemblies contained freehold peasants, but not townsmen or clerics.[51] In contrast, from at least the fourteenth until the early nineteenth centuries, the national and provincial diets were usually meetings of several estates.

The nobility's privilege of parliamentary membership entailed either the right of personal attendance or the right to elect deputies to the noble estate. In the local diets, the nobility tended to enjoy a right of personal attendance, whereas in the national and provincial assemblies membership of the noble chamber was frequently by deputation. This was the case, for example, in Hungary and Poland where an original corporate right of personal attendance had been confined by the mid-sixteenth century to the local diets which elected deputies to the national or provincial assemblies.[52] A similar practice developed in fifteenth-century Bohemia but was terminated in the early sixteenth century by Ferdinand I's insistence that the nobles should attend the provincial diet either in person or not at all. By the seventeenth century the election of deputies was also practised by the nobilities of Brandenburg, Hesse-Cassel, Saxony, Brabant, Hainault, Normandy and East Prussia;[53] and where national as well as provincial diets existed, as in France or the Low Countries, an elected membership to the national diet was the rule.[54] On the other hand, throughout the history of the national and provincial estates assemblies,[55] some nobilities retained the right to attend them in person. In these cases, membership of the noble chamber was usually subjected to highly restrictive qualifications. In most diets the privilege of personal attendance was a property right. In the provincial assemblies established in late

eighteenth-century Russia, membership was conditional on the possession
of land in the relevant province.[56] Elsewhere the property qualification was
more exacting. In Upper Austria and Bohemia, the possession of an estate
legally defined as noble was the means of admission.[57] In Naples, Sicily,
Friuli and Sardinia, a fief held of the Crown was the primary requirement,
while in the Piedmontese parliaments the feudatories of nobles as well as of
the Crown were entitled to a personal seat.[58] The ownership of a noble estate
(*Rittersgut* or fief) also justified personal attendance in the diets of several
German principalities and in some of the provincial diets of the Low Countries and France.[59] In a number of diets—for example, in Saxony, Dauphiné
and Limbourg—a noble estate only awarded its owner the right of parliamentary attendance if it possessed certain rights of jurisdiction.[60] Occasionally additional restrictions were imposed, largely to forestall the entry of
parvenus. Thus by the eighteenth century the fief-holding families in the
Lower Rhine duchies of Cleves, Mark, Jülich and Berg needed at least four
generations of nobility on both sides to warrant the right of attendance.
Some of the French and Low Countries provincial assemblies placed similar
restrictions upon the fief holders.[61] Besides the property qualification, there
was the limitation which confined personal attendance to the titled nobility,
as in the provincial assembly of Languedoc, the national diet of Hungary
from 1608 to 1919, in England from the fourteenth century and in Scotland
from the late sixteenth century until elected deputation was substituted by
the union of 1707, and again from 1963.[62] Another limitation restricted
personal membership of the noble chamber to the nobles of ancient lineage,
as in the Breton provincial diet where the original property qualification for
membership gave way to the requirement that at least one hundred years of
undisputed nobility was necessary to award admission.[63] Originally the right
of personal attendance had often been conditional on the receipt of a royal
summons, and vestiges of this condition survived, but the overriding tendency was for this restriction to wither away and for nobles to attend by
automatic right rather than by royal favour.[64] Qualifications additional to
noble status could determine not only the noble's right of personal attendance
but also his right of parliamentary membership by deputation. In the German
principalities, for example, the right to elect the deputies to the noble
chamber belonged exclusively to the owners of noble estates.

Nevertheless, several states resorted neither to deputation nor special
qualification. Thus, noble status alone conferred the right of personal attendance in medieval Hungary and Poland and over a much long period in
Sweden, Aragon, Catalonia and Valencia. In Spain this was made practicable
by the existence of several provincial assemblies within the one state, ensuring that the number of nobles qualified to attend each assembly was relatively
small. In Sweden where a national diet allowed all nobles the right of

personal attendance, the power to speak was limited after 1626 to one member of each noble family and voting was by family (each family having one vote) not by head, the vote to be cast by the member with the right to speak. These restrictions must have reduced the numbers wishing to exercise their attendance rights.[65]

The states which confined the noble estate in parliament to specially qualified nobles left many nobles completely without the parliamentary privileges of their order. Even in those states which allowed the whole nobility the right of attendance (Sweden, the provinces of the Crown of Aragon, Hungary and Poland), the right was restricted to part of the representative system, as in Poland and Hungary where for the bulk of the nobility it was soon confined to the local assemblies. Or it was eventually taken from certain elements within the nobility. In Sweden, newly created nobles were excluded from the noble chamber after 1762 unless they could gain entry by replacing a family which possessed the right of attendance or unless the process of extinction reduced the family membership of the *riksdag* to 800 or below. Furthermore, after 1809 all the male members of qualified families were no longer admitted, and admission was confined to one representative from each family. In Valencia, minor nobles of recent extraction were excluded from the *cortes* in 1626. Following its annexation by Austria in 1775, the minor nobility of Galicia lost their parliamentary rights, In this respect, the English aristocracy was not alone in being divided between those with and those without noble parliamentary privileges. By 1800 landless and poor nobles, or nobles whose estates were not definably noble, commonly lacked the parliamentary privileges of their order. In some states, elements within the nobility lacked most of them. In Hungary by the late eighteenth century, landless nobles or those occupying smallholdings were excluded from the county diets and formed no more than a part of the electorate which selected the noble deputies for the national diet. In Russia individual voting rights in the provincial and district noble assemblies were confined initially to nobles with government office and a landed income of at least 100 rubles and from 1831 to nobles with more than 100 serfs or with at least 8,000 acres of uninhabited land.[66]

In many estates parliaments there was one noble chamber, as, for example, in Sweden, several of the German states, Tyrol, Sicily, Naples, Catalonia, Valencia, England and Denmark. On the other hand, in Hungary, Poland, Aragon, Bohemia, East Prussia, Saxony and all the Austrian territories but for Tyrol, there were two noble chambers.[67] This imparted a further distinction of privilege within the nobility. It allowed the noble order to be divided not only between those with and those without the right to parliamentary privileges, or between those with a right of attendance and those with no more than a right of deputation (as in Normandy, Saxony and Hungary, where the two rights coexisted[68]), or between those with full parliamentary rights and those with but a few of them (as in Hungary and Russia), but also between those with the right to attend the first and those with the right to attend the second noble chamber.

In contrast with the local assemblies where it was often possible for both commoners and nobles to sit by hereditary right,[69] in national and provincial diets attendance by birthright was usually confined to the nobility. Most unusual was the Scottish system which gave freeholders an inheritable right to attend parliament in person. This right, however, came to be restricted to the peerage in the course of the fifteenth and sixteenth centuries.[70] Safeguards were erected to prevent commoners from enjoying the nobility's parliamentary privileges. In a number of states, lands which conferred parliamentary membership could only be owned by nobles or, as in Brittany and Burgundy, could only confer parliamentary membership if held by a nobleman.[71] Except in the states which allowed commoners to acquire parliamentary privileges through landownership,[72] non-nobles secured only a personal as opposed to an hereditary membership of the noble chamber. And this happened very infrequently in spite of the emergence of a middle-class in the early modern period—essentially due to the professionalisation of the government machinery, rather than to any economic development—which could not be slotted into the traditional 'estates' categories and might have been more rationally accommodated within the noble rather than the burgher estate in view of its outlook, aspirations and function. Yet, except in Sweden, this group was given some privileges of nobility but not its right of parliamentary membership. Moreover, in Sweden noble parliamentary privilege was conferred only on commoner army officers, not on commoner civil servants. The royal ordinance of 1617 initially gave the Swedish army officers their own estate, but this failed to establish itself, largely because a high proportion of officers were nobles and, therefore, entitled to attend the noble chamber. Then after 1664, the commoner officers were allowed to attend the noble chamber, although without voting rights.[73] In Hungary, commoners came to attend the noble chamber in parliament simply because the commoner estate was not given parliamentary membership in its own right. To allow the commonalty direct representation without destroying the diet's exclusively noble membership, royal boroughs were allowed to define themselves as collective nobles.[74] Finally, in the *cortes* of Aragon commoners gained membership of the noble chamber simply because in the middle ages the representatives of five small towns were allowed to sit with the nobles instead of with the other urban representatives.[75]

Thus the noble parliamentary privileges accessible to commoners were extremely limited. When acquired, the privileges differed in kind from those enjoyed by the nobility, lacking birthright and sometimes, as in Sweden and

Hungary, imparting fewer rights of parliamentary participation.[76] On the other hand, rarely were the nobles barred from membership of the other chambers. In several estates parliaments the nobility was the presiding force not only because of its noble rights but also because noblemen were frequently the elected representatives of the other estates.[77]

Connected with their parliamentary membership, nobles enjoyed several other privileges which, like that of membership, were not simply the rights of M.Ps. but belonged specially to the nobility. In a number of diets where voting was by head rather than by chamber—for example, in Hungary, Bohemia and the Austrian territories—the noble members had the right of a personal vote whereas the non-noble members could only vote collectively.[78] Over much of Europe the membership privileges of the nobles included the natural right to represent the inhabitants of their domains. As a result, the only non-noble element in parliaments, apart from the clergy, tended to be the delegates of royal townships and, much less frequently, the deputies of peasants who were freeholders or Crown tenants. The tenantry and townships of the nobility gained access to parliament only by virtue of their landlord's right of parliamentary membership.[79] In addition, the nobility's parliamentary privileges sometimes included the right of favoured representation in the standing committees which parliaments employed to look after their affairs in between sessions. Thus in Lower Austria and Carinthia, the membership of the parliamentary committee was limited to the nobility even though direct representation in the diet was enjoyed by the commonalty. In other states, notably Bavaria and Sweden, the nobility was allowed a disproportionate number of committee seats.[80]

Noble privilege outlived the estates assembly. As a result of the parliamentary reforms of the nineteenth century, the nobles retained special rights: seats continued to be reserved for them, to be occupied either by right of personal attendance or by deputation, in Great Britain, Portugal, Hungary, Bohemia, Austria, Russia, Prussia and several other German states, while Hungarian nobles were exempted from the franchisal qualifications required of the rest of the electorate. However, rarely did the reforms of the nineteenth century permit noble privileges to be held by corporate right. In most cases they were imparted by the special qualifications of entitlement and landownership.[81]

(a) Location and life span

The privileges which local diets allowed the nobility had a very long history, except in Russia where they were first introduced in the late eighteenth century, in Bohemia where local diets were abolished in the course of the seventeenth century and in France where some diets faded away with the rise of provincial assemblies in the late middle ages and others, notably the seneschalsy and *recette* assemblies of Guyenne, either lost their noble membership in the sixteenth century or went under in the early seventeenth century, roughly at the same time that the provincial assembly of Guyenne ceased to meet.[82]

Having largely originated in the fourteenth and fifteenth centuries, these local diet privileges were quashed latterly: in the late eighteenth century in Austrian Poland; in the nineteenth century in Prussian and Russian Poland, the German states and Hungary; and in 1917 in Russia.[83] Yet outside Eastern Europe they were never very common. In this respect, the presence of local diets in Guyenne, Burgundy and Languedoc was unusual for Western Europe and their absence in Moravia, Silesia and the Austrian territories was exceptional for Eastern Europe. In the Austrian territories the *Kreis* was adopted as a unit of local government in the eighteenth century but, in contrast to its traditional equivalent in Bohemia and Brandenburg, its character was bureaucratic not representative.[84]

Much more frequently found were the noble privileges associated with national and provincial parliaments, especially between the thirteenth and nineteenth centuries. In many cases the appearance of the estates diets had been preceded by occasional gatherings of vassals or other leading subjects summoned to counsel and assist the king.[85] These essentially noble assemblies developed into estates diets through the addition of deputies from the clerical and communal estates. The primary purpose of these enlarged assemblies was to grant taxes. In spite of their right of fiscal exemption, the nobles continued to attend them because it was felt that feudal law made their consent necessary for validating the taxes which the Crown levied on their tenants: hence the close connexion between noble parliamentary privileges and fief ownership. In contrast, a nobility's enjoyment of parliamentary privileges as a corporate rather than a property right tended to stem either from its traditional liability to direct taxation, as in Poland, or from its membership of parliaments with long-standing legislative powers, as in Hungary and the provinces of the Crown of Aragon.

However, noble parliamentary estates were not universally found in Europe and many, after flourishing in the middle ages, died long before the nineteenth century. Russia developed a noble parliamentary estate at the national level only temporarily in the late sixteenth and early seventeenth centuries and belatedly in 1905; and acquired provincial and local assemblies representing the noble order only with the reforms of 1785 and 1864.[86] Several states possessed long-established parliaments from which the noble estate was absent. In a number of South German principalities—for example, Baden, Württemberg, the Palatinate, Bamberg and Trier—the nobles, if ever present in parliament, soon withdrew and acquired the right of non-attendance by securing the status of imperial free knights.[87] In the Alpine states of the Swiss confederation and Vorarlberg, and in the Pyrenean province of Quatre Vallées, representative assemblies traditionally admitted no privileges of nobility.[88] In Castile, the noble estate never established itself as an integral part of the *cortes*, failing to secure a right of summons for its members, who attended only by government appointment or as elected representatives of the urban communes. Likewise in Belgian Flanders.[89] Furthermore, in the assembly of the March of Ancona, the noble estate disappeared in the late fourteenth century, although the assembly continued to meet as a gathering of estates until the eighteenth century.[90]

Of the noble rights attendant on parliamentary membership, committee privileges were not widely found, nor were special voting rights.[91] On the other hand, almost coincident with the range of parliaments with noble estates was the right of nobles to be the sole parliamentary representative of those subjected to their lordship.[92]

Under the old regime the termination of a representative assembly deprived several nobilities of their parliamentary privileges. In large parts of Northern and Central France, provincial assemblies had expired by the mid-fifteenth century.[93] The last Piedmontese estates parliament sat in 1560. In the seventeenth century alone, estates parliaments met for the last time in Denmark (1660), Brandenburg (1667), Bavaria (1669), Naples (1642), Portugal (1698), Sardinia (1698), the French provinces of Périgord (1612), Dauphiné (1626), Normandy (1655) and Alsace (1683), in the *généralité* of Guyenne (1635) and in the Government of Lyonnais, where the assemblies of Forez, Beaujolais and the Plat Pays of Lyonnais expired in the course of Louis XIV's reign. In Franche-Comté and the Crown of Aragon the traditional diets were eliminated in the early years of the eighteenth century.[94] Yet monarchs who took rigorous action against the parliaments of the pre-revolutionary period were not in every case opposed to the existence of the nobility's parliamentary privileges. In many instances the Crown's attitude resembled the one it adopted towards fiscal privileges. It was prepared to uphold them so long as they did not hinder the government. Moreover, its reform of parliament mainly concerned the latter's authority, not noble privilege. Prior to the nineteenth century the Crown rarely excluded the noble order from parliament; nor did it challenge the right of noble members to represent their tenants and dependants. Consequently estates parliaments and their noble privileges could survive not only where royal government remained straitjacketed by constitutional precedent but also in monarchies such as Bohemia and the Austrian territories in the seventeenth and eighteenth centuries where the Crown liberated itself from the traditional restraints upon its powers.[95] They also survived in France: provincial assemblies with a noble estate persisted until the Revolution in French Flanders, Artois, Brittany, Navarre, Béarn, Languedoc, Burgundy and Provence.[96] In the Prussian monarchy the nobility retained parliamentary privileges not only in the parts where diets continued to meet but even in the territories such as Brandenburg where the provincial diets ceased to sit. Here the tax-granting function of the diet was transferred to the *Kreistage*, the local assemblies in which the owners of noble estates sat by right.[97] In Bavaria the estates parliament no longer met after 1669, but a vestige of its noble privileges was preserved in the continued existence of its standing committee, half of whose membership had to be noble.[98] In falling prey to royal absolutism in the late eighteenth century, Poland was not immediately bereft of its estates assemblies. Parliamentary reforms initially replaced one estates assembly by another: thus in 1815 both the Russian and Prussian governments authorised estates assemblies in the parts of Poland which they had annexed, while in 1775 the Habsburgs instituted an Austrian type of estates parliament in Galicia. What disposed of the Polish nobility's parliamentary privileges was not simply its subjection to royal absolutism but a nationalist opposition to foreign overlordship which provoked the Russian government to terminate the parliamentary system in the Congress Kingdom and eventually persuaded the Austrian and Prussian governments to substitute a democratic parliament in Galicia and Poznania.[99]

The estates parliaments had largely gone by 1850. After that date they lingered on only in Sweden and in the duchies of Mecklenburg-Schwerin and Macklenburg-Strelitz, the former until 1866, the latter until 1918.[100] Responsible for their disappearance was not only the capacity of royal absolutism to develop a political organisation which had no need of parliament, but also the emergence of assertive social groups which the estates parliament had failed to represent. The chief of them was a class of professionalmen and government officials, who, in the revolutionary circumstances of the late eighteenth and early nineteenth centuries, acted decisively to force the abolition of the estates structure of parliament and to replace it by a system of privilege which, instead of specifically favouring nobles and the owners of noble estates, showed partiality for the appointees of the Crown.[101] Yet prior to the twentieth century the pressures of revolution did not totally dispose of the traditional organisation. The nobility reaped great benefits from the parliamentary reforms of the nineteenth century not only because of the electoral importance which the new constitutions awarded property-owners but also because in a number of states nobles retained an hereditary right to parliamentary membership, exercisable by personal attendance or deputation. Thus in the Habsburg Empire, the reforms of 1848 disposed of the traditional estates assemblies but those of 1861 preserved noble privilege as an integral part of the parliamentary system, in having an upper chamber both in the *Reichsrat* and in the reformed Hungarian parliament where titled nobles enjoyed the right of personal attendance. Also maintaining it was the curial system of election to the *Landtage* (the unicameral provincial assemblies) and the lower house of the *Reichsrat*. Until 1907 the parliamentary electorate in certain provinces was divided into four curias, the first being confined to the owners of noble estates (estates registered as *landtäflich*). This arrangement applied to all the provinces except for Tirol, Dalmatia and Bohemia where the first curia electorate was determined by property size or tax liability, Vorarlberg which lacked the first curia just as under the old system it had lacked a noble estate, and Hungary where the curial organisation was not adopted.[102] Noble privilege in Hungary resided in the titled nobility's right to sit in the upper house, a right which became conditional on a tax liability of at least 3,000 florins in 1886 and was converted into a right of deputation in 1926, and the untitled nobility's privilege to cast a vote by 'ancestral right' in the election of members to the lower house. This privilege exempted all nobles from the property and educational qualifications which determined the commonalty's right to vote. Eventually it lost meaning with the establishment of universal suffrage.[103]

In the territories of the Hohenzollerns noble parliamentary privileges partly resided in the *Herrenhaus* which the Crown imposed upon the Prussian diet in 1853 by introducing to the upper chamber the counts, life members elected by groups of long-established owners of noble estates and the representatives of a limited number of noble families each of whom had been awarded the right, conditional upon royal approval, to provide one member of the *Herrenhaus*. This undid the democratic reforms of 1848, 1849 and 1850 which, in creating a national parliament without noble privilege and by abolishing the traditional provincial and local assemblies, had allowed the nobility to assert itself in parliamentary matters only by means of its wealth and influence. In the same year (1853) the Crown restored the provincial diets (*Landtage*), originally revived in the 1820s with a proportion of their seats reserved for the delegates of the noble estate owners. Likewise, the local noble assemblies (*Kreistage*) were also restored in 1853 and remained a source of noble parliamentary privilege until 1872.[104]

Several other German states retained a strong element of noble privilege throughout the nineteenth century. In the Kingdom of Hanover, the estates parliament was revived in 1814 by royal decree, after its abolition by the French. Then in 1833, the old system was replaced by a parliament with an upper chamber in which the higher nobility had the right of personal attendance and the lesser nobility the right to elect thirty-five deputies. Rejected in 1848, this system was re-established in 1855. In Saxony, the constitutional reforms of 1831 which ended the estates parliament provided an upper chamber in which certain nobles had the right of attendance. Although repudiated in 1848, the system was restored in the reaction of the following decade. An upper chamber with a special place for some of the nobility was

featured in the constitutions introduced in 1818 for Bavaria and Baden, in
1819 for Württemberg and in 1820 for Hesse-Darmstadt. In Baden and
Württemberg the nobility thus acquired a privilege which it had not enjoyed
for centuries.[105] The constitutional reforms of the nineteenth century also
created a chamber of nobility in Portugal (1826) and Sicily (1812 and 1848)
and preserved one in Great Britain. In each case, the members attending by
noble right were titled.[106]

The most blatant example of the latter-day creation of parliamentary
privileges occurred in Russia. The reforms of the late eighteenth century and
after created rather than preserved noble privilege, giving the hereditary
nobles the right of attendance in provincial and district assemblies in 1785,
the right of electing noble deputies in the provincial and district *zemstvos* in
1864 and the right to elect deputies from the provincial noble assemblies to
the Council of State in 1905–6.[107]

Thus, in the course of the nineteenth century constitutional reforms demo-
lished the estates system and favoured the commonalty by extending its right
of electoral representation. Yet, in many instances, they preserved part of
the traditional system for the special benefit of the nobility. In some respects
the removal of the nobility's parliamentary privileges resembled the abolition
of its fiscal privileges; certain rights were taken either from the nobility as a
whole or from elements within it, while in compensation a vestige of privilege
was retained and further rights bestowed. Unlike most of the fiscal privileges,
however, the parliamentary ones were still strongly entrenched in 1900.
Their final elimination only came with the establishment of republican
systems of government, in Portugal in 1910, in Russia in 1917, in Germany,
Bohemia and Austria in 1918 and in Hungary in the 1940s, a coincidence
which confirms the ascendant role of monarchy in their maintenance.[108]

After 1918, noble parliamentary privilege survived only in Great Britain
and Hungary, in the former because the house of lords was shorn of most of
its traditional authority in 1911, conservative governments had much to gain
from its continued existence, labour governments, for a complexity of
reasons, could always convince themselves that more important matters
demanded their prime attention and because the large-scale creation of life
peers after 1958 made the Lords seem not so much a bastion of birthright as
a means of rewarding commoners for meritorious service.[109] In Hungary,
noble parliamentary privilege survived because the revolution of 1919 was
defeated by the old order with the military aid of the Rumanian monarchy.
This victory gave the traditional society, under a regency if not a reigning
monarch, an extension of life which was terminated by the Russian armies
at the end of the Second World War.[110]

(b) *Value and effect*

The impact of the nobles' parliamentary privileges depended upon the powers possessed by a parliament, the extent to which a nobility's privilege allowed it to take charge of these powers and the nobility's alternative means of influencing parliamentary affairs.

Only a handful of estates parliaments exercised as a legitimate right an executive control of government. In sixteenth- and seventeenth-century Poland, for half a century in eighteenth-century Sweden, in England following the revolutions of the seventeenth century, in the Dutch Republic and incipiently in sixteenth-century Bohemia, parliaments secured the right to determine government policy. They did so by severely restricting the royal prerogative and by establishing a system of ministerial responsibility.[111] In addition, the diets of Denmark, Brandenburg, East Prussia, Pomerania, Saxony and Bavaria acquired, and also lost, in the period from the fifteenth to the seventeenth centuries, the right to decide aspects of government policy, although, except in Brandenburg, this right was confined to foreign affairs.[112]

Furthermore, only a few of the estates parliaments acquired a control of legislation. The Bohemian diet possessed this authority between 1310 and 1627, the Swedish *riksdag* acquired it in the course of the sixteenth and seventeenth centuries, while in the fifteenth or sixteenth centuries it was exercised by the national diets of Piedmont, Hungary and Poland. It was also held by the *cortes* of Catalonia, Aragon and Valencia between the thirteenth and early eighteenth centuries, by the English parliament from the fourteenth century, by the Scottish parliament from the mid-fifteenth century until 1707, by the States General of the Dutch Republic and by the parliament of Friuli in the fourteenth and early fifteenth centuries.[113] Yet legislation remained beyond the competence of the diets of the Southern Netherlands, most of the German principalities, Austria, France, Portugal, Naples and Denmark, that is, apart from authorising taxation, offering advice on legislative matters or petitioning the government for legislation. In several instances a parliament's capacity to make laws, as in sixteenth-century Sicily or Sardinia, was only an alternative to, not a replacement for, legislation by royal decree.[114]

The commonly held tax-granting powers of many of the estates parliaments were also limited. As governments could often call upon substantial non-parliamentary revenues and because parliamentary taxes were frequently of an irregular and extraordinary nature, rarely was a government's financial resources completely subjected to parliamentary control. In a number of states (for example, Denmark, Sicily, Hungary, Portugal, France, Castile) from the fifteenth century onwards only a small proportion of the government's income was granted by parliament. Most of it derived from highly profitable regalian rights: the Crown's monopoly of mining and salt production in Hungary; the royal income from overseas empires in Portugal and Castile; the king's prerogative to impose indirect taxes as in Hungary, Naples and Sicily or direct taxes, as in the French *pays d'élections*. Governments also escaped parliamentary control because of the resources which could be drawn from the Crown's rights of landownership, as in eighteenth-century Prussia, or because of grants of permanent taxes which, unless altered, could be levied without further recourse to parliament. This was the case with most indirect taxes in France, the Prussian monarchy, Castile and Sicily.[115]

Imposing a further limit upon the estates parliaments was the absence of a right of regular assembly. Parliaments normally sat by royal permission. Few secured the right to sit irrespective of the royal summons, and very few were granted the right of regular and frequent convocation. The rights which the Aragonese *cortes* secured between 1292 and 1307 for either biennial or triennial meetings and the right of triennial assemblies granted to the Hungarian diet in the fifteenth century were exceptional concessions.[116] Certain parliaments, such as those of the Austrian territories, Bohemia and a number of German states met annually in the seventeenth and eighteenth centuries; at times those of Naples met biennially and the Sicilian parliament met triennially; the provincial assemblies of France met between once a year or once every three years. But these regular meetings were a consequence of the Crown's inability to exact regular direct taxation without recurring parliamentary consent.[117] The convocation of estates parliaments tended to rely simply upon the need of the Crown to raise extraordinary taxes or, in a limited number of instances, to make new laws or repeal old ones. Neither ensured regular sittings.

Furthermore, in the course of the early modern period, the estates parliaments, if not eliminated, were forced to forfeit many of their powers to the Crown, so much so that by the late eighteenth century, apart from the parliaments of England and the Dutch Republic which had progressively increased their authority, the Hungarian diet was one of the few to retain most of its traditional powers. Yet they were frozen for long periods between 1765 and 1867 as the Habsburgs allowed years to pass without it meeting.[118] By the outbreak of the French Revolution, in most European states, laws tended to be made by royal edict, taxes tended to be levied either without parliamentary consent or with a right of consent which failed to alter the government's demand, and government policy tended to be decided by ministers who were solely responsible to the Crown. Since this subjection was often achieved without the abolition of parliament or the removal of the noble chamber, the nobility's parliamentary privileges consequently suffered devaluation rather than termination.

Nevertheless, although the powers of the estates assemblies rarely matched those of modern democratic parliaments, their existence at the national, provincial or local level, from at least the fourteenth century onwards, had awarded important functions to the small proportion of society which they directly represented. These functions included the widely enjoyed granting of taxes and the petitioning of government as well as the less frequently enjoyed right of resistance and the power to make laws, serve as high courts of justice, determine policy, appoint government officials, administer, even appropriate, government supplies, elect kings and ennoble. To buttress their powers and to take care of their business in between parliamentary sessions, estates parliaments in many cases developed their own standing committees and permanent administrations.[119]

The authority of the estates parliaments was probably at its greatest in sixteenth- and early seventeenth-century Poland. By the early seventeenth century the *sejm*, the national diet of Poland, had acquired a complete control over legislation and taxation. It had also forced the monarch to seek its consent if he wished to travel abroad, to create new noblemen or to make war or peace. In addition, the Crown could appoint to certain offices of state only candidates nominated by the *sejm*. Moreover, from the late sixteenth century there existed a standing senatorial committee. Elected by the *sejm*, this body decided government policy in consultation with the king and had to report its business to the *sejm* for authorisation. As a result, the government's policy-making was firmly placed under direct parliamentary control. Complementing the right to direct the executive was the legitimate right of rebellion, a right first established in 1574. Underpinning the whole system of parliamentary power was the *sejm*'s right to elect the king's successor.[120]

Few of these powers were unique. A control of ennoblement was possessed in the sixteenth century by the Bohemian diet and in the eighteenth century by the Swedish *riksdag*.[121] Several assemblies acquired the right to some control of foreign policy, notably in the German principalities, between the fifteenth and seventeenth centuries.[122] Standing committees were possessed by the estates parliaments of Saxony, Bavaria, East Prussia, Brandenburg, the March of Ancona, Mecklenburg, the Crown of Aragon, Sicily, Portugal, Bohemia, Austria, Sweden and of the French provinces, although not often with ministerial responsibility.[123] Most of the committees were administrative organs, responsible for looking after the interests of parliament, particularly the allocation, appropriation and collection of taxes, rather than for running the state.[124] Much less common, but quite extensively enjoyed nonetheless, was the right of resistance. Both the diets of Bavaria and Aragon possessed it in the fourteenth century, while the right of the East Prussian diet to summon the assistance of the king of Poland in the late sixteenth century if the government infringed its privileges, implies its existence in yet another form. In the late seventeenth century the right was finally terminated in Hungary, having been enjoyed by the noble estate since 1222.[125] Control of, or influence over, the succession to the throne was a right of the Hungarian parliament until 1687, of the Bohemian diet until 1627, of the Swedish *riksdag* as a result of the failure of the ruling line in the early eighteenth and early nineteenth centuries, of the Portuguese *cortes* following the revolution of 1640 and of the Sicilian parliament for a time in the fifteenth century.[126] Likewise, the right to appoint public officials was widely held by estates assemblies and was found in Russia, Denmark, the Crown of Aragon, France, Austria, Sicily, Bohemia, a number of German principalities (for example in East Prussia, Pomerania, Brandenburg, Mark and Cleves), the French *pays d'états* as well as in Poland.[127] What distinguished the Polish diet was the range of powers which it simultaneously enjoyed over a long period of time, and the way the nobility's right of membership allowed it to use these powers for restricting the rights of Crown and commonalty and for enlarging its own privileges.

The local diets which emerged in Poland in the late fourteenth and early fifteenth centuries also enjoyed considerable powers, but throughout the sixteenth and well into the seventeenth centuries, they were restricted by their subjection to the national *sejm*. In this period their basic function was to elect to the *sejm* representatives who, after 1496, were endowed with full powers.[128] In contrast, the county assemblies of Hungary retained control over their delegates to the national diet. They could legitimately dismiss and replace those who failed to abide by their instructions.[129] A similar relationship existed between the local and provincial diets of Bohemia.[130] However, in the course of the seventeenth century, the local diets of Poland came to the fore as parliaments in their own right with the authority to grant taxes and to pass laws. This happened as magnate factions and their use of the *liberum veto* to terminate parliamentary sessions, frequently before any laws could be enacted, paralysed the national *sejm*.[131] Among local diets, the county assemblies of Hungary most closely resembled those of Poland, especially after 1608 when the national diet allowed them to determine changes in the legal relationship between lord and serf. Although undone by the Crown's intervention during the reigns of Maria Theresa and Joseph II, the arrangement was revived in 1790 and reaffirmed in the 1820s.[132] In Bohemia the local diets acquired similar legislative and fiscal powers to the local diets of Poland but only during the interregnum of 1439 to 1458.[133] Likewise the Swedish local assembly (*haradsting*) was a means by which the government could comply with the 1350 land ordinance requiring it to seek popular consent for new taxes and laws. However, this consent could also be given by other representative bodies, notably the provincial assembly (*landsting*) in the middle ages, and the national assembly (*riksdag*) in the modern period.[134] The local assemblies of Brandenburg lacked legislative authority but possessed the right to elect deputies to the provincial diets, a function also shared by the local assemblies of East Prussia and Saxony.[135] In Brandenburg the demise of the provincial diet in the late seventeenth century elevated the local assembly in importance by making it the sole tax-consenting body for the rural areas.[136]

In the late sixteenth century the local diets in Poland acquired the right to elect local government officials.[137] This right was frequently exercised by the local assemblies of other states. From at least the early sixteenth century and until the 1840s in Hungary, the county administration essentially resided with noble officials elected in the local assemblies.[138] The chief exception was the head of the county administration, the *foispan*, who was a royal appointment. Further powers and functions acquired by this county administration included the standing army established in 1715, as well as the population surveys which the Crown promulgated in the eighteenth century.[139] Although repeatedly challenged by the Crown, the Bohemian local assemblies managed to acquire some control of local administration through the appointment of officials; but unlike the Hungarian and Polish local diets, they failed to establish themselves as an integral and durable part of the political system. Having been legalised in 1494, they were placed at the mercy of the Crown in 1528 when their meetings were made dependent upon a royal summons. Thereafter they were rarely convened.[140] The local assemblies of Brandenburg, Sweden and Russia all enjoyed important functions in electing local officials, although the Swedish local diets lost the right to appoint the *häradshövding* (sheriff) as early as the mid-fourteenth century, while the local diets in Brandenburg only acquired the important right to nominate candidates for the office of *Landrat*, the government's chief administrative official at the circle level, in 1769.[141]

The nobles of pre-partitioned Poland successfully used their representative authority to resist any attempt to increase the power of the Crown, as well as to maintain the monarchy in a politically primitive condition, decentralised and deprived of the extensive professional bureaucracy and large standing army which other states acquired as a result of their subjection to royal absolutism. Thus, by means of the powers of parliament, the Polish nobles upheld their traditional public functions. In addition, they were able to serve their own interests as merchants, passing laws which handicapped the commerce of the native bourgeoisie, and as landlords, enacting a body of legislation which, by the mid-seventeenth century, had left the peasantry with fewer rights than anywhere else in Europe outside of Russia.

Eventually the Polish parliamentary system fell a prey to royalty, following the partition of the kingdom by three Crowns which had already imposed upon their own realms absolutist systems of government. After the partition, new estates assemblies replaced the *sejm* in Austrian and Prussian Poland— the last estates diets to be created—and a diet with a special provision for the nobility was created in Russian Poland, while local assemblies were retained in Russian and Prussian, but not in Austrian, Poland. Yet, although noble privilege was thus preserved, it was severely reduced in value as the powers of both types of assembly were dramatically reduced: those of the local diets as a result of the bureaucratisation of local government which converted the officials elected by the diets into the advisers of bureaucrats over whom the diets had no control, those of the provincial diets, through losing the *sejm*'s traditional control of taxation and legislation and becoming bodies which could only advise and petition as in Prussian and Austrian Poland, or which enjoyed some legislative competence but no capacity to withstand the Crown as in Russian Poland.[142]

The impact of royal absolutism upon the nobility's parliamentary privileges was conditioned by the range of powers possessed by parliaments and how soon the Crown was able to strike them down. Thus, the effect was considerable in Bohemia[143] not only because of the actions of Ferdinand II following his victory at White Mountain (1620), but also because of the parliamentary rights which John of Luxemburg had granted in 1310 in return for his election to the throne. They awarded the Bohemian diet the power to elect the king's successor as well as to control legislation and government finance. In addition, by the sixteenth century it had acquired some control over ennoblement and over the appointment of leading judicial and administrative officials in central and local government.[144] But Ferdinand II dissolved the law-making and electoral capacities of the Bohemian diet in 1627 and, with the later help of Maria Theresa and Joseph II, the government weakened so effectively its traditional grip on the administration that by the 1780s the only diet-appointed officials in the central administration were two officials attached solely as advisers to the *Gubernium*.[145] Likewise, the diet's control of local government disappeared in 1751 when the circle captains were converted into salaried royal officials. Furthermore, its traditional fiscal rights were seriously reduced in the course of the seventeenth and eighteenth centuries. The right to grant and administer taxes was narrowly restricted between 1659 and 1763 as the Crown transformed several diet taxes into royal taxes which could be levied without parliamentary consent and were collected by the king's officials rather than by those of the diet. The fiscal powers of the diet were reduced even further when the Crown insisted in 1749 that the remaining diet taxes should be granted decennially. Moreover, if Joseph II's reform of the land tax had not been undone by his successor, Leopold II, the whole system of taxation would have become independent of the diet. As it was, the Bohemian diet in the eighteenth century ceased to question the royal demands for revenue and so in practice renounced its right to determine taxation. It continued to meet annually and preserved the right to apportion and collect, as well as to grant, certain taxes. It successfully pressurised Leopold II to abandon some of Joseph II's reforms. But by 1800 it was a faint shadow of its former self.[146]

Other notable victims of royal absolutism were the diets of Brandenburg, Denmark, Sweden, the Crown of Aragon, Austria and certain French provinces. Between the fifteenth and late seventeenth centuries, the Brandenburg diet had acquired some control over government policy, in spite of its lack of legislative powers, and had developed a standing committee and a bureaucracy for administering the taxes which it was authorised to grant. All was swept away in the course of the seventeenth century as the government established a general excise in 1667 which did not require diet consent for its renewal, invested the local assemblies with the right of consent to the land tax and made the collection of taxes the responsibility of royal rather than diet officials.[147] The diets of Bavaria and East Prussia were similarly treated.

In Sweden, a system of parliamentary government operated between 1720 and 1772. Prior to that, the evolution of parliament was retarded. Although first appearing in the fourteenth century, it was not until after 1660 that it fully controlled the system of fiscal and legislative consent. Hampering its development was the existence of traditional provincial and local assemblies, folk rather than 'estate' in character, through which the government could obtain the necessary consent for new laws and new taxes. Initially the development of the *riksdag* came of the Crown's need for a counterweight to the magnate-dominated *riksråd*. Then, as a result of the noble revolt against royal absolutism on the death of Charles XII, from 1720 to 1772 the *riksdag* came to dictate government policy through the *riksradet* whose membership was appointed by the parliamentary estates, and through a committee of secret matters which represented all the estates except for the peasantry.[148] In Sweden, royal absolutism did not reduce parliament to a permanent state of passive impotence. Having survived the absolutism of Charles XI and XII with its fiscal powers intact, the *riksdag* retained a great deal of power after being subjected to the absolutism of Gustavus III and his successor. Moreover, as the legislative authority which was lost in the late seventeenth century and again in the late eighteenth century was shortly afterwards restored (in 1720 and 1809), the only permanent victim of royal absolutism was ministerial responsibility which the Swedish parliament eventually recovered in the early twentieth century.[149] In contrast, the Danish parliament was terminated as a result of the establishment of royal absolutism and ceased to meet from 1660 until 1849. Although the traditional estates parliament never acquired the legislative authority or ministerial control of the Swedish *riksdag*, and its powers in practice were severely limited by the private resources of the Crown which until the early seventeenth century made it largely independent of parliamentary taxation, it was equipped from the mid-fifteenth century with an impressive range of rights which included not only fiscal consent, but also a role in the appointment of state officials and a say in the declaration of war.[150]

As decisive, was the impact of Bourbon absolutism upon the *cortes* of the Crown of Aragon. These were abolished in the early eighteenth century. Instead, the three provinces were given representation in the much less powerful *cortes* of Castile. From the fourteenth century, the *cortes* of Catalonia, Aragon and Valencia possessed the sole right to authorise taxation and to make changes in the law. They had standing committees to supervise the observation of laws and to administer public funds, an administrative machinery to collect taxes and a rule of either biennial or triennial sessions. They never acquired the right to control government policy, only the right to discuss questions of war and peace and to ratify treaties, but nonetheless they gave their members a decisive voice in the affairs of state, especially under the Habsburgs when the Castilian orientation of the monarchy left the Aragonese provinces largely to their own devices. In addition, the *cortes* of Aragon held the right to investigate all infringements of the law by the king and government officials. In spite of Philip II's reprisals against the Aragonese, following the revolt of 1591, and Olivares' attempts, in the 1620s and 1630s, to tax the provinces appropriately, very few of their traditional powers were quashed before Philip V's act of abolition.[151]

Besides reducing and terminating the rights of traditionally powerful assemblies, royal absolutism was also responsible for limiting and eliminating the powers of parliaments whose authority had always been comparatively slight. In the provincial diets of Austria, for example, there was a long history of standing committees, diet-run bureaucracies and annual sessions, but the legislative function of the diets was traditionally restricted to the granting of taxes and to advising the government on other legislative matters. Their essential powers were financial and they came under strong attack in the late eighteenth century. All that was left by 1800 was the right to consent formally every ten years to the taxes determined by the Crown and to participate in their allocation and collection. The diets, in addition, had also acquired some political force through their permanent committees, but the powers of these bodies came to be severely limited during the seventeenth and eighteenth centuries as provincial administrations became the complete responsibility of the *Gubernia* which by 1780 were fully established as bureaucratic boards. In contrast to the standing committees which had been entirely elected by the diets, only two members of each *Gubernium* needed to be diet-elected and their function was merely advisory. Whereas the Bohemian diet retained the right to elect the diet president, in the Austrian territories the subjection of the provincial diets to bureaucratic monarchy was symbolised by the fact that the *Landeshauptmann*, the head of the *Gubernium*, was automatically president of the provincial diet.[152]

Other victims of royal absolutism, among the parliaments with traditionally limited powers, were the provincial diets of the French *pays d'élections* whose establishment in the fourteenth century accompanied the development of a national system of taxation and which ceased to meet in the period from the fifteenth to the seventeenth centuries, although as important as the strength of the Crown in bringing them to an end was the traditional scantiness of their powers which hardly justified the inconveniences of assembly.[153]

Finally, a group of estates parliaments were largely unaffected by royal absolutism. They included the provincial assemblies in the parts of France which remained *pays d'états*, the national parliaments of Hungary, England and Scotland, the provincial diets of the Low Countries and the States General of the United Provinces.

In Hungary the powers of the national diet were successfully maintained not only because of the strength of the parliamentary opposition, but also because they were not too much of an impediment upon the actions of the Crown. Between 1437 and 1457, the Hungarian diet became a regularly meeting body with the power to authorise all legislation and direct taxation. In the course of time it also acquired the right to consent to a general levy of the noble militia.[154] In addition there fell to it the right to elect the successor to the throne, and in 1606 it became responsible for electing the palatine who headed the government of Hungary in the king's absence. Of these basic rights, only those of regular assembly and electing the successor to the throne were taken away: the Habsburgs made the Crown hereditary in the male line in 1687 and the female line in 1723 and dispensed with parliament for decades at a time in the late eighteenth and early nineteenth centuries.[155]

Nevertheless, the considerable powers of the Hungarian parliament remained firmly framed by the royal prerogative since the Crown kept the right to decide foreign policy, to determine the tariffs on foreign trade, to administer the considerable income from the regalia, to ennoble, to summon and prorogue the diet at will, to initiate all legislation and to make key appointments in central and local government. Parliamentary government was not introduced until after 1867.[156] The part of the king's authority which was subjected to parliamentary consent in pre-partitioned Poland was largely left untouched in Hungary. Mainly responsible for this difference in political development was the long-term policy of the Habsburgs, the reputation which they gained for defending and liberating Hungary in the war against the Turk and also the small proportion of government revenues dependent upon diet consent which never formed more than one-third of the revenues drawn by the Habsburgs from the Hungarian lands.[157] Such factors countered in Hungary the political circumstances of the late medieval period when, in both Poland and Hungary, kings were forced to make political concessions to ensure their election to the throne and to attract noble support for their wars. On the other hand, the Habsburg monarchy failed to impose itself on the Hungarian diet with the success which it achieved in the remainder of its territories. While succeeding in transforming the state from an elective to an hereditary monarchy, the Habsburgs could not, as they could in Bohemia, affect a revolution in government. Defeating their political designs was the intransigence of the Hungarian nobles who proved highly effective not so much in limiting the powers of the Crown as in preventing their extension. A pattern of political events was reiterated over the centuries: an attempted extension of royal power was followed by an aristocratic revolt and a royal compromise. The revolt of 1790 against the absolutism of Maria Theresa and Joseph II which resulted in a concord upholding the customary rights of the Hungarian nation was only a repeat of what had happened prior to the settlements of 1606, 1681 and 1711.[158] In Hungary the attempt to impose royal absolutism only made for periods without parliament (from 1765-80, 1811-25, 1849-60 and 1861-5), not a loss of the diet's constitutional authority. Similarly, prior to the late nineteenth century, the attacks on the county diets only led to their temporary suspension, not to a reduction of their powers or their elimination.

The Hungarian nation only managed to throw off the royal control of the Habsburgs in 1867 when, almost twenty years after the demise of its estates parliament, it established a system of parliamentary government. A similar achievement occurred in England with the revolutions of the seventeenth century which abolished strong monarchy. Among estates assemblies in the modern period the English parliament was exceptional in managing to impose severe restraints upon the authority of the Crown. However, prior to the seventeenth century, its achievement was only to maintain the powers which it had originally acquired in the fourteenth century. Compared with those of many continental assemblies, these were extremely limited in number. Lacking was the right to appoint officials, to elect a standing committee, to employ its own bureaucracy, to approve domestic or foreign policy. Summoned at royal will, it had no right of regular attendance. The source of its strength was the Crown's dependence upon parliamentary taxation, a consequence of the inadequacy of the king's ordinary revenues. In addition, the limited authority of royal proclamations rendered parliamentary statutes the basic means of altering the common law. By the eighteenth century, parliament had transformed its political position. Not only had royal absolutism been defeated but, in the struggle against it, parliament had also ceased to be merely a body summoned to grant extraordinary revenue and to make changes in the law: instead it had become essential to everyday government and, therefore, in frequent and regular session.[159]

The Scottish parliament had enjoyed roughly the same powers that the

English parliament had traditionally exercised. From the fifteenth to the eighteenth century it controlled legislation and taxation. In contrast with the provincial *cortes* of the Crown of Aragon, its abolition in 1707 as an independent assembly did not reduce the value of the noble's right of parliamentary participation since it involved incorporation with a parliament, that of England, whose powers by this time were considerably greater than those of the Scottish parliament. What changed was the nature of the privilege; the Scottish peerage's right of personal attendance was replaced by the right to elect deputies.[160]

Also unaffected by royal absolutism were the provincial assemblies of the Low Countries. Those of the north were safeguarded by the establishment of the Dutch Republic, those of the south were maintained by the incapacity of the Spanish and Austrian Habsburgs to deny them their basic rights. In the south the only assembly to go was the States General which failed to meet between 1632 and 1790 when a revolt against royal absolutism resulted in its revival. In the United Provinces, the States General took over much of the authority of monarchy in the late sixteenth and seventeenth centuries but failed to deprive the provincial diets of their traditional powers which were preserved and enlarged by a system of deputation. Lacking in full powers, the deputies of the States General remained fully answerable on every matter to the provincial diets.[161] In the Southern Netherlands the traditional powers of the provincial diets, essentially tax-granting and administrative, remained untouched. As in Hungary, the absolutism of the Austrian Habsburgs met its match. Joseph II's repeal in 1789 of the 1356 charter of Brabant, a reaction to the refusal of the Brabant and Hainault diets to grant supplies, met with effective revolt. Although challenged from below as well as above, these provincial diets retained their traditional powers until the old regime was toppled by the French Republican Army in 1792.[162]

Finally, in France royal absolutism encountered representative assemblies whose powers were probably more limited than anywhere in Europe. They lacked legislative authority and several (the diets of the *pays d'élections* with the exception of Normandy) lacked tax-granting powers. Moreover, those with the right to grant taxes (the diets of the *pays d'états* plus Normandy) tended to comply with the tax demands of the Crown. However, many of the diets did acquire and retain a habit of regular assembly, meeting every one, two or three years. This contrasted with the national diet which, having met only six times in the fifteenth and sixteenth centuries, assembled but twice in the seventeenth and eighteenth centuries. In addition, some of the provincial assemblies acquired standing committees and their own administrations for the collection of taxes. Essentially responsible for the limited nature of their powers was the extended emergency of the Hundred Years War which helped to justify as necessary and normal the arbitrary authority of the Crown. But also contributary was the fact that by 1500 the provincial assemblies with tax-granting powers covered less than one-half of the realm. With the remainder providing revenues which were independent of parliamentary grant, the Crown had less need to make concessions to the tax-granting parliamentary assemblies in order to raise supplies. Limited from the start, the powers of these provincial diets remained largely undiminished throughout the era of royal absolutism, a consequence not of the failure of royal policy but of the diets' traditional weaknesses which made them and their powers tolerable to the government and not worth the trouble of confiscation.[163]

Parliamentary privilege allowed the nobility either to share the powers of parliament with the rest of the membership or to take charge of them. The latter occurred in the estates parliaments of Poland, Hungary, Bohemia, Austria and Naples where the disparity between the parliamentary privileges of the nobles and those of the commonalty and the clergy made the nobility's domination of parliament a natural right rather than something secured by enlisting the support of the other estates. In the diets of Hungary, Poland and Naples, the commonalty lacked its own parliamentary chamber and, obliged to attend the same house as the nobles, was subsumed by their overwhelming majority. By 1600 the non-nobles had been totally excluded from the Polish system of representation. At all levels, national, provincial and local, with the exception of the provincial assembly of West Prussia, it was a noble preserve.[164] Whereas clergy and townsmen retained a right of membership in the Hungarian diet, it appertained only to a minority of seats in the lower chamber. Non-nobles in Hungary were completely excluded from the local assemblies and only attended the national diet, an officially recognised noble institution, through an arrangement which granted them temporary noble status. Added to the disadvantage of being in a small minority and lacking representation as estates, the clergy and townsmen suffered from a voting system which by 1800 gave every noble member an individual vote and restricted the urban and clerical delegates to one collective vote for each group. Earlier, when the towns first gained admission in the mid-fifteenth century, their delegates had attended only as observers.[165] The noble members of the Neapolitan parliament were similarly favoured. Under the Angevins, commoners and clergy had ceased to attend and it became a gathering of barons. Alfonso I restored to the parliament its original estates character in the early fifteenth century but this made little practical difference. Under the Habsburgs it was attended only by the barons and the representatives of the city of Naples, all of whom sat in the same chamber, made decisions by majority vote and, because of the barons' numerical ascendancy, operated in the noble interest.[166] For a time in the French provincial diet of Dauphiné the system of deliberating and voting in one house and the rights of membership which ensured a numerical predominance for the nobles awarded the noble order a natural domination of parliamentary business, that is, until the late sixteenth century when voting by order and deliberation in separate chambers was substituted.[167]

The non-noble members of the Bohemian and Austrian diets possessed their own parliamentary chambers, yet the system of membership and voting again guaranteed domination by the nobility. In the provincial diet of Bohemia, the clerical estate was without membership from the early fifteenth to the early seventeenth centuries, as was the commoner estate from 1485 to 1508 and from 1547 to 1564. Then the admission of the clerical estate to membership in the 1620s was accompanied by the almost complete exclusion of the commonalty which, as in Hungary, Poland and Naples, had consisted only of the delegates of certain royal boroughs. Before 1620, 30 of these royal cities were represented in the diet. After 1627 their number was reduced to six; and after 1755 only Prague had the right to send deputies who could attend for the whole session. The deputies of the other cities merely stayed to hear the royal *postulata* and then departed. In 1846, on the eve of the diet's termination, the disparity of privilege ensured that 90% of the diet membership was noble, with seven urban deputies, fourteen clerics and 194 nobles. Before 1620 each chamber was allowed one vote and the majority of votes determined parliamentary business. In the absence of the clerical estate and the occasional absence of the urban estate, the nobility had enjoyed an advantage which was only complicated by disagreements between the two noble chambers. The reappearance of the clerical chamber in the early seventeenth century necessitated a change in the voting system in order to uphold the noble advantage. Under the new arrangement, the nobility and the clergy were allowed personal votes while the attenuated urban membership was given one collective vote. With voting by head substituted for voting by chamber—the collective vote of the urban deputies counting for no more than one head—an overcareful safeguard was erected to prevent the urban delegates from acquiring voting powers disproportionate to their numbers.[168]

In the provincial diets of the Austrian territories, the numerical excess of nobles over non-nobles was also staggering. Except in Tyrol and Vorarlberg, each diet possessed four chambers, two of them reserved for the nobility. In the Vorarlberg diet the nobles were unrepresented, while in Tyrol there was only one noble chamber. The diets of Tyrol and Vorarlberg were also unusual in possessing a peasant estate. In the other Austrian diets, the non-nobles were solely the delegates of royal towns. They were easily swamped by the noble membership. For example, in Lower Austria by the early nineteenth century, the parliamentary membership comprised 338 nobles and thirty-eight urban delegates. The diet of Upper Austria contained eighty-one nobles and the delegates of ten townships whose numbers could not have exceeded twenty. But, as with Hungary and Bohemia, the nobility's control of these diets lay in the system of voting. Besides possessing two chambers to the commoners' one and an overwhelming numerical advantage, the noble members enjoyed personal votes while the urban delegates had, at the most, one collective vote and, in some cases, no vote at all. As in Bohemia, the voting system, in which parliamentary decisions rested on the consent of the majority of members not of chambers, licensed the nobility to determine matters in their own interest.[169]

Yet in most of the estates parliaments, the system of privilege awarded the nobility the right to occupy the majority of seats, in spite of its smallness as a social group, but not to dominate parliament; and, in many instances, even placed it at a disadvantage for controlling parliamentary affairs.

Usually voting by chamber rather than by head neutralised the nobility's numerical preponderance. Furthermore, in East Prussia where the noble exceeded the number of non-noble chambers, the advantage was countered by the constitutional rule that, to authorise a parliamentary decision, the three chambers should be in unanimous agreement.[170] In other states the nobles gained no advantage from its parliamentary privileges because the noble and non-noble chambers were equal in number, as in the English parliament, the provincial assembly of Gelderland, the *cortes* of Aragon and also in the diets of several German principalities after the Reformation had excluded the clerical estate;[171] or, and this was usually the case, the nobles were at a clear disadvantage because the noble estate occupied by right only a minority of the chambers. In Denmark before 1626 and Sweden, the ratio of noble to non-noble chambers was one to three.[172] Yet rarely was the minority greater than one to two, and in Catalonia, Sardinia and Sicily this disadvantage was countered by the voting procedure which, like that of the East Prussian diet, insisted on the chambers being in unanimous agreement.[173] Also disadvantaging the noble estate was the voting system of certain Low Countries assemblies which gave more votes to the urban deputies than to the noble estate. This amounted to three votes against one in Flanders, six votes against one in pre-Revolt Holland, eighteen votes against one in Republican Holland and seven votes against one in Zeeland.[174] In the provincial diet of Languedoc where the third estate had as many votes as the noble and clerical estates combined, a similar counterweight against noble privilege operated.[175]

Especially valuable in upholding the nobles' parliamentary position was their right to represent those under their lordship. Most of the commonalty was represented in parliament not by elected deputies but by their seigneurs. Direct peasant representation was rarely found in assemblies with a noble estate. At the provincial or national level it existed in Sweden, Denmark (before 1626), East Friesland, Tyrol and England and at the local level in

East Prussia and the Grand Duchy of Poznan. Otherwise, peasant representatives tended to be found only in parliaments which lacked a noble estate,
as in the margravate of Baden or the province of Vorarlberg. Furthermore,
in the few parliaments where it was found, the peasant's right of direct
representation did not deny the lord's right to represent his tenants in
parliament since the peasant's right was confined to the freeholders and
Crown tenants. For example, in the Swedish estates parliament, the peasant
chamber merely represented these two independent groups. The same was
true of Denmark, while peasant representation in East Friesland and East
Prussia was restricted to the freeholders, as it originally was in England
(subjected to a forty shilling property requirement).[176] In most diets the
commoner estate consisted exclusively of the deputies of royal townships.
Townships in the possession of nobles were normally represented by their
lords. In Piedmont a number of communes enjoyed direct representation
even though they were owned by feudatories and by other communes, but
this was an exception.[177]

A central feature of the estates parliaments was that, like the democratic
parliaments before the adoption of universal suffrage, they never directly
represented more than a small fraction of society. As most of society was
incorporated in parliament only through the nobility's or the Crown's privilege to stand as its natural representative, a great deal of anti-noble resentment, particularly the sort which the seigneurial system generated between
landlord and tenant, was kept out of parliamentary debates. The commoner
members, whether townsmen or freehold peasant, tended to be free of such
grievances while the noble members tended not to press an issue which
accused their own kind and threatened their own livelihood.

Also highly beneficial to the nobility was its privilege of favoured representation on parliamentary standing committees, not so much in Lower
Austria and Carinthia where the nobility's control of parliamentary business
was already assured by the parliamentary system,[178] but in Sweden and
Bavaria where this type of privilege reduced the nobility's disadvantage of
occupying only a minority of the chambers in the diet. It did so by permitting
voting by head rather than by order in the committee, by allowing the
committees' decisions to be reached by a majority vote and by reserving for
the nobility a substantial number of committee seats.

In Bavaria the nobility's disadvantage of being in a voting minority in the
diet, in spite of comprising the majority of its membership, was countered
after 1508 by its right to a delegation on the diet committee which equalled
the combined representation of the non-noble estates. In the course of the
seventeenth century this privilege became additionally important when parliamentary business was totally vested in the standing committee as a result
of the diet's demise in 1669.[179] Buttressing the position of the Swedish nobles

in the *riksdag*, where the noble estate had to cope with three non-noble estates, was firstly the right of the noble chamber's speaker to serve as marshal of the diet, and secondly the noble right of double representation on all *riksdag* committees. Since the peasant estate was omitted from the secret committee of the *riksdag* that operated in the period 1720–72, the nobility's privilege allowed it to occupy half the seats on that committee.[180] In East Prussia, the nobility's right to a majority of seats on the diet committee helped to compensate for the voting system whose principle of unanimity undid the nobility's advantage of occupying the majority of chambers and seats in the diet.[181]

Nevertheless, in most cases the nobility's domination of parliament had little to do with privilege but depended essentially on the deference of the clerical and commoner members, and the degree to which the nobles could influence them, notably through patronage and by acquiring membership of their estates. In this respect, the English aristocracy's traditional control of parliament was in keeping with what had prevailed in much of Europe. From the fifteenth until the late nineteenth centuries, both houses of the British parliament had a preponderantly aristocratic membership. Paradoxically, until the multiplication of titles in the closing decades of the eighteenth century, the membership of the Commons was more aristocratic than that of the Lords. This was due on the one hand, to the bishops' and, before the Henrician Reformation, the abbots' right to sit in the upper chamber and, on the other, to the large numbers of gentry in the lower house, 88% of whose membership was aristocratic in 1584 and 76% as late as 1865. Originally a gathering of tenants-in-chief and leading royal officials, the upper house quickly became the exclusive chamber of the peers and the leading clergy, whereas aristocratic membership of the lower house continued to rest not on privilege but solely on the ability to get elected. Moreover, since the majority of Commons seats were borough and not county, an aristocratic majority in that house depended upon the gentry's ability to persuade independent townsmen to accept them as their parliamentary representatives. The English aristocracy's control of parliament had little to do with their right to dominate the upper house. The principle of consent by both houses soon established itself which, when breached in the late seventeenth century for finance bills and in 1911 for most legislation, worked against rather than in favour of noble privilege by permitting a unilateral decision of the Commons, subject to the assent of the Crown, to authorise statutes of this nature. From the late middle ages, the direction of parliamentary business came to reside with the Commons and, therefore, depended on the exercise of political influence rather than of parliamentary privilege. Nonetheless, over the centuries, privilege did endow a section of the aristocracy, the peerage, with an essential role in the legislative process, a role which ceased to be inevitable in 1911 but retained importance in the amendment and postponement of legislation.[182]

The election of nobles to parliament by the non-noble estates not only occurred in England. The nobles were prominent in the urban, clerical and noble chambers in Sicily, Portugal and France, while in the Castilian *cortes* the representation of the towns by *hidalgos* helped to make up for the nobility's lack of representation as an estate. In early nineteenth-century Sweden nobles were frequently chosen to represent the smaller towns in the urban estate of the *riksdag*. The nobles entered the commoner estate in the same way in the part of Poland which first became the Duchy of Warsaw and later the Congress Kingdom. By infiltration, and by manipulating the deference of commoner and clerical representatives, nobles could compensate for the shortcomings of their parliamentary privileges, securing in practice as much control over parliamentary business as certain nobilities traditionally obtained by virtue of their privileges.[183]

Since the nobility used its powers and influence to impose itself in parliament throughout the nineteenth century, the reduction of noble privilege in the revolutionary era seems not to have seriously affected the nobles' ability to direct parliamentary affairs. Even in those parliaments which privilege had placed in noble hands, noble control easily outlived the loss of it. Furthermore, the elimination of a noble's sole right to represent his tenantry was deprived of immediate effect by the restrictions which literacy and property qualifications initially placed upon the electorate of the reformed parliaments. Occasionally combining with those noble privileges which survived the abolition of the estates structure of parliament, the nobility's capacity of leadership and its political and economic resources preserved the class as a powerful force in parliamentary affairs.

It was not very difficult for nobles to enjoy a decisive voice in the parliamentary assemblies of the late nineteenth century even though they were no longer aided by the traditional estates system. In Hungary, the surviving importance of the nobility as a political elite and an electoral system which confined the vote to 6% of the population, produced in the very first election of the reformed parliament a house of representatives 72% of whose membership was noble. Sustained by the vestigial estate privilege residing in the upper house and in the nobility's exemption from the franchisal qualifications, by an electoral system which strongly favoured property-owners and by a reputation earned as the saviour of the nation against the might of Habsburg absolutism, the Hungarian nobles were strongly placed to dominate parliamentary politics well into the twentieth century. In 1910 58·4% of the house of representatives remained noble.[184] In Bohemia, Austria and Prussia, the retention of noble parliamentary privileges and a franchise which favoured property owners ensured that the nobility's control of parliament outlived the abolition of the estates diets in 1848.[185] Moreover, in France, Sicily and Sweden where the abolition of the estates system left the nobles completely without parliamentary privilege, their influence in parliament persisted long afterwards.[186]

What finally deprived the nobility of parliamentary influence was not the elimination of privilege since a good deal of parliamentary power remained with the nobles after 1848. More important was the elimination of a franchise narrowly restricted to favour property owners and the rich. The days of the nobility as a parliamentary force were only numbered when the establishment of universal suffrage gave freedom of expression to the old social antagonisms (which chiefly concerned landlordship) and created an outlet for new anti-noble sentiments which could be nationalistic as in the Austrian Empire, or could stem from a democratic disbelief in birthright or from conflict between the agrarian and industrial interest. By presenting him with the unpalatable need to pay 'court to unwashed majorities', the extension of the franchise persuaded the noble to retire from politics. His place was taken by the professional politician. Consequently the parliamentary elite became bourgeois in character.[187]

The development of representative systems of government owed something to the nobility's parliamentary privileges. Their privilege of membership gave them an interest in preserving parliament even when its limited powers and their fiscal immunity provided them with little cause to concern themselves with parliamentary matters. Their appreciation of parliament was certainly no safeguard against the reduction of its authority. However, out of respect for noble privilege, absolute monarchs tended to preserve a system of representation even when it had little practical point. On the other hand, nobles seemed to have no sympathy for democracy. As they valued it, representation was primarily by right of privilege, not election. Privilege directed the nobility to value political systems in which representative bodies had some part to play; and to counter popular opposition to their privileged position, nobles in the nineteenth century conceded extensions of the franchise; but privilege turned them against systems of parliamentary government based upon universal suffrage.[188]

V

Honorific privileges

These privileges entailed (1) formal recognition of rank, notably by means of public precedence and salutation; (2) exclusive membership of, or the right to use, certain chivalric, ecclesiastical, academic and banking institutions; (3) the insignia of sword-wearing, special garments and coats of arms and (4) titles, predicates and forms of address. In keeping with most noble privileges, many of the honorific rights were state authorised. They were either granted or confirmed by the government. Some, however, were private creations. The privilege of special access to military orders, monasteries, cathedrals and private schools was created independently of the government whose role in the development was only to imply approval by failing to make objection.

The longevity of some of the honorific privileges, notably coats of arms and titles, helped to preserve for the nobility a distinctive identity well after it had lost its ruling function and had adopted a bourgeois way of life. Besides juridically distinguishing noble from commoner, they also made social distinctions between the members of a nobility. They not only helped to identify noble status by forming an important part of the corporately-held privileges, but also determined that the noble order should be stratified by a hierarchy of titles rather than simply by wealth and function. Nevertheless titles were only one form of status differentiation within a nobility. There was also the distinction between old and new creations, the feudal distinction between vassal (tenant-in-chief) and vavasour (vassal of a vassal) and the social distinction between nobles of the blood royal and the rest of the nobility. In parts of France and Germany a distinction persisted until the thirteenth century between free and unfree knights (*ministeriales*). In early modern France a further demarcation existed between nobles elevated for civil service (*noblesse de robe*) and nobles elevated for military service (*noblesse d'épée*).

By definition the honorific privileges were of less material or political importance to the nobility than their other privileges. Unlike the fiscal or seigneurial rights, no direct financial advantage normally accrued to them, and, in comparison with what was imparted by seigneurial rights, reserved offices and parliamentary privileges, their contribution to the nobility's political function was negligible. Yet they cannot be regarded as having merely a decorative or definitive value. Where representative assemblies contained houses of lords or *Ritterstand* chambers, a title awarded a special political function through conferring the right of parliamentary attendance. In England, Spain, France and the empire of the Austrian Habsburgs, entitlement imparted privileges of material benefit such as easy access to the royal company or the reservation of office.[1] Noble academies provided considerable opportunities for those planning to pursue careers in the civil service and army, while financial benefits came of the low interest rates and generous lending policy of the noble banks.[2]

The interconnexion between privilege and the possession of a noble estate could confine fiscal, parliamentary and seigneurial privileges to a part of the nobility. In contrast, many of the honorific privileges belonged to every member of the noble order. This was even the case in England where the gentry shared with the peerage the right to bear coats of arms and special noble insignia, although firmly excluded from the peerage's indemnity and parliamentary rights. As corporate rights, the honorific privileges ensured that the nobility should contain a broad range of wealth which encompassed the extremes of riches and poverty and also a wide spectrum of occupation and social activity.

The honorific privileges were not beyond the possession of the commonalty. Commoners managed to secure coats of arms and eventually to assume the lesser designations of nobility.[3] Preserved, however, exclusively for the nobility was membership of many of the chivalric orders, sometimes because membership automatically imparted nobility, the right of attendance at noble academies, the right to use noble banks, the higher titles and normally the right of precedence and salutation.

1 Rank

The rights in this category laid down a sitting and walking order and imposed upon commoners an obligation to salute noblemen. They could be both noble and seigneurial.[4] Besides distinguishing noble from commoner, they also made distinctions within the nobility. In England, for example, peers and baronets had public precedence over the gentry and by the mid-fourteenth century a gradation of precedence was established within the peerage to determine the seating arrangement in the upper house of parliament. In France, barons and the rest of the higher nobility preceded knights; princes of the blood preceded dukes, counts and *pairs*, and nobles of the robe, according to Loyseau, preceded the untitled nobility. On the other hand, the humblest noble in France normally preceded the most prominent commoner. The exception to this rule occurred when the commoner was a magistrate and the noble was untitled. In this situation, the commoner had precedence over the noble. The privileges of rank had antecedents in the public precedence awarded the senators of Imperial Rome. Other probable origins were the rank always enjoyed by freemen over slaves and the pre-eminence always accorded royalty.[5] By following ancient example, monopolising the rights of freemen and acquiring some of the rights of royalty, the nobility secured this particular privilege.

2 Exclusive membership and access rights

Establishing the nobility's exclusive membership privileges in the military orders and the orders of chivalry was the tendency of knighthood, the primary requisite for membership, to become confined to nobility. This happened when only nobles by birth were allowed to become knights. By 1250 the position of brother knight in the Order of the Templars required both knighthood, conferred by the ceremony of dubbing, and noble birth. The other military orders followed suit. Formed like the Templars in the twelfth century as organisations of knights dedicated to the protection of pilgrims and the crusade against the infidel, the Hospitallers, the Teutonic Knights and the Spanish and Portuguese military orders soon came to recruit their knights solely from the nobility.[6] However, because admission assumed nobility, membership as a brother knight in some of the orders, notably those of Spain and Portugal, was regarded as sufficient proof of noble status and so became a means of ennoblement or noble confirmation. The gigantic wealth at their disposal allowed the military orders to bestow more than honorific benefits upon their membership, largely through the reserved tenure of the orders' offices and estates.[7] The orders of Spain and Portugal thrived as a source of honour and material benefit until the nineteenth century, largely thanks to the protection offered them by the Crown.[8] The other orders had mostly withered away by 1600.

The orders of chivalry were less materially advantageous to their members, lacking the landed endowments of the military orders. Created by the Crown, the first of them appeared in the fourteenth century. The purpose was to honour leading subjects, and also to create a further distinction between members of the nobility; the means was to make a ritual of the chivalric ideal. In this way, the English Order of the Garter, the French Order of the Star, the Burgundian Order of the Golden Fleece, the Austrian Order of the Salamander, the Castilian Order of the Sash and the Sicilian Order of the Cross came into being, all with an exclusively noble membership. Some of the orders, such as the French Order of the Star and the Austrian Order of the Salamander, died an early death; others became simply orders of merit, especially after the seventeenth century, with membership awarded to deserving subjects irrespective of their social background.[9] But in their original form as associations of noblemen honoured by the Crown, several still flourished in the nineteenth century. For example, in Austria there endured the Order of the Golden Fleece whose membership was confined to the high nobility, and several orders of a much later creation. The Order of Maria Theresa was founded in 1757 and the Order of Leopold and the Order of the Iron Crown were established in the first decade of the nineteenth century. In each case noble birth was the condition of entry.

Like the military orders, the orders of chivalry provided a means of social promotion for commoners. The regulations restricting membership to the nobility could not prevent commoners from gaining admission. By doing so they automatically acquired noble status. Membership of the Orders of Leopold and the Iron Crown could confer membership of the *Ritterstand*, while membership of the Order of Maria Theresa could impart the title of baron. In this respect, membership of these orders could socially elevate noblemen. Normally membership of the chivalric orders had only an honorific value. The exceptions were found in the Austrian monarchy prior to the parliamentary reforms of 1848 where the orders conferring the title of *Ritter* awarded the recipients special parliamentary rights, and in Castile where membership of the Orders of the Golden Fleece and Carlos III could carry large pensions.[10]

Another source of honorific privilege were those cathedral chapters and religious houses which admitted to their membership only the offspring of noblemen. Initially, admission had depended upon free status, but from the thirteenth century the right to become a monk, nun or canon in many instances was exclusively annexed by the nobility (a further example of a noble privilege beginning as a freeman right). By 1600 the noble monopoly of membership was widely found—for example, in France, Germany, Austria, Italy, the Low Countries and Poland—although it seemed largely absent in post-Conquest England; and occasionally the rules of membership barred admission not only to the sons of commoners but also to new nobles and their children. It was another honorific privilege which could confer material benefits. The places reserved for the noble-born in convents, for instance, allowed lords to dispose of their surplus daughters without the expense of giving them away in marriage. Furthermore, the insistence that canons and monks should be of noble birth ensured places in cathedrals and monasteries for the younger sons of the nobility. This avoided the need to find them a livelihood, helped to uphold the integrity of the family estate and sometimes reduced the burden upon it of annuities.[11]

The academic privileges of the nobility largely concerned schools reserved for the sons of noblemen. Some were private, but several were state-owned. Occasionally, but not often, the academic privileges applied to university education. In Russia a decree of 1850 reserved the bulk of university places for the noble-born; and traditionally in France and Spain, the sons of nobles were allowed to graduate in less time than the sons of commoners.[12]

Schools for nobles developed comparatively late in the day. Essentially they stemmed from the value placed upon an academically educated nobility by the Italian Renaissance and from the professional needs of royal absolutism which required well-trained bureaucrats and army officers but remained unwilling to dispose of the traditional ruling class. Noble schools appeared, then, some founded by the government, in response to the Crown's attempt to improve the efficiency of the state without needing to abandon its traditional belief that the sons of nobles were the best recruits for officers and officials. They sprang up principally in the seventeenth and eighteenth centuries. In this time several German principalities, Prussia, Russia, Austria, Sicily, Lombardy, Spain, Portugal and Venice acquired them. The development was basically over by 1800.[13] Moreover, with one or two exceptions—notably in Russia which preserved the privilege until 1913 and in Bavaria where the *Pagerie* endured as a noble academy until 1918, the academic privileges had disappeared by the mid-nineteenth century, a consequence of the changing nature of social elites, the personnel needs of the government which could no longer be adequately met by the nobility and, as far as the private noble academies were concerned, the persuasiveness of bourgeois wealth.[14] Although four degrees of nobility were required for admission to the French military academies, the *école royale militaire* and the *école de la marine*, normally noble birth was a sufficient entry ticket. The advantages to the nobility were substantial: the *alumni* were often qualified to start their service careers at a higher grade than commoners.[15]

Royal absolutism established banks as well as schools for nobles. In every case they were mortgage institutions whose facilities were only available to noblemen. In Russia they were state-run. Elsewhere they were private mutual credit organisations. Traditionally the Crown had acted as the fairy godmother of noble debtors, allowing them the privilege of indemnity from imprisonment for debt, cancelling their debts to the state, and reducing the interest on private loans.[16] Innovating, but acting in this protective tradition, the Crown in eighteenth-century Russia and Prussia authorised the establishment of banks designed to make loans to noblemen on the security of their estates (and in Russia's case also on the security of their serfs). Thus in 1754 the Tzar created a state noble bank, which having gone through several vicissitudes in the early nineteenth century was revived in 1885 to 'make more easily accessible to the hereditary nobility the means of preserving for

their posterity the estates in their possession'.[17] In 1770 Frederick II authorised the Silesian nobility to establish a mortgage bank for its members. This
became the basic model for other noble banks: for example, the one which
Frederick allowed the Pomeranian nobles to form in 1781, the one the Tzar
authorised for the nobles of the Kingdom of Poland in 1825, the one allowed
by the Habsburgs for the Galician nobility in 1841 and those established in
Denmark and the Baltic provinces.[18] Like the noble academies, the noble
banks were attempts by absolute rulers to equip the nobility with the means
of fulfilling its function as a ruling elite. They tended to be established in
situations of dire hardship caused by the subjection of chronic noble poverty
to an economic crisis: for example, the aftereffects of the Seven Years War
and of the Napoleonic War and the agrarian depression of the late nineteenth
century. Frequently they came of a noble appeal for greater credit facilities.
Governments, however, sometimes refused to comply fearing, as in the
Austrian Empire, that the establishment of noble banks would curtail investment in government stock.[19] In supporting noble banks, the government's
basic consideration was to prevent nobles from losing their estates to commoners as a result of money-lenders foreclosing on mortgages.[20] The effect
of noble banks was neither to strengthen the nobility nor to prevent the flow
of noble estates into commoner hands. Generally it encouraged nobles to
adopt a commercial attitude to their property and to regard their estates as
little more than security for loans, while the generous lending policy of the
banks, their low interest rates and their unwillingness to foreclose encouraged the nobles to indulge in acts of gross extravagance and irresponsibility.[21]

In addition, there was the obvious privilege of Court access. The royal
company, needless to say, was frequently confined to nobles, presence at
Court requiring at least noble status and often the qualification of royal
kinship and a long noble lineage. This privilege had very early origins and
tended to live as long as the monarchy. As a means of receiving royal
patronage, or securing control of it, its benefits were undoubtedly material
as well as honorific.[22]

3 Special insignia

The insignia privileges allowed nobles an exclusive right to carry or use
arms, initially swords and lances and eventually crossbows and handguns;
to wear apparel forbidden to the rest of society; to sport badges of nobility;
and to bear coats of arms. The weapon right originated as the right of
freemen. In early Germanic societies it distinguished freeman from slave and
derived from the freeman's obligation to respond to the ruler's call to arms.[23]
By the end of the ninth century it had already ceased to be the normal right
of freemen in parts of France where the military obligation had become

confined to enfeoffed vassals and the weapon right had been similarly restricted. In the following three hundred years it frequently became confined to the freemen of noble status. Responsible for this restriction was the rise of knighthood and its monopoly of the weapon right available to commoners, the annexation of knighthood by the nobility and the consequent disappearance of the commoner knight, and the substitution of the payment of taxes for what remained of the freeman's original military obligation. The right finally materialised as an exclusive noble privilege when it became divorced from military service. Thus, wearing certain arms, notably swords, became the right not only of those in military service but also of nobles irrespective of whether they were fulfilling a military function.

Although the weapon right remained predominantly a freeman privilege in 1000, by 1500 it was well-founded as a noble privilege, prevailing in France, Germany, Scandinavia and Austria.[24] Yet it did not take this course throughout Europe; and the nobilities in possession of the right did not always hold it corporately. In France, for example, the sword-wearing right did not extend to the *noblesse de robe*; in the Austrian territories the full *Waffenrecht* was limited to the *Ritter-* and *Herrenstände*, and in England the weapon right created in the sixteenth century by statutory regulations on the use of the crossbow and handgun applied only to the peerage.[25] However, in some of its forms it went simply with noble status. For example, in 1601 all French nobles were given a special right to use the arquebus; and in the Austrian territories there existed a lesser and greater weapon right, the lesser conferred by noble status, the greater by additional qualifications.[26]

The weapon right was yet another noble privilege which commoners could secure special permission to enjoy. It was awarded in late fifteenth-century Portugal to a group of commoners, the legists, along with fiscal exemption and indemnity from certain forms of punishment. In 1767 the wholesale *négociants* of Orléans obtained the nobles' sword-wearing right, while rentier bourgeois shared the French nobility's arquebus right of 1601.[27] Stemming from the weapon right was the noble's exclusive right to participate in tournaments and to acquit his honour in the duel. By making duelling the preserve of the nobles, the weapon right obliged them to respond to the challenge of other nobles but safeguarded against the need to respond to commoners.[28]

In Tyrol there was a uniform of nobility, red in colour, which the *Ritter-* and *Herrenstände*, the nobles with rights of parliamentary membership, were entitled to wear. Similarly in England the peerage acquired a distinctive parliamentary dress of ermine and scarlet with the grades of peerage distinguished by bars of white.[29] Specific noble dress stemmed either from parliamentary privilege or dubbed knighthood. For example, the English knights were entitled to a green tunic and the French knights to a distinctive *baudrier*, golden spurs and gilded horse harness.[30] Privileges of this nature undoubtedly echo Roman practices, notably the special dress of the senators (red shoes and a toga with a broad purple stripe) and *equites* (a toga with a narrow purple stripe). Accompanying the red uniform of the Tyrolese nobles was a badge of nobility.[31] Badges indicative of noble status, however, did not usually exist. In their place were coats of arms and the badges of the military and chivalrous orders. Moreover, much more common than the noble right to wear special clothes was the noble right to wear clothes made of special materials, especially furs such as ermine, silk, velvet, cloth of gold or garments adorned with precious stones. This type of privilege derived from the sumptuary regulations which governments authorised usually to curtail extravagance in dress, but also to prevent 'the confusion of degree where the meanest are as richly dressed as their betters'.[32] This sort of regulation was frequently made between the fourteenth and seventeenth centuries and rarely before or since. Sumptuary laws often restricted the use of finery by nobles as well as commoners, but they could also impose regulations upon society from which the nobility was indemnified. On occasions governmental regulations which aimed to promote manufacturing also created apparel rights. Thus, the English statute of 1571 requiring all subjects to wear a woollen cap on holidays and Sundays made an exception of peers and public officials.[33]

There is little evidence for the successful enforcement of sumptuary legislation. Furthermore, complicating the privilege's capacity to distinguish noble from commoner was that sumptuary legislation could grant the same rights to some commoners as they granted to the nobles. In England the regulation of apparel, like some of the firearms regulations, could grant immunity not only to aristocrats but also to subjects with a certain degree of wealth. Sumptuary regulations could create distinctions of class as well as degree.[34]

Heraldry was another noble privilege established by the transformation of knighthood from a military occupation to a denotion of noble status. Coats of arms were initially a compensation for the failure of the knightly title to become hereditary. This failure meant the emergence in the twelfth and thirteenth centuries of devices whereby knighthood could nonetheless transmit its status to future generations. On the one hand, it was soon established that only the offspring of knights could normally attain knighthood; on the other, there developed formal indicators of a family's lineal association with knighthood, the chief of which was the coat of arms. As an hereditary right, the coat of arms was first held by royal families. Its connexion with knighthood began with the adoption of personal insignia to distinguish armoured knights from each other in battle or in the tournament. It became an hereditary right of subjects in response to the regulation that only the sons of knights could participate in tournaments.[35]

Coats of arms were normally restricted to the nuclear family of lord, wife and sons. However, in Poland the same coat of arms was possessed by every member of a clan. Admission to the clan and the acquisition of its escutcheon served as an informal means of ennoblement. Coupled with the absence of an effective heraldic register of authentic bearings, this practice helps to account for the relative populousness of the Polish nobility.[36] A lack of strict governmental surveys allowed the adoption of a coat of arms to serve an ennobling purpose in several other states. Like the possession of noble estates, or the purchase of office, or admission to military or chivalric orders, it provided commoners with a means of ennoblement which was independent of government authorisation. Apart from the titles, a coat of arms was the honorific privilege with the longest history, originating in the twelfth century in Western Europe, fully establishing itself as a noble right by 1400 and surviving into the twentieth century. However, in parts of Eastern Europe it emerged at a much later date: in Hungary not before the fifteenth century and in Russia it was first introduced by Peter the Great.[37]

The ownership of a family coat of arms did not always coincide with the possession of nobility. In Poland before the fourteenth century and throughout the history of the French nobility, many commoners legitimately owned family escutcheons. Louis XIV's registration of armorial bearings in 1696 found that only 25,000 of the 110,000 registered escutcheons belonged to noble families. In France nobles and commoners were distinguished from the fourteenth century onwards only by the nobles' right to a special type of escutcheon, one surmounted either by a helm or a crown. The French nobility's possession of other corporately held privileges made coats of arms inessential for the denotion of nobility. In contrast, in thirteenth-century Brandenburg where noble rights were largely confined to coats of arms, escutcheons were a crucial indicator of noble status.[38] Similarly in England, the traditional absence of noble privileges, apart from those of the peerage and of the seigneurs, rendered coats of arms a vital means of identifying the bulk of the aristocracy as noble. However, only in the brief period of the heraldic visitations (from 1529 to the late seventeenth century) when an official register of authenticated escutcheons was kept, was the ruling rigorously upheld that only aristocrats could bear family coats of arms. At other times, from its foundation in the fifteenth century to the present, the college of heralds merely adjudicated the disputed and dubious claims brought to its attention; and in the nineteenth century coats of arms were widely adopted by the English bourgeoisie. A much more definite association between nobility and armorial bearings existed in eighteenth- and nineteenth-century Scotland. This followed the 1672 act of parliament which revived and extended an earlier act of 1592 and declared coats of arms illegal unless approved by Lyon King of Arms.[39]

The importance of armorial bearings to the nobility was determined by its alternative means of social distinction. Where many nobles were too poor to maintain an aristocratic way of life, as, for example, in Poland, Spain and Sicily, coats of arms were outstandingly important as the indicator of nobility and the justification for the rightful enjoyment of noble privilege. Frequently in these states the escutcheons displayed over the threshold or fireplace, or on seals, family portraits and tombstones were the only tangible expression of nobility.[40] In fact, where the nobles were not distinguished from the commoners by their wealth and occupation, where nobles were poor and occupied as artisans, shopkeepers, labourers and farmers, the escutcheon was the essence of their social identity. As the removal of privilege erased the other means of noble identification, they became increasingly important. And where other corporately held privileges were vestigial or non-existent— a common feature of the late nineteenth-century nobility and a traditional feature of the English aristocracy—armorial bearings were also responsible for providing the nobility with a common juridical character. Within the ranks of nobility, coats of arms were of greater value to the lesser, than to the higher, nobility and more important to the *parvenus* than to the long-established members, serving as a means of status definition and a device for obtaining noble status without formal ennoblement.

Finally, mention has to be made of the special insignia conferred upon high-ranking nobles by the liberties permitted in royal residences and the royal presence. Thus in Spain, the *grandes* were distinguished by the right to remain hatted in the company of the king and to have free access to royal palaces; likewise the *duc et pairs* of France were privileged to enter any royal palace without the need to dismount or to get out of the carriage at the front gate, and their wives were authorised to be seated on a footstool in the presence of the queen.[41] It is noticeable that the titles with which these rights were associated had initially been the exclusive possession of the royal family, and in all likelihood they originated as licences granted by the king to his own kith and kin. Needless to say, although only a minute proportion of nobles enjoyed them, they were of great value in structuring the upper echelon of the noble order.

4 Titles, predicates and forms of address

Eventually, most nobilities acquired hereditary titles. Even in pre-partitioned Poland where the government never recognised the noble title and only granted noble status, titles were in use: princely titles sported by the Lithu-anian descendants of Rurik and Gedymin, titles conferred by foreign auth-orities such as the Emperor and the Pope and the titles of baron and count which certain families claimed on the grounds of long usage.[42] Nevertheless,

although prevalent by the eighteenth century, in much of Europe the governmental practice of awarding noble titles had been a late development. By the
mid-fifteenth century it had yet to be established in Hungary, Russia, Sweden,
Denmark and Poland. In Hungary the first hereditary count was created as
late as 1453. Until the sixteenth century the Hungarian nobility resembled
that of Poland in being stratified neither by titles nor privileges but only by
the differing degrees of wealth enjoyed by its members. Then, introduced as
a device for imposing imperial control on a recalcitrant and alien nobility,
the Habsburgs established a peerage. Subjects were awarded the titles of
prince, count and baron and the law of 1608 gave them, alone among the
Hungarian nobles, personal membership of the national diet. By 1800 this
higher nobility consisted of 300 families and possessed a function and authority similar to that of the English peerage. Apart from the use of the ducal
title for members of the royal family, peerage titles were unknown in Sweden
until Eric XIV introduced them in 1561; and even then, it was not until the
reigns of Christina and Charles XI that they were created with any frequency.
Prior to this development, the higher nobility in Sweden had consisted of the
royal family and the members of the *riksråd*. Similarly in Denmark the noble
ranks were differentiated only by wealth, royal connexion and membership
of the *rigsraad* until titles followed the establishment of royal absolutism in
1660. In Russia noble titles, other than those of prince (*kniaz*), were first
implanted by the westernising policies of Peter the Great which substituted
a noble structure determined by titles of European type such as count and
baron for the traditional one in which the beneficiaries of the *méstnichestvo*
system, the princes and the boyars, were distinguished from the rest of the
nobility, the *dvoriáne*. In Poland the creation of officially recognised titles
only followed the partition. For example, in Galicia noble titles were introduced by the Habsburg reforms of 1786 which divided the Polish *szlachta*
into the titled and the untitled.[43]

Elsewhere in Europe there was a much longer tradition of titles and
entitlement. One of its bases was the personal title of knight. Knighthood
was not conferred as an automatic birthright but depended upon the ceremony of dubbing. Nonetheless, the capacity to be dubbed tended to become
an inheritable right. Furthermore, although knighthood was not initially
confined to the nobility, from the twelfth century onwards it was frequently
awarded in the West as a noble title rather than simply as a military honour.[44]
A second base was the titles connected with the fief or the lordship. They
derived both from the feudal process of enfeoffment which created the title
of baron and from certain officials of state, notably the Carolingian count,
duke and marquis. Predating the establishment of feudalism, these officials
were incorporated within the feudal system as their offices became territorial
and hereditary. The capacity of subjects to hold the fiefs and offices by

hereditary right produced the higher titles of nobility.[45] A third base, the original source of hereditary entitlement, was the princely titles. They derived from the ruler's need to honour his family and from the demotion of rulers to the status of subjects.[46] The earliest higher titles dispensed by rulers tended to be reserved for the royal kin. A further source of higher nobility was the immediate nobility of the Holy Roman Empire. In their origins and through being tied to territory, they were closely related to the titles which had stemmed from the Carolingian offices of state, but differed from them in being subject only to the Emperor, not to an intermediate authority. For centuries, the imperial titles were more princely than noble, their holders resembling sovereign rulers rather than subjects, and since the older titles, the dukes, margraves, landgraves and palsgraves, could not be increased by imperial gift, they were not a means of entitlement except by birth. However, by the late seventeenth century new imperial titles had come into being—princes, counts and barons—which formed part of the patronage dispensed by the Habsburgs to loyal subjects.[47] A final source of early entitlement came of the vassals' right to be tried by his peers rather than by the ruler's judges. In France this produced a group of princes and great feudatories, originally twelve in number, with the function of trying those subjects who were protected by the right of trial by peerage. In imitation of the French, a similar category of higher nobility developed in eleventh-century Flanders and Navarre.[48]

Nevertheless, until at least the fourteenth century, these sources of entitlement produced only a very small number of lords with hereditary titles. This was because knighthood remained a life honour and because the major source of new recruitment to the hereditary honours remained the royal family. In France the hereditary titled element increased in the eleventh and twelfth centuries as viscounts and castellans were converted from officers to landed lords, but the major breakthrough only came when the Crown, after 1297, decided to create further *pairs*, rather than to abide by the original twelve, and to make additions to the hereditary titles imparted by land ownership. The latter was accomplished by changing the dignity of certain estates: either new fiefs were erected or old ones were awarded new titles.[49] Notably in the sixteenth and seventeenth centuries a massive creation of hereditary titles occurred, realised by the territorial means devised in the fourteenth century and the Crown's abandonment of the traditional practice of awarding the title of *duc et pair* sparingly and usually only to princes of the blood and foreign princes. The willingness to grant these exalted titles to subjects of non-royal backgrounds ensured that non-princely subjects held as many as fifty-two out of seventy-six titles of *duc et pair* in 1723, whereas they had held only eleven out of forty titles in 1589.[50]

The fourteenth century also marked an important stage for the development of the higher title in England, especially because of the range of titles made available for the first time to subjects who were not of the blood royal, the consequent enlargement of the titled element and its acquisition of privileges from which the rest of the noble order was excluded. A 'rise of the peerage' thus occurred. In the course of the fourteenth and fifteenth centuries, largely on account of Edward III's generosity in making new creations and the development of the upper house in parliament, the English peerage ceased to fade away, increased its membership from thirteen to sixty and enlarged its privileges and authority. Further decisive increases in the number of peers occurred in 1603–28 when the willingness of the Crown to raise revenue by selling titles doubled the peerage's size, and in the closing years of the eighteenth century when the abstemiousness of the previous century in the granting of titles was suddenly remedied, and the peerage was yet again doubled.[51]

Critically important in the development of the higher titled nobility was the Crown's ability to create titled nobles whose origin and function had no direct connexion with feudal obligation or membership of the royal family. This happened extensively between the fourteenth and fifteenth centuries, not only in England and France but also in Scotland, for example, with the emergence in the late fourteenth and early fifteenth centuries of a higher nobility of personal rather than territorial titleholders, a development which culminated in the establishment of an English-style parliamentary peerage in the second quarter of the century and which was permitted by the fact that the Crown no longer needed to depend upon the tenurial title for raising armed forces and was unwilling to create new political enclaves in the kingdom by granting further territorial titles.[52] In Sicily a non-tenurial element in the higher nobility originated in the fifteenth century when Alfonso created the first non-royal duke. In the course of the sixteenth and seventeenth centuries it became a substantial group. Alongside an increase in the tenurial baronage promoted by a multiplication of fiefs (from seventy-two in 1556 to 277 in 1810), a peerage of personal titles blossomed. In the mid-sixteenth century the few peerage titles, sixteen in all, were exclusively held by the tenurial baronage; yet by 1800 there were 2,153 titles (prince, duke, marquis and count) against 277 fiefs, and consequently many fiefless peers. Responsible for this spectacular growth of the higher titles was the Crown's readiness to sell them, and its willingness in the late sixteenth and seventeenth centuries to sell them in profusion.[53] The Neapolitan nobility followed roughly the same course. Until the mid-fourteenth century the higher nobility was the tenantry-in-chief. However, by the end of that century personal titles such as the marquisate had been created, and subjects had also obtained the personal title of duke which was formerly reserved for the royal family. The work of the Angevins in creating new titles was complemented by the

Habsburgs' lavish dispensation of them, especially in the early seventeenth century. Thus, whereas the tenurial baronage only grew from 470 in 1586 to 493 in 1669, the personal titleholders rocketed from 118 in 1590 to 434 in 1675.[54] In Lombardy a substantial titled nobility was initially formed by the divisibility of estates and their associated titles. It had emerged by the end of the twelfth century. The titles were count and marquis. Relics of the Carolingian Empire, they had originated as hereditary offices and eventually became territorial titles. With the termination of the republic in the late fourteenth century, the titled element was further enlarged as a result of the Visconti and the Sforza practice of creating titles by granting new fiefs with titles attached. Finally, the higher titled nobility became a numerous class after the establishment of Habsburg rule in 1535, particularly with the lavish conferment of count and marquis as personal titles in the seventeenth century. As in Naples and Sicily, the higher titles of nobility became a widely enjoyed privilege in Lombardy because of the Spanish Habsburgs' readiness to use them for raising revenue and for creating allies within alien elites.[55]

In all these instances a titled nobility grew upon a firm feudal base. But higher titles could also develop independently of a native feudal system, although usually in imitation of states which had experienced feudalism. Non-feudal Hungary gained its peerage when the Habsburgs applied to the lands of the Crown of St. Stephen the system of titles employed in the feudalised Austrian territories. Moved by the English example, the Portuguese monarchy created its first duke in 1415, its first marquis in 1451 and its first baron in 1475. This marked the beginnings of a titled higher nobility which became a sizeable class under the rule of Habsburg Spain between 1580 and 1640. In Castile the Trastamaras, upon seizing the throne in 1368, established a titled higher nobility, apparently moved by French example. Only in Catalonia and Aragon had such a group formerly existed in the Iberian peninsula as a class rather than in the form of an occasional individual with an outlandish title. In Catalonia this was simply due to the state's former attachment to the Carolingian Empire and the fusion of fiefs with hereditary public offices. In Aragon, French influence had introduced a tenurial baronage which acquired its own parliamentary chamber. Elsewhere in Spain, prior to the emergence of the higher titles in the fourteenth century, the higher nobility had consisted of *ricos hombres*, a group of families clearly distinguished from the rest of the nobility by their power and wealth, not by their privileges. In the typical manner of a Spanish Habsburg possession, the higher titles increased enormously in the late sixteenth and early seventeenth centuries as the Crown used them to raise revenue and to reward nobles for providing it with troops. The number of *grandes* increased from twenty-five in 1520 to ninety-nine in 1600 to 113 in 1700, while the *títulos* increased from thirty-five in 1520 to 535 in 1787, with 419 new titles created in the seventeenth century.[56]

The higher titles thus originated in the royal family, the nobles' capacity to gain hereditary control of lands and offices and the ability of ex-chiefs to retain a superior status following their subjection to monarchical rule. Of outstanding importance in the development of the higher titles was the dispensation of personal titles by the Crown. It first used them to honour royal relatives but from the fourteenth century granted them to subjects unconnected with the royal family, bestowing them extensively either to raise revenue or to bind important subjects to the royal cause. By the eighteenth century the creation of personal titles was a well-established form of royal patronage in the European monarchies and, with the notable exception of Norway, continued to be exercised until the twentieth century when the practice was either stopped or confined in the medieval manner to honouring members of the royal family.

Impeding the development of higher titles were republican systems of government or principalities in which the rulers had not acquired the full authority of kingship. In both Germany and Italy, the dispensation of personal titles before the nineteenth century was restricted by the limited number of rulers with the power to grant them. At fault was the persistence of imperial and papal suzerainty, as well as the survival of communal republics. In North Italy these restraints were only removed when the Habsburgs acquired Lombardy in the early sixteenth century and Tuscany in the eighteenth century; when the rulers of Piedmont acquired the Sardinian monarchy and its powers of entitlement; and following the unification imposed them on the rest of Italy; when a national nobility was created in 1885 and when the republics of Venice and Genoa were eliminated in 1815.[57] The latter states had certainly possessed titled nobles. In the thirteenth century a number of Venetian families held the title of duke or count, having been enfeoffed with islands to the east; and within the Genoan Republic was the ancient tenurial baronage of Liguria and nobles with foreign titles, mostly awarded in the sixteenth and seventeenth centuries by the Spanish Habsburgs. But for centuries there was no such thing as entitlement by the government.[58]

In the German lands the ruler's authority to entitle was prohibited by the imperial monarchy. Little was achieved to escape this ban by any ruling dynasty except for the Habsburgs until 1660 when the Elector of Brandenburg-Prussia acquired the legal right of entitlement, the first of the German princes to receive it, apart from those who became emperor, since the Golden Bull of 1356 had confined it to the imperial authority. The Great Elector's entitling authority stemmed from his acquisition of East Prussia which stood outside the Holy Roman Empire. The outcome was that by 1800 one-sixth of noble landowners in Brandenburg had gained the rank of count or baron. Until the dissolution of the Empire and the conversion of the surviving principalities into independent monarchies in 1815, the right of hereditary entitlement in the German lands lay solely with the Emperor, the Habsburgs and the Hohenzollerns.[59] Then, with the extension of national monarchy in the early nineteenth century—in Germany with the conversion of princes into kings, in Italy with the elimination of the surviving republican forms of government, and in the Low Countries following the creation of the monarchies of Belgium (1831) and the Netherlands (1815)—the privilege of entitlement became much more widespread;[60] only to be suddenly ended in the twentieth century, usually along with the dramatic dismissal of monarchy.

The higher titles of nobility tended to be the last of the privileges to go. Never was nobility retained and the titles abolished. The disposal happened in two ways: governments either desisted from creating further titles or abolished the title as a juridical privilege. In many cases, the abolition of titles coincided simply with the removal of monarchy. In view of the birth-right principle to which both inevitably subscribed, and the Crown's neces-sary role in the process of entitlement, that was not surprising. Thus, the fall of the Habsburgs, the Romanoffs, the Hohenzollerns and the other German ruling dynasties in 1917 and 1918, and their replacement by republican governments, directly caused the elimination of noble titles in Germany, Russia, Bohemia, Austria and Poland. Transformed into a regency with the fall of the Habsburg monarchy, Hungary significantly retained its titled nobility until the 1940s when the eventual establishment of a republic brought it to an end. Likewise the nobility and its titles fell with the end of monarchy in Portugal in 1910 and Italy in 1946. The same happened in Spain in 1931 but titles, although not mere noble status, were revived in 1947 as part of the fascist plan to restore the monarchy.[61] The exception to this simple intercon-nexion between the abolition of monarchy and the termination of titles occurred in Norway where nobility was abolished under the Swedish mon-archy in 1821 but very much against the wishes of the Crown, in Denmark in 1910, and in France where titles were abolished in 1790 under the mon-archy and, having been revived by Napoleon, were re-abolished by the second republic in 1848 and, having been revived again in 1852, were toler-ated by the succeeding republics. Titles thus remain in France, but not entitlement. None of these exceptions detract from the ascendant role of monarchy in upholding the privilege of noble titles and the decisive part played by republicanism in destroying it.[62]

Complementing the abolition of titles has been the tendency of the surviv-ing monarchies in the late twentieth century to desist from making new hereditary titles except for members of the royal family, and to employ life titles, as in Great Britain after 1958, as the main means of entitlement. Thus in monarchical England, as in the French Republic, hereditary titles survive but their acquisition has become virtually impossible except by birth. This reversion to pre-fourteenth-century practices means that, deprived of new recruitment and dependent upon propagation for its survival, the hereditary peerage is destined to fade away. Monarchy also worked against the titled nobility by denying it the privileges traditionally associated with a title. Although the final removal of the titled nobility usually accompanied the establishment of republics, its more important privileges tended to be lost under monarchical rule. Thus the legislative authority of the British house of lords was severely attenuated in 1911; the reserved offices and parliamentary privileges of the Austrian and Bohemian *Hochadel* had been withdrawn by 1850; and the Sicilian house of lords, established by the revolution of 1812 and modelled on English lines, was quickly quashed by Bourbon absolutism.

By the close of the middle ages the higher titles of nobility were mostly inheritable.[63] In this respect, the extensive award of life peerages in England after 1958 has transformed the character of the English peerage. The higher titles tended to be transmitted by primogeniture, even in Prussia where the nobility subjected its estates to partible inheritance. However, this was not always the case. For example, in Sweden, Russia, certain parts of France, notably Lorraine, Franche Comté, Flanders and Artois, in Lombardy prior to Spanish rule and in other parts of Italy where fiefs descended by Lombard rather than Frankish law, all the male offspring of a lord had the right to inherit his title; and in Hungary titles of nobility passed to every direct offspring of the entitled family.[64] The higher titles tended to be confined to the male line, although there was a multitude of exceptions to this rule even in France where a royal edict of 1370 made nobility transmissible only by males, yet in Champagne and Franche Comté female inheritance remained possible. In England female succession was excluded in the course of the fourteenth and fifteenth centuries as the title in fee was replaced by the title in tail male. Other exceptions to exclusive male inheritance are found in Spain, Austria and, for princely titles, in the Belgian monarchy established in 1831.[65] Female inheritance of the higher titles, however, tended to occur only in default of a direct male heir.

The higher titles were either territorial or personal; that is, they were conferred by landownership, like the title of seigneur, or by the personal right of the titleholder. Responsible for the territorial title was the official and feudal origins of entitlement. However, in France where the territorial title prevailed, the personal title had an equally long history, mainly because of the practice of allowing younger sons to receive titles even though the family estate and its associated title was transmitted by primogeniture. Thus, in the early middle ages the title of baron was awarded to cadets of great families. The existence of these family titles permitted a separation of entitlement from land tenure.[66] In the course of time, as the fief lost its usefulness and rulers came to appreciate the title not as a means of imposing a special military and governmental function upon the recipient but as a type of cheap patronage, the territorial title gave way to titles which could be awarded without an accompanying donation of land. Exceptionally in France the traditional system continued to prevail, the major titles retaining an exclusively territorial character until the Revolution which, under Napoleon, brought the personal title to the fore.[67] In most of the states subjected to feudalism—in Italy, Germany, Bohemia, Austria, England and Scotland for example—the tenurial baronage became only a fraction of the higher nobility particularly when the ruler possessed the right to create personal titles. In England the one was totally supplanted by the other, and the privileges and functions of the higher nobility came to be imparted not by landownership but by the letters patent conferring peerage. In those states without a dominant feudal past—for example in Scandinavia, Russia, Poland, Hungary, Portugal and Castile—the personal title always predominated but as an hereditary title it emerged several centuries later than in the monarchies of the feudal system.

Whether the higher title was territorial or personal did not necessarily make much difference. Since only a fraction of the original estate needed to be retained to legitimise the title, a territorial title could be enjoyed merely through the possession of a family seat.[68] Moreover until at least the late nineteenth century, the owners of personal titles usually resembled the territorially entitled in being large landowners, their estates frequently donated by the Crown to permit a way of life appropriate to the title. A broad difference between personal and territorial titles only arose in states such as Sicily or Naples where the tenurial baronage retained special privileges which were denied the holders of personal titles, where many of the personal titleholders were virtually landless and extremely poor and where territorial titles could be acquired by the purchase of noble estates.[69] Whereas the personal title could only be granted by the Crown or inherited, the territorial title could be acquired independently of the Crown's agency. But this did not mean that the territorial title was more commercialised and easier to obtain, since governments, notably in the sixteenth and seventeenth centuries, frequently put personal titles up for sale.

In compliance with the earlier tradition of knighthood, the higher titles were normally reserved for subjects who had already achieved noble status. Prior to 1848, the lower orders in the Austrian territories were legally barred from acquiring the grades of *Ritter, Freiherr, Graf* and *Fürst*.[70] Elsewhere, the same exclusiveness prevailed, although not always upheld in the law. For example, of the titles of baron and above which the Prussian Crown created between 1871 and 1918, very few went to men from bourgeois backgrounds—

only twenty-six out of 221—and, in each of these instances, entitlement only proceeded ennoblement. In this period, and there is no good reason to believe that it marked a new departure in government policy, Prussian titles were not so much a reward for 'new men' as a device for reassuring the noble status of marginal members of the old landed nobility.[71] In England newly created peers and baronets traditionally came from the landed aristocracy. The main source of recruitment was the gentry and the baronetcy. Very rarely were men from other social groups the recipients. A change eventually came between 1886 and 1914 when at least half the 246 peerage titles created in that time went to non-aristocrats.[72] If popular deference towards the nobility was maintained by the prospect of social promotion, it owed very little to the award of the higher titles. Much more important was the commoner's opportunity to secure noble status or some of the associations of nobility, notably fiscal privilege, seigneurial rights and gentility.

In many cases the exclusiveness of the higher titles only deprived the commonalty of the chance to leapfrog socially the bulk of the nobility. Not often did the higher titles confer special material or functional benefits. Quite exceptional were the English peerage and the nobilities of the Austrian Habsburgs. In the course of the fourteenth century the English peers acquired privileges which were closed to the remainder of the English aristocracy. They included automatic membership of parliament, reserved offices, special judicial rights, exemption from some of the tasks and obligations of local government and certain fiscal privileges. They awarded the peerage not only a number of personal freedoms and allowances from state control but also a necessary role in the making and repeal of statutes. Such privileges were only seriously reduced in the twentieth century, notably in 1911 and 1949.[73] By the eighteenth century the *Hochadel* of the Austrian territories, Bohemia and Hungary were similarly distinguished by special privileges, enjoying access to the royal family, reserved offices in the provincial and imperial administrations and exclusive membership of the upper chamber in parliament.[74] Elsewhere the main privileges of nobility were traditionally imparted either by noble status or by the ownership of noble estates or by lineage, rarely by entitlement. The higher titles therefore tended to be only of honorific value. This was true, for example, of most French titles. An exception was the title of *duc et pair* which conferred automatic membership of the parlement and certain courtly advantages. It was also true of the range of Spanish titles, with the exception of the *grandes*, the creation of Charles V, who enjoyed the courtly right to be hatted in the royal presence, seated in the royal chapel, to enjoy precedence over archbishops and to have free entry to the royal palace. Where special privileges existed for the high nobility, they tended to be courtly or parliamentary. In the German principalities, as in the Austrian territories, some members of the high nobility enjoyed, by

virtue of their titles, an equality with the royal family. This conferred rights
of court access as well as some judicial privileges. It thus bore some affinity
to the specially privileged Spanish *grandes* and French *pairs* whose privileges
likewise stemmed from the close family connexions which had originally
existed between their membership and the Crown.[75] On the other hand,
before the nineteenth century the titled nobility's right to enjoy special
parliamentary privileges was not usually found, since the nobility's privileges
of parliamentary membership stemmed either from the possession of noble
status or a fief held directly of the Crown. Thus in the *cortes* of Aragon, the
membership of the upper chamber was reserved for tenants-in-chief, not the
títulos, and in Sicily prior to the revolution of 1812, and in Naples before the
demise of parliament in the late seventeenth century, the titled nobility
gained access to parliament only by right of fief-ownership or through
election to the third estate. Only in England and in the Austrian Empire did
houses of lords traditionally exist which admitted special membership to
subjects bearing the higher titles of nobility.[76]

Some of the last noble privileges to be created were conferred upon the
titled nobility. In this respect, the nineteenth century marked a highly crea-
tive, as well as a highly destructive, stage in the history of noble privilege.
These latter-day grants of privilege appertained to parliamentary rights: in
the course of the century houses of lords were established in Sicily, Portugal
and Prussia. Furthermore, of all the noble privileges, those of the titled
nobility have proved the most durable, surviving in Austria, Bohemia and
the German states until 1918–19, in Portugal until 1910, in Spain until 1931
with a revival in the 1940s, in Hungary where the parliamentary privileges of
the titled nobility underwent a short intermission from 1918 to 1926 and then
lasted until the fall of the regency in 1944, and in England where the peerage
retains its own parliamentary chamber and the judicial privilege of freedom
from arrest in civil actions. Not until 1911 was it deprived of its essential
role in the legislative process; and not until 1949 did it lose its privilege of
trial by peerage.[77]

Nobilities were also stratified by lesser titles, especially that of knight (*Ritter,
chevalier, caballero, cavaleiro*) and esquire (*ecuyer* or *damoiseau, escudeiro,
escudero*). Besides these designations of noble rank there were corporately
held predicates and forms of address which signified noble status: for example, the mediterranean 'don' (dominus), señor and signore, the English
'Mr' and 'gent', the French 'de' and 'gentilhomme' and 'monsieur', the
German and Austrian 'von' and 'Herr', the Low Countries 'van' and the
Hungarian suffix -y.[78]

Like the higher titles, knighthood emerged as either an awarded personal
honour or a territorial obligation of the feudal system. Initially knighthood

could be conferred by any other knight, but by the thirteenth century its creation was usually monopolised by the Crown. As a title conferred by landownership, it had a much more restricted history than the higher territorial titles. This was because a knight's fee in France, Italy and England did not impart knighthood.[79] Only in certain German principalities, Austria and Bohemia did the territorial knighthood develop, originally in connexion with military service and later with parliamentary membership, the qualification for admission to the noble chamber residing with the ownership of a *Rittersgut*.[80] As a personal title, knighthood differed from the higher personal titles in failing to become hereditary. It remained strictly the entitlement of those who were dubbed knights. In compensation for this limitation, knighthood was allowed to transmit to the next generation the title of esquire and the privileges of nobility; and further titles developed which in basic character were hereditary knighthoods like the English baronetcy, first introduced in 1611 and so lavishly granted that by the twentieth century its membership almost doubled that of the peerage.[81] Apart from the title, the baronet possessed no more privileges and functions than the gentry. Knighthood was originally the social status accorded mounted warriors under the Frankish monarchy. Between the twelfth and fourteenth centuries the nobility annexed it so totally—at the expense of ceding to the Crown the sole right to make new knights—that normally only nobles could be knighted and knighthood came to enjoy the range of corporately held noble privileges. By the sixteenth century, knighthood was a mere title without military or governmental function unless attached to a fief of *Rittersgut*.[82] Overall, it lacked the pervasiveness of the higher titles, firmly establishing itself in the West and the German lands but failing to take root in Hungary, Poland, Russia, Scandinavia and Southern Italy.

Closely associated with the knighthood was the title of esquire. Essentially it declared the capacity for knighthood. As this came to be determined by birth, the title of esquire acquired an hereditary character. Besides being the birthright of esquires' sons, it was the natural right of the untitled male offspring of title-holders and bearers of coats of arms, as well as the appellation of untitled office-holders.[83] The title of 'don' had a similar history, becoming, like the esquire, the designation of noble status rather than noble rank. However, in thirteenth century Flanders it was exclusively the title of all dubbed knights; in eleventh century France it was strictly reserved for owners of castles but by 1200 had also become a title of knighthood. In Sicily it was originally the automatic right of the younger sons of barons and personal title-holders. This was in imitation of Aragonese practice. Like the higher titles, the 'don' in Sicily could also be awarded by the Crown and many were sold in the seventeenth and eighteenth centuries. In Lombardy, prior to the imposition of Spanish rule, 'don' was the special appellation of untitled patricians; in seventeenth-century Catalonia it remained the right of a middling section of the nobility.[84] Only in the course of time did it come to embrace the whole of the non-titled nobility in the Iberian and Italian peninsulas. The predicates 'von' and 'de' served the same corporate purpose. Both indicated the noble status of untitled noblemen. They were obtained by the act of ennoblement or inherited by the younger sons of title-holders and all the sons of ordinary nobles.

Since they were not subjected to the rule of primogeniture and were freely granted by the Crown, the predicates and the other designations of noble status clearly had much more scope for expansion than the titles designating noble rank. Their expansiveness was eventually the cause of their downfall, especially when it resulted from their usurpation by non-nobles. By the late nineteenth century the European nobility was losing its traditional definition not only because of the reduction of corporately-held privileges but also because of the inroads made by the bourgeoisie into some of the surviving privileges, notably the lesser titles, predicates and forms of address. For this process of usurpation the government held as much responsibility as the social acquisitiveness of rising elites. While the higher titles were safeguarded as noble preserves until the abolition of nobility, non-nobles were allowed to annex the various designations of nobility especially when noble status no longer conferred material or political rights. In Sicily the bourgeois recipients of fiefs had traditionally enjoyed the title of don. After the conversion of fiefs into freeholds in 1812, the right was shared by the recipients of the fragments of former fiefs as they came to be broken up and put on the market.[85] The usurpation of the title of 'don' had a very long history. Only the scale of it changed in the nineteenth century. By 1900 'don' was widely used in Italy and Spain as a form of address and by sections of society in which the nobility formed only a small part. In this respect it no longer indicated nobility. In England the title of esquire went the same way. Although it continued to be granted as a noble honour by Victoria and endured into the twentieth century as the appellation of non-titled bearers of coats of arms and of J.P.s, it also became the designation of the middle classes.[86] Some of the predicates suffered from bourgeois usurpation. In post-revolutionary France, the usurpation of the particule was unrestrained. The *Adelspradikat* continued to be awarded in Germany and Austria until 1918, and on a very large scale. For example, of the 1,315 creations of nobility made by the Prussian monarchy in the period 1871 to 1918, all but 221 were awards of the 'von'.[87] However, the government's heavy reliance upon it as a form of patronage may have limited, but could not prevent, its informal adoption. The forms of address, especially those indicative of noble status rather than noble rank, also slipped into other hands, 'Mr', 'Signore', 'Señor', 'Herr' and 'Monsieur' becoming the common property of the citizenry and no longer the mark of nobility.

The confusion of degree which resulted from the reduction of privilege and the usurpation of noble designations subjected the nobility to a profound character change. It tended to become a peerage, as nobility was confined to the higher title-holders. As a result, the nobility became more vulnerable than ever before to attack and dismissal. Previously the exclusiveness of the higher titles had been alleviated by the accessibility of noble status. With the latter demeaned by the usurpation of its designations and the reduction of its privileges, the traditional safety valve of social mobility became blocked up. More of a caste than a class, the hereditary nobility in its new guise was condemned to decline either because of social and political ostracism or because it became socially peripheral in an elite, largely composed of the rich and the professional, which it could no longer subdue, convert or captivate by the process of ennoblement.

VI

Seigneurial rights

The nobility's privileges of indemnity and political participation primarily concerned the public relationship between subject and state. In contrast, seigneurial rights essentially concerned the private relationship between lords and their own subjects. Usually they were imparted by landownership, but not necessarily. Within the same society, some lands conferred seigneurial authority and others did not. Furthermore, lords could exercise seigneurial rights over men who were not their tenants by acquiring, either through alienation or usurpation, the bannal privileges of rulers. These regalian rights appertained, for example, to the castellan lordships of eleventh and twelfth-century France, to the non-territorial *señoríos* granted in seventeenth-century Castile, to the franchises of medieval England, to the donations of medieval Portugal, to the baronies established in sixteenth-century Sweden, to the hereditary sheriffdoms and regalities of medieval Scotland and to the *Gerichtsherrschaft* of the German principalities. In all these cases, seigneurial authority was coterminous not specifically with land-ownership but with a territory officially recognised as a sphere of alienated bannal right.[1] Tenancy was often part of the relationship between master and serf; bound to the land, the serf was subject to the owner of that land. But serfdom could also detach seigneurial right from landownership. In Russia and Poland seigneurial rights derived from the serf's personal bond to his master; the serf was obliged to his lord not because he was his tenant but because he was, in the manner of a slave, the lord's disposable chattel. Personal serfdom was by no means confined to Russia and Poland. For example, under the Capetians, it was common in Northern and Central France, although, undergoing in the course of time conversion to tenurial serfdom. The extent of personal serfdom is evident in the range of societies which permitted the sale of serfs without land. Serfs were sold in Bohemia, Hungary, Swedish Pomerania, Livonia and in several of the German principalities as well as in Poland and Russia.[2]

Commoners had acquired seigneurial rights as early as the thirteenth century in Northern Italy, the Low Countries and France, usually by land purchase.[3] At the close of the seigneurial system, they exercised them on a substantial scale either through the ownership of seigneurial estates or through leasing the right of seigneurial exaction.[4] Nevertheless, over the centuries the majority of privately owned lordships tended to adhere to the nobility. Safeguarding them as a noble possession was the practice in Eastern Europe and Scandinavia of excluding commoners from the ownership of seigneurial estates or serfs, and the practice in medieval France of allowing the ownership of seigneurial authority to confer nobility; yet, even in areas without these safeguards, lordships remained largely in noble hands. In late seventeenth- and early eighteenth-century Denmark a spectacular transference of land allowed commoners by 1720 to own 44% of all privately owned lordships. But before the nineteenth century this was exceptional. Even by 1855 Prussian nobles retained 55% of *Rittergüter* in the six eastern provinces. Throughout their history, seigneurial rights possessed a strong noble connotation, serving as a recognised sign, if not proof, of nobility, so much so that commoners acquired them for this very reason. Seigneurial rights also remained closely associated with the nobility because commoners more frequently gained control of them as the agents and lessees of nobles than by ownership.[5]

Yet many nobles failed to become seigneurs. This was the case in the populous nobilities of Poland, Hungary and Castile and also in absolutist Russia and Prussia, where nobility was frequently granted as a reward for civil or military service, and in seventeenth-century France, Sicily and Naples where the government's income became heavily dependent upon the sale of noble status.[6] In these instances, the supply of nobles easily outstripped the supply of lordships. However, like socially ambitious commoners, the aspiration of nobles was to secure or to retain rights of lordship. Although no part of the definition of nobility, the noble order accepted seigneurial right as an important feature of its true character.

1 *The range of rights*

Seigneurial rights served (1) to assert pre-eminence; (2) as a source of income; (3) as a means of tenant control. Seigneurial income derived from the lord's right to exact labour services, dues and taxes as well as from his monopoly and pre-emption rights and his right of patrimonial justice. The tenant control conferred by the seigneurial system rested upon the lord's private jurisdiction, his authority to determine the duration of a tenancy and his right to license the movement, marriage and occupation of his serfs. It also relied upon certain administrative functions which the state expected the seigneur to fulfil: principally the collection of state taxes, the selection of military conscripts and the appointment of public officials.

(a) *Public pre-eminence*

In most societies public pre-eminence was a right of nobility. Custom or law authorised the priority of nobles over commoners and an order of precedence within the nobility. In parts, public pre-eminence could be a seigneurial right, specifically conferring a seat on the front bench in church, or first place in religious processions, or the possession of a pew in the choir, or the right to be sprinkled with holy water separately from the rest of the congregation, or the right to receive a personal mention in the prayers of intercession, or the right to command silence and respect when entering or leaving the church. Frequently these rights accompanied a privately possessed bannal authority, notably that of justice, and clearly had a regalian origin. They were commonly found in France, where they were the special right of *haut justiciers*. They were also conferred by the *señorios* created in seventeenth-century Castile.[7]

(b) *Labour services*

Basically they consisted of the free services a tenant was obliged to provide his lord, the services he was bound to provide for a wage and the full-time services required of his children.[8] The services were not confined to farm-work. They could also include long and short distance transport duties, postal obligations, assistance with the lord's hunting and fishing, the cutting of firewood and planks, the spinning of flax and the picking of oakum, the manufacture of implements and garments, domestic service and night-watch—this could include beating the moat to prevent the frogs from croaking—, furnishing the lord with fuel for his fire and material for the repair of his property, and rearing and tending his livestock.[9] Outstanding for the range of their service obligations were the territories of the Carolingian Empire in the ninth century and those of the Austrian Empire in the seventeenth and eighteenth centuries.[10] The variety and extensiveness of the labour services, however, did not necessarily account for their oppressiveness. Farmwork remained the major exaction and the weight of labour services was essentially determined by the seigneur's farming activities. Much depended upon the size of the demesne, the extent to which it was directly farmed by the owner, the availability of other forms of labour and the type of farming.

Among the seigneurial obligations exacted in Western and Southern Europe, labour services featured prominently from the final years of the Roman Empire until the thirteenth and fourteenth centuries. In this time the landlords tended to operate large-scale farms on their extensive demesnes by means of tenant rather than slave or wage labour.[11] Heavy labour services also prevailed from the sixteenth to the nineteenth centuries in the *gutsherrlich* areas of Eastern Europe, notably Mecklenburg, Brandenburg,

Pomerania, East Prussia, Poland, Livonia, Bohemia and Hungary, where seigneurial rights provided the nobles with free labour for their capitalist farming. The weight of labour services clearly differed between areas where the seigneurial system principally provided the labour for demesne farming and areas where it provided an alternative or supplementary income in cash or kind to that of rent. Thus, within the Austrian Empire of the eighteenth century, a dramatic difference lay between *gutsherrlich* Bohemia and Hungary where the labour services amounted to several days a week and the *grundherrlich* Austrian territories where they amounted to several days a year.[12] Labour obligations in seventeenth and eighteenth century Royal Prussia and the duchy of Samogitia, both of them Polish territories of tenant farming and wage labour, were much lighter than in the parts of Poland where landlord farming predominated.[13] Within the territories of the Bohemian Crown, labour services in seventeenth-century Bohemia and Moravia, both of them *Gutsherrschaft* regions, were much heavier than in parts of Silesia where serfdom likewise existed but *Grundherrschaft* prevailed.[14] Labour services, moreover, were slight throughout the Bohemian lands, four to twelve days a year, until the development of demesne farming in the seventeenth and eighteenth centuries when they rose to three days a week.[15] Labour services were similarly light in Brandenburg and Pomerania until the introduction of demesne farming in the sixteenth and seventeenth centuries transformed a labour service of a few days a year into one of several days a week.[16] On the other hand, the decline of direct demesne farming in Western Europe between the twelfth and fourteenth centuries reduced labour services from two or three days a week to a few days a year.[17]

Since the exaction of labour services in the modern period differed from area to area within each of the eastern monarchies, its weight can be said to have relied upon the needs of the landlords rather than upon the nature of the political system. Opportunities for raising labour services existed because of the weakness of royal government both in late medieval Eastern and Western Europe, but it is significant that the seigneurs seized them only in the former. Furthermore, prior to the nineteenth century, the weight of labour services in the monarchies of Eastern Europe remained largely unaffected by the government, no matter whether it was constitutionally weak and bureaucratically primitive, as in Hungary and Poland, or absolutist and powerful, as in eighteenth-century Prussia and Bohemia. Labour services were certainly heaviest where the monarchy was weakest: the common requirement of five or six days a week of compulsory labour in parts of seventeenth- and eighteenth-century Poland was unmatched elsewhere. But week-work, as opposed to the annual requirement which had largely taken its place in Western Europe by 1400, also came to prevail in absolutist Prussia, Russia and Bohemia. In Brandenburg and Russia it predated the rise of royal absolutism but was tolerated by the latter. In Bohemia, the system of oppressive labour services developed under strong monarchy and with its authorisation.[18]

More important than the political factor was the extent of the landowners' farming operations, the availability of slave and wage labour and whether the farming was principally arable or pastoral. Although large in comparison with the *grundherrlich* areas of the Austrian territories, the amount of demesne land in late eighteenth-century Bohemia formed only 16% of the cultivated area. The remainder consisted of peasant tenures. In contrast, in Galicia 43.5% of cultivated land was demesne, while in Croatia, Inner Hungary and parts of Transylvania, it amounted to 40%. Of the *gutsherrlich* parts of the Austrian Empire, only in North and West Hungary, where the traditional tenures had not been upset by the Turkish occupation and the reconquest, were the proportions of demesne to peasant land similar to that of Bohemia. Elsewhere the proportion was at least twice as large and correspondingly greater were the labour services. In the mid-eighteenth century a maximum of three days a week existed in Bohemia, while four days a week was common in Transylvania and six days a week was known in Galicia.[19]

Another contribution to the weight of labour services was the close involvement of demesne farming with agriculture rather than with animal husbandry. Notably in Bohemia, demesne farming long preceded the imposition of week-work. However, while the lords' commercial activities were confined to pisciculture, timber and sheep, heavy labour services were not required, and only followed their adoption of corn growing at the turn of the sixteenth and seventeenth centuries. Similarly in Denmark labour services became considerable in Jutland as landlords in the late seventeenth and early eighteenth centuries transferred from pastoral to arable farming. The relative lightness of labour services in Hungary, as defined and authorised in the urbarial regulations of 1767, reflects upon the pastoral farming practised by the landlords.[20]

The density of the population and the legal status of the peasantry also influenced the weight of the labour services. Week-work was associated with serfdom. Although by the modern period there were many lightly burdened serfs in Western Europe, throughout the history of the seigneurial system it remained the custom that freemen did not perform week-work. The weight of labour services owed by serfs and freemen depended not only upon the availability of other forms of labour but also upon the availability of men under obligation to provide labour services. Depopulation could lead to an increase in the weight of labour services, especially when the landlords remained farmers and, as in seventeenth-century Poland and Bohemia, the tenant's servile condition prevented him from reaping any advantage from his scarcity value.[21]

Reducing the weight of labour services was technological advancement. This happened not so much in the modern period, when the mechanisation of farming followed the abolition of labour services, as in the early middle ages when the contraction of services in Western Europe between the ninth and twelfth centuries was partly due to the substitution of the plough for the hoe and to improvements in the harnessing of draught animals.[22] Labour services were also lessened by the availability of alternative sources of production and labour. The manufacturing services in Western Europe declined with the development of urban manufactures in conjunction with the greater availability of money.[23] In farming, the compulsory labour services required of tenants had increased with the decline of slavery—for example, in early medieval Western and Southern Europe and in early modern Russia[24]—but decreased when rapid population growth and the development of a money economy made hired labour a feasible proposition. When the availability of labour ensured low wages, seigneurs could regard wage labour as preferable to the social friction and inefficiency caused habitually by labour services. This was as true of Italy and Western Europe in the twelfth and thirteenth centuries as of Eastern Europe in the late eighteenth and nineteenth centuries.[25] Of outstanding importance in reducing or removing labour services was a shrinkage in the amount of land directly farmed by the seigneur. This could result from the creation of peasant tenures on demesne land or the expansion of existing tenures at the expense of the demesne, processes which reduced the actual size of the demesne, as in France from the tenth to the twelfth centuries.[26] Or more frequently, a reduction of the seigneur's farming operations resulted from leasing out demesne lands, a policy which kept the demesne lands intact but eliminated the need of labour services to work them. By 1300 demesne leasing was extensively practised in Western Europe and North Italy.[27] Promoted, if not initiated by depopulating plagues, it had caused the virtual collapse of landlord farming by 1400.[28] Thereafter, the rentier inclination of the landlords in Western Europe, Scandinavia and Italy ensured that farmwork services would be comparatively light and much less burdensome than rents and dues.

On the other hand, labour services could also be lessened in association with an expansion of the land directly farmed by the lord, especially when he became reliant upon hired labour and having relieved the peasants of their farmwork services, proceeded to relieve them of their tenures. This happened extensively in Eastern Europe during the late eighteenth and early nineteenth centuries. Seizing the opportunities stemming from rapid population growth to charge high rents and pay low wages, lords freed themselves and their peasants of compulsory farmwork either by leasing the demesne in the western manner or by working it with wage labour. The former preserved the peasantry, the latter turned it into a proletariat.[29]

Throughout most of Europe, labour services were a feature, if not always a prominent one, of the traditional agrarian system.[30] Except where the farming needs of the landlords dictated otherwise, they became confined to a few days a year: not more than twelve days p.a. in eighteenth-century France, not more than four to six days p.a. in sixteenth-century Bavaria, not more than fourteen days p.a. in sixteenth-century Upper Austria, not more than two to six days from the thirteenth century in Hainault.[31] In many parts, labour services underwent conversion to rent centuries before the abolition of the seigneurial system. Nonetheless, because of the willingness of landlords to participate in farming and because of their inability to find alternative sources of labour, compulsory labour services—as in the medieval West and the modern East—could become the most oppressive of seigneurial obligations. In Eastern Europe they became for this reason a vital element in the abolition of the seigneurial system, inciting massive popular opposition against the seigneur to which both counter-revolutionaries and revolutionaries needed to respond. Even in France, where labour services had become attenuated long before their complete abolition, they were a major cause of anti-seigneurial sentiment among the peasantry in 1789.[32]

(c) Seigneurial dues

A lordship usually consisted of the demesne on the one hand and the tenures on the other. The tenures were held in return for the fulfilment of seigneurial obligations which included dues as well as services. The regularly exacted dues consisted of either a proportion of the produce (*champart* in France, *terrage* in the Low Countries, *osep* in Poland, *nona* in Hungary, *Zehent* in Austria, *Teilfrucht* in Germany) or a rent (*cens* in France, *Gült* or *Grundzins* in Germany, *census* in Hungary, *czynsz* in Poland), payable in money or kind. Both were usually fixed by custom.[33] The *champart* form of payment was not found in Scotland, England and Bohemia, and in France it was never so common as the *cens*. Nonetheless, it became widely practised in Europe, with a history reaching back to the Romans.[34] It was extensively used in eleventh- and twelfth-century Western Europe as a means of exploiting reclaimed land.[35] In France it also developed as the task-work fields of the demesne were converted, in the tenth and eleventh centuries, to tenures owing *champart*.[36] With the leasing of demesnes on a share-cropping basis, it became a major source of revenue, although no longer a seigneurial one, in the states of the Mediterranean. In periods of inflation, the *champart* possessed a special value because, unlike the fixed money rent, it was not prone to devaluation. However, famine or depressed agricultural prices badly affected it. The proportion of the produce exacted by the lord varied from place to place. In Valencia, Portugal and Burgundy the share of the harvest annexed by the lord amounted to a quarter and a third. Elsewhere it tended to be a much smaller proportion. In Hungary it amounted to one-ninth but included livestock as well as crops; in Austria it was a tenth. Frequently it was as low as one-twelfth.[37]

The rent was usually an alternative to the 'proportion of the produce' exaction, although in Hungary both *nona* and rent were exacted of the tenures.[38] As early as the thirteenth century the rent could be well below the tenure's rental value. By the end of the sixteenth century it could be a nominal amount, important not for its direct yield but because, fixed by custom, it necessitated the imposition of compensatory exactions.[39] In much of Europe the fixed rent thus underpinned the complicated system of seigneurial dues.

Compensating for the fixed rent and supplementing the *champart* were firstly the gifts of food owed by each tenure at certain times of the year such as Christmas, Easter and St. Martin's Day. Regular donations of this nature featured commonly in the seigneurial system throughout Europe.[40] When paid in kind they acted as another useful hedge against inflation. Often, however, they were converted to a fixed money payment which time devalued. Secondly, there was the money paid in commutation of labour services. This frequently merged with the rent. Commutation of labour services was practised in Carolingian times. In the tenth century it is found in Burgundy and North Italy.[41] In Tuscany money payments had replaced labour services on many estates by the late twelfth century and on the remainder by the late thirteenth century.[42] Commutation occurred frequently in thirteenth-century France.[43] By the fourteenth century labour services had been widely transformed into a quitrent in Brandenburg, a process which was undone with the revival of demesne farming in the sixteenth and seventeenth centuries. By the sixteenth century a similar commutation had taken place in Saxony and Upper Austria. The determination of a seigneurial rent in eighteenth-century Portugal to accord with the yoke of oxen possessed by the tenant implies its origin as a labour service.[44] As population growth produced an excess of labour, notably in the twelfth, thirteenth, sixteenth and eighteenth/nineteenth centuries, commutation was correspondingly common.[45] And furthering the process in the late middle ages in Western Europe and in the late modern period in Eastern Europe, was the withdrawal of the landlord from direct farming. Frequently the labour service became a customary and regular rent, invariable and therefore devalued in the course of time by the process of inflation. A final source of regular income were the initially irregular exactions, the casualties, which came to be converted into regular, annual payments. In parts, this happened to tallage, transfer charges and the revenue from the lord's grinding and baking monopoly.[46]

Seigneurial casualties were exacted either on special occasions or in return for specific services. Some were due on the death of a tenant (heriot, *meilleur catel*, *Besthaupt*, *mainmorte*, *nuncio*). This type of exaction originated in

serfdom, stemming from the lord's ownership of the property and goods of
his serfs. It usually entailed the seigneur's acquisition of the deceased tenant's
best beast. Another casualty was the transfer charges which fell due when
the possession of a tenancy was renegotiated, perhaps to allow its sale or
exchange (*lods et ventes, laudemium, Lehngeld, Handlohn, Besitzwechsel-
gebühren*), perhaps to extend a family's tenure of it (entry fine, *gersuma*), or
perhaps to authorise the succession from father to son of a perpetual tenancy
(relief, *mortuarium, Hauptrecht*). The transfer charges originated in the
proprietorial rights of free tenants. Both forms of casualty were common in
Western and Central Europe from at least the twelfth century to the destruction of the seigneurial system in the late eighteenth and early nineteenth
centuries; and heriot became common in Eastern Europe in association with
serfdom.[47] Upholding transfer charges was the existence of hereditary,
fixed-rent tenancies; working against them was the landlord's right to evict
his tenants and to determine their rent. Thus, in the *Lassbauer* areas east of
the Elbe—for example, in post-1500 Brandenburg, Pomerania and Poland—
as well as in Bohemia and Hungary in the modern period, areas of serfdom
where tenant right was extremely limited, transfer charges were not very
common.[48] Elsewhere, their prevalence was mostly determined by the landlord's inability to replace hereditary, fixed-rent tenures by leaseholds and
tenancies-at-will. Notably in Brittany and Burgundy, the survival of ancient
tenures, their rents fixed in the middle ages and made nominal by the process
of inflation, left landlords heavily dependent upon such casualties until the
Revolution.[49] On the other hand, in parts of Scotland transfer charges had
largely disappeared by 1600 as landlords succeeded in converting the tenantry
into short-term leaseholders.[50] In England, the entry fine, a due paid on the
renegotiation of a tenancy, remained of prime financial importance to landlords in the sixteenth and seventeenth centuries, allowing them to ride
inflation in spite of the widespread custom of fixed rents and the decay or
disappearance of other seigneurial dues. But gradually English landlords
came to prefer a second safeguard against falling landed incomes. Instead of
raising entry fines, they substituted an economic for a fixed rent by incorporating the traditional tenures into the demesne and by leasing them to
tenants.[51] There were, however, exceptions to the conjunction of transfer
charges and hereditary, fixed-rent tenures. For example, in Sweden tenants-
at-will paid entry fines to renew their tenancies every six years.[52] In England
customary tenants for life and at will were liable to entry fines, while an
intermediate stage in the conversion of customary to leasehold tenancy in
England was the beneficial lease whose low rent was countered by the
landlord's right to exact a large entry fine when the lease expired.[53]

Another frequent casualty was the fee paid by the tenantry in return for a
grant of the lord's permission. In both the traditional serf societies of Western

Europe and the renovated serf societies of Eastern Europe, the landlord legally controlled the marriage, migration and occupation of his tenantry.[54] Especially where serfdom was retained but was not required for demesne farming, as in Burgundy, parts of Western Germany and the Austrian territories in the seventeenth and eighteenth centuries, these rights tended to be transformed simply into a source of income, notably if the lord lost the right to refuse permission upon payment of the requisite fee. In most of Eastern Europe, however, they remained a source of control as well as of revenue until their abolition.[55]

Established during the collapse of two empires, the Roman and the Carolingian, seigneurial dues eventually came to affect most of Europe, largely by a process of noble usurpation, royal concession, conquest and colonisation. Along with the labour services, they formed an integral part of the traditional agrarian system. Like the labour services, the exaction of seigneurial dues had been seriously limited by 1400, both in North Italy and Western Europe, because of the decline of serfdom, the need to attract tenants in a period of severe depopulation caused by plague, and the practice of incorporating tenures into the demesne, thus converting them to leaseholds.[56] Yet this process of limitation did not totally replace the range of dues by a simple rent. Dues survived especially if the rent remained fixed by custom and if the existence of perpetual tenures and the protection of royal justice prevented lords from turning the tenures into leaseholds.[57] Before the period of government abolition in the revolutionary era, it was only where lords could obliterate the customary tenures, as, for example, in parts of Tuscany, Lombardy and the Low Countries by 1300 and in England, Scotland and Southern Spain by the early eighteenth century, that seigneurial dues were terminated.[58] In many parts of Western and Central Europe, an extension or intensification of seigneurial dues continued to provide lords with an important means of preventing inflation from devaluing their landed incomes, as was shown in the thirteenth, sixteenth and eighteenth centuries.[59] Except in areas of demesne farming, where seigneurial dues were overshadowed by the profits made from farming, and except in areas of peasant freeholds and leaseholds, seigneurial dues remained a major source of landed income until the collapse of the seigneurial regime in the years after 1789.

Ending seigneurial dues was either the initiative of landlords or the compulsion of governments. The process of voluntary elimination was well under way by 1300 as lords replaced customary tenures by leaseholds and destroyed the dichotomy of demesne and tenure.[60] Promoting this process over the centuries was the pressure which inflation or depopulation brought upon landlords to increase their landed incomes, the vulnerability of tenures to inclusion within the demesne, the fiscal exemption imparted to a tenure once it became part of the demesne, and the availability of tenants prepared to rent demesne leaseholds. These tenants were provided either by the rise of agrarian capitalism, which produced farmers capable of renting large areas of demesne at an economic rent, or by a plenitude of sharecroppers, a feature of Mediterranean countries, prepared to lease demesne smallholdings. Not all demesne expansion, however, worked against the seigneurial system. When lords enlarged the demesne for their own farming operations, the tendency to rely upon compulsory rather than hired labour before the nineteenth century left them heavily dependent upon seigneurial exactions. This type of demesne expansion only reduced the area of land devoted to the tenures: it did not eliminate them. Furthermore, seigneurial demands could be made of sharecroppers and of commercial farmers even when they were merely demesne leaseholders. Nonetheless, the lord's reliance upon an economic rent allowed seigneurial exactions to fall into disuse. They did so most completely with the development of agrarian capitalism. The relative importance of the several factors is evident in the ability of English lords to liberate themselves more absolutely from the seigneurial system than their counterparts in many parts of France. Upholding the seigneurial system in France was the durability of customary tenures and the relative absence, except in the North-east and Paris Basin, of the large-scale commercial farmer. In his place was the demesne leaseholder who worked a small farm and the *fermier général* to whom the landlord leased the collection of his seigneurial exactions and whose livelihood depended upon maintaining rather than disposing of the seigneurial system. In France the exploitation of the demesne was certainly a device which lords employed to counter falling landed incomes, but the pressures and opportunities to enlarge it at the expense of the tenures were not so great as in England.[61]

Governments certainly proceeded against seigneurial dues prior to the French Revolution. Moved by fiscal considerations and physiocratic doctrine, governments in the eighteenth century sought to increase state revenues by restricting the seigneurs' means of tapping the peasantry's wealth; yet before 1789 they seemed mostly incapable of conceiving the abolition of the seigneurial system and succeeded only in defining and regulating it.[62] Seigneurial dues eventually disappeared in revolutionary circumstances and did so because a combination of peasant militants with anti-seigneurial aims and revolutionaries with anti-noble intentions either forced revolutionaries to make concessions to peasants in order to win popular support and to quell disorder, or persuaded the old order to act likewise to prevent its overthrow.[63]

(d) Monopoly and exemption rights

Another source of seigneurial income was the lord's sole right to the natural products of the countryside. Occasionally the right applied to the subsoil as well as the surface, awarding the seigneur the ownership of the mineral resources found upon his estate. In eighteenth-century Naples the right included manure and rainwater. In the Austrian territories landlords could charge a fee when granting their tenants permission to hunt, fish and collect nuts. In the Southern Netherlands, the use of woods and pastures could involve the payment of a seigneurial due. The same was true in sixteenth-century Poland and thirteenth-century England.[64] Often the lord's right was limited by the extensive rights of common available to the tenantry. However, exclusive hunting and fishing rights were widespread. In several states hunting was controlled not only by seigneurial custom but also by overlying state laws which prohibited it to the commonalty and sometimes confined the hunting of certain types of game to certain types of noblemen. Hunting could thus be a privilege of nobility, conferred by noble status or noble rank. But over much of Europe, the *droit de chasse* and the *droit de pêche* were seigneurial rights, created by the Crown's alienation of its regalia and imparted by landownership. Besides furnishing the lord with provisions, these rights could be a source of income in licence fees.[65] In addition to owning the natural products of the manor, lords could enjoy lawful possession of things lost and found and not reclaimed. This included escaped swarms of bees and animals.[66]

Further income came of the seigneur's commercial monopolies which encompassed the production of alcoholic drinks, the processing of farm produce (grinding, baking and slaughtering), the fertilisation of farm stock through the right of stud, the sale of provisions and the keeping of certain livestock such as swans, rabbits and pigeons. Occasionally the seigneur had sole right to authorise the weights and measures used by a community (*pesage*), and sometimes the sole right to mint coins.

Rights of commercial monopoly were found from at least the tenth and eleventh centuries in Northern Italy and Western Europe and from a somewhat later date, although certainly by 1600, in Eastern Europe; and persisted until the revolutionary era, except in Austria and Bohemia where they were abolished just prior to the French Revolution. In France they were especially common and wide-ranging. Sometimes they spread through contact with France, as in Angevin Sicily and Naples, or in imitation of the French, as in parts of medieval Spain. In Scandinavia, the commercial monopoly was virtually absent. Like the hunting right, commercial monopoly was a banality, alienated to subjects by the prince, and provided a source of income from both sales and licence fees since the lord's exclusive right to grind corn, bake bread, brew beer, press grapes and so on entitled him to charge a fee for the service.[67]

For centuries seigneurs throughout much of Europe enjoyed a considerable income from milling and baking rights. Less common, but more lucrative, was the right to manufacture alcohol. Brewing, wine-making and distilling rights could be a noble privilege, a monopoly imparted to nobles by the state's exclusion of commoners from the activity. Either in the form of a seigneurial or a noble right, it was widespread in modern Eastern Europe and was also found on the territorial *señoríos* of Spain, in France, England, a number of German principalities and parts of the Low Countries.

The sale of alcohol was another seigneurial monopoly which sometimes became a noble right. In Poland, Bohemia, Spain and Naples, the sale of alcohol on the estate became the exclusive right of the seigneur. In Hungary the seigneurs were privileged to sell wine throughout the year whereas, in contrast, the rest of society could do business only at certain times. A similar right of sale was enjoyed in France, Portugal and the Danubian Principalities, where the seigneurs had the sole right to sell wine for a number of days after the vintage. As for the provisioning monopolies, the Hungarian seigneurs were privileged to supply the villages on their estates with meat; in Sicily the seigneur controlled the village shop; in Poland salt, tobacco and herring had to be bought from the seigneur; in Bohemia the sale of salt was a seigneurial monopoly and in much of Western Europe the right of market was regularly in seigneurial hands. The rights of sale were often complemented by rights of pre-emption. This applied not only to property (*retrait lignager*, *Vorkaufsrecht*) but also to the products of the tenantry. It existed in at least Russia, Poland, Hungary, Bohemia, Austria, Sicily and Naples. All these rights were a considerable source of income, as rent if leased out, as fees for services rendered or permission granted, and because they allowed prices to be non-competitively set.[68]

Alongside these commercial monopolies was the highly profitable exemption of the seigneur from the regulations appertaining to common rights. In parts of France, Poland and Germany, for example, the number of beasts grazed by a lord on the common was unlimited whereas that of the tenants was fixed. Lords not only pastured large herds of sheep and cattle on the common but also leased out their right of exemption to commercial farmers. A related right in Sicily denied the tenantry the use of forests and common pasture for part of the year while the seigneur was entitled to free access at all times. Rights of exemption increased with the development of commercial farming. For example, *troupeau à part* in Lorraine had medieval origins but was confined to a handful of seigneurs until a growing market for wool and meat in the seventeenth and eighteenth centuries, and the appearance of capitalist farmers prepared to lease the seigneur's right, rapidly increased the number of seigneurs laying claim to it. Like labour services, this was an instance of capitalist farming extending and intensifying seigneurial privilege.[69]

(e) Taxes and the profits of justice

Seigneurial revenue also consisted of taxes, both direct and indirect, and the profits of justice. The regular direct taxation of serfs (chevage) existed in Western Europe as early as the tenth century; the direct taxation of the rest of the community by seigneurial right (tallage) developed somewhat later but was established by the close of the eleventh century, initially in the form of irregular and variable demands for specific purposes such as war, the lord's hospitality and, like the aid required of knightly vassals, to finance the lord's ransom, the marriage of his eldest daughter and the knighting of his eldest son. By the thirteenth century these tallages had become annual levies with no specified justification. In the same period private indirect taxation also emerged in the West. Like the judicial and monopoly rights, these fiscal privileges were mostly banalities ceded to subjects by the Crown. With one or two exceptions, the direct levies disappeared centuries before the final collapse of the seigneurial system, excluded by the development of national systems of taxation. Indirect levies—highway and bridge tolls, ferry charges, customs dues and sales taxes—had a much longer life. Highway tolls, for example, were only abolished in 1791 in the Kingdom of Naples, while tolls and taxes on the local transactions of tradesmen, fishermen and lawyers remained a source of seigneurial income in Portugal until the 1820s. Although threatened by Colbert, seigneurial tolls only ended with the Revolution in France. Before state taxation depressed their value, private taxes were a considerable source of seigneurial income.[70] The same was true of the profits of private justice, the sums exacted as fines in the seigneurial courts of law, especially by lords with rights of high and middle justice. The extension of royal justice eventually side-tracked a good deal of business and profit, but before that happened (as, for example, in twelfth-century France), the income from fiscal and judicial rights could easily exceed the income from seigneurial dues and could even exceed the income from direct farming.[71]

(f) Rights of jurisdiction

Some seigneurial rights were primarily a source of income; others were a means of control. The latter included the right of patrimonial jurisdiction, the right to determine tenancy, a series of rights intimately connected with serfdom, the right to administer the fiscal and military demands which the state made of a seigneur's subjects, and the right to influence the appointment of public officials.

The jurisdictional rights took two forms: one allowed a lord to dispense justice in his own court, and the other authorised him to nominate the judges in public courts. The latter was, for example, exercised in Capetian France where the appointment of *échevins*, royal officials of the Carolingians with a duty to judge minor causes, became the right of lords. It was widely distributed in Castile. It was also found in Lombardy where a number of fiefs retained in the eighteenth century the authority to appoint the *podestà*, the chief magistrate of the commune. In Portugal the right to nominate royal judges, or to ratify their appointment, replaced the right of private jurisdiction in 1790. A similar revision of seigneurial authority occurred in the Congress Kingdom of Poland between 1807, when private jurisdiction was abolished, and 1818, when the office of mayor was placed in seigneurial hands.[72]

Much more common was the right of private jurisdiction, although it was largely absent from Sweden, Frisia, the Basque provinces, Navarre, Württemberg, and the Rhine duchies of Cleves, Mark, Jülich and Berg.[73] From at least the eleventh century in the West, and from the fourteenth century in the East, seigneurs enjoyed the right to dispense justice in their own courts. Like the seigneurial monopolies and taxes, patrimonial justice was mostly created by the subject's assumption of regalian right. The right could encompass crimes, misdemeanours and civil cases—that is, matters which otherwise would have been the concern of public courts—as well as offences against manorial regulations. Frequently it permitted lords to order capital and corporal punishment as well as to impose fines and to forfeit tenancies.[74] The right to judge crimes (high justice) was featured in most seigneurial systems, but in some of them only a small proportion of seigneurs could exercise it. For example, in sharp contrast to Brandenburg, Pomerania and Prussia whose rulers in the late middle ages alienated their right of high justice to subjects on a massive scale, essentially to raise cash, the rulers of Saxony retained most of their criminal jurisdiction. The outcome was that in Saxony high justice was the prerogative of a few lords, the *Schriftsassen*. The majority of seigneurs, the *Amtsassen*, held only low justice.[75] Moreover, in certain states high justice was shortlived as a seigneurial right. In England the extension of royal justice in the twelfth century largely confined it to the franchises and the courts leet with view of frankpledge; and as a right of trial and punishment it was terminated in 1536 when the franchises lost their right of criminal jurisdiction.[76] Similarly, in Northern Italy criminal justice tended to be annexed by the communes and rendered public between the eleventh and the fourteenth centuries. In a number of countries, notably Castile and Bavaria, criminal jurisdiction never became a seigneurial right.[77] On the other hand, it was frequently and durably possessed by the seigneurs of Hungary, Bohemia, Austria, Poland, Brandenburg, Pomerania, Prussia, Russia, France, the provinces of the Crown of Aragon, Sicily, Naples, Scotland and the provinces of Holland, Zeeland and Utrecht, surviving until at least the eighteenth century and in some cases until the mid-nineteenth century.[78] However, its attendant rights sometimes ceased to be exercised long before they were abolished. Long before the government's prohibitive restrictions of 1788, private criminal jurisdiction in France did no more than to impart the honour of sporting the gallow tree close by the family seat; and when the Spanish monarchy abolished the right in 1716, the seigneurs of the Crown of Aragon had not exercised their powers of criminal jurisdiction for over a century. The same was true of the Austrian territories and of Poland. In the former the close supervision of royal officials and the government's traditional right to approve the death sentence passed in the private courts (*Bannleihe*) caused private criminal justice to cease operation long before its abolition. In Poland, the abolition of the seigneurial right of capital punishment in 1768 made little difference because earlier it had fallen into disuse.[79] Frequently the penalties of the private courts were subjected to state scrutiny. Thus in France the death sentence passed by a seigneurial court came to be invalid unless confirmed by a royal court. In Hainault the sentences of private courts in major causes from the fourteenth century onwards required the consent of the *grand bailli*. In the Prussian monarchy, royal absolutism tolerated patrimonial jurisdictions but insisted that in criminal matters the royal justices should pronounce sentence, the royal high court should approve it, and the king should authorise the penalties of capital punishment and exile.[80]

The seigneur's rights of criminal jurisdiction were never all-inclusive. As a rule they failed to include treason. Moreover, they were usually subjected to the defendant's right of appeal to a royal court. The right of seigneurs to hold a court of final appeal was rare. Private jurisdiction, then, was not often autonomous. It is true that in Poland peasants lost the right to appeal against the judgments of the seigneurial courts in 1518 and only retrieved it after the partition of the Commonwealth, and in the course of the seventeenth and eighteenth centuries each noble estate in Russia became a legal entity, the lord having the right to inflict the death penalty, the serf lacking after 1767 the right of appeal to the royal courts.[81] But these were exceptions. In the long development of patrimonial jurisdiction, some jurisdiction—either the right of appeal or the exclusive right to judge certain offences or to impose certain penalties—was reserved for an independent authority. This was the case with the Roman latifundist's jurisdiction over his colons, the Frankish immunist's jurisdiction over his free and unfree subjects, serfdom as it was practised in the medieval West and the feudal system in which appeal jurisdiction and the right of suzerainty interlocked.[82] Rather than creating them for the first time, the development of royal justice basically applied or extended rights of control which governments had long possessed. Private justice at times acquired a practical all-inclusiveness, but not normally as a legally enshrined seigneurial right since this all-inclusiveness usually resulted from the Crown's inability to assert its higher jurisdictional authority, or from the difficulties of commoners in making complaint to the higher courts against the judgments of their seigneurs.[83] In Brandenburg, for example, the peasant's right of appeal was countered before the nineteenth century by his lord's right to imprison him if his complaint proved to be false,[84] while in Bohemia and Hungary the jurisdictional powers of lords in the seventeenth and eighteenth centuries were almost as complete in practice as those of Poland and Russia. In Hungary, the official courts of appeal were the county courts for civil matters and the district courts of appeal and the *tabula regia* for criminal matters. In none of these courts could the serf bring an action, or bear witness, personally against a noble. His only course was to entrust his suit to a nobleman. Because of the composition of the appeal courts, it was then adjudged by a panel of noblemen. Some relief only came in 1836 when seigneurial courts were barred from judging cases to which the lord was a party and serfs were permitted to transfer their pleas to the county courts if the seigneurial court failed to act within fourteen days after presentation.[85] A similar system had operated in Bohemia but was subjected at a much earlier date to external restrictions. While the system remained intact in Hungary until the 1840s, in eighteenth-century Bohemia a series of measures were applied—notably the extension of the right of appeal, the development of a system of public supervision, the criminal ordinances of 1765 which reduced the number of private courts authorised to impose the death penalty from 381 to thirty—that severely curtailed, without completely abolishing, the right of private jurisdiction.[86] In other cases the seigneur's ability to exercise full or unquestioned powers of jurisdiction was not integral to the system but, resulting from the weakness of the Crown, was undone with the restoration of the latter's political effectiveness. This was the case in early medieval France when the collapse of the Carolingian regime enabled lords to annex full jurisdictional powers which the recovery of the Crown's political ascendancy between the twelfth and fourteenth centuries severely limited.[87]

The rights of private jurisdiction stemmed from two basic sources: land ownership and lordship. Under the Roman Empire landownership eventually conferred upon the latifundists the right to punish their tenantry moderately and for minor offences, while slave-ownership (lordship) conferred more extensive rights of private jurisdiction. This collection of rights long outlived the empire. They awarded jurisdiction not only over slaves and serfs but also over freemen, the former for reasons of lordship, the latter for reasons of landlordship.[88] Under the Merovingians and Carolingians the rights of jurisdiction enjoyed by landlords were enlarged and extended, particularly over freemen, by the grant of immunities. Immunities were associated closely with estates which, in belonging to the royal domain, were privileged to be independent of the state's formal machinery of government. Although mainly granted to ecclesiastical bodies, they came to be widely owned by laymen who received them either directly from the Crown or more commonly *via* the Church. Like the jurisdictional rights of the Roman landowner, the immunists' jurisdiction was originally of a lesser nature. Major crimes were the province of the count, a royal officer. However, between the ninth and eleventh centuries, the immunist acquired in practice the ability to judge major as well as minor causes; and as the office of count became the hereditary right of certain families the courts of the counts became private rather than public tribunals. This development allowed owners of the office to judge crimes not by right of landownership but by virtue of owning bannal lordship over a specific territory.[89]

By immunity and by acquiring the Crown's bannal authority, subjects obtained an extensive private jurisidiction over freemen as well as serfs. In the West this process was furthered by the fragmentation of bannal jurisdictions in the eleventh and twelfth centuries. As a result, rights of high justice became the possession not only of counts but also of castellans and lesser lords. Since they could be granted to lesser lords as the perquisite of a grant of land, many of these bannal rights were bestowed by landownership rather than by the lordship incumbent upon office-ownership. Meanwhile, the voluntary submission of freeholders to the jurisdiction of lords in return for their protection continued apace, a process under way in the closing years of the Roman Empire and revived as the Carolingian Empire fell into decay.[90]

Having been established in the West between the tenth and twelfth centuries by a combination of royal or comital grant, noble usurpation and peasant submission, the right of high justice was then extended to Eastern Europe principally in the course of the fourteenth and fifteenth centuries. Responsible was the Crown's willingness to alienate its bannal rights to subjects. However, as in the West, lordship and landownership became very closely linked. For example, in Brandenburg, Pomerania and Prussia prior to the fourteenth century, high justice was normally exercised through the ruler's court by his advocates while low justice was exercised by hereditary village mayors through public tribunals in which freemen were obliged to serve as jurors. Seigneurial rights of jurisdiction were founded as landlords annexed the office of village mayor and as poverty forced the ruler to sell them his powers of high justice.[91] Only stemming the tide of seigneurial justice was the preservation of peasant proprietorship, not as a perpetual tenancy as in England and France, but as an allod. Where allodial freeholders survived in large numbers, as in Sweden and Frisia, the ancient popular assemblies, which had traditionally dispensed justice through the agreement of the freemen, preserved their independence of the seigneur. The other alternative to seigneurial justice was the royal courts. The ruler's retention of his right of justice, however, did not prevent the development of seigneurial justice. It curtailed only the private possession of high justice. Low justice became a private right as a legacy of the Carolingian system which had allowed seigneurs to exercise it in the absence of *échevins*[92] and because of the capacity of seigneurs to convert popular public tribunals into private courts.

It would be wrong to regard seigneurial justice as an offshoot of the feudal system since its roots long preceded the latter's establishment. Moreover, by 1500 private justice comprehended a much wider area of Europe than that which had experienced feudalism. Nonetheless, feudalism certainly promoted private justice by converting allods into dependent tenures, notably in England following the Conquest, and by turning German chiefs into vassals while allowing their regal rights to survive in a seigneurial guise. Whether imposed by conquest as in Sicily and Naples, or by imitation as in twelfth- and thirteenth-century Portugal, Castile and Aragon where royal grants were modelled on French fiefs, feudalism was also the carrier of seigneurial justice. Essentially feudalism contributed to the development of seigneurial justice by recognising it as an integral part of the political system and by asserting its subjection to an independent appellate jurisdiction vested in the suzerain.[93]

It would be misguided to regard seigneurial justice simply as a medieval creation which withered away in the modern period. In the twelfth and thirteenth centuries it came under serious attack from the communes of Northern Italy and from the monarchs of England and France, although this onslaught restricted rather than abolished it.[94] Furthermore, private justice was briskly extended in the sixteenth and seventeenth centuries. In Brittany, for example, rights of high justice were usurped at the expense of the Crown and other seigneurs. In Castile the area of private jurisdiction was considerably enlarged as the Crown sold *señoríos*.[95] In Sicily and Naples, the process of extension, promoted by Crown sales, continued into the eighteenth century. In Sicily a notable stage in the extension of private justice occurred in 1621 when fiefholders received the right to purchase the right of jurisdiction on any fief in their possession. In Naples at the end of the fifteenth century 1,200 out of 1,500 communities remained free of seigneurial jurisdiction. By 1734 this number had been reduced to fifty. This alienation of justice was again the work of the Spanish Habsburgs. Unlike Castile, where the sale of jurisdictional rights had not conferred high justice, in Naples and Sicily it frequently did so.[96] Also responsible for the extension of private justice in the modern period were the Hohenzollerns, who between 1645 and 1652 granted civil and criminal jurisdiction of first instance to the nobility of Mark and Cleves, partly to raise revenue and partly to establish allies in the newly acquired duchies.[97] At roughly the same time the Danish Crown authorised the extension of seigneurial justice to Norway, while in the sixteenth century the Vasas introduced private justice to Sweden by creating a number of county franchises which survived until 1680.[98]

The process of outright elimination commenced in 1789 and was completed in the mid-nineteenth century when rights of patrimonial jurisdiction were abolished in the Hohenzollern, Habsburg and Romanoff lands. The survivor was the traditionally restricted and largely inoffensive rights of the English manorial court which lasted until 1926. Compelling the abolition of private justice was a combination of peasant militancy and the prospect of political revolution. Yet long before the revolutionary era, seigneurial justice was subjected to cancellation by seigneurs who wished to rid themselves of the cost and inconvenience of dispensing it and by governments who acted for the same revenue reasons that had once persuaded rulers to allow its extension. Not only in medieval England and France but also in the eighteenth-century empire of the Austrian Habsburgs, the Crown had confiscated jurisdictional rights in order to increase the profits of royal justice as well as to redress injustice.[99] Nonetheless, royal governments had proved remarkably capable of tolerating seigneurial justice, not only in the primitive monarchies of Poland and Hungary but also in the bureaucratic monarchies of eighteenth-century Prussia and Russia. In both types of state, seigneurial justice remained an integral part of the judicial system. Over the centuries royal government showed a deep and enduring respect for the seigneur. Patrimonial justice was not just a system of judicial administration but also a means of rapport between Crown and nobility. For this reason its maintenance owed much to the nobility's appreciation of it. The development of royal justice and government regulations could render the income from seigneurial justice less than the cost of its administration;[100] yet private justice remained useful to lords as a means of tenant control. Moreover, the nobility's identity as a ruling class depended heavily upon the right to dispense seigneurial justice. Along with the privileges of parliamentary membership and reserved office, this right preserved the nobility as something other than a professional elite, by allowing it a private, hereditary function in the running of the state.

(g) Serfdom

Seigneurial rights were at their most oppressive where serfdom prevailed. Yet the oppressiveness of serfdom differed from country to country and from period to period. It was comparatively mild, for example, in eighteenth-century Gelderland, Overijsel and Drente, in seventeenth-century Silesia and in thirteenth-century Prussia.[101] Furthermore, only rarely did the lord's control of the serf match that of the slave. Except in Russia after 1767 and in Poland after 1518, the ruler retained an appellate jurisdiction over serfs, and the serf-owner was obliged by law to regard the serf as something superior to mere property. Since the serf tended to be hereditarily bound to his lord's estate as well as to his lord, so that he was not normally disposable by sale apart from the estate to which his servitude ascripted him, his master was obliged to regard their relationship as a contractual one based upon land tenure. In this respect the serf was by nature a peasant rather than a piece of property. He was a landholder with proprietorial rights, sometimes rights of inheritance. Juridically distinct from the slave, the serf was also legally distinguished from tenants of free status and was subjected to restrictions and exactions from which the rest of the peasantry was usually free. Moreover, because the rights of lords to increase the exactions of the serf were less bound by custom, he was much more vulnerable to seigneurial exploitation. In matters of migration, marriage, change of occupation, schooling, the decision lay not with the serf's family but with its lord who also had the right of ownership over the movable goods acquired by a serf in his lifetime and much greater opportunities to enlarge the exactions made of serfs than of free tenants. Often a lord possessed the right of criminal jurisdiction over his serfs when lacking it over his other dependants. Serfdom placed the peasant firmly under the control of his lord since the serf's ability to secure his lord's consent and forbearance rarely became simply a money matter. The lord's rights to grant licence, to make arbitrary exactions and to confiscate property ensured the subjection of the serf to his master.[102]

Serfdom originated in the Roman practices of allowing slaves to hold land, of banning the separation by sale of agricultural slaves from the estates which they worked, and of attaching free peasants to the soil.[103] As a result of the rights acquired by the tenants of slave origin and the rights lost by the free tenants, serfdom emerged largely to furnish lords with a reserve of free labour for demesne farming. By the early tenth century it was common in parts of North Italy, France and Western and Southern Germany, reaching the peak of its development in the twelfth and thirteenth centuries when in Western Europe lords promoted a further extension of serfdom not for farming purposes but to extract greater seigneurial revenues from their peasantry.[104] Then serfdom underwent a profound collapse. In lowering wages and raising rents, rapid population growth gave lords a growing independence of labour services, making it profitable for them to cultivate their demesnes directly with wage labour or indirectly through leaseholders. Furthermore, rapid inflation forced lords to raise additional revenue by selling serfs their freedom at a time when the profitability of farming supplied serfs with the means of buying it. This process of emancipation was accelerated by the depopulation and economic regression of the fourteenth and fifteenth centuries which terminated direct demesne farming and persuaded lords to reduce seigneurial impositions in order to attract tenants and to deter their flight to other lords.[105] The process of elimination happened more rapidly and earlier in the Rhineland and North Italy than in England and

France; yet by 1400 serfdom had become a marginal feature of the agrarian system in the West, with a few pockets of survival, and later of revival, in parts of France, notably Franche-Comté and Burgundy, and of North-west Germany, which lasted until their formal abolition in the revolutionary era.[106]

Countering this process of emancipation in the West was a gigantic extension of serfdom in Eastern Europe. This happened from the fifteenth century onwards. The enserfment of the middle ages had been, to a large extent, a process of liberation, endowing former slaves with some of the legal rights of freemen. In contrast, the enserfment of the early modern period essentially deprived freemen of their liberties or further restricted the rights of the unfree. Completed in the eighteenth century, the process was then undone by government decree, whereas the first serfdom had wilted and withered away because of a voluntary change of relationship between lord and tenant. The second serfdom affected Denmark which had known serfdom in the thirteenth century and then saw it restored to the islands in the fifteenth century and, following its abolition in 1702, reimposed upon the whole realm in 1733.[107] Serfdom was not established in the rest of Scandinavia, but under Swedish rule became well founded in Estonia, Livonia and Swedish Pomerania.[108] In the course of the sixteenth and seventeenth centuries a serfdom became common in Hungary, Bohemia, Mecklenburg, Austria, Brandenburg, Prussia, Pomerania, Poland and Russia, which closely resembled the medieval serfdom of Western Europe, producing a mass of smallholders heavily obliged to pay labour services, dues, fees, fines and taxes to their lord and heavily restricted by their lord's extensive right of consent.[109]

The imposition of this serfdom cannot be explained simply in terms of an imbalance between the nobility and the Crown.[110] Serfdom was not always extended in periods of royal weakness and did not always contract in periods of royal strength. The process of emancipation in the West coincided with the weakness of the Crown in England and France. Although the second serfdom acquired a foothold in periods of royal weakness in Poland, Bohemia and Hungary, it developed and thrived in spite of the establishment of royal absolutism in Bohemia, Lower Austria, Russia and Prussia.[111] Nor can direct farming by the landlords be held wholly responsible for the second serfdom.[112] In most cases it was only partly responsible, and occasionally it was not the chief factor. In Russia the connexion between demesne farming and the imposition of serfdom was slight since the former was confined to certain regions while serfdom became general. In Brandenburg-Prussia, Bohemia and Little Poland, the introduction of serfdom preceded the extensive development of demesne farming.[113] Just as important in generating serfdom were the problems which underpopulation created for landlords, especially when intensified by the depopulating effects of famine, plague, war and migration.[114] The basic aim of serfdom in Eastern Europe was to secure the presence of peasants in sufficient numbers and to make them vulnerable not only to a weight of labour services but also to seigneurial exactions in cash and kind. A loss of population affected serfdom quite differently in Eastern Europe from Western Europe, promoting it in the former and discouraging it in the latter. Accounting for the difference was the fact that in the West the depopulation of the late middle ages followed a period of overpopulation, whereas in the East it intensified a chronic underpopulation. In Western Europe the emancipation process, initially a response to overpopulation, preceded the fall in population and, in failing to oppose the noble interest, was unstoppable. Furthermore, in Western Europe mortality was the basic cause of depopulation; and serfdom became the major cause of popular rebellion. The imposition or maintenance of serfdom therefore offered little solution. However, in Eastern Europe depopulation and protest often took the form of peasant flight. In binding peasants to the land or the lord, serfdom was an attempt at preventing this type of depopulation and revolt. Another response to depopulation in the East was demesne farming; in contrast, in the West depopulation drove lords to further the leasing of their demesnes.[115] For these reasons, the lord's attitude towards serfdom in the East was bound to differ from that of the West.

Although they responded differently to depopulation, both serfdoms were similarly undermined by rapid population growth. The eventual end of serfdom in Europe came by government decree, but easing its passage was the landlord's growing independence of the seigneurial system. This was due to overpopulation. The landhunger resulting from rapid population growth in the late eighteenth and nineteenth centuries raised the landlord's chances of drawing a thriving income from rents. Moreover, the resulting glut of landless labour encouraged lords to substitute wage for compulsory labour at a time when anti-seigneurial peasant revolt was persuading lords to regard serfdom as more of a liability than an advantage. However, there is no reason to believe that, without orders from the government, landlords would have terminated the second serfdom. Their dependency was too strong. For example, in both Hungary and Russia schemes for the voluntary cession of serfowner rights had little effect. By 1861 the ukase of 1803 which allowed lords to liberate their serfs had freed only 150,000 in a serf population of 10 million, while in Hungary a similar law of 1839 emancipated less than 2% of the serf class.[116] In terminating the second serfdom, enforcement by government decree played a vital role.

(h) The right to determine tenancy

The seigneurial system contained two types of ownership. On one level was the proprietorship of the seigneur. This conferred full ownership of the demesne and his final ownership of the tenures. His control of the demesne was restricted only by the agreements he made with those to whom he leased parts of it. The leases tended to be short-term and subjected to an economic rent. His control of the tenures entitled him to make exactions of their holders and was countered by their proprietary rights. This second level of proprietorship imparted rights of inheritance and sale. These rights were not the monopoly of free peasants since tenure in serf societies often became hereditary. Although not amounting to complete ownership, these secondary proprietorial rights considerably restricted the seigneur's tenurial authority to the extent that his control over the demesne tenants was much greater than over the holders of the tenures. Furthermore, in some regions where the tenant's proprietary rights remained frail, as in eighteenth-century Prussia, Hungary, Bohemia and Lower Austria, governments could impose restrictions upon the lord's ownership of land: for example, directed by fiscal considerations, they could forbid the absorption of the tenures into the fiscally privileged demesne.[117]

Yet not all tenures were hereditary. Serfdom often authorised lords to evict at will, or to alter arbitrarily the size, location and occupancy of the tenures.[118] And in many non-serf societies the terminal tenure provided the lord with an effective means of tenant control. In Sweden and Denmark, for example, the landlord traditionally had the right to evict at will and tenancy was often between one and eight years, while in most free societies many tenures either depended entirely upon the lord's paternalism or, held for life or lives, could eventually fall at the lord's disposal.[119] Even the perpetual tenures were not wholly safeguarded against the landlord's right of repossession. For the non-fulfilment of seigneurial obligations or for the neglect of the tenure, landlords frequently enjoyed the right of confiscation, and countering the hereditary rights of the French peasantry were the landlord's rights of *mainmorte* and *retrait lignager*. *Retrait* (the German equivalent was *Losungsrecht*, *Vorkaufsrecht* or *Näherrecht*, the Netherlands equivalent was *recht van naasting*, the Polish equivalent was *prawo retraktu* and in England the term was resumption) was the lord's option to purchase a tenure on his estate when it was sold; *mainmorte* awarded the lord the right of inheritance if the holders of the tenure failed in the main line.[120]

Although the seigneur's control of the tenures was not as great as his control over demesne tenancies, he, nonetheless, often possessed a right to determine the tenancy of the former, a right which came to an end only when the government's abolition of the seigneurial system converted the tenures into freeholds. The opposite was achieved when seigneurial rights were eliminated by the seigneur's incorporation of tenures within his demesne. Then the seigneur's limited control of the tenure gave way to the much greater tenurial control of the lessor.

(i) Rights of public administration

The seigneur's control of his tenantry was also upheld by his right to administer the collection of royal taxes and state conscription. This had Roman origins, the *dominus fundi* in the fourth and fifth centuries A.D. having had the responsibility to collect the taxes of his tenants and the authority to decide which tenants should do military service.[121] Like the right of parliamentary consent, the seigneurial right to collect royal taxes was a sop which medieval monarchs granted to lords in exchange for the extension of the right to tax their dependants. It was also a constituent of royal absolutism; in spite of the bureaucratisation of the state, landlords in the late eighteenth century collected the royal taxes owed by their tenantry in the Prussian monarchy, Austria, Bohemia and Russia, as well as in the administratively primitive monarchies of Poland and Hungary.[122] Royal absolutism likewise preserved the Crown's traditional reliance upon the landed nobles for the raising of troops. Conscription rendered unnecessary the private followings which the nobles had traditionally furnished for the government's use, yet its administration at the local level was frequently dependent upon the nobles, acting not in the capacity of state officials but as landlords. From 1544 until the late seventeenth century the Swedish landlords were allowed to determine which of their tenants should be conscripted. This became the usual practice in the seventeenth and eighteenth centuries where conscription was adopted: in Prussia, Bohemia, Austria, Russia and Denmark. The power which this right conferred upon the landlord was vividly portrayed by Alexander Herzen, the illegitimate son of a Russian noble, who recalled in his autobiography: 'at the summons of the landowner, a file of military police would appear like thieves in the night and seize the victim without warning; the bailiff would explain that the master had given orders the night before for the man to be sent to the recruiting office.'[123]

In addition, the appointment of certain public officials, state and ecclesiastical, became a seigneurial right. From the sixteenth to the nineteenth centuries prebends in Sweden were in the gift of the lord who owned the land upon which they were situated.[124] In Scotland the patronage act of 1712 gave noble landlords the right to nominate the ministers of the established church in the parishes located on their estates. The same lords were entitled to take part in the appointment of the parish school teacher and in the administration of poor relief.[125] In the Prussian monarchy the right of junkers to appoint village mayors and ministers survived until at least 1872.[126] In the Netherlands seigneurs possessed until 1922 the right to nominate pastors and in 1814, in compensation for the loss of patrimonial jurisdiction, they were awarded the right to present candidates for public office in the locality, a right which endured until 1848.[127] The seigneurs' control of ecclesiastical appointments was commonly found; their control of secular posts was much less extensive and usually concerned judicial matters.

The willingness of the state to make use of the seigneur for purposes of public administration, a practice revived and reinvigorated rather than reduced by royal absolutism, added to the landlord's domination of his tenantry, increasing the punitive measures at his disposal and allowing him to control the channels of popular indoctrination.

2 History of the seigneurial system

In all likelihood, the seigneurial system had pre-Roman origins. In France, for example, it stemmed from the rights which the village chiefs of ancient Gaul had enjoyed over their tribesmen. In Germany it had a similar derivation, emerging as tribal chiefs managed to retain some of their rights when converted into subject landowners. However, its basic structure, the demesne and the tenures, first formed in the latter days of the Roman Empire when large-scale commercial farming by slave labour was supplemented with the labour which tenants furnished as a condition of their landholding. With the decline of slavery, the conversion of slaves into tenants owing labour services, the submission of allodial peasants to lordship—a process promoted by the collapse of the Roman and Carolingian Empires—the seigneurial system was erected. By A.D. 1000 it was well established in much of Western Europe, both as an instrument of jurisdiction and exaction. Private justice also had ancient roots since the lord's jurisdiction over serfs derived from the jurisdiction Roman masters had exercised over their slaves; and the Roman lord's rights of jurisdiction over his *coloni* prepared the ground for the jurisdiction which seigneurs held over free tenants.[128]

Furthering the seigneurial system's development in the West was the ability of subjects to acquire regalian rights. Through the ruler's alienation and the subject's usurpation of these rights, subjects acquired rights of justice, labour services, dues, taxation, justice and monopoly. The willingness of rulers to sanction usurpations of bannal authority, to grant regalian rights to subjects as patronage and to raise revenue from their sale, brought the seigneurial system to completion.[129] It was then extended geographically by a process of imitation, conquest and colonisation. Only holding it at bay was the survival of societies of free peasants with allodial farms as in Central France and the Midi, Tyrol, Scandinavia, Frisia and East Prussia where the *Colmische Freie* held off the seigneur until the eighteenth century.[130] Yet where a nobility arose, a seigneurial system usually followed. In Sweden, for example, the demesne eventually emerged as the nexus of the noble estate in imitation of Danish practices; and, although manorial justice never developed, dues and labour services came to be exacted.[131] Rarely was the seigneurial system entirely excluded. The presence of peasant allods merely prevented it from embracing the whole community. Apart from the allod, only the landowner-ship of the Church and the Crown, both of them organised on a seigneurial basis, and the existence of royal free boroughs removed men from the sway of noble lords; and, like the allod, these forms of independence were mas-sively annexed by the nobility in the course of time.

The intensity and extensiveness of the seigneurial system depended upon the needs of the nobles and the degree to which the Crown was obliged to humour them. The Crown tended to be more generous in permitting the exaction of labour services and dues than in countenancing private taxes and patrimonial justice, basically because the latter meant a loss of government revenue. It had to weigh up whether more was to be gained by alienating fiscal and jurisdictional rights than by keeping them for itself. Often, how-ever, it had no choice; the weakness of the Crown's political position, as in eleventh-century France or fifteenth/sixteenth-century Bohemia, Hungary, Poland and Brandenburg allowed the nobles to take what they wanted and in some cases to give their actions parliamentary sanction. Especially when seigneurs managed to secure the Crown's licence to impose serfdom upon their tenants, as in Poland, Brandenburg, Russia, Bohemia and Hungary in the early modern period, the outcome was a great enlargement of the seig-neurial burden. Relieving the tenantry was the long-term ability of royal governments to encroach upon private fiscal and judicial rights. Moreover, in the course of the eighteenth century royal governments, notably Habsburg and Bourbon, proceeded against the seigneurial system, moved by a plan to improve the resources of the state through the renovation of society; but over the centuries the Crown inclined to favour the interests of the landlord before those of the tenant and therefore to uphold the seigneurial system, even though, moved by self-interest, it occasionally confiscated and limited seig-neurial rights.[132]

Faced with fixed-rent tenures and the pressures of inflation, landlords who lacked alternative sources of revenue were forced to enlarge their seigneurial exactions. Landlords with the chance to profit from demesne farming but without an alternative form of labour to compulsory farm-work had the same need. The poverty of seigneurs, whether natural or circumstantial, was another source of seigneurial oppressiveness, helping, for example, to account for the weight of exaction in modern Russia, Poland and Brandenburg-Prussia.[133]

Strongly influencing the nobility's attitude towards its seigneurial rights were the demographic factors of underpopulation, overpopulation, population growth and population contraction.[134] The need to attract settlers could produce a mild seigneurialism. This happened in the early medieval West as the area of cultivation was extended and also in the late medieval West to prevent depopulation from contracting the area of cultivation; it happened in Castile between the eleventh and thirteenth centuries as the Reconquest reclaimed territory from the Moors; it happened in Eastern Europe in the thirteenth and fourteenth centuries and in Sicily between the fifteenth and seventeenth centuries when the area of cultivation was much enlarged. The recovery and resettlement of the Danubian plain in eighteenth-century Hungary had the same effect; so did the settlement of the Ukraine by Polish nobles in the early seventeenth century and of parts of West and North-west Poland in the eighteenth century.[135] However, as an area became sufficiently populated, the initial mildness could give way to seigneurial harshness. Overpopulation, paradoxically, could have the same effect as underpopulation, especially in encouraging the abandonment of serfdom, as already mentioned.[136]

The effect of depopulation upon the seigneurial system was largely determined by the practice of demesne farming. Thus, in fourteenth-century England depopulation coincided with the retirement of seigneurs from direct farming and led to a massive reduction in the weight of seigneurial exactions.[137] Yet where depopulation accompanied the introduction of demesne farming, as in fifteenth-century Brandenburg, or the survival of demesne farming, as in seventeenth-century Bohemia and Poland, it had the opposite effect.[138] Rapid population growth could lighten the seigneurial burden by preparing the way for the remission of serfdom. However, in societies which were largely free of serfdom, the inflation resulting from rapid population growth could cause lords to exploit rigorously their seigneurial rights.[139] Rapid population growth could also undermine the seigneurial system by reducing the landlord's dependence upon it, as well as by intensifying the hostility of the peasantry for their lords, as in late eighteenth- and early nineteenth-century Eastern Europe.[140] Relieving the peasantry of seigneurial exaction was the ability of lords to find other sources of landed income. These usually came in the form of leasehold rent or hired labour. Their adoption in place of seigneurial dues and labour services was encouraged by low wages and land-hunger among the peasantry, the fruits of a rapid increase in the rural population.

After causing friction between lord and tenant for centuries, the system collapsed, essentially because the French Revolution transformed the language of popular protest by replacing a traditional demand for the reduction of seigneurial rights with a novel demand for their complete elimination. By the 1860s, largely as a result of the revolutions of 1848, the seigneurial system had virtually disappeared. Yet for several centuries prior to its collapse, it had suffered deterioration, its rights reduced by the voluntary actions of landlords and the compulsion of governments. Certainly in North Italy and the Rhineland the seigneurial system was in serious decay by 1300, principally because of the decline of direct demesne farming with compulsory labour and because of the extension of leasehold tenancy. In the course of the twelfth and thirteenth centuries the demesne tended to swallow the tenures and was either farmed by the landlord himself with hired labour or, more commonly, leased. Consequently labour services and seigneurial dues became unnecessary.[141] Accompanying these decisive changes in estate management was the submission of patrimonial justice to royal or communal jurisdiction.[142] A further serious blow was the high mortality of the late middle ages which finally disposed of demesne farming in the West and forced landlords to attract or to retain tenants by reducing seigneurial obligations.[143] Then a further encroachment upon seigneurial justice occurred between the sixteenth and eighteenth centuries, the work of royal governments; and on the eve of the French Revolution a number of governments abolished serfdom, notably in Baden (1783), Savoy (1771), Denmark (1788), Austria-Bohemia (1781), Sicily (1789).[144] Nevertheless, these onslaughts neither eliminated private jurisdictions nor completely erased seigneurial exactions. The system of royal justice which had developed in England, France and Spain by 1600 still allowed a function for the patrimonial court; the disposal of serfdom did not terminate seigneurial right; and only in parts did the spread of leasehold completely transform the landlord-tenant relationship into one of rent. Neither the prevalence of sharecropping in Southern Europe nor capitalist tenant farming in the North-west ended seigneurial obligation which survived in the form of rights of jurisdiction, dues and services.

Upholding the seigneurial system in modern Europe was not only its survival in the West, but also its spectacular introduction or reconstruction in the East, a process extending from the fifteenth to the eighteenth centuries. There it flourished, both in the aristocratic republics of Poland and Hungary and in the absolute monarchies of Prussia and Russia. Of the East European absolute monarchies, only that of Austria-Bohemia proceeded rigorously against the seigneurial system prior to having its hand forced by the threat of revolution. The Habsburg government abolished and regulated. Abolished were some of the rights of monopoly (1738), the permission rights concerning marriage, migration and occupation (1781), labour services (1789) and heriot (1673). Regulated were patrimonial jurisdictions (1756, 1769 and 1781) and the range of seigneurial dues (1771 in Silesia, 1772 in Lower Austria, 1775 in Bohemia, 1778 in Styria and Carinthia, 1782 in Carniola and 1781 and 1786 in Galicia). Mostly, it was the work of Maria Theresa, Joseph II and their ministers. While the abolition of labour services was undone by Leopold II, his refusal to comply with the Bohemian diet's demand for the cancellation of all reforms introduced after 1745 allowed the Crown's radical alteration of the seigneurial system to stand.[145] This attack on seigneurial right was principally a response to a growing shortage of government funds and the humiliating defeats suffered by the Habsburgs in the War of the Austrian Succession and the Seven Years War. In Bohemia's case it was also a reprisal against the nobility, an act of punishment for its attempt in the 1740s to transfer the allegiance of the Bohemian state to the electorate of Bavaria. The Crown's essential aim was to reform society so that the government's military needs could be more satisfactorily met and so that the internal security of the state was less troubled by popular revolt. This was to be accomplished by replacing the serf by a prosperous free peasantry which, in being less oppressed by seigneurial demands, would be a better provider of government revenue and less prone to insurrection.[146] The reforms did not spring from any questioning of the nobility's ruling function, or even from a disbelief in the seigneurial system. In a long tradition it envisaged regulation rather than extermination.

Before the French Revolution abolition of the seigneurial system resulted not from government order, except in Tuscany and Piedmont, but only from the piecemeal arrangements which landlords privately reached with their tenants.[147] Nevertheless, government action in the eighteenth century marked an important, if not a culminating, stage in the removal of seigneurial right, especially through generating an atmosphere of criticism from which the seigneurial system could never again escape.

The initial conflicts of the French Revolution had nothing to do with the seigneurial system. They principally concerned a confrontation between Crown and the nobility on the issue of fiscal exemption and another between the second and third estates over parliamentary procedure. Seigneurial right was introduced as an issue only by the popular revolts of July and August 1789. Peasant uprisings were a familiar feature of the old regime and had been often regarded as revolutionary in aim, although most merely called for the intervention of a just king to reduce state taxes and to lower seigneurial dues and rents. The tradition of French peasant disturbances certainly showed a good deal of hostility towards seigneurs, but popular uprisings tended to be ineffective unless they received aristocratic support. When the local nobility opposed it, peasant revolt had little chance. For this reason large scale uprisings were not ostensibly against the nobility and their privileges but against the policies of the government, their political rather than social aims giving them a greater chance of receiving noble sympathy. Since most revolts were terminated by force rather than concession, their ineffectiveness was ensured.[148]

The limitations of the past were lost when in July and August 1789 peasant revolt combined with a political crisis which split the establishment as never before. In these revolutionary circumstances rebellious peasants acquired a remarkable effectiveness and a revolutionary forcefulness, but not because they had become intrinsically revolutionary. Their initial complaint seemed to be against the weight rather than the existence of the seigneurial system. In all likelihood their revolutionary impact in 1789 stemmed from the fact that, irrespective of their normal conservative nature, they were traditionally regarded as the spectre of revolution, and also because a divided establishment was constrained to follow a course of appeasement. Moved by traditional concepts of peasant rebellion and requiring to restore order, but not at the expense of forfeiting popular support, the National Assembly awarded the peasants much more than they were demanding. Faced by widespread peasant disturbances, the National Assembly on 4th August committed a radical act against noble privilege by sweeping away a range of seigneurial rights. Educated by this legislative decision, it became much easier for peasants to conceive an agrarian system free of seigneurialism, and peasants expressed their belief in the new agrarian order, and so promoted its realisation, by ceasing to pay seigneurial dues and by refusing to make the redemption payments required by law to release them from seigneurial obligation. Spurred on by rural revolt and intransigence, the process of demolition was continued in August 1792 and was completed in July 1793 when the redemption payments were formally abolished. Crucial to the process was the incapacity of the government to mount a campaign of suppression and the capacity of the peasantry to switch the focus of their revolt from government taxation to seigneurial exactions.[149]

The coincidence of peasant militancy and political revolution in 1848 further dismantled the seigneurial system, almost to the point of completion. Revolutionaries decreed abolition; and, as in France, the old order when back in control could not afford to retract what revolution had granted or promised. To quell disorder created by peasant militancy and to acquire popular support, revolutionary and conservative forces were constrained to act alike. The inevitable victim was the seigneurial system.[150]

In the destruction of seigneurial rights the years 1789 and 1848 were of decisive importance, the events of 1789 making the idea of abolition socially and politically acceptable; those of 1848 applying it throughout large parts of Europe. In the intervening years, rights were abolished or abandoned, often in the atmosphere created by the French Revolution and sometimes compelled by the presence or proximity of the French revolutionary armies. French annexation led to the annulment of rights in the Low Countries after 1795, in Lombardy after 1796 and in Savoy after 1792.[151] Terminating the seigneurial system in Naples was the French rule of the kingdom between

1806 and 1815. French occupation disposed of seigneurial rights in the German states on the left bank of the Rhine, in some of the Austrian territories and in that part of Poland which became the Duchy of Warsaw and later the Congress Kingdom.[152] The removal of serfdom in Prussia in 1807 was precipitated by military defeat but also stemmed from the abolition of serfdom by Napoleonic decree in the adjacent Kingdom of Westphalia and in the Duchy of Warsaw.[153] The abolition of seigneuries in Spain in 1811 seemed heavily influenced by Napoleon's promise of emancipation in 1808.[154] The near presence of the French helped to dispose of the seigneurial regime in Sicily, although also responsible were the Bourbon reforms of the late eighteenth century and the presence of the British who backed the reforms of 1812 releasing the peasantry from seigneurial obligation and patrimonial justice.[155] The French Revolution also put an end to the extension of seigneurial right: in the late eighteenth century the Russian Tzar had allowed the imposition of serfdom on the Ukraine, the Crimea and the Caucasus, whereas in the early nineteenth century he prevented the spread of serfdom to newly acquired Finland and Bessarabia.[156]

Counter-revolution was unable to recover what revolution jettisoned; it could only delay the process of dissolution. Rights were restored but minimally and ephemerally. Thus in the Low Countries rights were revived in 1814 but mostly removed in 1848. In Portugal the liberal reforms of 1821–3 were partially undone in the following years but fully and permanently restored in 1832. In Spain the reaction of Ferdinand VII in 1814 modified the decree of 1811, but was undone by the legislation of 1820–3 and 1837. The reaction in the 1850s to the 1848 revolution in the Prussian monarchy restored only a little of the seigneurial system—essentially policing powers and the right to approve village officials—and this had gone by 1891.[157] By restoring seigneurial rights the old order risked losing popular support and inflaming rural revolt. For this reason, its capacity to withstand revolution depended upon proceeding against seigneurial rights or of confirming revolution's elimination of them. Even the Russian government made no attempt to revive the rights rejected by Napoleon in the Duchy of Warsaw when it fell into Russian hands in 1815; and the Habsburgs who became more respectful of seigneurial right after witnessing the French Revolution, nonetheless did not restore seigneurial justice to the French-occupied Austrian territories when they returned to their possession in 1814. Moreover, in Spain Ferdinand VII's hostility to the edict of 1811 did not persuade him to restore rights of private jurisdiction.[158] The seigneurial system was finally condemned when the removal of seigneurial rights became the old order's essential device for opposing revolution.

Promoting the termination of seigneurial privilege were three elements of the old order. Firstly, royal governments took action, seeking in the late eighteenth century to make greater demands of the peasants by reducing the demands made of them by nobles, and attempting in the early nineteenth century to stem the tide of revolution.[159] What was done was mostly in imitation of other governments.[160] Then there was the peasant seeking liberation from seigneurial control and made militant by land-hunger, landlord oppression and the news that emancipation had occurred elsewhere. Thirdly, in Eastern Europe, notably Prussia, Poland, Estonia, Mecklenburg and Swedish Pomerania, farming nobilities abetted, if not initiated, the destruction of the seigneurial system in order to enlarge their farms at the expense of the peasant holdings.[161] The nobility in Poland, Bohemia, Austria and Hungary urged reforms upon the government and implemented reforms to get rid of useless or troublesome practices, such as labour services and rights of jurisdiction, to avoid jacqueries and to benefit from the compensation which tended to accompany emancipation.[162] Nobles could advocate reform in the attempt to persuade peasants to support nationalist movements or to enlist popular support for their struggle against royal autocracy. Thus in the 1830s and 1840s the Hungarian nobles ordered the abolition of the seigneurial system, an achievement which the Habsburg monarchy confirmed in the 1850s in an attempt to regain credit with the Hungarian peasantry. Czech nationalists operated in the same way as the Hungarian nobles. In their struggle against the Russian protectorate, Rumanian nobles pressed for seigneurial reform in the 1830s and 1840s. Polish nobles promoted seigneurial reforms from the 1790s to the 1860s, seeking to secure a unified nationalist opposition to Russian domination. To outbid the Polish nobility, the Russian government in 1864 terminated the seigneurial system in the Congress Kingdom on terms highly favourable to the peasantry. Rebelling against autocracy in the 1820s the Decembrists, a party of reformist nobles, sought the emancipation of the Russian serf, while struggling against Bourbon despotism, Sicilian nobles were heavily involved in the emancipation settlement of 1812.[163]

Less evident in the termination of the seigneurial system is the bourgeois capitalist. He certainly played a part in the earlier erosion of seigneurial rights through encouraging landlords to replace customary tenures by demesne leaseholds, though not in every case for lords frequently replaced the customary tenures not by commercial farmers but by small sharecroppers and peasant leaseholders. The bourgeois capitalist also helped to end the practice of seigneurial exactions since they tended to continue after their legal abolition in areas of peasant farming but not in areas of large-scale capitalist farming. However, in the legal abolition of the seigneurial system he seemed to play a marginal role. Governments did not outlaw seigneurial rights in response to the rise of agrarian capitalism. They largely proceeded against them in a traditional world dominated either by peasant or noble farming.[164]

In spite of the opposition and lack of support, seigneurial rights showed a remarkable capacity to survive. Substantially preserved in the early nineteenth century, they lingered on in the late nineteenth and even into the early twentieth centuries. In Prussia and Bohemia some of the administrative and policing powers of the seigneur managed to survive the reforms promoted by the revolutions of 1848. These were only removed in Prussia in 1872 and 1891 and in Bohemia in 1868. A serf system endured in Russia until 1861 and in Rumania until 1864. Private rights of jurisdiction survived in Mecklenburg until 1877 and in Holstein until 1866. In the Austrian Empire the monopoly of distillation and the sale of spirits survived as seigneurial rights until the 1860s. Labour services continued to be exacted in the Congress Kingdom of Poland until 1864 and in the Baltic Provinces of Livonia, Estonia and Kurland until 1868.[165] A number of rights persisted in the twentieth century. In the Netherlands the seigneurial right to nominate pastors lasted until 1922; and hunting and fishing rights lasted until 1923. In Sweden and Denmark labour services were never abolished, eventually fading away through their conversion to rent. In England, the seigneurial system endured until the 1920s when copyholds were transformed into freeholds and manorial jurisdiction was terminated. In Scotland the seigneurial right of pre-emption in relation to property still survives.[166]

The durability of seigneurial rights in the nineteenth century was, to some extent, a reaction against the achievement of the French Revolution. In the Austrian Empire, the progressive approach shown by the Crown towards seigneurial reform in the reigns of Maria Teresa and Joseph II ended in the 1790s and its attitude remained reactionary until the 1840s.[167] Because abolition seemed so total and decisive in France, elsewhere the tendency was to promote a partial and gradual elimination.[168] This policy of moderation also stemmed from the government need to offer sops to the old order in compensation for what was taken away. In addition, it was heavily influenced by the view that some seigneurial rights were inseparable from rights of property. The distinction between rights wrongly held and rights which were an integral part of landownership was originally made by the deputies of the French National Assembly in 1789. Although removed for freeholders by the general abolition of July 1793, the distinction was retained for leasehold and sharecropping tenancies and lasted until popular opposition persuaded landlords to abandon it.[169] In a number of states which the French occupied in the 1790s and in the opening years of the nineteenth century— for example, in Lombardy, the Austrian territories and parts of Poland— proprietorial exactions were left untouched and action was only taken against serfdom and rights of private jurisdiction.[170] In both Spain and Portugal, the interconnexion of seigneurial and property rights allowed

seigneurial rights to survive until the 1830s.[171] Furthermore, emancipation
settlements were often made dependent upon the peasant's desire and ability
to purchase his freedom. In the Austrian Empire and the Congress Kingdom
of Poland emancipation was mandatory from the start, but elsewhere it was
rarely so. Thus, the endurance of certain seigneurial rights was due to the
peasants' inability or unwillingness to afford their redemption.[172] In some
instances, seigneurial rights survived because their failure to incite popular
hostility did not force nobles or governments to abolish them. Sometimes
the demands which lordship made of the commonalty were too minor to
provoke much wrath, as in nineteenth-century England; and sometimes, as
in Sweden, anti-aristocratic movements were directed by sections of society,
freehold rather than a tenant peasantry, who were personally unaffected by
seigneurial rights and enlisted popular support with other issues.[173] In Russia
massive peasant opposition was provoked by the survival of the seigneurial
system but, lacking the opportunity to benefit from a revolutionary rift
within the political nation, it failed for years to persuade the government to
take action.[174] Finally, seigneurial rights could be exacted long after their
formal abolition by virtue of the power traditionalist landlords held over
their tenantry and because the government was unable to enforce its anti-
seigneurial laws. For this reason, the seigneurial system had an afterlife, the
result of an impetus created by the past which took time to expire.[175]

3 Value to the nobility

Seigneurial rights played little part in determining nobility. Many nobles did
not possess them; and rarely did a subject become a legitimate nobleman
because he was a seigneur. Where the ownership of a lordship was conditional on noble status, a subject exercised seigneurial rights because he was
a noble. Elsewhere seigneurial authority and nobility were closely connected
only because most lordships were owned by noblemen. France was highly
unusual in allowing the ownership of a *fief* or *seigneurie* to confer nobility.
However, for most of France a royal edict closed this means of social
promotion in 1579.[176]

Yet for the nobility seigneurial rights were of considerable benefit, imparting character, wealth, power, function and social distinction. A nobleman's identity relied heavily upon seigneurial rights since the ruling function
associated with the nobility involved not only the professional and paid
tenure of appointed offices but also an unpaid, aristocratic fulfilment of
public service by right of a privately owned, inheritable authority. Seigneurial
right was an outstanding feature of the nobility's public function. Because of
the state's dependence upon landlords to appoint public officials, to administer justice in their own courts, to collect taxes and, with the emergence of

standing armies, to organise the conscription of their tenantry, nobles could enjoy an important share in the machinery of local government even when they had not received appointment to public office. Countering the development of centralised, beureaucratic monarchy and its tendency to professionalise the system and personnel of government, seigneurial right preserved for the nobility its traditional identity as a class which ruled by private right.

With a few exceptions, seigneurial dues and services remained an essential source of noble income, or at least an important supplement, until the abolition of the system, the jurisdictional and administrative rights of the seigneur remaining an effective means of ensuring their payment. The persisting importance of these exactions was not only because landed income provided the nobility with the bulk of its financial resources but also because rarely before the revolutionary era were seigneurial dues and services completely converted to rent. The traditional organisation of the lordship showed a remarkable durability, its demesne worked directly by the lord or leased to farmers or sublet to an intermediary lessor, its customary tenures with their fixed rents making the lord dependent upon the compensatory income which his officials extracted from dues, monopolies, taxes and labour services. Reducing the lord's dependence upon seigneurial revenues was his growing dependence upon demesne rents. However, if the lord chose to farm the demesne himself, the seigneurial system remained of enormous value to him, especially by providing free labour, as in the early medieval West and in much of modern Eastern Europe. Seigneurial income derived from taxes and fines as well as dues and services. The fiscal and judicial income of seigneurs was considerable in twelfth-century Western Europe, so much so that it persuaded some to withdraw from demesne farming;[177] but as a source of cash it was eventually limited by the growth of royal taxation and royal justice. Generally in Eastern Europe, seigneurial exactions remained a substantial source of noble income until the early nineteenth century. Especially valuable were the labour services and the rights to manufacture and sell alcohol.[178] In Western Europe, the dues and fees rather than the services remained of great value. In periods of rapid inflation, they became a major device for raising revenue to counter the depreciation of landed incomes; and in normal circumstances they provided noblemen with a substantial part of their landed income. In the diocese of Toulouse, an area reckoned to have a limited dependence upon the seigneurial system by the eighteenth century, the nobility, nonetheless, drew 8% of its income from dues and banalities. The remainder came from demesne rents and from the sale of produce grown by demesne sharecroppers. In parts of eighteenth-century Saintonge, seigneurial rights furnished 63% of the nobility's landed income; in the duchy of Nemours, 75%; in the diocese of Rennes, 57%. Notably in the provinces of Brittany and Burgundy the financial resources of nobility remained heavily reliant upon the seigneurial system until the Revolution.[179] Less dependent upon the system were the nobles who abolished the tenures, substituted a revisable for a customary rent and leased rather than farmed the demesne. By the eighteenth century, this had occurred extensively in much of Italy, in Southern Spain and Southern Portugal, in England, Scotland and parts of France.[180]

Seigneurial privilege was also valuable to the nobility as a counteraction to the rights of the peasantry. The seigneurial exactions compensated for the fixed rent of the tenures while seigneurial rights of forfeiture and resumption compensated for the existence of perpetual tenancies.[181] This compensatory role was less needed in the serf societies of Eastern Europe simply because the seigneurial system placed fewer impediments upon the lord's ability to exploit the peasant.

The seigneurial system awarded the nobles power over the tenantry through rights of private jurisdiction, tax collection, the administration of conscription, the determination of tenancy and the exercise of banality and servile rights. However, banality and servile rights tended to become a source of income rather than of control, the lord readily ceding a licence for a fee; the right to decide tenancy came to be restricted by the extensive development of the hereditary tenure; and by the late eighteenth century judicial rights had suffered badly from the oversight and interference of royal justice. Nonetheless, the opportunities for reprisal and discipline which the control of rights offered remained important to landlords until the end of the system. Yet seigneurial rights not only upheld the landlord's power over his tenantry but also weakened it. They were a major cause of tenant disobedience. In societies with a strongly ingrained sense of deference towards the nobility, seigneurial rights were responsible for a long tradition of popular hostility towards noblemen. Of all the noble privileges, the seigneurial rights, especially those associated with serfdom, were the most capable of provoking popular antagonism in the forms of violence against the persons of nobles and their officials, the destruction of property, livestock and records, dilatory and incompetent work for the lord, the refusal to pay dues and flight.[182] Their capacity to generate social conflict gave seigneurial rights a large share in the nobility's downfall, especially through enlisting the peasantry on the side of revolution, notably in 1789 and in the Hohenzollern and Habsburg Empires in 1848. In the onslaught upon the old regime, seigneurial rights gave revolutionary parties a rapport with the bulk of the population and thus helped to ensure their success. On the other hand, in focusing the popular opposition upon privilege rather than wealth, seigneurial rights helped the nobility to survive as landlords. The movement for land reform gathered momentum only after the removal of seigneurial right. In diverting popular hostility from fixing upon more fundamental social discrepancies, seigneurial privilege gave the noble landowners an extra lease of life.

Finally, seigneurial privileges were of honorific value to the nobility. They declared an order of social superiority which was not simply a consequence of wealth. Even when of limited material value, they could still be beneficial, especially to *parvenus* greedy for social status and to poor nobles in danger of being socially overlooked.[183]

The wealth and power of the nobility easily outlived the destruction of lordship. Long before emancipation, nobles were ceasing to summon their courts and were transforming dues and services into rent. The government's abolition of the seigneurial system merely completed this development. Lordship was then replaced by landlordship. Under the new system income was readily furnished by economic rents, while short-term leases and the prospect of eviction or the non-renewal of the lease provided an effective means of tenant control. Moreover, the elimination of seigneurial rights only ended the lord's final ownership of the tenures, turning proprietary tenants into complete owners; it did not adversely affect the ownership of the lord's demesne. In some cases it enlarged it. Only where the demesnes were small, as in parts of Austria, was the proportion of land owned by the nobility seriously altered.[184] Otherwise, the nobles retained as landlords considerable private power and wealth until the land reforms of the twentieth century deprived them of their estates.[185] Nevertheless, the farming concerns of the nobility could be retarded by the removal of labour services, not so much in the medieval period when lords abandoned them because they were no longer needed, but certainly in the nineteenth century when governments ordered their elimination. However, sometime beforehand, noble farmers in Prussia, Bohemia, Hungary and parts of Poland had substituted hired for serf labour.[186] Badly damaged by the termination of seigneurial rights were the poor nobles, notably of Poland and Russia, who, deprived of seigneurial rights, could not farm commercially because their poverty left them without the necessary resources and who could not thrive as rentiers because the prevalence of subsistence farming among their tenantry made it difficult to extract much in rent. For the nobles caught in this poverty trap, the abolition of the seigneurial system was a disaster.[187]

4 Impact

Seigneurial rights played a part in the modernisation of the state and the economy. The stage of political modernisation represented by revolution owed much to the peasantry's seigneurial grievances and the use that revolutionaries could make of them to win popular support. In addition, the earlier rise of bureaucratic monarchy was aided by royal absolutism's respect for seigneurial rights. Prussian and Russian absolutism were strongly dependent on the *droit de seigneur*, while the restrictions imposed upon the seigneurial system by royal absolutism in France or the Austrian Empire failed to sweep it away. The nobility's concurrence with this stage in the modernisation of the state owed something to the Crown's tolerance of seigneurial rights. However, the very existence of seigneurial rights and their enduring role in the administration of justice, the collection of taxes and the organisation of conscription gave the absolutist state a primitive base. The Crown's willingness to accommodate the seigneur meant that the political modernisation achieved by royal absolutism could apply only to certain aspects of the state, notably its centralisation and the professionalisation of its civil and military services.

Seigneurial rights cannot be regarded simply as a source of economic retardation.[188] In the modern period, they sustained the development of the European economy in the sense that until the nineteenth century the granary of Western Europe was large parts of Eastern Europe where corn production was dependent upon labour services. Here was a form of agrarian capitalism flourishing within the seigneurial system. Some modern industrial enterprise likewise relied upon seigneurial rights, notably the early development of factory production in eighteenth-century Bohemia and in eighteenth- and nineteenth-century Russia.[189] Seigneurialism was not, of necessity, the enemy of productive farming. In Western Europe, for example, the seigneurial system allowed the peasantry considerable security of tenure. The nature of their tenancy, especially if it was customary and not demesne, gave peasants every incentive to make long-term plans rather than to regard farming shortsightedly as a means of immediate exploitation. Furthermore, as some seigneurial dues were fixed by custom, the peasant had the chance to accumulate capital, especially in periods of high inflation.[190] In fact, commercial farming with labour services, the leasing of banalities and seigneurial rights of common, as well as fixed rents, all directly generated capital.

In much of Eastern Europe seigneurial rights imposed insecurity of tenure and heavy obligations upon the peasantry, but this had little adverse effect upon farming because commercial agriculture was in the hands of the nobles who were either seigneurs or immunised against the payment of seigneurial exactions if they were tenants. Frequently, it was the short-term lease, not seigneurial dues and obligations, which was the root cause of low agricultural productivity.[191] Since the contraction of the seigneurial system often resulted in the proliferation of short-term leases, the release of agriculture from seigneurial right did not necessarily cause a growth in production. Compared with other types of tenant, peasants subjected to seigneurial rights tended to suffer little disadvantage, apart from the inconvenience of services. Like other forms of tenancy, the seigneurial tenure only appears at a decisive disadvantage when it is compared with full ownership. In this respect, the advantage conferred upon farmers by the abolition of the seigneurial system was often the conversion of tenancy to freehold rather than the liberation of farming from the impositions of seigneurialism.

Basically responsible for the long-term backwardness and the low productivity of farming was, on the one hand, a lack of capital, a consequence of the prevalence of peasant farming and the disinclination of lords to use their wealth for purposes of agricultural improvement, and, on the other, an inadequate refertilisation of the soil, the consequence of a shortage of manure which sprang from the lack among arable farmers of animal stock.[192] These restraints outlived the seigneurial system, especially when its abolition perpetuated peasant farming. However, while the incapacity of farmers to develop commercial operations owed something to the way the seigneurial system syphoned resources into the seigneur's pocket, the latter always happened in conjunction with church tithes and state taxes. The peasant's oppression resulted not simply from seigneurial exploitation but also because heavy demands were coincidentally made of him by church and state.[193] Furthermore, seigneurial exactions were not necessarily more exploitative of a peasantry than leasehold rent. In this respect, if the peasant's release from the seigneurial system was achieved by incorporating the tenures within the demesne, it could increase the proportion of his resources which the landlord was able to assume. Clearly, labour services were time-consuming for the serf and provided the seigneur with inefficient labour; but the low productivity of demesne farming cannot be wholly attributed to the seigneurial system. Where demesne farming was practised in the plains of Eastern Europe, farming techniques failed to change because the plenitude of good land and the foreign demand for corn rendered the traditional methods sufficient.[194] As for the peasant farmers of the seigneurial system, their resources were restricted not simply by the demands made of them by seigneur, church and state but also by the smallness of the typical holding, their concern with subsistence rather than capital accumulation and investment, and their appreciation of traditional rather than innovatory farming methods.

Seigneurial rights could profoundly affect the social structure of farming and the social relationships of the countryside. Unless nobles were directly involved in farming, their reliance upon the seigneurial system persuaded them to favour a multitude of smallholdings, rather than the creation in their place of a few large farms, since the latter appeared to restrict the profitability of seigneurial dues whose yield arguably depended upon the incidence with which the casualties fell due and therefore upon the number, not the size, of the holdings. Thus in England, the early decay of the seigneurial system promoted the emergence of large-scale farming, whereas the survival of lordship in parts of France helped to maintain the smallhold as the basic unit of agriculture. Only when the lords were able to substitute an economic rent for the payment of seigneurial dues did they have the incentive to encourage large-scale farming; when seigneurial dues remained of importance to the landlord so did small-scale farming. The outcome was not necessarily of great economic significance: until machinery was applied to farming in the course of the nineteenth century, small-scale and large-scale cultivation of the same product were equally labour intensive, and the economic rent of demesne leases could be more burdensome than the seigneurial exactions of the tenures. It could not therefore be said that the one always possessed a cost or productive advantage over the other, although the seigneurial system's close association with peasant farming and the rentier attitude of many seigneurs worked against the development of agrarian capitalism and the reform of agriculture. On the other hand, where seigneurs continued to farm, the seigneurial system was closely associated with agrarian capitalism and farming was starved of capital only by the poverty or extravagance of the lords. Moreover, the decay of the seigneurial system could uphold peasant farming when the incorporation of the tenures within the demesne produced a farming community of sharecroppers and smallhold lessees. So could the termination of the seigneurial system when the terms of emancipation gave peasants the right to own their farms.

The impact of seigneurial rights upon social relations was clearly of tremendous importance in view of their influence upon the course of events in the revolutionary era. In allowing the people to regard the landlord with great hostility, seigneurial rights helped to enlist a conservative-minded peasantry—significant because it formed the bulk of the population—on the side of revolution or, at least, deterred it from embracing the cause of counter-revolution. A different state of affairs existed in late eighteenth- and early nineteenth-century England where the farmers tended to be commercial operators, not peasants, and, released from the seigneurial system, showed a remarkable tolerance of the landlords. In England the conflict raging in the countryside was between a proletariat of farmhands and a middle-class of tenant farmers. Thanks to the fading away of seigneurial exactions, the rise of agrarian capitalism and the landlord's aversion to direct involvement in farming, rural conflict was basically a struggle between employees and employers over wages which only involved the minority of lords who farmed their estates.[195] Thus, upholding the old order in nineteenth-century England was a class conflict within the commonalty and an absence of the tenant-lord conflict which the seigneurial system naturally generated. On the Continent, the conflict between tenant and lord helped to determine the character and success of revolution. It allowed political revolution to precede economic revolution by persuading the majority of the traditional society, the peasants, to permit the disposal of an elite which for centuries had been found accept-able. It also ensured that this stage of revolution should be a war on privilege rather than on wealth, that *égalité* should have a juridical, not a material, meaning.

Privileges of landownership

Landownership awarded the nobility a large number of privileges. As we have seen, parliamentary, fiscal and titular privileges, as well as seigneurial rights, could all stem from the ownership of an estate. In addition, there was a separate category of privileges which concerned the actual manner in which land was owned. Within this category, rights to inherit, alienate and exploit landed property and the seigneurial right of final ownership were essentially the rights not of the nobility but of landowners. In contrast, the acquisition of land, the impartible or preferential descent of property and the use of legal devices for maintaining an estate's integrity could be reserved to the nobility and therefore were noble privileges.

As a specific noble privilege, landownership rights had been mostly dissolved by the 1860s. Generally, they were overthrown or conceded in the circumstances of revolution. The emergence of the land acquisition privilege had resulted from the need to protect the land market from the competition of commoners, but had also stemmed from the nobility's fiscal, parliamentary, seigneurial and titular rights which, when conferred by landownership, could best be restricted to the nobility by laws which prevented commoners from acquiring privileged estates. Some landownership rights grew out of the feudal system and its decay. Primogeniture, a concept alien to Roman Law, was a by-product of the fiefholder's military obligation, while the nobility's rights of inheritance to land became fully developed as the originally conditional tenure of the fief was made as absolute as the allod. However, the nobility's exclusive right to acquire land developed in its most extreme form in states where feudalism never became an integral part of the social and political structure, and failed to develop in some states which were subjected to the feudal system. Of decisive importance in the creation of this privilege was the nobles' ability to impose their wishes upon the Crown.

The right of final ownership provided seigneurial income; and subsoil rights could be highly profitable. However, some landownership rights were a source of noble poverty. Where noble status was imparted to every direct heir, the right of property inheritance, whether it be primogeniture or partible inheritance, could produce the poor noble. The exclusive land acquisition right confined the competition for land to a small minority, but retarded the capital value of land by limiting its selling price. This right did not necessarily determine the social composition of landownership. Without the privilege, nobles were capable of securing and retaining a large share of private land; and despite the privilege, commoners managed to acquire noble estates.

The contribution which landownership rights made to the development of the state was relatively minor, apart from limiting the authority of royal absolutism. Their contribution to the development of the economy depended upon the restrictiveness of final ownership rights and subsoil rights. If final ownership rights promoted *métayage* or limited the area of cultivation by preserving land for hunting purposes, they could impede agricultural growth, but if they permitted the development of large, leasehold farms or peasant tenures which were lightly burdened with seigneurial exactions, they could promote agrarian capitalism. Moreover, no adverse correlation existed between the nobility's subsoil rights and the exploitation of mineral resources for industrial purposes. Although an agrarian society was their natural habitat, nobles had no difficulty in placing their mineral wealth at the disposal of industrialisation.

1 Nature of the rights

In Poland, Russia and Hungary, the noble's exclusive right to acquire land applied to all privately owned estates; whereas in parts of the Prussian monarchy, the Austrian territories, Bohemia, Sweden, Denmark, Bavaria and Savoy, it applied only to estates which were legally classified as noble.

In Poland, the privilege endured from 1496 to 1791 with a brief prolongation following the partition; in Hungary it lasted from 1514 to 1843; and in Russia the nobility acquired a legitimate monopoly of private land in the course of the seventeenth century and held it over uninhabited land until 1801 and over inhabited land until 1861.[1] Yet because of exceptions in the law and problems of enforcement and because the law specified acquisition rather than ownership, in none of these states were commoners completely denied the right to own land or the opportunity to add to their landed possessions. From the start, the burghers of Cracow enjoyed the right to buy land and in 1538 this right was awarded the towns of Royal Prussia, then a Polish dependency. Commoners in Poland could also acquire the lands which had been granted to townships by royal charter. Moreover, the repeated re-enactments of the 1496 statute which created the privilege—in 1538, 1543, 1580 and 1611—suggests not only the persistence of parliamentary interest in the measure but also the problems of applying such an act.[2] Hungarian law excepted the royal boroughs and certain autonomous communities of free peasants. By the 1780s the boroughs owned more than 1% of the cultivated land, and the peasant communities owned 4% of it.[3] In Russia the regulations creating the privilege admitted a host of exceptions. These were severely reduced between 1730 and 1758 but not to the extent of denying the right to the *odnodvortsy*, a sizeable social group subjected to the tax obligations of the peasantry and the service obligations of the nobility. Moreover, the exceptions were extended in the late eighteenth century when the right to purchase land was granted to state peasants (1788) and to peasants on the personal estates of the imperial family (1766). Further extensions followed when in 1801 all subjects but for serfs were authorised to own uninhabited land and in 1848 the serfs were admitted to this right. In addition, Russian serfs were always able to buy land in their master's name.[4] However, in all three states, the opportunity of commoners to acquire land had little effect on private landownership which remained overwhelmingly noble.[5]

In none of the three cases was the privilege established in order to prevent commoners from acquiring fiscal and parliamentary privileges. Essentially, the three nobilities enjoyed these privileges by right of noble status, not landownership.[6] Moreover, since seigneurial rights in Poland and Russia were conferred by the ownership of serfs and not of lands, the landownership privilege was no means of making them a noble preserve in these two states. That could only be achieved by preventing commoners from owning serfs. Much depended on the willingness of the nobility to obtain the privilege and its capacity to secure the Crown's sanction. Where the possession of their privileges was not at stake, the nobles' interest sprang from the need to exclude the bourgeoisie from the land market.

Not as all-inclusive but almost as extreme were the landownership privileges of the Brandenburg, Pomeranian and East Prussian junkers and of the nobilities of Bohemia and some of the Austrian territories. In these parts the privilege did not deny free commoners the right to acquire land, barring them only from the acquisition of noble estates (*Rittergüter* in the Hohenzollern territories and *landtäflich* estates in the Habsburg lands). But as the serf status of the peasantry disqualified it from landownership and it was not too difficult to get land registered as noble, noble estates came to incorporate most privately owned land. In Brandenburg the customary confinement of *Rittergüter* to the nobility was supported by the Recess of 1653 which allowed the nobles pre-emption rights in the purchase of *Rittergüter* and awarded nobles who sold their estates to commoners a right of redemption. It was also upheld by Frederick II who prohibited commoners from acquiring this type of estate. Since the ownership of a Brandenburg *Rittergut* conferred exemption from the land tax, parliamentary membership and seigneurial rights, the landownership privilege in all likelihood developed to preserve these privileges for the nobility. The Crown supported it to protect its tax revenues. It was a device to prevent the wealth of commoners from sheltering behind fiscal immunity. Furthermore, since the noble estate was a unit of local government and the Crown remained imbued with the belief that the nobility was the natural ruling class, the government backed the privilege in the cause of good governance. These motives were evident in the policy of Frederick II who was prepared to allow certain commoners to own *Rittersgüter* on condition that they did not enjoy the attached privileges. In contrast, the landownership privileges of the Polish, Hungarian and Russian nobles bestowed no benefit upon the Crown and were attained as a result of the pressure which nobles could exert upon the government in periods of royal weakness. A breakthrough for the Brandenburg commoners came in 1807 when, as a concession made to stem a revolutionary crisis, the landownership privilege was eliminated while the privileges conferred by noble estates were retained. Consequently, for the next fifty years commoners were able to acquire the rights and functions of noblemen simply through the purchase of property.[7] 1807, however, only opened the gates wide to the common enjoyment of *Rittersgut* privileges. Earlier commoners had managed to squeeze through. The acquisition of noble estates by commoners speeded up after the Seven Years War when the Crown granted commoners permission to foreclose on the mortgaged estates of bankrupted nobles. By 1800 nineteen of the 206 owners of noble estates in the *Kreisen* of Uckermark, Niederbarnum, Lebus and Ruppin were commoners. Furthermore, commoners took over *Rittersgüter* in Brandenburg by using dummy nobles to serve as the *de jure* owner, or by leasing them from nobles, particularly from royal officials who had been posted to regions distant from their estates. In 1800 9% of all *Rittersgüter* in Kurmark were leased to commoners.[8]

Except in Tyrol and Vorarlberg which were regions of peasant freeholders, most private landownership in the Austrian territories was confined to the nobility by virtue of its sole right to acquire noble estates. The privilege was initially dissolved by Joseph II in 1786 but, after its restoration by Leopold II, survived until 1848. The privilege had a similar history in Bohemia. Long before its abolition commoners made large-scale inroads into the possession of noble estates. Traditionally the four royal boroughs in Bohemia had been excepted from the law and allowed to own noble estates. By 1802 they owned 111. By the same date individual commoners had acquired a further 163 while the nobles possessed 640. In both Austria and Bohemia, noble estates conferred noble as well as seigneurial privileges. The nobility's sole right to acquire noble estates therefore had a special role as protector of noble privilege, although the limited nature of the nobility's fiscal privileges in the eighteenth century gave the Crown little financial incentive to maintain this protection. That noble privilege was responsible for reserving noble estates to noblemen is evident in the distinctions originally made in the Austrian territories between the *Herrengut* and the *Edelmanngut*, each of them a noble estate. Since the possession of the one conferred different rights of parliamentary membership from the other, the owners of *Edelmanngüter* were denied the right to acquire *Herrengüter*. Thus, because of the nature of parliamentary privilege, the possession of certain noble estates was denied to some nobles as well as all commoners. This distinction lasted until the sixteenth century when the right of membership in the upper chamber of the provincial diets came to rest upon personal rather than territorial titles and the two types of noble estate were categorised as one and made available to all of noble status. As in Brandenburg, the privileges conferred by a noble estate in Bohemia and Austria outlived the nobility's exclusive right to acquire noble estates but by a much shorter period of time. In 1848 commoners were allowed the same right as nobles to own noble estates. However, by 1870 the noble estate had been abolished as a provision in the law.[9]

From 1669 until the French occupation in the early nineteenth century, the Bavarian nobles also enjoyed the sole right to acquire noble estates, a concession granted by the prince in response to noble complaints about the commoners' accumulation of noble estates. A similar concession was sought by the Saxon nobility in the course of the sixteenth and seventeenth centuries but failed to be granted.[10] In Savoy, Sweden and Denmark, the privilege was established in the middle ages; in Savoy it applied to fiefs; in Denmark and Sweden to fiscally privileged estates. In all these cases the prevalence of peasant freeholds ensured that the commonalty retained ownership rights over much of the land. In Denmark the privilege was removed in 1660, a consequence of the imposition of royal absolutism and the middle class alliance upon which it initially rested. Abolition followed an earlier relaxation of the privilege in 1641 which authorised nobles to sell their estates to commoners in order to acquit their debts but permitted commoners to hold them only on condition that, if they put them up for sale, they should be sold to a nobleman. This appeared to favour the nobility rather than the commonalty, allowing them a release from the constraints of privilege to help them solve their financial problems. In Savoy the privilege was also removed before the revolutionary era; in 1771 the government abolished noble estates in order to end the privilege of fiscal exemption. In Sweden the privilege was finally eliminated in 1810, a concession yielded by the old order in a bid to retain their fiscal privileges. By allowing the bourgeoisie the chance to enjoy these fiscal privileges through the ownership of a privileged estate, it was felt that they would stand a better chance of survival. However, the landownership privilege had been narrowed down in the previous hundred years. From the 1720s the bourgeoisie was allowed to acquire non-manorial noble estates, and in 1789 the peasantry was also admitted to this right.[11]

In Western Europe, similar privileges could be found but only on a very limited scale. In twelfth-century Leon-Castile, to safeguard against the extension of fiscal immunity, commoners were prevented from acquiring noble estates and nobles were prevented from acquiring commoner estates; but these prohibitions soon faded away. In France the complete confinement of noble estates to the nobility was prevented by the inability of fiefs to ennoble their owners immediately; and the commoner's likelihood of owning noble estates was increased by the edict of Blois (1579) which abolished their ennobling powers. Nevertheless, certain landownership privileges appertained to noble estates in France. First, there was the nobility's exemption from the *franc-fief*, a tax falling upon all fief-owning commoners. Secondly, the estates imparting titles of higher nobility—the dukedoms, the marquisates, countships, viscountcies, baronies and castellanies—were reserved for noblemen.[12]

Although the privilege had sometimes developed when the monarchy was too weak to withstand the nobility's demands, strong monarchy was not its enemy, except in Denmark, where the abolition of the privilege accompanied the establishment of royal absolutism, in Piedmont, where absolute monarchy abolished the privilege in 1770 and briefly in the Austrian Empire when Joseph II abolished the *Einstandsrecht* in 1786. In Sweden, Bohemia, Austria, Prussia, Russia and Bavaria, royal absolutism tolerated the privilege. In Bavaria it created it; in Prussia Frederick the Great refined it; in Bohemia and Austria Joseph II's successor revived it; in Poland the privilege was restored by the absolute monarchs among whom the Commonwealth was partitioned. Only in the revolutionary circumstances of the nineteenth century did these absolute monarchies erase the privilege.

In Sweden, Hungary and Poland the initiative and dynamism for its abolition came from the nobility, while in France there had been widespread advocacy from the nobility for the abolition of the *franc-fief* in the closing years of the old regime.[13] The motive for directing or accepting action against the privilege was a double one. In one sense it resembled that of the Crown. Terminating the privilege was the attempt of the birthright element, kings and nobles, to preserve itself by making concessions to revolutionary pressure groups in a bid for popular support. The old order's advocacy of abolition was especially an attempt to quell the revolutionary sentiment of the bourgeoisie by granting it access to the range of noble privileges which a noble estate conferred. Significantly, the abolition of the privilege preceded the termination of the fiscal, parliamentary and seigneurial rights which derived from landownership. In Poland and Hungary, nobles also supported abolition in order to consolidate the nationalist opposition to foreign overlordship. In addition, nobles were moved by financial considerations. In maintaining the distinction between noble and commoner estates and in permitting the commonalty the right to own both, abolition of the privilege ensured that, sustained by the attached privileges, noble estates would enjoy a market value far in excess of commoner lands. Even when no noble privileges were conferred by landownership, the open competition for land created by the privilege's abolition caused a rapid appreciation of the nobility's capital assets. By restricting the competition to noblemen, the privilege had favoured the nobles as buyers of land, but had disadvantaged them as vendors. Having a strong need to sell, the nobles naturally turned against the privilege. Thus nobles advocated or accepted abolition either to enlarge their financial resources or to improve the relationship between them and the commonalty.

Sometimes accompanying, sometimes in place of, the nobility's sole right to acquire land were several other exclusive landownership rights. They concerned the hereditary transmission of landed estates. Thus in parts of France the *partage noble* determined how much of a nobleman's estate should descend to his eldest son. The system was not one of strict primogeniture except in Normandy and the Bordelais and only when a family held but one fief which the rule of indivisibility assured to the eldest son. Elsewhere in France the degree of preference shown the eldest son by the *partage noble* varied considerably from the two-thirds partition in Brittany, Maine, Anjou and Touraine, the one-half partition found in Paris, Orléans and Berry and the one-fifth partition in Saintonge and Angoumois. Complementing the *partage noble* was the *partage roturier* which, as embodied in the Custom of Maine, laid down 'that no person who is not noble may make the condition of any of his heirs presumptive worse or better for one than another'. In French Flanders, Normandy, Brittany, Touraine, Anjou and Maine there was one law of inheritance for nobles and another for the commoners. The noble law favoured the eldest son; the commoner law insisted upon a partible descent of equal benefit to the heirs male. Helping to preserve this transmission privilege as a monopoly of the nobility was its ennobling capacity. In eighteenth-century Brittany, for example, three successive *partages nobles* were regarded as proof of nobility. On the other hand, the unwillingness in Brittany to allow the practice of the *partage noble* until families had held their nobility for three generations meant that the privilege was not always a corporately-held right, but sometimes depended upon lineage.[14]

This privilege was not found throughout France. In the Midi both nobles and commoners legimately practised the preferential transmission of property rights.[15] Moreover, beyond France an equivalent of the *partage noble* did not seem to exist. Primogeniture became a common form of inheritance among nobilities but peasants and burghers used it as well. The same was true of partible inheritance. Where the law insisted upon the one or the other it made no distinction between commoner and noble.

Legal devices to prevent the fragmentation of the estate by partible inheritance or alienation became common in Italy, the Austrian Empire with the exception of Hungary, and in most of Western Europe in the sixteenth and seventeenth centuries. This followed a development reaching back to the twelfth century in France, and to the thirteenth and fourteenth centuries in England, Italy and Spain. However, although these devices were closely associated with the noble estate, to the extent that the attack on the nobility in the nineteenth century singled out one of them, the entail, as an unnecessary evil, in very few states were they ever legally confined to the nobility. In Spain the Laws of Toro (1585) which provided a general authorisation of the *mayorazgo*, permitted non-nobles the opportunity to entail their landed property; and in the parts of France where customary law allowed entails, both commoner and noble were free to use them. This was also true of the English estate tail and the strict settlement, and of the *fideicommissum* in Italy and Germany. In France the entail only became a noble privilege when the ordinance of 1561 banned the use of the perpetual entail for all estates except the *duchés-paires*. However, this created a privilege closed to most of the nobility as well as the whole of the commonalty.[16] In Bohemia and Austria the *fideicommissum* became a right legally confined to men of noble status and remained so until 1848. Under Habsburg rule, the *fideicommissum* also become an exclusive noble right in Tuscany, but its use was shortlived. Introduced by Neri during the regency, the privilege came to an end when Gianni abolished all *fideicommissi* in the 1780s.[17] That seemed to be the extent of this privilege. Since the *partage noble* was an even rarer phenomenon, the landownership privileges of the nobility mostly concerned the exclusive right of acquisition and this right, while common in Eastern and Central Europe and Scandinavia, was infrequently found in Western Europe and Italy.

Although they failed to distinguish nobility from commonalty, several other landownership rights were important to the nobility, either because they protected its interests from state interference or allowed it to override the proprietary interests of the peasantry. These rights helped to characterise the European nobility by distinguishing it from the ruling classes of many traditional non-European societies.

In feudal or ex-feudal societies the nobles' rights of landownership were countered both by the lower proprietary rights of the peasant and by the higher proprietary rights of the Crown. The latter sometimes derived from the ruler's suzerainty over lands held of him in fee. The conditional nature of feudal tenure did not, initially, allow the tenant rights of inheritance and gave the ruler the right of confiscation if the tenant's obligations were not fulfilled. The ruler's final landownership right was not confined to feudal or ex-feudal societies. In Hungary and Russia, for example, the suzerain's overlordship was equalled by the sovereign's right to confiscate his subjects' property and to possess the resources of the subsoil. Authorised by regalian right, rulers confiscated property arbitrarily as in Russia, or confiscated it for the failure to provide military service, as in Hungary and Poland. The nobles' landownership rights were created as they succeeded in restricting, eliminating or annexing these suzerain or regalian rights, and managed to establish both perpetual possession of their estates and full ownership of the estate's natural products which, in many instances, were originally the ruler's preserve. The early acquisition of proprietorial rights by the fiefholders meant that a contrary development which in twelfth- and thirteenth-century France and Flanders transformed allods into fiefs, had little practical effect upon the nobility's landownership.[18]

The persistent process of transferring landownership rights from ruler to subject is encapsulated in the history of Russian landlordship. At the start of the fifteenth century landownership was allodial, lacking conditional obligations but subjected to the Tzar's patrimonial right of arbitrary confiscation. It had been so since the dissolution of the Kievan state in the twelfth century. During the fifteenth and sixteenth centuries it became strictly conditional on service to the Tzar. However, because of a relaxation of Tzarist control in the seventeenth century, the conditional tenure (*pomestye*) was by the late seventeenth century as securely hereditary as the allodial tenure (*votchina*) which it had replaced. Under Peter the Great the service obligations which he required of the nobility reinforced the conditional element in landownership, but within the space of fifty years service had ceased to be obligatory. The Charter to the Nobility of 1785 confirmed the implications of the 1762 decree which had abolished compulsory service: no longer was landownership conditional on state service. In addition, the Charter surrendered the Tzar's traditional rights of arbitrary confiscation as well as his ownership of the land's timber and mineral resources.[19]

Elsewhere estates mostly escaped from the ruler's final right of ownership at an earlier date and without the dramatic reassertions of regalian right that periodically had happened in Russia.[20] It took place in three stages. First, the hereditary landownership of fiefs was established; then the Crown's rights of appropriation and interference were reduced. Finally, the subject's ownership rights were extended to the subsoil.

The first stage was largely completed by the fourteenth century. In France, Bohemia, parts of Germany, Flanders and England it had occurred by 1200. As a result fiefholders as well as allod-holders could expect to alienate their estates or to transmit them to their offspring (even if they were minors or women and so incapable of personal military service), and even to collateral heirs.[21] The second stage was completed by the eighteenth century with the abolition in 1723 of the traditional penalty of loss of life and property for the Hungarian nobility's failure to serve in the *insurrectio*, and with the Tzar's grant of allodial rights to the Livonian fiefholders in 1783 and to the Russian landowners in 1785.[22] By the time of the French Revolution the landed nobility throughout Europe had been relieved of its service obligations and, except in the case of family extinction or conviction for a heinous crime, was fully assured in its hereditary landownership. Such rights were not simply extracted from an unwilling Crown by an overpowerful nobility. Often the Crown relinquished its rights in order to raise revenue. In place of the right of appropriation there developed a range of feudal dues: a relief falling due when the estate passed from father to son, a fee for the right to alienate, and sometimes the profitable right of wardship and marriage when the heir was a minor.[23] In place of the service obligation there developed a liability to taxation. In the eighteenth century some rulers, notably of Prussia and Hungary, were prepared to abolish the conditions of tenure in order to override the tax immunities which they had traditionally justified, while in Russia full proprietorial rights were granted as part of the Crown's attempt to strengthen the nobility. In England the Crown abandoned its feudal claims in 1660 partly to restore harmony between the Crown and the landlords but also to secure a compensatory grant of supplies from parliament. Moved by political and fiscal considerations, governments in the course of time tended to make fiefs and other conditional tenures practical freeholds.[24]

The third stage in the process, the transference from ruler to subject of the ownership of timber and mineral resources, was strongly countered by both Roman and feudal law, a stubborn tradition of regalian right and eventually by nationalisation, and therefore occurred in a much more complicated and less progressive manner and on a much more limited scale. In Bohemia, Austria, Hungary, Naples, Lombardy and Piedmont, it never occurred.[25] In several states it happened either belatedly or ephemerally. Furthermore, it rarely awarded to the landlord every mineral resource upon his estate. Usually gold and silver remained a royal preserve. In Poland rock salt was also retained by the Crown; in Sweden, copper.[26]

In England the right was assured to the private landlords in the late sixteenth and late seventeenth centuries. In 1568 a judgment in the courts ruled against the Crown's ownership of non-metallic minerals, thus endowing the landlords with a fully sanctioned right to mine the coal on their estates, but it asserted the Crown's right to metallic minerals which were likely to contain gold and silver. Acting upon this judgment, the governments of Elizabeth I and James I laid claim to the ownership of copper, and Charles I extended it to lead. As a result, licences were granted by the Crown authorising the mining of these minerals and not always to the owners of the land upon which they were found. Not until the Glorious Revolution was the matter resolved in the landlord's interest. Then his ownership of the subsoil was fully established, but gold and silver remained in the Crown's possession. By this time the landlord's right to mine the minerals on his estates was fairly common on the Continent.[27] In Spain John I in 1387 had given the landlords free mining rights on their estates, rights which even included gold and silver, in return for two thirds of the profit. In 1584 the Crown reclaimed its ownership right, but in the meantime the *fuero* of Viscaya, enacted in 1452 and confirmed in 1527, had authorised the landlords of that province to mine the mineral wealth of their estates subjected only to the payment of a fee, and this continued to stand. In France the seigneurial rights of *haut-justiciers* included mining. In 1413 the seigneurs were authorised to exploit the subsoil in return for a one-tenth royalty. In 1610 the Crown ceded this royalty. Landlords in the coalfields stretching from Liège to the Borinage, and also in the Ruhr and the Saar, had the right to mine. In some of these instances the ruler retained a right to a proportion of the product but ceded to the landlord the right to determine the mining operation. In Eastern Europe, Silesian and Polish landlords held similar rights, while in Sweden the nobles acquired ownership of the iron on their estates subjected in the seventeenth century to a one-thirtieth royalty.[28]

A further extension of subsoil rights occurred in the late eighteenth and early nineteenth centuries, as landlords acquired them in Italy, Spain and Russia. In Sicily the Crown had traditionally owned the subsoil, although to raise revenue and to dispense patronage, it had occasionally granted mining rights to favoured individuals. However, as a result of a royal concession in 1808 and the revolution of 1812, the right was totally transferred to the landlords. In North Italy, the persistence of Roman Law which reserved the subsoil for the state, was decisively countered in the late eighteenth century when, responding to physiocratic doctrine, the ruler of Tuscany granted ownership of the subsoil to the owner of the surface. In Russia, an ownership right, relating to timber as well as minerals, was conceded in 1782, while in Spain the right to mine coal was conferred upon the estate owners in 1785 and 1791.[29]

The eighteenth and nineteenth centuries, however, were also a period in which the state successfully reclaimed subsoil rights. In France mining was quashed as a seigneurial right when in 1744 an *arrêt du conseil* proclaimed the king sole proprietor of the subsoil. In Silesia the law of 1769 made mining dependent not on the permission of the landlord but the government. In 1825 a similar mining law, restoring ownership to the Crown, was imposed on the landlords of Spain. In the Southern Netherlands the landlords' mining rights disappeared with the abolition of the seigneurial system in 1810. As a result of this legislation, the mine owner was no longer the landlord but the *concessionaire*. In the Saar, the duke of Nassau-Saarbrucken took mineral ownership completely out of the landlords' hands. Existing mines were annexed and in 1754 the right to open new mines became a princely prerogative. When the Prussian monarchy acquired the Saar, this arrangement was left to stand. In this case the mines were not only owned but also worked by the state. As a result of these latter-day reclamations, English mining, which remained until nationalisation the untrammelled right of the landlord, became highly unusual in Europe, although not unique.[30]

As well as safeguarding the noble against state exploitation, landownership rights also allowed him to overcome the protective proprietary rights of the tenantry. The feudal principle of *nulle terre sans seigneur* and the tenurial security acquired by the tenantry had produced in much of Western Europe by 1300 a two-tiered system of landowning in which peasant proprietorship was accompanied by the final ownership of the seigneur. Thus, even in societies where peasants possessed perpetual tenures and rights of alienation, the seigneur retained rights of ownership which allowed him to exact dues and services and, in cases of the failure of a family line, negligence or the non-payment of dues, to reclaim the tenure. Although commoners could possess these final ownership rights, the close connexion between seigneurial ownership and the nobility ensured that in England, France and parts of Italy and West Germany, the nobility owned as large a proportion of private land as in the parts of Europe where land acquisition was an exclusive noble privilege. The rights of final ownership depended not only upon the survival of the seigneurial system but also upon the manner of its dissolution. When governments forced seigneurs to grant their tenants freeholds, a process initiated by the French Revolution and furthered by the revolutions of 1848, the final ownership right of the landlord was obliterated. However, if the seigneurial system was disposed of by incorporating the tenures into the demesne, leasehold was substituted for the customary tenure and the nobility's landownership was preserved and enlarged.[31]

2 Value and effect

The landownership rights reserved for the nobility—the *partage noble* of Western France, the *fideicommissum* of Austria, Bohemia and Tuscany, the land acquisition rights of the Scandinavian and East European nobles—were much less widespread than the indemnity, political participation, honorific and seigneurial privileges. In fact, except for the exclusive land acquisition privilege, they were extremely rare. Nearly all were conferred by noble status and therefore, along with the other corporate privileges, gave meaning to nobility.

Since similar forms of descent were widely practised in the parts of France without the *partage noble*, the effect of the privilege *per se* upon the French nobility is open to question.[32] Nevertheless, its influence can be roughly measured by comparing the areas of France subjected to the privilege with those where it failed to take root. The *partage noble* was not usually descent by strict primogeniture.[33] Normally, it allowed preference, not monopoly, for the eldest son. For this reason it did not automatically produce a landless nobility of cadet lines. The eldest son received the larger share of the estate, but a proportion was also reserved for younger sons. What produced landless nobles, apart from ennoblement by office, was the conjunction of strict primogeniture in the transmission of the estate and the inheritance of noble status by all the direct line. Arguably, the *partage noble* created a high proportion of poor landed nobles, especially in Brittany where it awarded the eldest son two thirds of the estate.[34] But the privilege differed considerably from province to province, in parts allowing as much as half the estate to descend to scions of the family. A poor landed nobility was frequently found in traditional Europe. Where its existence owed something to the system of inheritance, the responsibility lay not with noble privilege but with the absence of primogeniture in the transmission of noble status coupled with the partible inheritance of property, as in Poland, Hungary, Prussia and Russia. In denying the commoners impartible or preferential transmission of landed property, the *partage noble* probably affected the peasantry more profoundly than the nobility, especially when accompanied by a customary ban on the entail, as in Brittany and Normandy.[35] Unless countered by capitalistic opportunities, peasant farms in these areas were likely to be smaller, less economically viable and more prone to subsistence farming than elsewhere, having no legal safeguards against subdivision.

In assessing the value of the *fideicommissum* as a noble privilege one needs to take into account the extensive use of legal devices for protecting the integrity of estates and the fact that, although rarely a noble privilege, these devices were, nonetheless, mostly confined to the nobility. Thus in Austria and Bohemia the noble privilege of *fideicommussum* excluded commoners from a right which in other states was normally available to them, but only awarded the nobles the exclusive use of a device which would have been confined to them even if it had not been a privilege. The advantage to be gained from the privilege partly depended on whether or not the nobility transmitted its estates by primogeniture. Since primogeniture was traditionally practised by noble landowners in Austria and Bohemia the advantage of the *fideicommissum* privilege lay not in excluding younger sons from the inheritance of noble estates but in banning alienation. This could safeguard against wanton extravagance, but it could also tie up capital. Little was affected by the privilege's abolition since *fideicommissi* continued to be monopolised by the nobility long after that event.[36]

As a result of exceptions in the law and by means of legal subterfuges, commoners gained possession of estates which privilege reserved for the nobility. But to what extent? What effect did the privilege have on the social composition of landownership? And what benefit did the nobility derive from the privilege? The answers rest upon the ability of non-nobles to acquire estates protected by noble privilege, upon the way the privilege's abolition affected the relative proportions of land owned by nobles and commoners and upon the proportion of land held by nobles in states where the privilege did not exist. Moreover, as the privilege was designed to deny the commonalty a range of other privileges conferred by landownership, its effectiveness depended upon the degree to which it succeeded in that purpose.

The capacity of commoners to acquire estates reserved for the nobility varied in accordance with the exceptions in the law, the numbers of commoners able to evade the law and the numbers of nobles enforced by circumstance to sell their lands to the highest bidder, no matter what the law. The poverty of nobles and the wealth and aristocratic aspirations of the bourgeoisie were crucial factors. On the eve of the privilege's abolition in 1660, 2.6% of noble estates in Denmark were already commoner-owned. By 1800 13% of noble estates had fallen to the commonalty in Brandenburg. By 1802 30% of noble estates belonged to commoners in Bohemia and in 1780 1.4% of cultivated land was owned by commoners in Hungary.[37] Thus in some instances the privilege had rigorous effect; in others it was extremely lax. It cannot be said that the privilege actually preserved the bulk of private land for the nobility since prior to the twentieth century nobilities which had never held the privilege also tended to remain the major owners of private land. Rather, the privilege ensured for the nobility a larger share of the land than it would otherwise have possessed. Notably, at the close of the eighteenth century the proportion of commoner to noble owners of noble estates was twice as high in Silesia where the privilege was not to be found as in Brandenburg where it remained in force.[38] Moreover, in states where the privilege related to noble estates rather than to all lands, the proportion of land which it confined to the nobility depended on how much land was incorporated in noble estates. The prevalence of peasant freeholds in Sweden, Denmark, Bavaria, Vorarlberg and Tyrol kept a large portion of the land outside the possession of the nobility, their privilege notwithstanding. In some cases this exceeded the proportion of land which commoners owned in states where the privilege did not exist, especially when in these countries the nobles as seigneurs possessed the right of final ownership. Certainly, commoners in the seventeenth and eighteenth centuries owned a greater share of privately owned land in Sweden than in England or France.[39]

The privilege also failed to bestow upon the nobility a monopoly of the other privileges which landownership conferred. Where parliamentary membership was at stake, the privilege generally fulfilled its purpose of excluding commoners, especially when backed by a ruling that commoners with noble estates should not enjoy the attached privileges. However, governments appeared less restrictive when the attached privileges were seigneurial or fiscal.

A further indication of the privilege's importance in determining land-ownership and in confining noble privileges to the nobility is the effect of its abolition. This was at its most spectacular in Denmark where commoners increased their ownership of noble estates from 2.6% in 1660 to 44% in 1710. In the six eastern provinces of the Prussian monarchy, only 55% of noble estates remained in noble hands in 1855 and only 32% in 1889. In Russia the nobility's share of the land slid dramatically following the settlement of 1861, reaching 22% in 1877 and 11% in 1917.[40] These changes in landownership, however, did not simply result from the abolition of this privilege. In Denmark, the dramatic increase in the ownership of noble estates by commoners partly reflected the Crown's parsimony in creating new nobles, whereas in both the Prussian monarchy and the Austrian Empire the Crown's generous ennoblement policy helped the nobility to retain a sizeable share of the land in spite of the purchases of noble estates by commoners-born.[41] Working against the nobility's domination of landownership was the competition for land provided by peasant rather than bourgeois purchasers because the former were less likely to be ennobled. Peasant acquisitiveness helped to explain the slump in noble landownership in late nineteenth-century Russia. The nobility's share of the land in the nineteenth century also depended upon the terms offered the peasantry when emancipated from the seigneurial system and upon the size of the demesne. Where the demesne was small in proportion to the traditional peasant tenures, as in Bavaria and most of the Austrian territories, the termination of the seigneurial system rendered a large proportion of the land peasant freehold; but where the demesne lands were relatively large, as in parts of Poland, in the Prussian provinces east of the Elbe, in Hungary and in Bohemia, a great deal of land remained in noble hands until the land reforms of the twentieth century.[42]

The loss of noble landownership directly caused by the government's termination of the seigneurial system was accompanied and followed by the large-scale transference of noble estates from noble to bourgeois or peasant hands. The latter process depended upon both the noble's need to sell and the commoner's ability to buy. Generally in the nineteenth century, the nobilities of Europe were under pressure to sell lands in order to clear debts contracted either from an increase in current expenditure or from a contraction in income. The bad periods for the nobles followed the Napoleonic War when farming was seriously affected by a fall in farm prices and also occurred in the closing decades when European agriculture suffered the competition of American grain and beef. A bourgeois and peasant ability to buy was sustained by profits made in industry or commerce or farming.[43] It stemmed only partly from the removal of the nobility's exclusive land acquisition privilege. The process of land transference, already underway before the privilege was abolished, was certainly speeded up once the privilege had been removed, but just as important in promoting it were the conditions which reduced nobles to dire poverty and enriched bourgeois and peasant.

Its rights of inheritance and alienation over land were of crucial importance in allowing the European nobility to develop a character quite distinct from the traditional ruling elites of pre-colonial Africa and Asia,[44] and in distinguishing royal absolutism in Europe from Oriental and African despotism.

The political authority which subjects could legitimately exercise by birthright, an outstanding feature of the European nobility and monarchical state, depended not only upon hereditary functions imparted by noble status but also upon the private possession of estates and the legal capacity of subjects to transmit them from one generation to the next. Such a system of landlordism, although common in Europe from at least the twelfth century, was rare outside it unless imparted by European colonialism, influence or example. Where land was plentiful and so low in productivity that the area of cultivation required constant alteration—a common phenomenon in tropical Africa and India—there was little cause for landownership to develop. Moreover, when individual landownership did exist rights of inheritance tended not to be as firmly established as in traditional European societies, the ruler having the legitimate right to confiscate and to realot. In this respect, where individual landownership existed it tended to be not a natural inheritable right but reliant upon the grace of the prince. This was the case not only in many African societies but also in the imperial monarchies of Islam, the Moghul, Persian and Ottoman empires. Moreover where individual and inheritable landownership developed with a security of tenure equal to Europe, as, for example, in Imperial China, it tended not to confer political authority. Outside Europe grants of authority tended to go not with lands but with tax assignments. This was true of the Ottoman *timar*, the Persian *iqta*, the fief in the African kingdom of Nupe and the *zamindari* of the Moghul Empire.

Landlordism in pre-colonial Africa rarely emerged. This was because of the high availability of land in proportion to the population, the low productive quality of tropical soils and a technological backwardness centring on the absence of the plough. Low soil fertility necessitated shifting cultivation which the availability of land encouraged and so worked against the establishment of rights of permanent landownership. Tribalism, moreover, meant that when settlement occurred, communal landownership prevailed. Furthermore, even where individual landownership existed, as in Buganda,

Barotseland, Dahomey and Ethiopia, hereditary rights were not so strongly established as in traditional Europe. Thus, government officials in these societies could be granted estates but not the hereditary ownership of them; and their estates conferred power, influence and wealth but not legitimate authority. Traditional African and European societies certainly had much in common, especially because government resting upon the hereditary rights of a prince became a commonly found polity in both continents. But whereas in Europe the hereditary rights of the prince permitted the hereditary rights of a ruling class, in African societies, rulers tended not to grant to subjects hereditary titles, hereditary landownership and hereditary political functions. In African societies hereditary rights remained to a much greater extent the exclusive possession of the prince. This meant that the hereditary rights of subjects emerged as acts of usurpation, dependent for their survival upon the government's inability to repudiate them. Legitimate inheritable rights were not much in evidence. The nearest a traditional African elite came to resembling a European nobility was in Ethiopia but, apart from princely titles, its privileges, offices and lands were not awarded on an hereditary basis. Noble titles were only for life and the Emperor possessed the right to realot lands and offices at will. Europeans frequently noted the absolute authority of the Crown. Alvarez, a sixteenth-century Portuguese commentator, wrote: 'the Prester John deposes them and appoints them whenever he pleases, with or without cause ... I saw great lords turned out of their lordships and others put into them ...' In the seventeenth century, another Portuguese, d'Almeyda, reported: 'And it is so usual for the Emperor to chop, change and take the lands any man has and to bestow them on another'. Hereditary succession to offices and lands was basically reliant on the capacity of the monarchy to exercise its legitimate right to deny them. In the period 1769–1855 this was lost because of the weakness of the Crown's political position, but in the late nineteenth and early twentieth centuries it was recovered. This sort of royal authority was normal in the African monarchies. The legitimate despotism of the Ethiopian emperor was equalled by the Kabaka of Buganda, the Mekama of Bunyoro and by the kings of the Kongo Kingdom.

The enormous armies raised by the Ottomans and hurled against Europe in the sixteenth and seventeenth centuries consisted partly of the troops provided by the timar-holders, or occupants of military fiefs. But, in contrast with the development of feudalism in Western Europe, the *timar* was a grant of revenue and it did not become hereditary in the fief-holder's family. Upon the holder's death, the fief was redistributed; and on the accession of a new sultan there tended to be a general redistribution of *timars*. The Ottoman Empire certainly possessed private individual landownership, although hereditary rights depended on the grace of the sultan until 1867, and the landowners were prevented from becoming a European-type ruling class by a sophisticated bureaucratic system manned by slaves which only with its decay in the seventeenth and eighteenth centuries, allowed subjects to acquire political power through landownership. Like the Ottoman Turk, the Chinese Empire possessed a class of substantial landowners who for a long period of time lacked the opportunity to become a ruling class because the government enjoyed alternative means: in this case a salaried civil service selected by merit not birth, and also staffed by eunuchs, and a means of raising armed forces which did not have to depend on the co-operation of landlords. Chinese property rights, especially because of their sanctity against state confiscation and their hereditability, were much closer to European practice. However, landed political authority was lacking and political power was attained by the landlords only with the collapse of the system in the late nineteenth and early twentieth centuries; and then, only in local government. There was no equivalent in any of these societies to the European landlord who was given a role in central government by the parliamentary member-ship to which his landownership entitled him.

Likewise in India and Persia landlordism developed not as a natural part of a traditional system of government but because of the traditional system's collapse. In India landlordship developed because British rule sanctioned it through mistaking the former bureaucracy of the Moghuls for a European-type landed nobility. In this manner they legitimised rights which had been usurped during the period of decline and collapse in the Moghul Empire, especially by the *zamindars*, class of tax officials who had laid hereditary claim to the tribute assignments originally awarded them as payment for their services. By regarding this right as a right of landownership, by mistak-ing the tribute for rent, British rule gave birth to a landed nobility. European influence had a similar effect in Persia where nineteenth-century rulers sought to withstand colonial rule by adopting European ways and created a western form of hereditary landownership by ceding their traditional right of arbi-trary confiscation.

In contrast, Japanese society seemed to possess a ruling elite closely akin to the European model. But especially in the matter of landlordship, there appeared to be basic differences. For example, the majority of lesser nobles (*samurai*) were not landed but received rice allotments as a payment for their services. While the status of *samurai* and their sword-bearing privilege were hereditary, the land or rice incomes of the *samurai* were held only by the grace of their lords (*daimyo*). The conditional nature of tenure, as defined in the Hojo code of 1232, was more persistent than in Europe. Moreover, the Emperor, and after 1603 the Tokugawa Shogunate, held a constitutional right to dispossess or move the *daimyo*. The Japanese ruling elite came to resemble the nobilities of traditional Europe because of the overlords' unwillingness to exercise in any rigorous or systematic manner their rights of dispossession.

Landownership rights in Europe also influenced the development of the state, largely by restricting its powers over subjects. Whereas the rights of the ruler worked against the development of European-type nobilities outside Europe, the rights of the European nobles helped to prevent the absolutism of European monarchs from becoming a form of Oriental or African despotism. Royal absolutism, as it developed in Europe between the sixteenth and eighteenth centuries, was strongly influenced not only by an extension of central government's authority and power but also by the enduring rights of subjects which survived to limit the actions of the Crown. Prominent in this category of rights were the privileges of nobles and the rights of landlords.[45] In becoming a royal absolutism of the European type, an achievement which involved the creation of noble privileges and landownership rights, the Russian monarchy, previously an Asian despotism, underwent a limitation of its powers.

The right of final ownership over peasant tenures was an integral part of the seigneurial system. For nobles it was a source of income, a means of overcoming the proprietary rights of the tenantry and, ostensibly, a device for ensuring peasant deference. However, final ownership also placed restrictions upon what seigneurs could do to their tenants. The right of final ownership, which entailed respecting hereditary rights and rents fixed by custom, fell far short of the rights of the lessor who could revise tenancy and charge an economic rent. For this reason, many lords seized the opportunity to substitute the one right for the other by incorporating the tenures into the demesne.[46] Furthermore, final ownership rights were not only a means of tenant subordination but also a source of tenant hostility. Except for this privilege, the landownership rights were not in themselves all that socially provocative. Apart from the seigneurial complaint, what aroused the commoners against the nobles as landlords was the amount of land owned by the nobility and the settlements used to keep it intact and in the family.

The importance of the nobility's right to the subsoil depended upon the existence of mineral resources, the extent of the demand for them and the policy adopted by the Crown towards its own mining rights. Since the Crown had frequently granted its rights of mineral exploitation to the owners of the estates upon which the minerals were found, rather than mining them directly or granting the right of exploitation to other interests, the landlord's right of ownership had been of no decisive advantage. Authorised by royal licence, the landlord who merely owned the surface could exploit the mineral resources of his estate as effectively as the landlord who owned the subsoil. The gains to be made from the right of ownership lay not in the opportunity to exploit, but in a greater freedom from government exaction and a greater independence of royal authority. In the nineteenth century certain England lords became outstandingly wealthy within the community of European nobles, a reflection of the size of their landownership and the profitability of capitalist farming, urban property development and mining. But the profits they made from mining were not a simple consequence of owning the subsoil of their estates. It rather depended upon the massive demand for raw materials which industrialisation created. Likewise, certain Sicilian nobles in the nineteenth century drew great wealth from the mining of sulphur, not only because the subsoil had been granted to the landowners in 1812 but also because Sicily was one of the few places in the world where deposits of the mineral were known to exist at a time when the discovery of the Leblanc soda process had created an excess of demand over supply.[47]

The nobility's actual ownership of mineral wealth did not always encourage them to mine it themselves. In fact, although there were many exceptions, the tendency was for nobles to remain true to their rentier nature and to extract a profit from leasing out their rights rather than by direct exploitation.[48] Thus the exploitation of mineral resources took four forms: it was mined by *concessionaires*, licensed either by the noble landlords or by the state. Alternatively it was owned and directly mined either by the state or by the landlord. Since no one form was more productive than the other, it cannot be assumed that mineral resources were made more available by state or noble ownership. A ready supply of mineral resources was clearly a necessary ingredient of industrialisation and nobles with mineral ownership rights and agrarian predilections might have impeded the process by prohibiting or limiting mineral production. However, the allure of profit easily outweighed the fear of a defaced countryside.

Conclusion

Between 1200 and A.D. 1500 most European societies acquired a social elite, the nobility, with a membership determined not by wealth, occupation or royal lineage but by the legitimate possession of hereditary privileges. So important were these privileges that without them nobility was commonalty. However, as commoners could enjoy some of them without undergoing ennoblement, nobility depended not only upon the possession of privileges but also upon the manner in which they were granted and held.

The privileges of nobility were conferred either by noble status or by landed, titular or lineage qualifications. A noble estate awarded its owner both *dominium* over the tenantry and *libertas*: rights of immunity and participation in relation to the state. Because of its rights of *libertas*, some of the privileges imparted by a noble estate closely resembled the privileges conferred by noble status, lineage and entitlement. The status privileges gave definition to the nobility by distinguishing noble from commoner; whereas the estate, lineage and titular privileges created hierarchy within the noble order by distinguishing one noble from another. Thus, both the identity and structure of the European nobility were determined by privileges, the one by the privileges which all nobles enjoyed and the other by the privileges confined to some of them. The outcome was not a caste-like society. Commoners could attain the privileges of nobility not only by ennoblement but also through the purchase of noble estates and by means of the special concessions which the Crown was capable of granting to individuals; and nobles could attain the privileges confined to part of the noble order either by entitlement, dynastic survival, or the acquisition of a noble estate.

As well as structuring and defining the nobility, privilege profoundly affected the composition of the noble order by allowing nobles to exist who lacked, apart from privileges, all the noble characteristics. Although traditionally conceived as a ruling class, the nobility could contain members who had no ruling function whatsoever, and whose way of life was indistinguishable from that of the commonalty. An outstanding feature of most nobilities was a membership which reflected the whole social spectrum: as well as nobles with impressive titles, great estates and important political functions, there were noble shopkeepers, peasants, artisans, shepherds, labourers, professionalmen and officials. Responsible for this variegated composition was the role of privilege as the primary characteristic of nobility, and its tendency to descend to every member of the family. However, central to the European nobility's identity was not only privilege, but also a noble ethos which emphasised a distinct way of life and the possession of a private income. Thus, although privilege was essential to nobility, it fell short of providing the ideal nobleman.

By the mid-twentieth century noble privilege was little more than an honour, except in Great Britain and there the political and legal benefits conferred by privilege had become of small importance. Yet for centuries privilege had formed the core of the nobility's power and wealth. Seigneurial rights, for example, were a source both of political authority and of income. The seigneur's right of private jurisdiction and public administration were as integral to the political system in the absolute monarchies as in the feudal regimes. Also upholding the nobility's political function was its right of parliamentary representation and the existence of offices of state which were reserved for nobles. Thus, in local and central government the privileges of nobility preserved for it an important role in the running of the state. In addition, the parliamentary and seigneurial privileges allowed nobles to enjoy a ruling function which was quite independent of government appointment and the influence exerted by their wealth and power. Likewise reliant on privilege was the nobility's major source of wealth, its landed income. The slow development of wage labour in agriculture left noble farmers heavily dependent upon the labour services of the seigneurial system. The equally slow emergence of rent as the sole payment for tenancy left the nobles who drew their income from peasant farming heavily reliant upon seigneurial exactions. Privilege could also be of material benefit to the nobility by exempting it from taxation and the billeting of royal troops, by awarding it the fees of reserved office and by giving it access to noble banks.

And yet the political and economic advantages of the nobility were never merely the fruit of its juridical privileges. For this reason the former could outlive the latter. Even when it was sustained by privilege, the nobility's control of representative assemblies usually depended on its ability to direct the non-noble chambers, while its control of the state which essentially relied upon the exclusion of commoners from important official positions, frequently stemmed from the government's natural inclination to prefer noblemen. This preference caused it either to select nobles for high office or to ennoble the commoners who attained high office. Quite exceptional were the monarchies of Poland and Hungary where noble privilege defined the polit-

ical nation, where privilege alone ensured the noble domination of parliamentary assemblies and where the tenure of most public offices was legally
restricted to noblemen. Furthermore, the basic source of noble wealth was
not seigneurial right *per se* but the ownership of land. The importance of the
seigneurial system to the nobility as a source of wealth depended upon the
method of estate management. By leasing the demesne or by farming it with
wage labour, landlords became less reliant for their income upon seigneurial
rights. Seigneurial rights were a means of tenant control as well as of revenue.
However, their tendency was to become merely sources of income, with
permission automatically granted for the payment of a fee, and the judicial
rights of the seigneurs becoming seriously circumscribed by government
regulation and the remedy offered in the royal courts. Moreover, the landlord's control over his tenants basically resided in his powers of eviction.
These could be extreme or slight within the seigneurial system. The decisive
factor was whether or not the tenant was a serf. What is more, the seigneurial
rights were as much a source of disobedience as obedience, breeding dissi-
dence among the peasantry towards the landlords rather than respect and
adherence. This was evident in a long history of riots and rebellions in which
the target was the landlord and the grievance was the way he exercised his
seigneurial rights. Finally, fiscal exemption rarely protected nobles from the
range of taxation, and, long before its abolition, the liability of nobles
rendered tax evasion of greater benefit to them than their privilege of fiscal
immunity.

Until the late eighteenth century the commonalty showed a remarkable
tolerance of noble privilege. With the exception of seigneurial rights, the
criticism of noble privilege had come from the government rather than from
the people. This capacity for acceptance persisted well into the nineteenth
century in spite of the acts of abolition which revolutionary or conservative
governments committed in the wake of the French Revolution of 1789, even
to the extent of permitting privileges to be restored. Upholding the people's
faith in noble privilege was the fact that the belief in birthright, upon which
noble privilege rested, failed to accept birth as the only means by which
noble privilege could be obtained. Of outstanding importance in maintaining
popular respect for noble privilege was the commoner's chances of acquiring
for his children a birthright to it. Either by ennoblement or the acquisition of
a noble estate, this was easily obtainable throughout most of the history of
privilege on account of the generosity of princes, the existence of informal
means of entry which lay outside the state's control and because nobility
consisted of mere status as well as entitlement. Permitting the extensive
promotion of commoners into the nobility was the hierarchical structure
imparted to the nobility by the coexistence of corporately held and special
privileges. This structure allowed nobility to remain accessible and exclusive

at the same time. As a result it was possible to please the commonalty by allowing massive admission to the nobility without offending important elements in the nobility who could remain distinguished from the new arrivals by the privileges conferred by lineage and titles. Because the process of ennoblement won over to the noble cause the wealthier and more dynamic elements of the commonalty, because the exclusiveness of certain privileges allowed the more powerful elements within the nobility to accept the inflation of honours and its likely debasement of noble status, and because ordinary nobles had some prospect of acquiring the non-corporate privileges, noble privileges retained a great deal of influential support.

Social promotion, however, only partly accounts for society's acceptance of the noble order. Moreover, it serves less well to explain the peasantry's acceptance of seigneurial right than to account for the bourgeoisie's acceptance of it; and as access to the titled nobility was extremely difficult for commoners, entitlement could have played little part in persuading commoners to regard favourably the privileges of the higher nobility. The same was true of the privileges conferred by lineage. Furthermore in many cases the parliamentary and fiscal privileges which were imparted by the possession of a noble estate were also difficult for non-nobles to obtain. They were either barred from ownership or, if ownership was allowed, commoners were denied the attendant privileges. Basically the seigneurial and noble privileges continued to exist because there was no popular articulation of the need for their total abolition. This did not mean that opposition was absent. However, until the late eighteenth century the limited protests made by the peasantry against the abuse of the seigneurial system were effectively countered with minor concessions or military force, and the criticism offered by the occasional intellectual lacked general appeal. Nor did it mean that complete abolition simply followed the acquired ability of the people to conceive a society without noble privilege. Arguably the abolition of privilege initially preceded the popular demand for its abolition and created rather than was created by that demand. In revolutionary France the National Assembly overreacted to peasant rebellion and gave the peasantry more than it was demanding. The resulting abolition of privilege affected the whole of Europe creating a fashionable social ideology which condemned noble privileges as an irredeemable evil and to which revolutionary and counter-revolutionary parties needed to respond in the competition for popular support.

From the late eighteenth century, the privileges of nobility came to be regarded as retrogressive, a serious impediment on the process of modernisation. Yet much of the machinery of the modern state developed long before the abolition of noble privilege. Moreover, a factor in the development of professional bureaucracies and standing armies were nobilities rendered compliant with the designs of royal absolutism by the preservation or extension of their privileges. The nobility's interest in representative assemblies, which was sustained by their rights of membership, had a part to play in the long-term development of parliamentary government, notwithstanding their antipathy to democracy. Seigneurial rights were not an inevitable restraint on agricultural progress: rights of inheritance and low rents, which the seigneurial system often awarded when serfdom had withered away, could allow the tenantry opportunities for long-term planning and the accumulation of capital. The seigneurial system could provide the means for large-scale commerical farming both on the demesne and the tenures. Rather than the seigneurial system, economic backwardness was due to inadequate techniques and reactionary attitudes. Moreover, farming could be handicapped by the abolition of the seigneurial system especially when it led to the creation of small peasant freeholds with limited market possibilities or to the development of short-lease farming. Noble privilege was an integral part of traditional Europe but not a guarantor of its preservation. Modernisation long preceded its abolition and was not necessarily promoted by its demise. This was also the case with social relations. Privileges provided the framework of the estates society but did not determine its social attitudes. The estates society was a shell within which class relations grew, not an alien or even an alternative social organisation to the class society.

Central to the meaning of noble privilege was a body of rights which protected the subject and his possessions from the actions of the state. As they developed in Europe, human rights rested upon the fact that, on account of its privileges, the dominant class had a vested interest in withstanding rather than merely imposing the state. In this respect democracy was born of noble privilege and came to fruition not simply by destroying it but by converting it into the rights of the citizenry.

Notes

Chapter I. Noble privileges in general

1 This does not mean that all estates owned by nobles were juridically different from estates owned by commoners. It refers to estates which were officially recognised as conferring noble privileges or seigneurial rights.

2 General: S. J. Woolf, 'The aristocracy in transition: a continental comparison', *Econ. H. R.*, 2nd ser., 23 (1970), pp. 525-6; J. Meyer, *Noblesses et pouvoirs dans l'Europe d'ancien régime*, pp. 64 ff; *N.C.M.H.* IV, pp. 20-1 (Cooper) and R. Barber, *The Knight and Chivalry*, pp. 32-3. On individual nobilities, see W. Dworzaczek, 'Perméabilité des barrières sociales dans la Pologne du XVIe siècle', *Acta Poloniae Historica*, 24 (1971), p. 34, and J. C. Miller, *The Nobility in Polish Renaissance Society*, pp. 51 and 110; G. Richard, *Noblesse d'affaires au XVIIIe siècle*, pp. 25 ff, J. Meyer, *La noblesse bretonne*, p. 138, P. S. Lewis, *Later Medieval France*, p. 175, and F. L. Ford, *Robe and Sword*, pp. 25-6; M. Roberts, *Gustavus Adolphus*, II, pp. 129-30, and G. Ohlin, 'Entrepreneurial activities of the Swedish aristocracy', *Explorations in Entrepreneurial History*, 6 (1953), p. 153; A. Dominguez Ortiz, *La sociedad española en el siglo XVII*, I, p. 226, W. J. Callahan, *Honour, Commerce and Industry in Eighteenth-Century Spain*, pp. 3, 5-6 and 15-18, and R. Herr, *The Eighteenth-Century Revolution in Spain*, p. 97; J. Roberts, 'Lombardy', in *The European Nobility in the Eighteenth Century*, ed. A. Goodwin, p. 65, and A.-E. Sayous, 'Aristocratie et noblesse à Gênes', *Annales*, 9 (1937), p. 378; M. Raeff, *Origins of the Russian Intelligentsia*, p. 114, and P. Dukes, *Catherine the Great and the Russian Nobility*, pp. 8-9; L. W. Muncy, *The Junker in the Prussian Administration under William II*, p. 20.

3 Meyer, *Noblesses et pouvoirs . . .*, p. 33; R. Pipes, *Russia under the Old Regime*, p. 181; P. S. Wandycz, *The Lands of Partitioned Poland*, pp. 18 and 126; R. Bonney, *Political Change in France under Richelieu and Mazarin*, pp. 436-8, and A. Dominguez Ortiz, *La sociedad española en el siglo XVIII*, pp. 83-4.

4 The subject is conveniently treated in three books of essays: G. Duby, *The Chivalrous Society*, especially chs. 3, 5, 6, 9, 11, and 13; F. L. Cheyette (ed.), *Lordship and Community in Medieval Europe*, especially the essays by Schlesinger, Duby and Genicot; and T. Reuter (ed.), *The Medieval Nobility*, especially chs. 1, 2, 5, 6, 7 and 8. Also see the introduction of E. Warlop's *The Flemish Nobility before 1300*, L. Verriest, *Noblesse, chevalerie, lignage*, K. Leyser, 'The German aristocracy from the ninth to the early twelfth century',

Past and Present, 41 (1968), and E. Lourie, 'A society organised for war: medieval Spain', *Past and Present*, 35 (1966) and J. Martindale, 'The French aristocracy in the early middle ages: a reappraisal', *Past and Present*, 75 (1977). For the 'Roman nobility', Matthias Gelzer's *The Roman Nobility* was seminal and remains essential. Also see C. Nicolet, 'Les classes dirigeantes romaines sous la république: ordre sénatorial et ordre équestre', *Annales d'histoire E.S.*, 32 (2) (1977).

5   Genicot (Reuter), pp. 25–8.

6   Irsigler (Reuter), p. 106; Werner (Reuter), p. 183; Schlesinger (Cheyette), p. 82; Gelzer, op. cit., pp. 153–4, and Nicolet, op. cit., p. 727.

7   Werner (Reuter), pp. 160–1 and p. 183; Schlesinger (Cheyette), pp. 72–9, and Reuter, op. cit., p. 11.

8   They contrast in this respect with the consular privileges which seem to be of monarchical origin, see Gelzer, op. cit., p. 50.

9   Irsigler (Reuter), pp. 123–4; Werner (Reuter), pp. 142–5, 160, 179–80 and 183; Tellenbach (Reuter), p. 208; Schmid (Reuter), p. 50, Genicot (Reuter), pp. 21, 23–5 and 27; Genicot (Cheyette), p. 134 and Duby, op. cit., pp. 79–80.

10   Genicot (Cheyette), p. 130–1; Warlop, op. cit., pp. 254–5 and 324; Duby (Cheyette), pp. 147–50; J. Beeler, *Warfare in Feudal Europe*, p. 17, and Genicot (Reuter), p. 22.

11   Genicot (Reuter), p. 28.

12   Warlop, op. cit., pp. 300–3, 320 and 327; Barber, op. cit., pp. 16–17; M. Bloch, *Feudal Society*, pp. 321–2; Genicot (Reuter), p. 28, and Lourie, op. cit., pp. 72–5.

13   Bloch, op. cit., pp. 330–1; R. H. Hilton, 'Freedom and villeinage in England', in *Peasants, Knights and Heretics*, ed. Hilton, pp. 174–6, and S. Painter, 'Feudalism, liberty and democracy' in *Feudalism and Liberty*, ed. F. A. Cazel, p. 263.

14   Duby, op. cit., p. 174 and Genicot (Reuter), p. 24.

15   Schmid (Reuter), p. 54; Genicot (Reuter), pp. 26–7; Tellenbach (Reuter), pp. 219–20; Warlop, op. cit., p. 333, and Genicot (Cheyette), pp. 130–3.

16   Genicot (Cheyette), p. 134 and Genicot (Reuter), pp. 21–2.

17   Miller, op. cit., ch. 1; A. Bruce Boswell, 'Poland', in *The European Nobility in the Eighteenth Century*, ed. Goodwin, pp. 156–7; *N.C.M.H.* I, p. 382 (Macartney) and A. Marongiu, *Medieval Parliaments: a Comparative Study*, pt. IV, chs. 1–3.

18   R. J. Kerner, *Bohemia in the Eighteenth Century*, p. 10.

19   Miller, op. cit., ch. 1, especially pp. 48–52, 97 and 119; *N.C.M.H.* I, pp. 382–3 (Macartney); ibid., II, pp. 473–4 (Betts); J. Bardach, 'Gouvernants et gouvernés en Pologne au moyen-âge et aux temps modernes', *Recueils de la Société Jean Bodin*, 25 (4) (1965), p. 267; *Cambridge History of Poland*, I, p. 260; G. V. Vernadsky, *Russia at the Dawn of the Modern Age*, pp. 194 and 196–8, and O. P. Backus, 'The problem of feudalism in Lithuania, 1506–1548', *Slavic Review*, 21 (1962), pp. 644 and 651.

20   C. A. Macartney, 'Hungary', in *The European Nobility in the Eighteenth Century*, ed. Goodwin, pp. 118–22; J. Blum, *Noble Landowners and Agriculture in Austria*, p. 35; B. K. Király, *Hungary in the Late Eighteenth Century*, pp. 24–5, and *A History of Hungary*, ed. E. Pamlenyi, pp. 82–3.

21   For a broad and convincing, if imperfect, treatment of the noble/absolute monarch relationship, see Perry Anderson's *Lineages of the Absolutist State*.

22   P. du Puy de Clinchamps, *La noblesse*, pp. 118 ff; T. F. Hamerow, *Restoration*,

Revolution, Reaction, chs. 7, 10, and 11; C. A. Macartney, *The Habsburg Empire,* chs. 9, 10 and 11, and *A History of Hungary,* ed. Pamlenyi, ch. 9.
23　See below, pp. 201-4.

Chapter II. Fiscal privilege

1　See below, pp. 35-9.
2　British Isles: R. S. Rait, *The Parliaments of Scotland,* pp. 211 and 489-90; J. R. Strayer, *On the Medieval Origins of the Modern State,* p. 44; and also see n. 7; Silesia: The *Historical Essays of Otto Hintze,* ed. F. Gilbert, p. 47; East Prussia: see n. 6; Tuscany: D. Herlihy, *Pisa in the Early Renaissance,* pp. 76-7 and E. Cochrane, *Florence in the Forgotten Centuries,* p. 487; Venice: P. Burke, *Venice and Amsterdam, a Study of Seventeenth-Century Elites,* p. 18 and J. Georgelin, *Venise au siècle des lumières,* pp. 532-7.
3　F. L. Carsten, *The Origins of Prussia,* pp. 170-1, 188 and 195-7; F. Martiny, 'Die Adelsfrage in Preussen vor 1806', *Vierteljahrschrift für Sozial-und Wirtschaftsgeschichte,* 1938 (Beheit 35), p. 10, and *The Historical Essays of Otto Hintze* (Gilbert), p. 59.
4　The Great Elector introduced commutation in 1663 and 1665 but afterwards restored the obligation of actual military service (Carsten, op. cit., pp. 197-8); ibid., pp. 171 and 188, and Martiny, op. cit., p. 10.
5　C. A. Macartney, 'Hungary', in *The European Nobility in the Eighteenth Century,* ed. Goodwin, pp. 119-20, and J. Blum, *Noble Landowners and Agriculture in Austria,* pp. 34-5; C. A. Macartney, *The Habsburg Empire,* pp. 338 and 444; J. Bérenger, *Finances et absolutisme autrichien,* p. 319; H. Marczali, *Hungary in the Eighteenth Century,* p. 125, and B. K. Király, *Hungary in the Late Eighteenth Century,* pp. 24-5 and 69-70.
6　Carsten, op. cit., pp. 207 and 220 ff; *The Historical Essays of Otto Hintze* (Gilbert), p. 47, and A. Goodwin, 'Prussia', in *The European Nobility in the Eighteenth Century,* ed. Goodwin, pp. 86-7.
7　A. S. Turberville, *The House of Lords in the Reign of William III,* pp. 62-3. For the immunity from the danegeld, see G. L. Harriss, *King, Parliament and Public Finance in Medieval England to 1369,* ch. 1.
8　N.C.M.H. I, p. 385 (Macartney); ibid., III, p. 381 (Skwarczyński); A. Wolowski, *La vie quotidienne en Pologne au XVIIe siècle,* p. 42; *Cambridge History of Poland,* I, pp. 431 and 450; J. K. Hoensch, *Sozialverfassung und politische Reform,* pp. 57-8, and J. C. Miller, *The Nobility in Polish Renaissance Society,* pp. 350-62.
9　F. L. Carsten, *Prince and Parliaments in Germany,* ch. 5.
10　S. Adler, *Das adelige Landrecht in Nieder-und Oberösterreich und die Gerichtsreformen des XVIII Jahrhunderts,* pp. 43; Macartney, *The Habsburg Empire,* p. 51; Bérenger, op. cit., pp. 327-30, 334 and 340, and H. Hochenegg, *Der Adel in Leben Tirols,* p. 15.
11　Hoensch, op. cit., p. 58.
12　M. A. Ladero Quesada, 'Les finances royales de Castille à la veille des temps modernes', *Annales d'histoire E.S.,* 25 (1) (1970), pp. 780-2, and A. Mackay, *Spain in the Middle Ages: from Frontier to Empire, 1000-1500,* pp. 145-6; Ladero Quesada, op. cit., pp. 776-7; J. N. Hillgarth, *The Spanish Kingdoms,* I, p. 292, and A. Dominguez Ortiz, *Política y hacienda de Felipe IV,* pp. 203-4. Although liable to state indirect taxes, it seems that the nobles enjoyed some

exemption from municipal indirect taxes (see J. Lynch, *Spain under the Habsburgs*, II, pp. 134, and N. Salomon, *La campagne de nouvelle Castile à la fin du XVIe siècle*, p. 289, n. 1).

13   S. de Moxó, *La Alcabala*, p. 45; R. Herr, *The Eighteenth-Century Revolution in Spain*, p. 97; Dominguez Ortiz, op. cit., p. 232; H. Kamen, *The War of Succession in Spain*, ch. 9, especially pp. 205–6; Dominguez Ortiz, op. cit., pp. 227–8, and I. A. A. Thompson, *War and Government in Habsburg Spain*, pp. 146–7.

14   S. G. Payne, *A History of Spain and Portugal*, p. 130; H. V. Livermore, *A New History of Portugal*, pp. 133 and 209, and A. H. de Oliveira Marques, *History of Portugal*, I, pp. 392–3.

15   J. F. O'Callaghan, *A History of Medieval Spain*, p. 288; Hillgarth, op. cit., p. 278; Kamen, op. cit., pp. 255, 323, 335–7, 348–9, 358–60, and Herr, op. cit., p. 129.

16   D. E. Zanetti, 'The patriziato of Milan from the domination of Spain to the unification of Italy: an outline of the social and demographic history', *Social History*, 6 (1977), p. 747.

17   Bérenger, op. cit., pp. 321, 328 and 340–1; R. J. Kerner, *Bohemia in the Eighteenth Century*, pp. 27 and 47.

18   J. Blum, *Lord and Peasant in Russia*, pp. 234–5 and 464; Blum, 'Russia', in *European Landed Elites in the Nineteenth Century*, ed. D. Spring, pp. 76 and 79; P. Dukes, *Catherine the Great and the Russian Nobility*, pp. 5 and 9, and H. Seton-Watson, *The Russian Empire*, pp. 248 and 529.

19   M. Roberts, *Gustavus Adolphus*, II, pp. 51–3 and 60, and *Sweden's Age of Greatness*, ed. M. Roberts, pp. 79, 106 and 120–1.

20   B. J. Hovde, *The Scandinavian Countries*, p. 286; I. Andersson, *A History of Sweden*, p. 393; D. V. Verney, *Parliamentary Reform in Sweden*, p. 102; Roberts, *Gustavus Adolphus*, II, pp. 156–7; P. Jeannin, *L'Europe du nord-ouest et du nord aux XVIIe et XVIIIe siècles*, pp. 130–1; *Sweden's Age of Greatness*, ed. Roberts, pp. 79, 105, 121 and 252–3, and M. Roberts, *The Early Vasas*, p. 37.

21   Hovde, op. cit., pp. 285 and 551–2; *N.C.M.H.* V, p. 525 (Rosén), and Jeannin, op. cit., pp. 127 and 133.

22   For exemption from direct taxation, see B. Behrens, 'Nobles, privileges and taxes in France at the end of the ancien regime', *Econ. H. R.*, 2nd ser., 15 (1963), pp. 451–75, and the debate between Behrens and G. J. Cavanaugh in *French Historical Studies*, 8 (1974), and 9 (1976). For exemption from indirect taxes, see M. Wolfe, *The Fiscal System in Renaissance France*, pp. 325–6 and 328, and G. T. Matthews, *The Royal General Farms in Eighteenth-Century France*, p. 152.

23   J. B. Henneman, *Royal Taxation in Fourteenth-Century France*, p. 318; Behrens, op. cit., pp. 460–1; J. Meuvret, 'Fiscalism and public opinion under Louis XIV', in *Louis XIV and Absolutism*, ed. R. Hatton, pp. 218–22; J. Beeler, *Warfare in Feudal Europe*, p. 41; P. Deyon, 'The French nobility and absolute monarchy', in *France in Crisis, 1620–1675*, ed. P. J. Coveney, p. 235; J. Meyer, *La Noblesse bretonne au XVIIIe siècle*, p. 780; R. Bonney, *Political Change in France under Richelieu and Mazarin*, pp. 184, 187 and 203, and P. J. Coveney (ed.), op. cit., p. 15.

24   Wolfe, op. cit., pp. 317–26 and Matthews, op. cit., pp. 85–6, 90, 91 n. 9 and 152.

25 Frêche calculated that noble estates amounted overall to about 10% of the land while noble possessions amounted to about 45% of the land in the eighteenth century ('Compoix, propriété, foncière, fiscalité et démographie historique en pays de taille réelle', *Revue d'histoire moderne et contemporaine*, 18 (1971), pp. 330 and 342–3).

26 Deyon, op. cit., pp. 232–3, and D. J. Sturdy, 'Tax evasion, the *faux* nobles, and state fiscalism; the example of the *généralité* of Caen, 1634–35', *French Historical Studies*, 9 (1976), pp. 564–5.

27 O. Ranum, *Richelieu and the Councillors of Louis XIII*, p. 137; Meyer, op. cit., pp. 429–30; F. L. Ford, *Robe and Sword*, p. 111, and Meuvret, op. cit., p. 210; see n. 96.

28 Carsten, *Princes and Parliaments in Germany*, ch. 3.

29 D. Mack-Smith, *A History of Sicily*, pp. 155, 255–6, 274 and 318, and H. Koenigsberger, *The Government of Sicily under Philip II of Spain*, pp. 124–7; P. Colletta, *History of the Kingdom of Naples*, I, pp. 131 and 133–4, and II, p. 4.

30 Frêche, op. cit., pp. 337–8. E. Esmonin's impression that noble status in the course of the seventeenth and eighteenth centuries came to determine fiscal immunity throughout France since in the regions of the *taille réelle* all estates held by nobles tended to be regarded, from a fiscal point of view, as noble estates (see *Études sur la France des XVIIe et XVIII siècles*, pp. 172–3) is effectively contradicted by Frêche, who shows that, at least in Languedoc, the eighteenth-century noble remained heavily taillable (pp. 330 and 338) and that, rather than *roturier* estates becoming noble estates, there was a reduction in the proportion of land held as noble estates between the sixteenth and the eighteenth centuries (see pp. 341–3). Also see Deyon, op. cit., p. 234.

31 Naples: A. F. C. Ryder, *The Kingdom of Naples under Alfonso the Magnanimous*, p. 210, G. Coniglio, *Il regno di Napoli al tempo di Carlo V*, pt. III, ch. 1, and Colletta, op. cit., I, p. 131; Sicily: Mack Smith, op. cit., p. 318; Saxony: Carsten, *Princes and Parliaments in Germany*, p. 221; Piedmont: S. J. Woolf, *Studi sulla nobilta piemontese nell' epoca dell' assolutismo*, p. 139; Brandenburg: H. Rosenberg, *Bureaucracy, Aristocracy, Autocracy*, p. 219, Carsten, op. cit., p. 221, and Martiny, op. cit., pp. 25–6 and 40; Bohemia: Bérenger, op. cit., pp. 321–3; France, see n. 30; Jülich and Berg: Carsten, op. cit., p. 282; Sweden: Roberts, *The Early Vasas*, pp. 35 and 37, and *Gustavus Adolphus*, II, p. 53; Denmark: Hovde, op. cit., p. 285, and Jeannin, op. cit., p. 133.

32 See nn. 12 (Castile), 14 (Portugal), 5 (Hungary), 29 (Naples) and 8 (Poland). In Russia the system of exemption passed through several stages: in the sixteenth and seventeenth centuries it related to noble estates; in the early eighteenth century it seemed conditional on state service and by the late eighteenth century it had become the permanent right of those with noble status (see n. 18).

33 J. Meyer, *Noblesses et pouvoirs dans l'Europe d'ancien régime*, p. 33; R. Pipes, *Russia under the Old Regime*, p. 181; T. Emmons, *The Russian Landed Gentry and the Peasant Emancipation of 1861*, pp. 15–16; Seton-Watson, op. cit., p. 240; P. S. Wandycz, *The Lands of Partitioned Poland, 1795–1918*, pp. 18 and 126; Bonney, op. cit., pp. 436–8, and A. Dominguez Ortiz, *La sociedad española en el siglo XVIII*, pp. 83–4.

34 Macartney, 'Hungary', in *The European Nobility in the Eighteenth Century*, ed. Goodwin, p. 125; Marczali, op. cit., p. 167; J. Kovacsics, 'The population of Hungary in the eighteenth century', *3rd International Conference of Eco-*

nomic History, IV, p. 139, and Király, op. cit., pp. 24 n. 2, 37, 52 and 72–3.
35   See chapter VII.
36   Koenigsberger, op. cit., pp. 106 and 109; Frêche, op. cit., p. 338; P. Contamine, 'The French nobility and the war', in *The Hundred Years' War*, ed. K. Fowler, p. 144, and Ford, op. cit., p. 28. According to Frêche this did not happen on a large scale, the nobility and the clergy retaining the bulk of the noble estates (93% against 5% in bourgeois hands). Greater openings for commoners to acquire fiscally exempt properties lay in the acquisition of ecclesiastical estates (see Frêche, op. cit., pp. 345–6).
37   Wolfe, op. cit., pp. 310–11; Behrens, op. cit., pp. 464–5, and Matthews, op. cit., pp. 151–4. There were other towns which paid an '*abonnement*' in lieu of the *taille*. This was often raised through indirect taxes (see N. Temple, 'French towns during the ancien regime', in *State and Society in Seventeenth-Century France*, ed. R. F. Kierstead, pp. 75–6).
38   S. de Moxó, *La Alcabala*, p. 45, and Behrens, op. cit., p. 465.
39   B. Croce, *A History of the Kingdom of Naples*, p. 86; Mack Smith, op. cit., p. 255; Miller, op. cit., p. 350; de Moxó, op. cit., p. 45; Matthews, op. cit., p. 89 and pp. 148–9; Meuvret, op. cit., pp. 211–12, and J. Russell Major, *Representative Government in Early Modern France*, pp. 108, 126–7 and 134.
40   Wolfe, op. cit., pp. 326–7; Henneman, op. cit., pp. 311–12; J. H. Shennan, *Government and Society in France*, pp. 50–1, and Matthews, op. cit., p. 91 n. 9.
41   Rosenberg, op. cit., p. 101; J. Hassell, 'Implementation of the Russian table of ranks during the eighteenth century', *Slavic Review*, 29 (1970), pp. 283 and 286. Arguably, however, the Russian officials were noble by right of their inclusion in the table of ranks (see Blum, 'Russia', in *European Landed Elites in the Nineteenth Century*, ed. Spring) and only ceased to be in 1832 when those below the ninth rank were awarded 'honoured citizenship' instead of nobility (see Seton-Watson, op. cit., p. 240).
42   J. Blum, *The End of the Old Order in Rural Europe*, p. 23, and *Sweden's Age of Greatness*, ed. M. Roberts, p. 79.
43   See nn. 50–1 and 78.
44   De Oliveira Marques, op. cit., I, p. 183; A. Marongiu, *Medieval Parliaments: a Comparative Study*, p. 199; Dominguez Ortiz, *La sociedad española en el siglo XVIII*, p. 107, and Colletta, op. cit., I, p. 131.
45   De Oliveira Marques, op. cit., p. 289; Mack Smith, op. cit., p. 164; Dominguez Ortiz, op. cit., p. 107; Shennan, op. cit., pp. 50–1; *N.C.M.H.* IV, p. 22 (Cooper), and Seton-Watson, op. cit., p. 240.
46   *Sweden's Age of Greatness*, ed. Roberts, pp. 63–4, 105, 267 and 270; Roberts, *The Early Vasas*, pp. 35 and 37, and Roberts, *Gustavus Adolphus*, II, p. 53.
47   V. R. Gruder, *The Royal Provincial Intendants*, p. 122–3, and P. Goubert, *The Ancien Regime*, p. 123; for Russia, see n. 41.
48   De Moxó, op. cit., pp. 45–7, and Matthews, op. cit., p. 91 n. 9.
49   *N.C.M.H.* IV, p. 22 (Cooper), and Seton-Watson, op. cit., p. 240.
50   E. Lourie, 'A society organised for war: medieval Spain', *Past and Present*, 35 (1966), pp. 55–8 and 72–4; *Diccionario de historia de España*, I, p. 611; O'Callaghan, op. cit., pp. 178 and 470; Livermore, op. cit., p. 63; Hillgarth, op. cit., p. 65 and Dominguez Ortiz, op. cit., pp. 104–6.
51   Miller, op. cit., pp. 48–52; W. Dworzaczek, 'Perméabilité des barrières sociales dans la Pologne du XVIe siècle', *Acta Poloniae Historica*, 24 (1971), pp. 22–3;

Király, op. cit., pp. 34–5, and Lourie, op. cit., pp. 57–8.

52 Jeannin, op. cit., pp. 127 and n. 1 and p. 133; Roberts, *Gustavus Adolphus*, II, pp. 51–2, and *Sweden's Age of Greatness*, ed. Roberts, p. 106.

53 Rait, op. cit., pp. 211 and 505–6; H. Miller, 'Subsidy assessments of the peerage in the sixteenth century', *B.I.H.R.* 28 (1955), p. 19, and R. S. Schofield, 'Parliamentary Lay Taxation, 1485–1547' (Cambridge Ph.D., 1963), pp. 141–50, 174 and 222.

54 The citizens of the *villes franches* in the eighteenth century enjoyed along with fiscal exemption, exemption from militia service and the state *corvée* (Behrens, op. cit., p. 464). Likewise, the students of Salamanca university in 1492 were given exemption from militia service as well as from all personal taxation (M. Defourneaux, *Daily Life in Spain in the Golden Age*, p. 165). Officers of the law courts had obtained a like combination of exemption in eighteenth-century France (Ford, op. cit., p. 28 n. 17). The honoured citizens in Russia were free of recruitment for military service and exempt from corporal punishment as well as immune from the poll tax (Seton-Watson, op. cit., p. 240).

55 E.g. in Sweden: *Sweden's Age of Greatness*, ed. Roberts, p. 268, and in Spain: Kamen, op. cit., p. 212.

56 For the distinction between assignment and tax farming, see G. Parker, 'The emergence of modern finance in Europe', in *The Fontana Economic History of Europe*, II, pp. 562–3.

57 P. S. Lewis, *Later Medieval France*, pp. 318–19 and 223–4; P. Wolff, 'The Armagnacs in Southern France', *B.I.H.R.* 20 (1943–5), p. 187; E. Perroy, 'Feudalism or principalities in fifteenth-century France', ibid., pp. 183–4; Henneman, op. cit., p. 317; J. R. Strayer and C. H. Taylor, *Studies in Early French Taxation*, pp. 47–8 and 54, and Wolfe, op. cit., p. 321.

58 Hillgarth, op. cit., pp. 104–5 and 389–90; Dominguez Ortiz, *La sociedad española en el siglo XVIII*, pp. 301–2; his *The Golden Century of Spain*, pp. 155–6; and his *El regimen señorial y el reformismo borbonico*, pp. 11–12; Kamen, *The War of Succession in Spain*, p. 207; Ryder, op. cit., pp. 50–1; Mack Smith, op. cit., pp. 206 and 256; R. Villari, *La rivolta antispagnola a Napoli*, pp. 280–1; *N.C.M.H.* IV, pp. 48–51 (Cooper), and Colletta, op. cit., II, pp. 36–7.

59 *The Marcher Lordships of South Wales*, ed. T. B. Pugh, pp. 145 and 148; *Sweden's Age of Greatness*, ed. Roberts, pp. 86–8 and 106–7; A. Silbert, *Le Portugal méditérranéen à la fin de l'ancien régime*, I, pp. 143–5, and de Oliveira Marques, op. cit., p. 86.

60 G. Fourquin, *Lordship and Feudalism in the Middle Ages*, p. 123; G. Duby, *Rural Economy and Country Life in the Medieval West*, pp. 225–6; Király, op. cit., p. 65; Wolfe, op. cit., p. 51; C. Stephenson, *Medieval Institutions*, pp. 61, 67–8, 97–8 and 120–1; J. Q. C. Mackrell, *The Attack on 'Feudalism' in Eighteenth-Century France*, pp. 4 and 49 and Silbert, op. cit., I, p. 145.

61 Duby, op. cit., pp. 224 ff.

62 France: Henneman, op. cit., ch. 4; Sweden: G. Ohlin, 'Entrepreneurial activities of the Swedish aristocracy', *Explorations in Entrepreneurial History*, 6 (1953), p. 156; Bohemia: Kerner, op. cit., pp. 240 and 267–8; Denmark: Hovde, op. cit., p. 285; Russia: Blum, 'Russia', in *European Landed Elites in the Nineteenth Century*, ed. Spring, pp. 79–80.

63 Poland: Hoensch, op. cit., pp. 55 and 57; Miller, op. cit., p. 97, and Wolowski, op. cit., p. 42; Venice: Georgelin, op. cit., p. 536; Austria: Bérenger, op. cit., p. 334; Macartney, *The Habsburg Empire*, p. 51 and n. 3, and B. Waldstein-

Wartenberg, 'Osterreichisches Adelsrecht, 1804–1918', *Mitteilungen des österreichisches Staatsarchivs*, 17–18 (1964–5), p. 141; Silesia and West Prussia: *The Historical Essays of Otto Hintze* (Gilbert), p. 47; Hesse and Saxony: Carsten, *Princes and Parliaments in Germany*, pp. 184, 209 and 221.

64   See chapter VII.

65   Carsten, op. cit., pp. 193–4 and 426; Stephenson, op. cit., pp. 112 and 120, and Carsten, *The Origins of Prussia*, pp. 39, 95 and 98.

66   See chapter IV.

67   For Sweden, see n. 19; for Poland, see n. 63.

68   For a fuller elaboration and referencing of this section, see chapter IV (2).

69   A. S. Turberville, op. cit., pp. 188–9.

70   France: Henneman, op. cit., p. 317; the Habsburg territories: H. Feigl, *Die Niederösterreichische Grundherrschaft*, p. 100, Bérenger, op. cit., pp. 322 and 327–8, and E. M. Link, *The Emancipation of the Austrian Peasant, 1740–1798*, p. 40; Prussia: Goodwin, 'Prussia', in *The European Nobility in the Eighteenth Century*, ed Goodwin, p. 94; Russia: R. E. Jones, *The Emancipation of the Russian Nobility*, p. 20; Blum, *Lord and Peasant in Russia*, pp. 234–5; Denmark: Jeannin, op. cit., p. 134; Poland: Hoensch, op. cit., p. 58.

71   Turberville, op. cit., pp. 189–90; Miller, 'Subsidy assessments of the peerage ...', op. cit., p. 16; Schofield, op. cit., pp. 213 and 232; Mack Smith, op. cit., pp. 131, 190 and 318, and Blum, 'Russia', in *European Landed Elites in the Nineteenth Century*, ed. Spring, p. 76.

72   Iberian peninsula: Ladero Quesada, op. cit., p. 780, and O'Callaghan, op cit., p. 288; France: Meuvret, op. cit., pp. 199–200, and Lewis, op. cit., pp. 104–7 and 175; Brandenburg: originally confined to a demesne of no more than six *Hufen* but, in the following centuries, applied irrespective of demesne size (W. Görlitz, *Die Junker*, p. 25, and Carsten, *Origins of Prussia*, pp. 24–5 and 77); Hungary: Macartney, 'Hungary', in *The European Nobility in the Eighteenth Century*, ed. Goodwin, p. 20, and Blum, *Noble Landowners and Agriculture in Austria, 1815–1848*, pp. 34–5; Sweden: Roberts, *Gustavus Adolphus*, II, p. 53, and *The Early Vasas*, p. 37; Austria: Adler, op. cit., pp. 9, 15 and 42–3; Poland: Hoensch, op. cit., p. 58; Bavaria: Carsten, *Princes and Parliaments in Germany*, p. 364; Northern Italy: Herlihy, op. cit., pp. 71–7.

73   Wolfe, op. cit., p. 1, and Stephenson, op. cit., pp. 99–100.

74   Carsten, *The Origins of Prussia*, pp. 247–9; Jeannin, op. cit., pp. 127 and 133.

75   Carsten, op. cit., p. 170 (Brandenburg); Carsten, *Princes and Parliaments in Germany*, pp. 373 (Bavaria), 294 (Jülich and Berg) and 253 (Saxony); Hoensch, op. cit., pp. 57 and 59 (Poland).

76   See n. 6; Bérenger, op. cit., pp. 321–3.

77   Sicily and Naples: Ryder, op. cit., pp. 9–10, 210 and 259–60; Brandenburg and Pomerania: Carsten, *Princes and Parliaments in Germany*, p. 221, and Martiny, op. cit., pp. 25–6; France: see n. 30.

78   Spain: *Diccionario de historia de España*, I, p. 611, and O'Callaghan, op. cit., p. 178; Sweden: Roberts, *The Early Vasas*, p. 35; Hungary: Király, op. cit., pp. 34–5; Portugal: Livermore, op. cit., p. 68.

79   Beeler, op. cit., p. 41; Wolfe, op. cit., p. 1; Stephenson, op. cit., pp. 98–9; Strayer and Taylor, op. cit., p. 9; Henneman, op. cit., pp. 19–20; G. Duby, *The Chivalrous Society*, pp. 92 and 105–8; K. Fowler, *Age of Plantagenet and Valois*, pp. 99–100.

80   Henneman, op. cit., p. 318; Strayer and Taylor, op. cit., pp. 77–8, 80 and 88–9,

and Russell Major, *Representative Government* . . ., p. 29.

81 Strayer, *On the Medieval Origins of the Modern State*, p. 43; Ryder, op. cit., pp. 9–10.

82 A. Lewis, *Knights and Samurai*, pp. 61–2 and his *The Development of Southern France and Catalan Society, 718–1050*, ch. 19 and conclusion; Henneman, op. cit., pp. 309–10.

83 Henneman, op. cit., p. 5; Frêche, op. cit., pp. 337–8, and Lewis, *Later Medieval France*, p. 262.

84 France: Beeler, op. cit., p. 41, and Deyon, op. cit., p. 235; England: Stephenson, op. cit., p. 120; Naples: Ryder, op. cit., p. 259; Sicily: Mack Smith, op. cit., p. 256; Saxony: Carsten, *Princes and Parliaments in Germany*, pp. 232 and 236; Spain: Kamen, *The War of the Succession in Spain*, p. 206; Brandenburg: Martiny, op. cit., p. 10.

85 See above, section (2).

86 See above, section (3).

87 See ibid.

88 Herlihy, op. cit., pp. 72–6, and Wolfe, op. cit., p. 47.

89 Bavaria: Carsten, *Princes and Parliaments in Germany*, pp. 364 and 418; Mark and Cleves: ibid., p. 272; Sweden and Norway: Jeannin, op. cit., p. 127 n. 2 and p. 131; Denmark: ibid., p. 133; Saxony: Carsten, op. cit., pp. 246 and 252; Aragon: Herr, op. cit., p. 129, and Kamen, op. cit., pp. 359–60; Bohemia: Kerner, op. cit., pp. 239–40; Poland: Hoensch, op. cit., p. 58; Lombardy: Zanetti, op. cit., p. 747; Prussia: Hintze, op. cit., p. 47, and Goodwin, 'Prussia', in *European Nobility in the Eighteenth Century*, ed. Goodwin, p. 87; Hungary: Király, op. cit., p. 70; Galicia: Wandycz, op. cit., p. 12.

90 See chapter IV (2).

91 Italy: B. S. Pullan, *A History of Early Renaissance Italy*, p. 123, and Herlihy, op. cit., pp. 76–7; Spain: O'Callaghan, op. cit., p. 612; the Netherlands: H. G. Koenigsberger, 'The States General of the Netherlands before the Revolt', *Xth International Congress of Historical Sciences*, Rome (1955), p. 151; Germany: Carsten, *The Origins of Prussia*, pp. 170 and 235, and his *Princes and Parliaments in Germany*, pp. 219 ff, 281–2 and 396; Sweden: Roberts, *Gustavus Adolphus*, II, pp. 150–3, and *Sweden's Age of Greatness*, ed. Roberts, p. 251; Dauphiné: E. Le Roy Ladurie, *Carnival, a People's Uprising at Romans*, pp. 38 and 46–7, and Russell Major, *Representative Government* . . ., pp. 78–80 and 325–7.

92 Poland: S. Kieniewicz, *The Emancipation of the Polish Peasantry*, ch. 1; Hungary: Macartney, *The Habsburg Empire*, pp. 279–81, 315–18 and 337–8.

93 Prussia: *The Historical Essays of Otto Hintze* (Gilbert), p. 59; Sweden: Verney, op. cit., p. 102; Russia: Blum, *Lord and Peasant in Russia*, p. 464; for houses of lords, see ch. IV (2).

94 England: J. Z. Titow, *English Rural Society*, p. 63; A. Fletcher, *A County Community in Peace and War*, pp. 202–5; L. Stone, *The Crisis of the Aristocracy*, p. 54; J. T. Cliffe, *The Yorkshire Gentry from Reformation to Civil War*, p. 142, and W. R. Ward, *The Land Tax in the Eighteenth Century*, ch. 7; East Prussia: Goodwin, 'Prussia', in *European Nobility in the Eighteenth Century*, ed. Goodwin, p. 86; Spain: G. Brenan, *The Spanish Labyrinth*, p. 9.

95 Behrens, op. cit., pp. 451 and 463–4; R. Forster, *The Nobility of Toulouse in the Eighteenth Century*, p. 39; G. E. Mingay, *English Landed Society in the Eighteenth Century*, pp. 81–3; Ward, op. cit., ch. 7, and P. Mathias and P.

O'Brien, 'Taxation in Britain and France 1715-1810 . . .', *Journal of European Economic History*, 5 (1976), pp. 611 ff.

96 Behrens, op. cit., pp. 461-2, and Wolfe, op. cit., pp. 58 and 318. A reversal of its importance only occurred transiently in the late seventeenth century, a consequence of the schemes of Colbert and of the public disorder created by direct taxation in the early seventeenth century (Bonney, op. cit., pp. 424-5 and 433). Also see Meuvret, op. cit., pp. 199-201 and 215-16, and Mathias and O'Brien, op cit., pp. 625-8.

97 Regular direct taxation was widespread in the German territories at the close of the twelfth century, but, in the thirteenth and fourteenth centuries, freedom from it was extensively purchased (Stephenson, op. cit., p. 112, and Carsten, *Origins of Prussia*, pp. 39, 95 and 98). Exceptional instances of direct taxation serving as a source of ordinary supply in 1400 are to be found in Sweden (*Sweden's Age of Greatness*, ed. Roberts, p. 79) and Poland (Wolowski, op. cit., p. 42) and Castile, where the *moneda* was regularly exacted every seven years (see n. 12). For the development of regular taxation after 1400 see Mackay, op. cit., p. 146; Henneman, op. cit., pp. 4-5, and Wolfe, op. cit., chs. 1 and 2; Rosenberg, op. cit., pp. 35-6, and Carsten, *Princes and Parliaments in Germany*, pp. 184 and 232; and Bérenger, op. cit., pp. 320 ff.

98 C. M. de la Roncière, 'Indirect taxes or "gabelles" at Florence in the fourteenth century: the evolution of tariffs and problems of collection', in *Florentine Studies*, ed. N. Rubinstein, pp. 140-1; Mackay, op. cit., pp. 145-6; Livermore, op. cit., p. 133; Payne, op. cit., p. 130; Bérenger, op. cit., pp. 340-1; Carsten, *Princes and Parliaments in Germany*, pp. 168-9 and 225 ff; Carsten, *Origins of Prussia*, p. 218; and *N.C.M.H.* V, pp. 31-2 (Coleman).

99 Mackay, op. cit., p. 146; Kamen, *The War of the Succession in Spain*, ch. 9; J. Lynch, *Spain under the Habsburgs*, II, pp. 3-4 and 92; Defourneaux, op. cit., p. 98, and Herr, op. cit., p. 110.

100 See n. 15.

101 Koenigsberger, *The Government of Sicily under Philip II of Spain*, p. 125, and Mack Smith, op. cit., p. 130.

102 Hungary: Z. P. Pach, *Die ungarische Agrarentwicklung im 16-17 Jahrhundert*, pp. 21-2; German states: Carsten, *Origins of Prussia*, pp. 132-3 and 170, and *Princes and Parliaments in Germany*, pp. 364, 368-9, 373, 387 and 396; Holstein: H. Kellenbenz, 'German aristocratic entrepreneurship: economic activities of the Holstein nobility in the sixteenth and seventeenth centuries', *Explorations in Entrepreneurial History*, 6 (1953-4), p. 106; Sweden: Roberts, *Gustavus Adolphus*, II, p. 60; France: Matthews, op. cit., p. 152; Poland: Miller, op. cit., pp. 350-64.

103 *N.C.M.H.* III, p. 143 (Hurstfield); Meyer, *La Noblesse bretonne au XVIIIe siècle*, p. 780; Martiny, op. cit., p. 10; and see n. 29.

104 See chapter VI (1(i)).

105 See chapter IV (2(b)).

106 See chapter VI (1(e)).

107 See *N.C.M.H.* IV, p. 19 (Cooper); J. P. Cooper, 'Differences between English and continental governments in the early seventeenth century', *Britain and the Netherlands*, ed. J. S. Bromley and R. H. Kossmann, p. 85; A. Milward and S. B. Saul, *The Economic Development of Continental Europe*, pp. 45 and 99; H. Kamen, *The Iron Century*, pp. 150-1; and H. Hauser, 'The characteristic features of French economic history from the middle of the sixteenth to the

middle of the eighteenth century', *Econ. H.R.* 4 (1933), pp. 262–3.
108 J. Blum, *The End of the Old Order in Rural Europe*, pp. 77–8.
109 Hungary: Marczali, op. cit., pp. 319–20; Prussia: Otto Büsch, *Militärsystem und Sozialleben im Alten Preussen*, p. 5.
110 W. Doyle, *The Old European Order, 1660–1800*, p. 108; Blum, *Lord and Peasant in Russia*, pp. 234–5; Bérenger, op. cit., p. 322 and Meuvret, op. cit., p. 202; Hoensch, op. cit., p. 58.
111 Blum, *The End of the Old Order in Rural Europe*, pp. 72 and 77.
112 Lynch, op. cit., pp. 91–2, 141–2 and 144. For the incidence of noble exemption see A. Molinie-Bertrand, 'Les 'hidalgos' dans le royaume de Castille à la fin du XVIe siecle', *Revue d'histoire economique et sociale*, 52 (1) (1974). In 1591 10% of the population of Castile was noble (p. 62), with areas of remarkable noble density such as Asturias, where 75·9% of the population was noble (p. 66) and in Burgos and Leon where 46·5% of the population was noble (p. 62).
113 Herr, op. cit., pp. 128–30.
114 France: see n. 27; Spain: Dominguez Ortiz, *The Golden Century of Spain*, pp. 156–7; Naples: Villari, op. cit., pp. 189–91; Sicily: Koenigsberger, op. cit., pp. 137–8; Mack Smith, op. cit., pp. 157, 206–8, 220, 256 and 284, and F. Braudel, *The Mediterranean*, pp. 731–2.
115 For the 'noble bent' of the bourgeoisie, see Braudel, op. cit., ch. 5 (I and II); Kamen, *The Iron Century*, ch. 5; Doyle, op. cit., pp. 146–7; J. H. Hexter, 'The myth of the middle class in Tudor England', in *Reappraisals in History*, ch. 5; L. Stone, 'Social mobility in England, 1500–1700', *Past and Present*, 33 (1966); D. C. Coleman, 'Gentlemen and players', *Econ. H.R.*, 2nd ser., 26 (1973); G. V. Taylor, 'Non-capitalist wealth and the French Revolution', *A.H.R.* 72 (2) (1967); E. G. Barber, *The Bourgeoisie in Eighteenth-Century France*, chs. 4 and 5; T. Zeldin, *France 1848–1945*, I, ch. 1; Macartney, *The Habsburg Empire*, pp. 59–60, 301 ff and 711–12; Marczali, op. cit., p. 156; Mack Smith, op. cit., pp. 427–8 and 478–9; E. Sagarra, *A Social History of Germany*, ch. 13; J. J. Sheehan, 'Conflict and cohesion among German elites in the nineteenth century', *Imperial Germany*, ed. Sheehan, and A. János, 'The Decline of Oligarchy . . .', in *Revolution in Perspective*, ed. János and W. B. Slottmann, pp. 33–4.
116 F. Redlich, 'European aristocracy and economic development', in *Steeped in Two Cultures*, by Redlich, pt. II (2); Kamen, *The Iron Century*, ch. 4; R. Pike, *Aristocrats and Traders; Sevillian Society in the Sixteenth Century*, ch. 2, and Dominguez Ortiz, *La sociedad española en el siglo XVII*, I, p. 226, and W. J. Callahan, *Honour, Commerce and Industry in Eighteenth-Century Spain*, pp. 16–20; Stone, *The Crisis of the Aristocracy*, ch. 7.
117 M. Malowist, 'The problem of the inequality of economic development in Europe in the later middle ages', *Econ. H. R.*, 2nd ser., 19 (1966), pp. 23–8; Malowist, 'Poland, Russia and western trade in the fifteenth and sixteenth centuries', *Past and Present*, 13 (1958), p. 30; Malowist, 'The economic and social development of the Baltic countries from the fifteenth to the seventeenth centuries', *Econ. H.R.*, 2nd ser., 12 (1959), pp. 180–8; E. Wallerstein, *The Modern World System*, pp. 159–60 and 321–3; *N.C.M.H.* III, pp. 380–1 (Skwarczyński); J. Topolski, 'Economic decline in Poland from the sixteenth to the eighteenth century', in *Essays in European Economic History, 1500–1800*, ed. P. Earle, pp. 137–9.
118 See R. Mousnier, 'Research into the popular uprisings before the Fronde', in *France in Crisis*, ed. P. J. Coveney, pp. 145 ff.

119 Ward, op. cit., ch. 1.
120 See ch. IV (2).
121 The relationship is studied generally by Anderson in *Lineages of the Absolutist State*, Blum, *The End of the Old Order in Rural Europe*, ch. 10, and Wallerstein, op. cit., pp. 157 ff. For particular studies, see Carsten's *Origins of Prussia* and his *Princes and Parliaments in Germany*, Jones's *Emancipation of the Russian Nobility* and Deyon's essay 'The French nobility and absolute monarchy in the first half of the seventeenth century', in *France in Crisis, 1620–1675*, ed. P. J. Coveney.
122 Carsten, *Origins of Prussia*, pp. 247–8, and *Princes and Parliaments in Germany*, pp. 308–9.
123 Both the consent and assessment rights were taken away in the late seventeenth century (see above, pp. 45 and 46).

Chapter III. Judicial, service and seigneurial indemnities

1 M. Raeff, 'Imperial Russia: Peter I to Nicholas I', in *An introduction to Russian History*, ed. R. Auty and D. Obolensky, p. 169; B. K. Király, *Hungary in the late Eighteenth Century*, p. 219.
2 H. Koenigsberger, *The Government of Sicily under Philip II of Spain*, p. 118; D. Mack Smith, *A History of Sicily*, pp. 295–6.
3 M. Bloch, *Feudal Society*, pp. 283–4; J. Miller, *The Nobility in Polish Renaissance Society*, p. 51.
4 J. N. Hillgarth, *The Spanish Kingdoms*, p. 63; G. V. Vernadsky, *Russia at the Dawn of the Modern Age*, p. 198, and J. C. Lassiter, 'Defamation of peers: the rise and decline of the action of *scandalum magnatum*, 1497–1773', *American Journal of Legal History*, 22 (1978).
5 R. Baldick, *The Duel*, p. 78; Lassiter, op. cit., p. 222.
6 R. F. Leslie, *Polish Politics and the Revolution of November 1830*, p. 55, and Vernadsky, op. cit., p. 198.
7 C. Loyseau, *Traicte des Ordres*, p. 58, and A. Dominguez Ortiz, *The Golden Century of Spain*, p. 116.
8 H. V. Livermore, *A New History of Portugal*, p. 230.
9 P. Dukes, *Catherine the Great and the Russian Nobility*, p. 6.
10 J.-P. Labatut, *Les noblesses européennes*, p. 36; Loyseau, op. cit., p. 58, and Dominguez Ortiz, op. cit., p. 116.
11 Spain: J. M. Elliott, *The Revolt of the Catalans*, p. 101, and A. Dominguez Ortiz, *La sociedad española en el siglo XVII*, p. 180; Denmark: J. H. S. Birch, *Denmark in History*, p. 239; England: M. Graves, 'Freedom of peers from arrest: the case of Henry second Lord Cromwell, 1571–72', *American Journal of Legal History*, 21 (1977).
12 R. J. Kerner, *Bohemia in the Eighteenth Century*, p. 168.
13 Dominguez Ortiz, op. cit., p. 180.
14 A. Dominguez Ortiz, *La sociedad española en el siglo XVIII*, p. 118, and J. P. Cooper, 'Patterns of inheritance and settlement by great landowners from the fifteenth to the eighteenth centuries', in *Family and Inheritance*, ed. J. Goody and others, p. 250.
15 M. Roberts, *Gustavus Adolphus*, II, p. 156.
16 Loyseau, op. cit., p. 58.
17 Baldick, op. cit., pp. 12–31, 54–68 and 151.

18 France: M. Marion, *Dictionnaire des institutions de la France aux XVIIe et XVIIIe siècles*, p. 397; F. L. Ford, *Robe and Sword*, p. 28, and P. Goubert, *The Ancien Régime*, pp. 162 f; Spain: J. H. Elliott, *Imperial Spain*, p. 104, and his *Revolt of the Catalans*, p. 101; Prussia; H. Rosenberg, *Bureaucracy, Aristocracy and Autocracy*, p. 101; Bohemia-Austria: B. Waldstein-Wartenberg, 'Österreichisches Adelsrecht, 1804–1918', *Mitteilungen des österreichisches Staatsarchivs*, 17–18 (1964–5), p. 140.

19 R. Boutruche, *Seigneurie et féodalité*, II, pp. 185–6.

20 G. Fourquin, *Lordship and Feudalism in the Middle Ages*, pp. 109–10; J. F. O'Callaghan, *A History of Medieval Spain*, p. 469, and Elliott, *Imperial Spain*, p. 104; C. A. Macartney, *The Habsburg Empire*, p. 126.

21 Boutruche, op. cit., II, p. 308.

22 Brandenburg: F. L. Carsten, *The Origins of Prussia*, pp. 82–3 and 97–100; Saxony: Bloch, op. cit., p. 372, and F. L. Carsten, *Princes and Parliaments in Germany*, p. 194.

23 F. B. Palmer, *Peerage Law in England*, pp. 146–9; L. G. Pine, *The Genealogist's Encyclopedia*, p. 249, and M. L. Bush, *The Government Policy of Protector Somerset*, pp. 132–3.

24 Roberts, op. cit., I, pp. 333–4, and II, p. 156; I. Andersson, *A History of Sweden*, p. 293, and M. Roberts, *Essays in Swedish History*, p. 41.

25 *N.C.M.H.* IV, pp. 19 (Cooper), and 586 (Jablonowski).

26 Hungary: J. Blum, *Noble Landowners and Agriculture in Austria*, p. 35; Király, op. cit., pp. 89–90, and A. János, 'The decline of oligarchy', in *Revolution in Perspective*, ed. A. János and W. B. Slottmann, p. 16; Bohemia-Austria: Macartney, op. cit., p. 51 and 126, and Kerner, op. cit., pp. 49–50 and 172–5.

27 R. E. Jones, *The Emancipation of the Russian Nobility*, pp. 227, 278 and 285.

28 Bohemia-Austria: Macartney, op. cit., p. 51; England: Graves, op. cit., p. 1; Palmer, op. cit., pp. 150 and 152, and L. Stone, *The Crisis of the Aristocracy*, p. 54; Spain, see n. 10.

29 J. Bardach, 'Gouvernants et gouvernés en Pologne au moyen-âge et aux temps modernes', *Recueils de la Société Jean Bodin*, 25 (4) (1965), p. 262, and A. Zajaczkowski, 'En Pologne: cadres structurels de la noblesse', *Annales d'histoire E.S.*, 18 (1) (1963), p. 89; Blum, op. cit., p. 35, and H. Marczali, *Hungary in the Eighteenth Century*, pp. 174–5.

30 Poland: nn. 6, 25 and 29; Hungary: nn. 26 and 29; England: nn. 11 and 23; France and Spain: nn. 7, 11 and 18.

31 In 1296 Sicily acquired a court of twelve nobles and 'prudent men' nominated by parliament to judge the criminal cases of feudatories and vassals (A. Marongiu, *Medieval Parliaments: a Comparative Study*, p. 116), but it had gone by the late sixteenth century (Koenigsberger, op. cit., p. 118) and was not replaced by any other procedural privilege. For non-noble judicial privileges in Sicily see Mack Smith, op. cit., pp. 164 and 258–9.

32 G. Duby, *Rural Economy and Country Life in the Medieval West*, p. 188; G. Duby, *The Chivalrous Society*, pp. 36, 39, 42 and 56–7; Carsten, *The Origins of Prussia*, pp. 97–100; Bloch, op. cit., pp. 328 and 368–70, and E. Warlop, *The Flemish Nobility*, pp. 324–5.

33 L. Genicot, 'Recent research on the medieval nobility', in *The Medieval Nobility*, ed. T. Reuter, and Duby, *The Chivalrous Society*, pp. 95 ff.

34 Fourquin, op. cit., pp. 109–10.

35 See nn. 9 and 27 and Jones, op. cit., pp. 196–7.

36 See nn. 20, 24 and 26.
37 P. du Puy de Clinchamps, *La noblesse*, pp. 67–70; Rosenberg, op. cit., p. 211; Waldstein-Wartenberg, op. cit., p. 140; J. Blum, 'Russia', in *European Landed Elites in the Nineteenth Century*, ed. Spring, pp. 79–80, and Pine, op. cit., p. 257.
38 P. S. Wandycz, *The Lands of Partitioned Poland*, p. 8; Blum, op. cit., p. 79, and Palmer, op. cit., p. 145.
39 The extent of this privilege seems somewhat exaggerated by Doyle and Blum (J. Blum, *The End of the Old Order in Rural Europe*, p. 67, and W. Doyle, *The Old European Order*, p. 110). France: ibid. and Blum, op. cit., pp. 67–8; Scandinavia: B. J. Hovde, *The Scandinavian Countries*, pp. 284 and 551.
40 Stone, op. cit., p. 54, and Palmer, op. cit., p. 151.
41 Russia: Jones, op. cit., p. 283; Hungary: Blum, *Noble Landowners and Agriculture in Austria, p. 35; Marczali, Hungary in the Eighteenth Century*, p. 169; France: Loyseau, op. cit., pp. 57–8; Spain: Dominguez Ortiz, *La sociedad española en el siglo XVIII*, p. 118; Prussia: Carsten, *The Origins of Prussia*, p. 227.
42 General: Blum, *End of the Old Order* ..., pp. 69–70; Bohemia-Austria: Blum, *Noble Landowners* ..., p. 23, and Waldstein-Wartenberg, op. cit., p. 140; Spain: I. A. A. Thompson, *War and Government in Habsburg Spain*, pp. 142 and 146; Russia: Blum, op. cit., in *European Landed Elites in the Nineteenth Century* (ed. Spring), pp. 75 and 79; Sweden: see n. 45; Denmark: Blum, *End of the Old Order* ..., p. 219; France: Doyle, op. cit., p. 111, and Ford, op. cit., p. 28; England: Stone, op. cit., p. 54.
43 Macartney, op. cit., p. 15; Marczali op. cit., pp. 130 and 355; Blum, *Noble Landowners* ..., p. 35.
44 Fourquin, op. cit., pp. 122–3; E. Lourie, 'A society organised for war: medieval Spain', *Past and Present*, 35 (1966), p. 60; M. Roberts, *The Early Vasas*, p. 244, and his *Gustavus Adolphus*, II, pp. 211–12.
45 Stone, op. cit., p. 54; Roberts, *The Early Vasas*, p. 244.
46 L. Verriest, *Noblesse, chevalerie, lignages*, ch. XI; Marion, op. cit., p. 397, and Király, op. cit., p. 219.
47 Duby, *The Chivalrous Society*, pp. 57, 127, 168 and 178; Duby, *Rural Economy* ..., pp. 188–91.
48 See vol. II.
49 Goubert, op. cit., pp. 162 f, and Rosenberg, op. cit., p. 101.
50 Hillgarth, op. cit., p. 65; Lourie, op. cit., pp. 56–7; Genicot (Reuter), p. 28, and Duby, *The Chivalrous Society*, p. 170.
51 Blum, *Noble Landowners* ..., p. 39.
52 Wandycz, op. cit., p. 8, and W. J. Callahan, *Honour, Commerce and Industry in Eighteenth-Century Spain*, pp. 48–9.
53 B. Behrens, 'Nobles, privileges and taxes in France at the end of the ancien régime', *Econ. H.R.*, 2nd ser., 15 (1963), p. 453; G. Lefebvre, 'Urban society in the Orléanais in the late eighteenth century', *Past and Present*, 19 (1961), p. 47.
54 Callahan, op. cit., pp. 48–9.
55 Macartney, op. cit., p. 50 n. 1.
56 Király, op. cit., p. 219.
57 Duby, *The Chivalrous Society*, pp. 57, 106–7 and 170.

Chapter IV. *Rights of political participation*

1 See below, pp. 84–5.
2 N.C.M.H. V, p. 524 (Rosén); J. H. S. Birch, *Denmark in History*, pp. 240 and 296–7, and E. Ekman, 'The Danish Royal Law of 1665', *Journal of Modern History*, 29 (1957), p. 103.
3 V. R. Gruder, *The Royal Provincial Intendants*, p. 122; P. Contamine, 'The French nobility and the war', in *The Hundred Years' War*, ed. K. Fowler, p. 143; P. du Puys de Clinchamps, *La noblesse*, p. 26.
4 P. Goubert, *The Ancien Régime*, pp. 181–4; F. L. Ford, *Robe and Sword*, pp. 63–4; Gruder, op. cit., pp. 119–25, and Du Puys de Clinchamps, op. cit., p. 25.
5 Ibid., p. 24; Gruder, op. cit., pp. 121–4, and J. Meyer, *La Noblesse bretonne au XVIIIe siècle*, pp. 428–9.
6 M. R. Raeff, *Origins of the Russian Intelligentsia*, pp. 38–9; J. Blum, *Lord and Peasant in Russia*, pp. 346–7, and R. Pipes, *Russia under the Old Regime*, pp. 123–4.
7 Raeff, op. cit., pp. 65 and 68, and Pipes, op. cit., pp. 90 and 125.
8 T. Emmons, *The Russian Landed Gentry and the Peasant Emancipation of 1861*, pp. 12–4; G. L. Yaney, *The Systematisation of Russian Government*, pp. 369–72; J. Blum, 'Russia', in *European Landed Elites in the Nineteenth Century*, ed. D. Spring, pp. 88–9, and J. Blum, *The End of the Old Order in Rural Europe*, p. 416.
9 M. Raeff, 'Imperial Russia: Peter I to Nicholas I' in *An Introduction to Russian History*, ed. R. Auty and D. Obolensky, p. 167; Raeff, op. cit., ch. 3; Pipes, op. cit., p. 124, and Blum, *Lord and Peasant in Russia*, p. 346.
10 H. Seton-Watson, *The Russian Empire*, p. 106; J. Hassell, 'Implementation of the Russian table of ranks during the eighteenth century', *Slavic Review*, 29 (1970), pp. 288–9 and 293.
11 P. Dukes, *Catherine the Great and the Russian Nobility*, p. 159, and Hassell, op. cit., pp. 292–3.
12 Seton-Watson, op. cit., pp. 106 and 112; J. Keep, 'Imperial Russia: Alexander II to the Revolution', in *An Introduction to Russian History*, ed. Auty, p. 231, and P. Anderson, *Lineages of the Absolutist State*, p. 346.
13 Hassell, op. cit., pp. 286–7.
14 C. Lucas, 'Nobles, bourgeois and the origins of the French Revolution', *Past and Present*, 60 (1973), pp. 102, 105–6, 110 and 116; Meyer, op. cit., p. 931, and Goubert, op. cit., pp. 163–4.
15 Prussia: Lamar Cecil, 'The creation of nobles in Prussia, 1871–1918', *A.H.R.*, 75 (1969–70), p. 794, and H. Rosenberg, *Bureaucracy, Aristocracy, Autocracy*, pp. 140–1; Austria: B. Waldstein-Wartenberg, 'Österreichisches Adelsrecht, 1804–1918', in *Mitteilungen des österreichisches Staatsarchivs*, 17–18 (1964–5), pp. 127–8.
16 L. W. Muncy, *The Junker in the Prussian Administration under William II, 1888–1914*, p. 21, and Rosenberg, op. cit., pp. 105–6, 144–5, 160 and 163–4.
17 C. A. Macartney, *The Habsburg Empire*, p. 54; H. Hochenegg, *Der Adel in Leben Tirols*, p. 15; S. Adler, *Das adelige Landrecht in Nieder- und Oberösterreich und die Gerichtsreformen des XVIII. Jahrhunderts*, p. 42, and see below, p. 89.
18 Rosenberg, op. cit., pp. 211–12 and 218.
19 See n. 39.

20 Cecil, op. cit., p. 794. For Austria, figures which separate nobles-born from commoners and elevated nobles show 57% of the posts in the administration held by the noble-born. A sharp contrast existed in the army, where only 6% of officers were of noble extraction. See N. von Preradovich, *Die Führungsschichten in Österreich und Preussen*, p. 66 and passim.

21 M. Roberts, 'Sweden', in *The European Nobility in the Eighteenth Century*, ed. A. Goodwin, p. 150; H. Kamen, *The War of Succession in Spain, 1700-15*, pp. 93-4, and W. Doyle, *The Old European Order*, p. 247.

22 See ch. V (2).

23 Russia: Pipes, op. cit., p. 106; Bohemia: R. J. Kerner, *Bohemia in the Eighteenth Century*, pp. 154-5; Sweden: B. J. Hovde, *The Scandinavian Countries*, p. 209; Denmark: A. R. Myers, *Parliaments and Estates in Europe to 1789*, p. 113, and Ekman, op. cit., p. 103.

24 See n. 37.

25 See above, pp. 80 and 84.

26 A. Zajaczkowski, 'En Pologne: cadres structurels de la noblesse', *Annales d'histoire E. S.*, 18 (1963), p. 89; P. S. Wandycz, *The Lands of Partitioned Poland, 1795-1918*, p. 8.

27 Macartney, *The Habsburg Empire*, p. 291; H. Marczali, *Hungary in the Eighteenth Century*, p. 158, and B. K. Király, *Hungary in the late Eighteenth Century*, pp. 208-9.

28 F. L. Carsten, *The Origins of Prussia*, pp. 168-9 and 205.

29 Ibid., pp. 166-7 and 169.

30 Kerner, op. cit., pp. 9, 61-2 and 154-5.

31 M. Roberts, *Essays in Swedish History*, p. 30, and Roberts, *Gustavus Adolphus*, I, pp. 255-6, and II, p. 163.

32 Roberts, *Essays in Swedish History*, p. 30; Roberts, 'Sweden', in *The European Nobility in the Eighteenth Century*, ed. Goodwin, pp. 147 and 150-1; Hovde, op. cit., pp. 193 and 209-10, and D. V. Verney, *Parliamentary Reform in Sweden*, p. 16.

33 A. Dominguez Ortiz, *La sociedad española en el siglo XVII*, I, p. 196; Sicily: H. J. Koenigsberger, *The Government of Sicily under Philip II of Spain*, pp. 106-7; D. Mack Smith, *A History of Sicily*, p. 292, and F. Braudel, *The Mediterranean*, p. 729.

34 Milan: D. E. Zanetti, 'The patriziato of Milan from the domination of Spain to the unification of Italy ...', *Social History*, 6 (1977), pp. 745-6, and J. Roberts, 'Lombardy', in *The European Nobility in the Eighteenth Century*, ed. Goodwin, pp. 64-5 and 75-6; Florence: R. B. Litchfield, 'Demographic characteristics of Florentine patrician families, sixteeenth to the nineteenth centuries', *Journal of Economic History*, 29 (1969), pp. 192-3; Genoa: A.-E. Sayous, 'Aristocratie et noblesse à Gênes', *Annales d'histoire E.S.*, 9 (1937), pp. 370, 372-3 and 375; Venice: J. C. Davis, *The Decline of the Venetian Nobility as a Ruling Class*, pp. 16-17 and 21-2.

35 Davis, op. cit., p. 19; Sayous, op. cit., p. 377; Roberts, op. cit., p. 64; Litchfield, op. cit., p. 194, and his article 'Les investissements commerciaux des patriciens florentins au XVIIIe siècle', *Annales d'histoire E.S.*, 24 (1969), pp. 687-8.

36 Davis, op. cit., pp. 23-4; Roberts, op. cit., pp. 64-5; Litchfield (*Annales*), pp. 686-8; Sayous, op. cit., pp. 375 and 379, and G. Martin, *The Red Shirt and the Cross of Savoy*, p. 32.

37 Genoa: Sayous, op. cit., pp. 379-80; Venice: Davis, op. cit., pp. 21-4; Lombardy:

Roberts, op. cit., pp. 64, 75-6 and 78-80, and Zanetti, op. cit., pp. 746-7; Tuscany: E. Cochrane, *Florence in the Forgotten Centuries*, pp. 172, 425-6 and 488, and Litchfield (*Journal of Economic History*), pp. 192-4.

38   Kamen, op. cit., pp. 92-3 and 383 (especially the offices of viceroy and governor); Dominguez Ortiz, op. cit., pp. 216-17, and W. J. Callahan, *Honour, Commerce and Industry in Eighteenth-Century Spain*, p. 7.

39   K. Richter, 'Die böhmischen Länder von 1471-1740' in K. Bosl (ed.), *Handbuch der Geschichte der böhmischen Länder*, II, p. 350; J. Blum, *Noble Landowners and Agriculture in Austria*, p. 22; E. Wangermann, *The Austrian Achievement*, p. 63. For the structure of the Austrian nobility, see Preradovich, op. cit., pp. 5-6, and Macartney, *The Habsburg Empire*, pp. 52-6.

40   R. Pipes, *Russia under the Old Regime*, pp. 90-2.

41   Goubert, op. cit., pp. 163-4; Lucas, op. cit., p. 102, and Meyer, op. cit., pp. 929 and 931.

42   Milan: Zanetti, op. cit., pp. 745-6, and Roberts, op. cit., pp. 62-5; Venice: Davis, op. cit., pp. 17-18 and 73, and Martin, op. cit., p. 30; Florence: Cochrane, op. cit., p. 205; Litchfield (*Annales*), p. 687, and Litchfield (*Journal of Economic History*), pp. 204-5 n. 22; Genoa: B. S. Pullan, *A History of Early Renaissance Italy*, p. 290.

43   O. H. Hufton, *Bayeux in the Late Eighteenth Century*, pp. 46-7 and 59; Gruder, op. cit., pp. 117-18 and 220-2, and R. B. Forster, *The Nobility of Toulouse in the Eighteenth Century*, p. 103.

44   Kerner, op. cit., pp. 154-5.

45   Roberts, *Essays in Swedish History*, pp. 16-17, 19 and 26-32; Hovde, op. cit., pp. 209-10.

46   P. Jeannin, *L'Europe du nord-quest et du nord aux XVIIe et XVIIIe siècles*, pp. 127-8 and 133; Ekman, op. cit., p. 103, and Myers, op. cit., pp. 113-14.

47   See nn. 36-7.

48   See nn. 38-9 and Blum, *Noble Landowners . . .*, pp. 31-2.

49   Wangermann, op. cit., p. 63; Rosenberg, op. cit., pp. 166-7; Muncy, op. cit., pp. 175-7, and Emmons, op. cit., pp. 12-14.

50   For French local estates, see R. Doucet, *Les institutions de la France au XVIe siècle*, I, pp. 340-1 and 353-6, and J. Russell Major, *Representative Government in Early Modern France*, pp. 59-60 and 108 ff.

51   Hungary: Macartney, *The Habsburg Empire*, p. 50; Poland: N.C.M.H. II, p. 465 (Betts); Brandenburg and Pomerania: Carsten, *Origins of Prussia*, p. 199; Hesse-Cassel: Carsten, *Princes and Parliaments in Germany*, p. 423; Bohemia: Bosl, op. cit., p. 345; Saxony: Carsten, *Princes and Parliaments in Germany*, p. 255; East Prussia: Carsten, *The Origins of Prussia*, p. 204, and *Princes and Parliaments in Germany*, p. 423.

52   Hungary: Király, op. cit., pp. 83 and 110-11; K. Górski, 'Les débuts de la représentation de la *communitas nobilium* dans les assemblées d'états de l'est européen', in *Anciens pays et assemblées d'états*, 47 (1968), p. 53, and G. Bonis, 'The Hungarian feudal diet', *Recueils de la Société Jean Bodin*, 25 (4), p. 294; Poland: Gorski, op. cit., pp. 40-2.

53   Bohemia: N.C.M.H. II, pp. 466 and 468 (Betts) and Bosl, op. cit., II, pp. 250-1; Normandy: Doucet, op. cit., pp. 342-3; Brandenburg: Carsten, *The Origins of Prussia*, p. 185; Hesse-Cassel and East Prussia: Carsten, *Princes and Parliaments*, p. 423; Saxony, ibid., p. 255; Southern Netherlands: J. Dhondt, 'Estates or powers: essays in the parliamentary history of the Southern Netherlands from

the 12th to the 18th centuries', *Ancien pays et assemblées d'états*, 69 (1977), p. 232.

54 Netherlands: R. Wellens, 'Les états généraux des Pays-Bas des origines à la fin du règne de Philippe le Beaux', *Ancien pays et assemblées d'états*, 64 (1974), pt II, ch. 2; France: Doucet, op. cit., pp. 316-17 and J. Russell Major, *Representative Institutions in Renaissance France*, p. 66.

55 Here the term estates parliament is conventionally used in contradistinction to the early folk assemblies of freemen or freeholders and to the democratic parliaments of the nineteenth and twentieth centuries in which the bulk of parliamentary members were elected by the enfranchised citizenry. In the estates parliaments the several orders of society were separately represented.

56 R. E. Jones, *The Emancipation of the Russian Nobility*, p. 283.

57 Blum, *Noble Landowners ...*, p. 25. This was generally true of the Austrian territories, although in Lower Austria, Styria and Carinthia non-landowning nobles could be admitted to membership of the noble chamber. For Bohemia: *N.C.M.H.* II, p. 468 (Betts), and Bosl, op. cit., p. 241.

58 Naples: B. Croce, *A History of the Kingdom of Naples*, p. 110, and A. F. C. Ryder, *The Kingdom of Naples under Alfonso the Magnanimous*, p. 125; Sicily: A. Marongiu, *Medieval Parliaments, a Comparative Study*, p. 164, and Koenigsberger, op. cit., pp. 150-1; Friuli: Marongiu, op. cit., pp. 186-7; Sardinia and Piedmont: ibid., pp. 139 and 202.

59 German states: Carsten, *Princes and Parliaments in Germany*, pp. 162, 268, 339 and 350-1; Low Countries: Dhondt, op. cit., p. 220, and J. Thielens, 'Les assemblées d'états du duché de Limbourg et des pays d'Outre-Meuse au XVIIe siècle', *Anciens pays et assemblées d'états*, 43 (1968), pp. 33-4; France: J. Richard, 'Les états bourguignons', ibid., 35 (1966), pp. 303 and 318-19; F. Dumont, 'La noblesse et les états particuliers français', *Etudes présentées à la commission internationale pour l'histoire des assemblées d'états*, XI (1950), pp. 153-4; Doucet, op. cit., pp. 344, and Russell Major, *Representative Government in early Modern France*, chs. 3-6.

60 Thielens, op. cit., pp. 33-4; Carsten, *Princes and Parliaments in Germany*, p. 255, and Russell Major, op. cit., p. 69.

61 Carsten, op. cit., p. 339; Richard, op. cit., p. 319, and Dumont, op. cit., p. 154; Thielens, op. cit., p. 33.

62 Languedoc: Russell Major, op. cit., p. 61; England: K. B. McFarlane, *The Nobility of Later Medieval England*, pp. 142-3, and P. A. Bromhead, *The House of Lords and Contemporary Politics*, pp. 6-9; Scotland: Rait, op. cit., p. 6, and F. Stacey, *The Government of Modern Britain*, p. 223; Hungary, Marczali, op. cit., p. 128.

63 Meyer, op. cit., ch. 4.

64 G. R. Elton, 'The body of the whole realm: parliament and representation in medieval and Tudor England', *Studies in Tudor and Stuart Politics and Government*, II, pp. 38-9.

65 Aragon: Marongiu, op. cit., pp. 66-75, and J. N. Hillgarth, *The Spanish Kingdoms, 1250-1516*, I, pp. 278-9; Sweden: Roberts, *Gustavus Adolphus*, I, pp. 294, and II, p. 159.

66 Sweden: Roberts, 'Sweden', in *The European Nobility in the Eighteenth Century*, ed. Goodwin, pp. 143-4, and D. Gerhard, 'Problems of representation and delegation in the eighteenth century', *Études presentées à la commission internationale pour l'histoire des assemblées d'états*, 27 (1963), p. 145; Valencia: A.

Dominguez Ortiz, *La sociedad española en el siglo XVIII*, p. 106; Poland: R. F. Leslie, *Polish Politics and the Revolution of November 1830*, p. 15; Hungary: Macartney, *The Habsburg Empire*, p. 57; Russia: T. Emmons, *The Russian Landed Gentry and the Peasant Emancipation of 1861*, p. 14, and Yaney, op. cit., p. 70-1. In Poland there emerged the rule of *scartabellat* in the seventeenth and eighteenth centuries, which denied a noble family some of the noble privileges until it was at least three generations old (J. K. Hoensch, *Sozialverfassung und Politische Reform*, p. 68).

67   Sweden: Verney, op. cit., pp. 24–5; Hungary: Blum, op. cit., pp. 37–8; Austria: ibid., p. 25; Aragon: Hillgarth, pp. 278–9; East Prussia: Carsten, *The Origins of Prussia*, pp. 204–5; Saxony: Carsten, *Princes and Parliaments in Germany*, p. 255; Bohemia: Bosl, op. cit., p. 249; Poland: *N.C.M.H.* II, pp. 467–8 (Betts); Sicily: Marongiu, op. cit., p. 164; Naples: ibid., pp. 151 and 155.

68   Normandy: Doucet, op. cit., p. 342; Saxony: Carsten, *Princes and Parliaments in Germany*, p. 255, and Hungary: see n. 52.

69   Thanks to rights conferred by landownership, as with the Prussian *Cölmer* (Carsten, *The Origins of Prussia*, p. 204), the commoner fief holders of Saxony (Carsten, *Princes and Parliaments in Germany*, p. 255) and the Swedish freeholders (Roberts, *Gustavus Adolphus*, I, pp. 324–5).

70   Rait, op. cit., pp. 5–6 and 195 ff.

71   See ch. VII; Richard, op. cit., p. 319, and Dumont, op. cit., p. 154.

72   E.g. Saxony (Carsten, *Princes and Parliaments in Germany*, p. 255), Prussia after 1807 (see chapter VII) and parts of France (Du Puys de Clinchamps, op. cit., p. 22).

73   Roberts, op. cit., p. 292–3.

74   Blum, op. cit., p. 38.

75   Hillgarth, p. 278, and Dominguez Ortiz, op. cit., p. 104.

76   For Sweden, see n. 73; for Hungary, see below, p. 114.

77   See below, pp. 118-19.

78   See below, pp. 114-16.

79   See below, pp. 116-17.

80   See below, p. 117-18.

81   See below, pp. 100-2.

82   Russia: Pipes, *Russia under the Old Regime*, p. 183, and Seton-Watson, *The Russian Empire*, pp. 18 and 351; Bohemia: Bosl, op. cit., II, p. 345; France: Russell Major, *Representative Government in Early Modern France*, ch. 4 (2) and p. 470.

83   Austrian and Prussian Poland: Wandycz, *The Lands of Partitioned Poland*, p. 12; Russian Poland: Blum, 'Russia', in *European Landed Elites in the Nineteenth Century*, ed. D. Spring, n. 12; Germany: R. M. Berdahl, 'Conservative politics and aristocratic landholders in Bismarckian Germany', *Journal of Modern History*, 44 (1972), pp. 9–10; Hungary: Macartney, op. cit., pp. 337–8; Russia: Blum, op. cit., p. 79, and J. L. Keep, *The Russian Revolution*, p. 266.

84   Doucet, op. cit., pp. 340–1; Russell Major, op. cit., pp. 108 ff; E. M. Link, *The Emancipation of the Austrian Peasant*, pp. 42–3, and Bosl, op. cit., II, p. 252.

85   Dumont, op. cit., pp. 148–52; Marongiu, op. cit., pt I (1) and pp. 52–3, and K. Górski, 'The origins of the Polish sejm', *Slavonic and East European Review*, 45 (1966), pp. 122–3.

86   M. Szeftel, 'La participation des assemblées populaires dans le gouvernement central de la Russie', *Receuils de la Société Jean Bodin*, 25 (4) (1965), pp. 346-62;

and see n. 82.
87   Carsten, *Princes and Parliaments in Germany*, p. 423.
88   A. R. Myers, *Parliaments and Estates in Europe to 1789*, p. 92; Blum, *Noble Landowners* ..., p. 25, and Russell Major, *Representative Government* ..., p. 134.
89   Hillgarth, op. cit., pp. 304–5; Myers, op. cit., p. 98, and Dhondt, op. cit., p. 231.
90   Morongiu, op. cit., pp. 172 n. 30 and 211.
91   See below, p. 117 (committee privileges) and pp. 114 and 115–16 (special voting rights).
92   See below, pp. 116–17.
93   M. Wolfe, *The Fiscal System of Renaissance France*, p. 42.
94   Bavaria: Carsten, *Princes and Parliaments in Germany*, pp. 411–15; Portugal: A. H. de Oliveira Marques, *History of Portugal*, p. 393; Naples: Croce, op. cit., p. 64; France: D. Ligou, 'Quelques recherches sur les états dans la royaume de France à l'époque moderne', *Anciens pays et assemblées d'états*, 70 (1977), pp. 438 and 440; R. Bonney, *Political Change under Richelieu and Mazarin*, p. 351, and Russell Major, op. cit., pp. 660–6.
95   Blum, *Noble Landowners* ..., pp. 23–4; Macartney, op. cit., pp. 27–9, and R. J. W. Evans, *The Making of the Habsburg Monarchy*, pp. 166–7 and 213.
96   Myers, op. cit., p. 104
97   Carsten, *The Origins of Prussia*, p. 199.
98   Carsten, *Princes and Parliaments in Germany*, p. 415.
99   Austrian Poland: Wandycz, op. cit., pp. 12, 72 and 215, and Waldstein-Wartenburg, op. cit., pp. 112–13; Prussian Poland: Wandycz, op. cit., p. 68; Russian Poland: Wandycz, op. cit., pp. 44, 75 and 122.
100 F. L. Carsten, 'German estates in the eighteenth century', *Receuils de la Société Jean Bodin*, 25 (4), p. 231, and Verney, op. cit., p. 1.
101 See L. O'Boyle, 'The middle class in Western Europe, 1815–1848', *A.H.R.* 71 (1966), and C. R. Lucas, 'Nobles, bourgeois and the origins of the French Revolution', *Past and Present*, 60 (1973).
102 Macartney, op. cit., pp. 513–14 and 605; Preradovich, op. cit., p. 60; Waldstein-Wartenburg, op. cit., pp. 142–3, and E. Anderson, *Poltical Institutions and Social Change in Continental Europe in the Nineteenth Century*, pp. 319–26.
103 A. János, 'The decline of oligarchy', in *Revolution in Perspective*, ed. János and W. B. Slottmann, pp. 6 and 9.
104 H. Holborn, A *History of Modern Germany*, *1840–1945*, pp. 78 and 105–7; Rosenberg, op. cit., pp. 219–20; Muncy, op. cit., pp. 73, 197–8 and 217, and Berdahl, op. cit., pp. 7–9.
105 F. Hertz, *The Development of the German Public Mind*, III, p. 127, 131–4, 139 and 142–3; T. Hamerow, *The Social Foundations of German Unification*, I, p. 206, and Holborn, op. cit., pp. 112–13.
106 S. G. Payne, *A History of Spain and Portugal*, p. 541, and Mack Smith, op. cit., pp. 343 and 418. Many other upper chambers came into existence, but not with membership as a right of nobility. The members were either appointed by the Crown or elected (see E. Lyon and A. Wigram, *The House of Lords*, pt II).
107 Blum, 'Russia', in *European Landed Elites in the Nineteenth Century*, ed. Spring, pp. 73, 79 and 80; Seton-Watson, op. cit., pp. 18 and 351, and M. Szeftel, 'The representatives and their powers in the Russian legislative cham-

bers, 1906-7', *Etudes presentées à la commission internationale pour l'histoire des assemblées d'états*, 27 (1963), p. 226 and n. 13.

108 Payne, op. cit., p. 560, and Rosenberg, op. cit., p. 220.

109 Bromhead, op. cit., pp. 15-16 and chs. 9 and 18, and Stacey, op. cit., ch. 9.

110 C. A. Macartney, *Hungary: a Short History*, p. 217.

111 Poland: see n. 120; Sweden: B. J. Hovde, *The Scandinavian Countries*, pp. 181-2; the Dutch Republic: Myers, op. cit., pp. 128-9; Bohemia: Bosl, op. cit., II, pp. 255-6, and *N.C.M.H.* I, pp. 389-90 (Macartney).

112 Denmark: Myers, op. cit., p. 88; Brandenburg: Carsten, *The Origins of Prussia*, pp. 166-7, and *The Historical Essays of Otto Hintze* (Gilbert), p. 41; Prussia: Carsten, op. cit., pp. 168-9; Bavaria: Carsten, *Princes and Parliaments in Germany*, pp. 353 ff; Saxony: ibid., p. 256; Pomerania: Carsten, *The Origins of Prussia*, p. 169.

113 Bohemia: Kerner, op. cit., pp. 8-9, and W. E. Wright, *Serf, Seigneur and Sovereign*, p. 13; Sweden: Roberts, *Essays in Swedish History*, pp. 7-9, and I. Andersson, *A History of Sweden*, p. 283; Piedmont: Marongiu, op. cit., pp. 197-8; Hungary: Bonis, op. cit., pp. 289-90 and 296-8; Poland: Hoensch, op. cit., pp. 61-2; the Crown of Aragon: Hillgarth, op. cit., pp. 278-9; Scotland: Rait, op. cit., p. 5; Friuli: Marongiu, op. cit., pp. 184-6.

114 Netherlands provinces: Koenigsberger, op. cit., pp. 145 ff; Germany: Carsten, *Princes and Parliaments in Germany*, p. 430; Austria: Macartney, *The Habsburg Empire*, pp. 27-8; France: Myers, op. cit., 72-3; Naples: Ryder, op. cit., p. 124; Sicily: G. Griffiths, *Representative Government in Western Europe in the Sixteenth Century*, pp. 83-4, and Marongiu, op. cit., pp. 164 and 168; Sardinia: Myers, op. cit., p. 94 and Marongiu, op. cit., pt IV (1).

115 Hungary: Marczali, op. cit., pp. 319-20; Sicily: Koenigsberger, *The Government of Sicily under Philip II of Spain*, pp. 127-8; Naples: Ryder, op. cit., pp. 124-5; Prussian monarchy: O. Büsch, *Militärsystem und Sozialleben im alten Preussen*, p. 5.

116 Myers, op. cit., p. 34; Marongiu, op. cit., pp. 73 and 75; Hillgarth, op. cit., p. 279, and Bonis, op. cit., pp. 289-90 and 296-8.

117 Austria and Bohemia: J. Bérenger, *Finances et absolutisme autrichien*, pp. 137-8, Blum, *Noble Landowners ...*, p. 27, and Link, *The Emancipation of the Austrian Peasant*, p. 19: German states: G. Benecke, *Society and Politics in Germany*, p. 70; Naples and Sicily: Marongiu, op. cit., pp. 156 and 162.

118 Hungary: see n. 155.

119 Myers, op. cit., pp. 33-4.

120 *N.C.M.H.* IV, pp. 585-6 (Jablonowski); Myers, op. cit., pp. 83-4 and 124; Dworzaczek, op. cit., p. 27; J. Bardach, 'Gouvernants et gouvernés en Pologne au moyen-âge et aux temps modernes', *Receuils de la Société Jean Bodin*, 25 (4) (1965), pp. 270 ff.

121 Evans, op. cit., p. 198; Bosl, op. cit., II, p. 241, and M. Roberts, 'Sweden', in *The European Nobility in the Eighteenth Century*, ed. Goodwin, pp. 143-4.

122 See above, p. 103.

123 Saxony: Carsten, *Princes and Parliaments in Germany*, pp. 255-6; Bavaria: ibid., p. 411; East Prussia: Carsten, *The Origins of Prussia*, pp. 204-5; Brandenburg: ibid., 166 and 185; Mecklenburg: Carsten, 'German estates in the eighteenth century', op. cit., p. 230; the Crown of Aragon: Anderson, *Lineages of the Absolutist State*, p. 64; Sicily: Koenigsberger, op. cit., pp. 159-60; Portugal: *N.C.M.H.* V, p. 391 (Magalhães Godinho); Bohemia: Bosl, op. cit., II, p. 43;

Austria: Blum, *Noble Landowners* ..., pp. 27–8; Sweden: Myers, op. cit., pp. 116–17, and the March of Ancona: Marongiu, op. cit., p. 212.

124 Myers, op. cit., pp. 154–5.

125 Bavaria: Carsten, *Princes and Parliaments in Germany*, p. 352; Aragon: Marongiu, op. cit., pp. 73–4; East Prussia: Carsten, *The Origins of Prussia*, p. 168; Hungary: Király, op. cit., pp. 24–5.

126 Hungary: see n. 155; Bohemia: W. E. Wright, *Serf, Seigneur and Sovereign*, p. 13, and Macartney, op. cit., pp. 13, 27 and 29; Portugal: *N.C.M.H.* V, p. 389 (Magalhães Godinho); Sicily: Myers, op. cit., p. 95.

127 Sicily: Marongiu, op. cit., p. 116; Denmark: Myers, op. cit., p. 88; Bohemia: Bosl, op. cit., II, pp. 255–6; Germany: Carsten, *The Origins of Prussia*, pp. 166–9, and Myers, op. cit., pp. 107–8; France: Myers, op. cit., pp. 154–5; Russia: Emmons, op. cit., p. 12, and the Crown of Aragon: Hillgarth, op. cit., p. 278.

128 J. Bardach, op. cit., p. 267; *Cambridge History of Poland*, I, p. 260, and Górski, 'The origins of the Polish sejm', op. cit., pp. 123–4. Reference here is to the district diets, of which there were thirty-seven in Poland and twelve in Lithuania (*N.C.M.H.* II, p. 465 (Betts), not to the provincial diets, of which there were seven (*N.C.M.H.* II, p. 466 (Betts).

129 Király, op. cit., pp. 83 and 112–13, and Blum, *Noble Landowners* ..., p. 38.

130 Kerner, op. cit., p. 8.

131 *N.C.M.H.* IV, p. 587 (Jablonowski), R. F. Leslie, *The Polish Question*, p. 7, and Bardach, op. cit., pp. 281–2.

132 Király, op. cit., p. 51, and Király, 'Neo-serfdom in Hungary', *Slavic Review*, 34 (1975) pp. 271–2.

133 *N.C.M.H.* II, p. 466 (Betts).

134 Sweden's *Age of Greatness*, ed. Roberts, p. 180, and Roberts, *The Early Vasas*, p. 39.

135 Brandenburg: Carsten, *The Origins of Prussia*, p. 185; East Prussia: ibid., p. 204, and Saxony: Carsten, *Princes and Parliaments in Germany*, p. 255.

136 Carsten, *The Origins of Prussia*, p. 199.

137 *N.C.M.H.* IV, p. 536 (Jablonowski), and A. Wolowski, *La Vie quotidienne en Pologne au XVIIe siècle*, p. 48.

138 Király, op cit., pp. 111–12, and Marczali, op. cit., p. 143.

139 Király, op. cit., p. 110.

140 *N.C.M.H.* II, p. 466 (Betts), and Bosl. op. cit., II, pp. 252–3.

141 Russia: Emmons, op. cit., p. 12; Sweden: Roberts, *Gustavus Adolphus*, I, p. 316; Brandenburg: Rosenberg, op. cit., pp. 166–7, and Muncy, op. cit., p. 20.

142 Austrian Poland: Wandycz, op. cit., pp. 12 and 72; Prussian Poland: ibid., p. 68; Russian Poland: ibid., pp. 18, 44–5, 75 and 125.

143 Reference is being made to the Bohemian diet, not to the Moravian diet, which was replaced by a nominated tribunal in 1632, nor to the Silesian diet, which conserved its rights unchanged throughout the seventeenth and early eighteenth centuries (*N.C.M.H.* V, p. 476 (Betts)), and nor to the general *Landtag* of the Bohemian lands (Bosl, op. cit., II, p. 250).

144 Kerner, op. cit., pp. 7–9 and 20.

145 Macartney, *The Habsburg Empire*, pp. 23 n. 1 and 27; Wright, op. cit., p. 13, and Kerner, op. cit., pp. 51–2. For some qualification of the effect of the 1627 *Landesordnung*, see Evans, op. cit., pp. 198–9.

146 Kerner, op. cit., pp. 9, 51, 61, 234–6, 238 and 241; Macartney, op. cit., pp. 23–4 and 28 n. 4.

147 *The Historical Essays of Otto Hintze* (Gilbert), pp. 41–3; Carsten, *The Origins of Prussia*, pp. 166–7 and 199–200, and Carsten, *Princes and Parliaments in Germany*, p. 429.
148 Roberts, *Essays in Swedish History*, pp. 7–8 and 32–8; Roberts, *The Early Vasas*, pp. 39–40 and 42–3; Myers, op. cit., pp. 116–17, and Roberts, 'Sweden', in *The European Nobility in the Eighteenth Century*, ed. Goodwin, pp. 137–8.
149 Andersson, op. cit., p. 283; Myers, op. cit., p. 116, and Verney, op. cit., ch. I and pp. 24 and 229–30.
150 Ekman, op. cit., p. 108, and Myers, op. cit., p. 88.
151 Ibid., pp. 63–5 and 99–101.
152 Blum, *Noble Landowners* ..., pp. 23 and 27–8; Link, op. cit., p. 19, and Macartney, op. cit., pp. 27–9.
153 Wolfe, op. cit., pp. 20–1 and 42–4; Myers, op. cit., pp. 72–3 and 104, and Russell Major, *Representative Government* ..., pp. 653 ff.
154 Myers, op. cit., p. 85; Bonis, op. cit., pp. 289–90 and 296–8.
155 The succession: Marczali, op. cit., p. 308 (retained was the right to determine the succession to the throne should the Habsburg line fail completely). Regularity of sessions: Marczali, op. cit., pp. 324–5, and Macartney, *The Habsburg Empire*, pp. 208 and 222–3.
156 Király, op. cit., pp. 78–80, and Macartney, op. cit., pp. 552–3 and 565–7.
157 Marczali, op. cit., pp. 319–20.
158 Király, op. cit., pp. 238–9.
159 J. S. Roskell, 'Perspectives in parliamentary history', *Bulletin of the John Rylands Library*, 46 (1963–4), pp. 448 ff; G. R. Elton, op. cit., ch. 22; J. P. Cooper, 'Differences between English and continental governments in the early seventeenth century', *Britain and the Netherlands*, I, ed. J. S. Bromley and R. H. Kossmann, pp. 74–7, and M. L. Bush, *The Government Policy of Protector Somerset*, pp. 146 ff. It is not quite true to say that parliament could not appoint officials in the continental manner. For a time the house of commons had the right to appoint the collectors of the fifteenth and tenth tax, but that right applied only to the period 1485–1547 and in that time the Crown preserved the authority to make supplementary or substitute nominations (see R. S. Schofield, 'Lay Parliamentary Taxation, 1485–1547' (Cambridge Ph.D., 1963), p. 65).
160 Rait, op. cit., p. 5.
161 Myers, op. cit., pp. 127–8.
162 Koenigsberger, 'States General ...', op. cit., pp. 145 and 154, and Myers, op. cit., p. 158.
163 Myers, op. cit., pp. 70–3; Wolfe, op. cit., p. 47, and Russell Major, *Representative Government* ..., pp. 138–59 and 630–52.
164 Myers, op. cit., p. 29, and *Cambridge History of Poland*, I, p. 437.
165 Myers, op. cit., p. 85; Blum, *Noble Landowners* ..., p. 38; Macartney, op. cit., p. 50; Bonis, op. cit., p. 296, and Király, op. cit., p. 49.
166 Ryder, op. cit., pp. 125 ff; Croce, op. cit., p. 114, and Marongiu, op. cit., p. 155.
167 Russell Major, op. cit., p. 69.
168 Kerner, op. cit., pp. 71 and 73–5; N.C.M.H. II, p. 469 (Betts); Macartney, op. cit., p. 23; Blum, op. cit., p. 27, and Bosl, op. cit., III, p. 24, and II, p. 441.
169 Blum, op. cit., pp. 25–8; Macartney, op. cit., pp. 23 and 58, and Link, op. cit., pp. 18–19.
170 Carsten, *The Origins of Prussia*, p. 204.
171 Gelderland: N.C.M.H. IV, p. 363 (Kossmann).

172   Denmark: Myers, op. cit., pp. 28 and 88; Sweden: Verney, op. cit., ch. 2.
173   Griffiths, op. cit., pp. 78 and 83, and Marongiu, op. cit., p. 139.
174   Myers, op. cit., p. 80, and Koenigsberger, 'States General . . .', op. cit., pp. 145–6.
175   Russell Major, op. cit., p. 62.
176   East Friesland; Myers, op cit., p. 76; Denmark: ibid., p. 28; East Prussia:
      Carsten, *The Origins of Prussia*, p. 204; Poznan: Wandycz, op. cit., p. 68;
      Baden: Carsten, *Princes and Parliaments in Germany*, pp. 423–4; Sweden:
      Roberts, *Gustavus Adolphus*, I, pp. 301–2.
177   Marongiu, op. cit., p. 202.
178   Blum, *Noble Landowners . . .*, p. 27.
179   Carsten, *Princes and Parliaments in Germany*, pp. 357–8 and 415.
180   Roberts, 'Sweden', in *The European Nobility in the Eighteenth Century*, ed.
      Goodwin, pp. 137–8; Hovde, op. cit., pp. 183–4, and Myers, op. cit., p. 157.
181   Carsten, *The Origins of Prussia*, pp. 204–5.
182   Lords: Bromhead, op. cit., chs. 1 and 9, and Stacey, op. cit., ch. 9; Commons:
      G. R. Elton, op. cit., p. 44, L. Stone, *Crisis of the Aristocracy*, p. 31, and W. L.
      Guttsman, *The British Political Elite*, p. 41.
183   Sicily: Mack Smith, op. cit., pp. 125–6; Portugal: *N.C.M.H.* V, p. 390 (Magalhães
      Godinho); Castile: Myers, op. cit., p. 98; Sweden: Hovde, op. cit., p. 183, and
      the Congress Kingdom: Wandycz, op. cit., p. 45. Of the 187 deputies of the
      third estate in the French Estates General of 1614, thirty-one were members of
      the nobility (see R. Mousnier, 'The development of monarchical institutions
      and society in France', in *Louis XIV and French Absolutism*, ed. R. Hatton, pp.
      38–9).
184   Macartney, op. cit., p. 378; *A History of Hungary*, ed. E. Pamlenyi, p. 339, and
      János, op. cit., pp. 6–7 and 9.
185   Bohemia and Austria: Macartney, op. cit., pp. 515 and 622; Prussia: Muncy,
      op. cit., pp. 217–19.
186   T. Zeldin, *France, 1848–1945*, I, p. 542; Sicily: Mack Smith, op. cit., pp. 449–50
      and 506, and Sweden: Andersson, op. cit., p. 360, and Hovde, op. cit., p. 537.
187   E. N. and P. R. Anderson, *Political Institutions and Social Change in Continen-
      tal Europe in the Nineteenth Century*, chs. 8 and 10, and Stendhal, *Scarlet and
      Black* (Penguin, 1953), p. 391.
188   Barrington Moore, Jnr., *Social Origins of Dictatorship and Democracy*, chs 7
      and 8; S. P. Huntington, *Political Order in Changing Societies*, ch. 3, and E. N.
      Anderson, op. cit., chs. 8 and 10.

Chapter V. Honorific privileges

1   See above, p. 89, see below, pp. 139–40.
2   See below, pp. 125–6.
3   See below, pp. 142–3.
4   See below, p. 146.
5   France: C. Loyseau, *Traicte des Ordres*, pp. 8, 57, 76 and 83; England: J. E.
    Powell and K. Wallis, *The House of Lords in the Middle Ages*, p. 402; L. O.
    Pike, *Constitutional History of the House of Lords*, pp. 113–16, and *Statutes of
    the Realm*, 31 Henry VIII, c. 10.
6   M. Bloch, *Feudal Society*, p. 320; D. Hay, *Europe in the Fourteenth and
    Fifteenth Centuries*, pp. 61–2; J. Riley-Smith, *The Knights of St. John of
    Jerusalem and Cyprus*, pp. 236–9; A. J. Forey, *The Templars in the Corona de*

Aragon, p. 2, and L. P. Wright, 'The military orders in sixteenth and seventeenth-century Spanish society', *Past and Present*, 43 (1969), pp. 34, 39 and 68–9.

7   Wright, op. cit., pp. 39–40, 47–8, 58 and 69; *N.C.M.H.* VII, p. 289 (Lindsay) and Riley-Smith, op. cit., pt. IV.

8   Wright, op. cit., pp. 41–2; R. Herr, *The Eighteenth-Century Revolution in Spain*, p. 96.

9   Hay, op. cit., p. 65; Loyseau, op. cit., p. 72; F. Bluche, *La vie quotidienne de la noblesse française au XVIIIe siècle*, p. 21, and P. du Puys de Clinchamps, *La noblesse*, p. 46.

10   B. Waldstein-Wartenberg, 'Österreichisches Adelsrecht, 1804–1918', *Mitteilungen des österreichisches Staatsarchivs*, 17–18 (1964–5), pp. 135 and 141; N. von Preradovich, *Die Fuhrungsschichten in Österreich und Preussen, 1804–1918*, pp. 25–7; Herr, op. cit., p. 96.

11   Bloch, op. cit., p. 328; L. Genicot, 'Recent research on the medieval nobility', in *The Medieval Nobility*, ed. T. Reuter, p. 22; *N.C.M.H.* IV, p. 20 (Cooper); C. A. Macartney, *The Habsburg Empire*, p. 51; Loyseau, op. cit., p. 56; D. Knowles, *The Monastic Order in England*, pp. 423–4, and K. Edwards, *The English Secular Cathedrals in the Middle Ages*, p. 34.

12   Russia: Blum, 'Russia', in *European Landed Elites in the Nineteenth Century*, ed. Spring, p. 76; France: M. Marion, *Dictionnaire des institutions de la France aux XVIIe et XVIIIe siècles*, p. 397; Spain: A. Dominguez Ortiz, *La sociedad española en el siglo XVIII*, p. 118.

13   Prussia and other German states: K. Demeter, *The Prussian Officer Corps*, pp. 67–8; France: Bluche, op. cit., pp. 122–30, and P. Goubert, *The Ancien Régime*, p. 164; Spain: Dominguez Ortiz, op. cit., p. 118, and J. Larios Martin, *Catálogo de los archivos españoles*, p. 24; Russia: Blum, op. cit., p. 81, and M. Raeff, *Origins of the Russian Intelligentsia*, p. 68; Tuscany: E. Cochrane, *Florence in the Forgotten Centuries*, p. 488; Sicily: D. Mack Smith, *A History of Sicily*, p. 253; Venice: J. C. Davis, *The Decline of the Venetian Nobility as a Ruling Class*, p. 77; Austria: H. G. Schenk, 'Austria', in *The European Nobility in the Eighteenth Century*, ed. Goodwin, p. 114; Portugal: M. Cheke, *Dictator of Portugal: the Life of the Marquis of Pombal*, p. 168, and A. Silbert 'Sur la "féodalité" portugaise et son abolition', *L'abolition de la féodalité*, I, p. 335.

14   J. Keep, 'Imperial Russia: Alexander II to the Revolution', in *An Introduction to Russian History*, ed. R. Auty and D. Obolensky, p. 231; Demeter, op. cit., p. 378 n. 2.

15   Raeff, op. cit., p. 68, and Bluche, op. cit., p. 130.

16   J. Blum, *The End of the Old Order in Rural Europe*, p. 168, and C. Jago, 'The influence of debt on the relations between Crown and aristocracy in seventeenth-century Castile', *Econ. H.R.*, 2nd ser., 26 (1973).

17   P. Dukes, *Catherine the Great and the Russian Nobility*, pp. 12 and 109–10; G. T. Robinson, *Rural Russia under the Old Regime*, p. 131; O. Crisp, *Studies in the Russian Economy before 1914*, pp. 117 and 132; W. K. Pintner, *Russian Economic Policy under Nicholas I*, pp. 36–8, and G. M. Hamburg, *Land, Economy and Society in Tsarist Russia*, pp. 81 and 98.

18   L. Muncy, *The Junker in the Prussian Administration under William II*, pp. 199–200; Blum, op. cit., pp. 168–9; S. F. Starr, *Decentralisation and Self-government in Russia*, p. 237.

19   J. Blum, *Noble Landowners and Agriculture in Austria, 1815–1848*, p. 116.

20   Blum, *The End of the Old Order in Rural Europe*, pp. 168–9; Muncy, op. cit.,
     pp. 20 and 199; Robinson, op. cit., p. 131, and Hamburg, op. cit., ch. IV.
21   Blum, op. cit., pp. 168–70.
22   E.g. J.-P. Labatut, *Les noblesses européennes*, p. 58.
23   R. Barber, *The Knight and Chivalry*, pp. 16–7; *C.E.H.*, pp. 652–3 (Bolin), and
     N. P. Brooks, 'Arms, status and warfare in late Saxon England', in *Ethelred the
     Unready*, ed. D. Hill, p. 83.
24   G. Duby, *The Chivalrous Society*, p. 163; G. Duby, *Rural Economy and
     Country Life in the Medieval West*, p. 191; Bloch, op. cit., p. 321; Goubert, op.
     cit, pp. 162–3; *C.E.H.*, I, pp. 652–3 (Bolin) and S. Adler, *Das adelige Landrecht
     in Nieder- und Oberösterreich und die Gerichtsreformen des XVIII. Jahrhun-
     derts*, p. 9.
25   France: Loyseau, op. cit., p. 57; Austria: H. Siegert (ed.), *Adel in Österreich*, p.
     21; England: *Statutes of the Realm*, 19 Henry VII, c. 4, and 2/3 Edward VI, c.
     14 (not repealed until 6/7 William III, c. 13). In the English case, other social
     groups were excepted also but qualified for this privilege not on grounds of
     aristocratic status but because of their degree of wealth.
26   Loyseau, op. cit., p. 58; Adler, op. cit., p. 42, and Siegert, op. cit., p. 21.
27   A. H. de Oliveira Marques, *History of Portugal*, I, p. 183; G. Lefebvre, 'Urban
     society in the Orléanais in the late eighteenth century', *Past and Present*, 19
     (1961), p. 49, and Loyseau, op. cit., p. 58.
28   Duelling: Bloch, op. cit., p. 328; Loyseau, op. cit., pp. 58–9; Siegert, op. cit., p.
     21; tournaments: A. R. Wagner, *Heralds and Heraldry in the Middle Ages*, p.
     71.
29   H. Hochenegg, *Der Adel im Leben Tirols*, p. 15, and K. B. McFarlane, *The
     Nobility of Later Medieval England*, pp. 122–3.
30   W. Camden, *Remaines Concerning Britaine*, p. 104; Loyseau, op. cit., p. 68.
31   Hochenegg, op. cit., p. 15.
32   Barber, op. cit., p. 85; F. E. Baldwin, *Sumptuary Legislation and Personal
     Regulation in England*, pp. 10 and 226.
33   N. B. Harte, 'State control of dress and social change in pre-industrial England',
     in *Trade, Government and Economy in Pre-Industrial England*, ed. D. C.
     Coleman and A. H. John, pp. 133–9; M. Defourneaux, *Daily Life in Spain in
     the Golden Age*, p. 56; Davis, op. cit., pp. 44–5; Cochrane, op. cit., p. 488; F. L.
     Ford, *Robe and Sword*, p. 68; Baldwin, op. cit., pp. 211–12, and L. Stone, *Crisis
     of the Aristocracy*, pp. 28–9.
34   Harte, op. cit., pp. 143–8; Baldwin, op. cit., pp. 218–19.
35   Bloch, op. cit., p. 328; Wagner, op. cit., ch. 3 and p. 47; A. R. Wagner, *English
     Genealogy*, p. 106, and Barber, op. cit., p. 31.
36   K. Górski, 'Les structures sociales de la noblesse polonaise au moyen âge', *Le
     moyen age* (1967), pp. 77–8 and 73; *Cambridge History of Poland*, I, p. 176; A.
     Zajaczkowski, 'En Pologne: cadres structurels de la noblesse', *Annales
     d'histoire E.S.*, 18 (1963), p. 89, and W. Dworzaczek, 'Perméabilité des barrières
     sociales dans la Pologne du XVIe siècle', *Acta Poloniae Historica*, 24 (1971), p.
     25.
37   J. H. Mundy, *Europe in the High Middle Ages*, p. 276; Wagner, *English
     Genealogy*, p. 106; L. G. Pine, *The Genealogist's Encyclopedia*, p. 194, and
     Wagner, *Heralds and Heraldry*, pp. 65–6.
38   Poland: Gorski, op. cit., pp. 77–8; France: Clinchamps, op. cit., p. 51, and
     Loyseau, op. cit., p. 48; Prussia: W. Görlitz, *Die Junker*, p. 24.

39 Wagner, *English Genealogy*, pp. 108-10; F. M. L. Thompson, 'Britain', in *European Landed Elites in the Nineteenth Century*, ed. Spring, pp. 31-2; and *Acts of Parliaments of Scotland*, VIII, pp. 95-6.

40 E.g. Elliott, *Imperial Spain*, pp. 103-4.

41 Labatut, op. cit., p. 61.

42 J. Miller, *The Nobility in Polish Renaissance Society*, p. 110; A. B. Boswell, 'Poland', in *The European Nobility in the Eighteenth Century*, ed. Goodwin, pp. 159-60, and Labatut, op. cit., pp. 37-8.

43 Hungary: ibid., p. 25; B. K. Király, *Hungary in the Late Eighteenth Century*, pp. 27-8; H. Marczali, *Hungary in the Eighteenth Century*, p. 128, and Macartney, *The Habsburg Empire*, p. 129; Sweden: M. Roberts, *The Early Vasas*, pp. 220-1; *Sweden's Age of Greatness*, ed. M. Roberts, p. 75, and Labatut, op. cit., p. 23; Denmark: ibid., p. 23; Russia: Dukes, op. cit., p. 2 n. 3; Raeff, op. cit., p. 14, and R. E. Jones, *The Emancipation of the Russian Nobility*, p. 14; Galicia: P. S. Wandycz, *The Lands of Partitioned Poland*, p. 12.

44 Bloch, op. cit., pp. 312-14.

45 Ibid., p. 335, and Clinchamps, op. cit., p. 55. The pre-Conquest English equivalent of the Carolingian official titles was that of earl (Wagner, *English Genealogy*, p. 89).

46 For the incorporation of Rhinish clan chieftains in the Frankish state by means of entitlement, see H. Gollwitzer, *Die Standesherren*, p. 15.

47 R. J. W. Evans, *The Making of the Habsburg Monarchy*, pp. 170-1.

48 Bloch, op. cit., pp. 333-5; E. Warlop, *The Flemish Nobility before 1300*, pp. 139 and 150-1, and Genicot (Reuter), p. 30 n. 13.

49 G. Fourquin, *Lordship and Feudalism in the Middle Ages*, p. 92; Bloch, op. cit., p. 335, and Clinchamps, op. cit., p. 55.

50 J. Russell Major, 'The Crown and the aristocracy in Renaissance France', *A.H.R.* 69 (1964), p. 631; Labatut, *Les noblesses européennes*, pp. 59-60, and Labatut, *Les ducs et pairs*, p. 69.

51 T. B. Pugh, 'The magnates, knights and gentry', in *Fifteenth-century England*, ed. S. B. Chrimes, ch. 5; L. Stone, *The Crisis of the Aristocracy*, ch. III (v); A. S. Turberville, *The House of Lords in the Age of Reform*, pp. 42-3, and J. Cannon, *Parliamentary Reform. 1640-1832*, p. 50.

52 This point was originally but crudely made by R. S. Rait in *The Parliaments of Scotland*, p. 195. For a more careful and complicated elaboration of the point see A. Grant, 'The development of the Scottish peerage', *Scottish Historical Review*, 57 (1978).

53 H. Koenigsberger, *The Government of Sicily under Philip II of Spain*, pp. 89 and 151, and D. Mack Smith, *A History of Sicily*, pp. 157, 206-8, 255 and 284.

54 A. F. C. Ryder, *The Kingdom of Naples under Alfonso the Magnanimous*, pp. 13 and 51-2; B. Croce, *A History of the Kingdom of Naples*, p. 118, and R. Villari, *La rivolta antispagnola a Napoli*, pp. 189-92.

55 F. Schevill, *History of Florence*, pp. 32 ff; J. K. Hyde, *Padua in the Age of Dante*, p. 18; D. E. Zanetti, 'The patriziato of Milan from the domination of Spain to the unification of Italy, *Social History*, 6 (1977), p. 745, and J. Roberts, 'Lombardy', in *The European Nobility in the Eighteenth Century*, ed. Goodwin, pp. 66-7.

56 Hungary: see n. 43; Portugal: De Oliveira Marques, op. cit., I, pp. 282 and 396-7, and II, pp. 25-6; F. Braudel, *The Mediterranean*, p. 732, and S. G. Payne, *A History of Spain and Portugal*, pp. 129 and 414; Spain: J. F. O'Callaghan, *A*

History of Medieval Spain, pp. 468 and 611; A. Mackay, *Spain in the Middle Ages*, pp. 46-7 and 97-8; J. N. Hillgarth, *The Spanish Kingdoms, 1250-1516*, I, p. 54; J. Lynch, *Spain under the Habsburgs*, II, p. 132; A. Domingues Ortiz, *La sociedad española en el siglo XVII*, pp. 209-13; J. H. Elliott, *Imperial Spain*, p. 103; Herr, op. cit., p. 96, and Clinchamps, op. cit., pp. 119-20.

57   Roberts, op. cit., pp. 66-7; A.-E. Sayous, 'Aristocratie et noblesse à Gênes', *Annales d'histoire E.S.*, 9 (1937), pp. 366 and 381; Mack Smith, op. cit., p. 37; Clinchamps, op. cit., pp. 122-3.

58   Venice: B. S. Pullan, *A History of Early Renaissance Italy*, p. 126; Genoa: Sayous, op. cit., pp. 366, 369 and 378.

59   H. Rosenberg, *Bureaucracy, Aristocracy, Autocracy*, pp. 139 and 147, and J. Meyer, *Noblesses et pouvoirs dans l'Europe d'ancien régime*, p. 119.

60   Clinchamps, pp. 119 and 123.

61   Ibid., pp. 118-20 and 124; H. Slapnicka, 'Die böhmischen Länder und die Slowakie, 1919-1945', in K. Bosl (ed.), *Handbuch der Geschichte der böhmischen Länder*, IV, p. 12; H. Siegert (ed.) *Der Adel in Österreichs*, pp. 74-5 and Payne, op. cit., p. 560.

62   Norway; T. K. Derry, *A History of Modern Norway*, p. 23, and B. J. Hovde, *The Scandinavian Countries*, p. 513; France: Clinchamps, op. cit., p. 69; Denmark: Blum, *The End of the Old Order in Rural Europe*, p. 419.

63   There were a few exceptions, as, for example, in eighteenth-century Portugal, where no noble could assume his father's title unless he secured a fresh grant of it from the king (Cheke, op. cit., p. 17).

64   Sweden: in the sixteenth century primogeniture seemed to have applied (Roberts, *The Early Vasas*, p. 36). Yet this soon gave way to a system whereby all the male children of a titleholder received their father's rank (see G. Ohlin, 'Entrepreneurial activities of the Swedish aristocracy', *Explorations in Entrepreneurial History*, 6 (1953), p. 149, and D. V. Verney, *Parliamentary Reform in Sweden*, p. 15); Prussia: F. Martiny, 'Die Adelsfrage in Preussen vor 1806', *Vierteljahrschrift für Sozial- und Wirtschaftsgeschichte*, Beiheit 35, p. 19; Russia: Raeff, op. cit., p. 181 n. 13, and R. E. Jones, *The Emancipation of the Russian Nobility*, p. 14; parts of France: Clinchamps, op. cit., p. 55; Lombardy: see above and, for application of strict primogeniture under Spanish influence, see Zanetti, op. cit., p. 750, and J. P. Cooper, 'Patterns of inheritance and settlement by great landowners from the fifteenth to the eighteenth centuries', in *Family and Inheritance*, ed. J. Goody and others, p. 282; Hungary: Marczali, op. cit., p. 123 n. 1.

65   Labatut, *Les noblesses européennes*, p. 22; England: Macfarlane, op. cit., pp. 272-4; France: Clinchamps, op. cit., p. 37; Spain: ibid., pp. 119-20; Austria: Waldstein-Wartenberg, op. cit., p. 127; Belgian monarchy: Clinchamps, op. cit., p. 119.

66   Ibid., p. 55, and Labatut, op. cit., pp. 60-4.

67   Clinchamps, op. cit., pp. 83-7.

68   Ibid., p. 59, Croce, op. cit., p. 118; Grant, op. cit., pp. 4-5; Labatut, pp. 18-23.

69   Mack Smith, op. cit., chs. 15 and 30.

70   Waldstein-Wartenberg, op. cit., pp. 131 and 133.

71   L. Cecil, 'The creation of nobles in Prussia, 1871-1918', *A.H.R.*, 75 (1) (1970), pp. 777 and 791.

72   F. M. L. Thompson, *English Landed Society in the Nineteenth Century*, pp. 7-12 and 294.

73 P. A. Bromhead, *The House of Lords and Contemporary Politics, 1911-1957*, chs. 1 and 9.

74 Macartney, op. cit., pp. 52 and 54. For the application to Galicia, see Wandycz, op. cit., p. 12.

75 Labatut, op. cit., p. 62; Loyseau, op. cit., p. 91; Clinchamps, op. cit., pp. 57-8 and 60; Dominguez Ortiz, op. cit., pp. 216-17; F. L. Ganshof, 'Nobility', in *Chambers Encyclopedia*.

76 See above, ch. IV (2).

77 For parliament, see pp. 100-2; for reserved office, see pp. 83-4 and 89; for judicial privileges, see pp. 68-9.

78 For the Hungarian designation, see W. O. McCagg, *Jewish Nobles and Geniuses in Modern Hungary*, p. 38 n. 37.

79 Bloch, op. cit., pp. 322-3; Barber, op. cit., p. 16; Wagner, *English Genealogy*, p. 103; Loyseau, op. cit., p. 70.

80 F. L. Carsten, *Princes and Parliaments in Germany*, pp. 162, 268, 339 and 350-1; Blum, *Noble Landowners and Agriculture in Austria*, p. 25, and Waldstein-Wartenberg, op. cit., pp. 131 and 133.

81 Stone, op. cit., ch. III (iv).

82 Bloch, op. cit., pp. 321 ff; Warlop, op. cit., pp. 300-3; Mackay, op. cit., p. 47; Barber, op. cit., pp. 16-17, and Wagner, op. cit., p. 103.

83 G. Duby, *The Chivalrous Society*, p. 183; Clinchamps, op. cit., p. 60, and J. T. Cliffe, *The Yorkshire Gentry*, pp. 7-8.

84 Warlop, op. cit., p. 301; Duby, op. cit., p. 174; Mack Smith, op. cit., p. 100, 154 and 207; Roberts, 'Lombardy', in *The European Nobility in the Eighteenth Century*, ed. Goodwin, p. 67; J. H. Elliott, *The Revolt of the Catalans*, p. 65, and Labatut, *Les noblesses européennes*, p. 10.

85 Mack Smith, op. cit., p. 427.

86 Pine, op. cit., pp. 232-3.

87 For the usurpation of the *particule* before the Revolution, see C. Lucas, 'Nobles, the bourgeois and the French Revolution', *Past and Present*, 60 (1973), p. 80; L. Cecil, op. cit., pp. 759-60.

Chapter VI. Seigneurial rights

1 B. H. Slicher van Bath, *The Agrarian History of Western Europe*, pp. 37-8 and 49-50; A. Dominguez Ortiz, *La sociedad española en el siglo XVIII*, pp. 301-2; T. C. Smout, *A History of the Scottish People*, pp. 33-4; A. Silbert, *Le Portugal méditerranéen à la fin de l'ancien régime*, I, pp. 138-43; M. Roberts, *Gustavus Adolphus*, I, p. 318; J. Blum, *The End of the Old Order in Rural Europe*, p. 51, and W. von Hippel, 'Le régime féodal en Allemagne au XVIIIe siècle et sa dissolution', *L'abolition de la féodalité*, I, pp. 290-1.

2 R. Rosdolsky, 'On the nature of peasant serfdom in Central and Eastern Europe', *Journal of Central European Affairs*, 12 (1952), pp. 133 and 136; C. A. Macartney, *The Habsburg Empire*, p. 62; S. Kieniewicz, *The Emancipation of the Polish Peasantry*, p. 15; Blum, op. cit., pp. 35-6 and 41-2, and M. Bloch, *French Rural History*, pp. 85-6 and 104-6.

3 G. Duby, *Rural Economy and Country Life in the Medieval West*, pp. 235-6 and 259, and P. J. Jones, 'From manor to mezzadria: a Tuscan case-study in the medieval origins of modern agrarian society', *Florentine Studies*, ed. N. Rubinstein, p. 207.

4   For leasing of rights: e.g. D. Mack Smith, *A History of Sicily*, p. 279; R. B. Forster, 'Obstacles to agricultural growth in eighteenth-century France', *A.H.R.* 55 (1970), pp. 1608–9, and Silbert, op. cit., II, p. 1040.

5   S. A. Hansen, 'Changes in the wealth ... of the Danish aristocracy, 1470–1720', *Third International Conference of Economic History*, IV, pp. 101–3; J. R. Gillis, 'Aristocracy and bureaucracy in nineteenth-century Prussia', *Past and Present*, 41 (1968), p. 113; G. Frêche, 'Compoix, propriété foncière, fiscalité et démographie historique en pays de taille réelle', *Revue d'histoire moderne et contemporaine*, 18 (1971), pp. 344–6; C. R. Lucas, 'Nobles, bourgeois and the origins of the French Revolution', *Past and Present*, 60 (1973), pp. 89–90; P. Léon, etc., 'Régime seigneurial et régime féodal dans la France du sud-est', *L'abolition de la féodalité*, I, pp. 156–7, and A. Dominguez Ortiz, *La sociedad española en el siglo XVII*, I, p. 197.

6   See vol. II.

7   Bloch, op. cit., p. 149; J. Q. C. Mackrell, *The Attack on 'Feudalism' in Eighteenth-Century France*, p. 4; R. B. Forster, *The Nobility of Toulouse in the Eighteenth Century*, p. 35, and A. Dominguez Ortiz, 'La fin du régime seigneurial en Espagne', in *L'abolition de la féodalité*, I, p. 317.

8   Blum, op. cit., pp. 50–8.

9   Ibid., and Slicher van Bath, op. cit., pp. 47–8.

10 Carolingian Empire: Duby, op. cit., pp. 40–1; Austrian Empire: J. Blum, *Noble Landowners and Agriculture in Austria*, pp. 72–4 and 76–8; Macartney, op. cit., p. 67 n. 4; E. M. Link, *The Emancipation of the Austrian Peasant*, pp. 16–17, and B. M. Király, *Hungary in the Late Eighteenth Century*, pp. 61–4 and 67.

11 Duby, op. cit., pp. 40–1, and bk. III, chs. 2 (1) and 4.

12 Blum, *Noble Landowners ...*, pp. 72–4.

13 Kieniewicz, op. cit., pp. 9–10; R. F. Leslie, *Polish Politics and the Revolution of November 1830*, pp. 55–6, and A. Kamiński, 'Neo-serfdom in Poland-Lithuania', *Slavic Review*, 34 (1975), pp. 256–7.

14 W. E. Wright, *Serf, Seigneur and Sovereign*, pp. 19–20.

15 W. E. Wright, 'Neo-serfdom in Bohemia', *Slavic Review*, 34 (1975), p. 248, and K. Mejdricka, 'L'état du régime féodal à la veille de son abolition et les conditions de sa suppression en Bohême', *L'abolition de la féodalité*, I, pp. 394–5 and 397.

16 F. L. Carsten, *The Origins of Prussia*, pp. 77–9, and ch. 11.

17 Slicher van Bath, op. cit., pp. 51–2, and Bloch, op. cit., pp. 91–2.

18 Bohemia: Mejdricka, op. cit., pp. 394–7 and 401; Prussian monarchy: H. Rosenberg, 'The rise of the junkers in Brandenburg-Prussia', *A.H.R.* 49 (1964), pp. 231–3, and Carsten, op. cit., pp. 156–8; Russia: J. Blum, *Lord and Peasant in Russia*, pp. 225–7 and 444–5; Poland: J. Rutkowski, *Le régime agraire en Pologne au XVIIIe siècle*, p. 59, and Kamiński, op. cit., p. 257.

19 Macartney, op. cit., pp. 66–7, 72–3 and 229 n. 1.

20 K. Richter, 'Die böhmischen Länder von 1471–1740' in *Handbuch der Geschichte der böhmischer Länder*, ed. K. Bosl, II, p. 217; *N.C.M.H.* V, p. 526 (Rosén), and Király, op. cit., p. 55 n. 21.

21 Mejdricka, op. cit., pp. 394–5, and Kamiński, op. cit., p. 262.

22 Duby, op. cit., p. 208.

23 Bloch, op. cit., pp. 91–3; Duby, op. cit., pp. 153 and 208, and E. J. Nell, 'Economic relationships in the decline of feudalism', *History and Theory*, 6 (1967), p. 343.

24 Duby, op. cit., pp. 53, 191-6 and 221-2; *C.E.H.* I, p. 251 (Bloch), and Blum, *Lord and Peasant in Russia*, p. 225.

25 Italy and the West: Jones, op. cit., *Florentine Studies*, ed. Rubinstein, pp. 193-4 and 198-9; *C.E.H.* I, p. 410 (Jones); Duby, op. cit., pp. 208 and 263, and Slicher van Bath, op. cit., pp. 51-2. Eastern Europe: Blum, *The End of the Old Order* ..., pp. 59 and 316; Macartney, op. cit., pp. 279-80, and B. Lesnodorski, 'Le processus de l'abolition du régime féodal dans les territoires polonais aux XVIIIe et XIXe siècles', *L'abolition de la féodalité*, I, pp. 464-5.

26 Bloch, *French Rural History*, pp. 95-6.

27 See Jones, in *Florentine Studies*, p. 214, and Duby, op. cit., pp. 273-8.

28 Ibid., pp. 305-11 and 317 ff, and Jones in *Florentine Studies*, pp. 203-4.

29 Blum, *The End of the Old Order* ..., p. 323; and R. A. Dickler, 'Organisation and change in productivity in Eastern Europe', *European Peasants and their Markets*, ed. W. N. Parker and E. L. Jones, pp. 280-1.

30 For the general picture, see Blum, *The End of the Old Order* ..., pp. 52-6.

31 Mackrell, op. cit., p. 4; F. L. Carsten, *Princes and Parliaments in Germany*, p. 351; L. Makkai, 'Die Entstehung der gesellschaftlichen Basis des Absolutismus in den Ländern der österreichischen Habsburger', *Studia Historica Academicae Scientiarum Hungaricae*, 43, p. 35, and R. Devleeshouwer, 'L'abolition des droits féodaux en Belgique', *L'abolition de la féodalité*, I, p. 210.

32 See Mackrell, op. cit., p. 4; also see n. 149.

33 Church tithes are not included within this category, although many became the possession of lay seigneurs.

34 G. Fourquin, *Lordship and Feudalism in the Middle Ages*, pp. 187 and 194-5.

35 Duby, op. cit., pp. 217-18.

36 Bloch, *French Rural History*, pp. 95-6.

37 A. Dominguez Ortiz, *The Golden Century of Spain*, p. 160; *N.C.M.H.* VI, p. 537 (Magalhães Godinho); P. Goubert, *The Ancien Régime*, p. 85; Király, op. cit., pp. 65-6; Blum, *Noble Landowners* ..., pp. 74-5, and Blum, *The End of the Old Order*, p. 60.

38 Király, op. cit., pp. 64-5.

39 Fourquin, op. cit., p. 191, and G. Bois, *Crise du Féodalisme*, pp. 203-4.

40 Hungary: Király, op. cit., pp. 66-7; Bohemia-Austria: Blum, *Noble Landowners* ..., pp. 76-7; England: K. Wrightson and D. Levine, *Poverty and Piety in an English Village: Terling, 1525-1700*, p. 27; Poland: Leslie, op. cit., p. 56; Portugal: *N.C.M.H.* VI, p. 537 (Magalhães Godinho) and, generally, Blum, *The End of the Old Order* ..., p. 64.

41 Duby, op. cit., pp. 44 and 51-2.

42 Jones, in *Florentine Studies*, p. 214.

43 Fourquin, op. cit., p. 196.

44 Carsten, *The Origins of Prussia*, pp. 78-9; Makkai, op. cit., p. 35, and Silbert, *Le Portugal méditerranéen* ..., I, pp. 145-6.

45 Duby, op. cit., pp. 203-11 and 263; J. Miller, *The Nobility in Polish Renaissance Society*, p. 387; Kieniewicz, *The Emancipation of the Polish Peasantry*, p. 12, and R. Rosdolsky, 'The distribution of the agrarian product in feudalism, *Journal of Economic History*, 11 (1951), p. 254, n. 15.

46 Fourquin, op. cit., p. 196; Blum, *The End of the Old Order* ..., pp. 64 and 77; Bloch, *French Rural History*, p. 83; Devleeshouwer, 'L'abolition des droits féodaux en Belgique', *L'abolition de la féodalité*, I, p. 213 and see immediately below and pp. 155 and 157.

47   Duby, op. cit., pp. 223 and 239–42; Fourquin, op. cit., pp. 188–90, and Bloch, op. cit., p. 88.
48   Blum, *The End of the Old Order* . . . , pp. 60–2; J. Blum, 'The condition of the European peasantry on the eve of emancipation', *Journal of Modern History*, 46 (1974), pp. 399–401, and Kieniewicz, op. cit., pp. 60–1.
49   J. Meyer, *La noblesse bretonne*, pp. 651–8; R. B. Forster, *The House of Saulx-Tavanes*, pp. 92–108, and Goubert, op. cit., pp. 83–7.
50   Smout, op. cit. pp. 137–8.
51   Entry fines: A. B. Appleby, 'Agrarian capitalism or seigneurial reaction?', *A.H.R.* 80 (1975), pp. 583–7 and 590–1; L. Stone, *The Crisis of the Aristocracy*, pp. 313 and 317; E. Kerridge, 'The movement of rents, 1540–1640', *Econ. H.R.*, 2nd ser., 6 (1953–4), pp. 16 ff, and R. B. Smith, *Land and Politics in the England of Henry VIII*, pp. 79–80; demesne extension: M. Spufford, *Contrasting Communities*, pp. 70–1; Stone, op. cit., pp. 308–9, 320–1 and 323–4; F. M. L. Thompson, 'Social distribution of landed property in England since the sixteenth century', *Econ. H.R.*, 2nd ser., 19 (1966), pp. 514–5; Wrightson and Levine, op. cit., p. 20; A. H. Johnson, *The Disappearance of the Small Landowner*, pp. 67 and 73, and R. Brenner, 'Agrarian class structure and economic development in pre-industrial Europe', *Past and Present*, 70 (1976), pp. 61–4.
52   Roberts, *Gustavus Adolphus*, II, pp. 51–2.
53   Stone, op. cit., ch. VI.
54   Duby, op. cit., p. 223, and Blum, *The End of the Old Order* . . . , pp. 65 and 83–4.
55   Ibid.; Goubert, op. cit., pp. 85–6, and Macartney, op. cit., p. 62.
56   Jones in *Florentine Studies*, pp. 202–3, and Duby, op. cit., pp. 317 ff.
57   Bloch, *French Rural History*, pp. 127–9.
58   See Jones in *Florentine Studies*, passim; *C.E.H.* I, pp. 402 ff (Jones); *C.E.H.* I, pp. 710 and 715 (Genicot); Duby, op. cit., bk. III, ch. 4, and bk. IV, ch. 2; Dominguez Ortiz, op. cit., *L'abolition de la féodalité*, I, pp. 318–19; Spufford, op. cit., p. 50, and Smout, op. cit., pp. 137–8.
59   Duby, op. cit., pp. 239–48; Bloch, *French Rural History*, pp. 112 and 129–33; F. Braudel, *The Mediterranean*, pp. 706–9; Blum, *The End of the Old Order* . . . , p. 206–7; W. Doyle, 'Was there an aristocratic reaction in pre-revolutionary France', *Past and Present*, 57 (1972), pp. 114 ff.
60   Duby, op. cit., pp. 257–8, and Jones, in *Florentine Studies*, pp. 198–204.
61   See n. 58 and Blum, *The End of the Old Order* . . . , pp. 206–9; Bloch, *French Rural History*, pp. 126 ff; R. B. Forster, 'Obstacles to agricultural growth in eighteenth-century France', *A.H.R.* 75 (1970), pp. 1604–9; B. Sexauer, 'English and French agriculture in the late eighteenth century', *Agricultural History*, 50 (1976), p. 503, and Brenner, op. cit., *Past and Present*, 70 (1976), p. 68.
62   Denmark: D. Tonnesson, 'Les pays scandinaves', *L'abolition de la féodalité*, I, p. 306; Austria: Blum, *The End of the Old Order* . . . , pp. 221–2; Prussia: ibid., p. 227; Spain: Dominguez Ortiz, op. cit., *L'abolition de la féodalité*, I, p. 318; Sicily: J. Rosselli, *Lord William Bentinck and the British Occupation of Sicily*, p. 3.
63   See below, pp. 174–5.
64   Blum, *Noble Landowners* . . . , pp. 75 and 78; Devleeshouwer, op. cit., *L'abolition de la féodalité*, I, p. 214; Miller, op. cit., p. 187; *C.E.H.* I, p. 603 (Postan); and also see Blum, *The End of the Old Order* . . . , pp. 64 and 83.
65   Ibid., pp. 82–3; L. Trenard, 'Survivances féodales et régime seigneurial dans les provinces septentrionales de la France au XVIIIe siècle', *L'abolition de la*

féodalité, I, pp. 188–9 and 195; *N.C.M.H.*, IV, pp. 26–7 (Cooper); Mackrell, op. cit., pp. 4–5; H. Rosenberg, *Bureaucracy, Aristocracy and Autocracy*, p. 219; Király, op. cit., p. 63, and I. J. Brugmans, 'La fin de la féodalité aux Pays-Bas', *L'abolition de la féodalité*, I, pp. 228–30, and Devleeshouwer, op. cit., p. 214.

66 Ibid., p. 212.

67 *C.E.H.* I, p. 262 (Bloch); Slicher van Bath, op. cit., p. 50; Blum, *The End of the Old Order* ..., pp. 80–1; Fourquin, op. cit., p. 95. For *pesage*, see Bois, *Crise du féodalisme*, p. 211 and Brugmans, op. cit., p. 232. For mintage; see Duby, op. cit., p. 249, Goubert, *The Ancien Régime*, p. 159 and J. Bérenger, *Finances et absolutisme autrichien*, pp. 302–3. For mining, see pp. 195–7.

68 Hungary: Király, op. cit., pp. 63–4; Austria: Blum, *Noble Landowners* ..., pp. 86–7; France: Bloch, *French Rural History*, pp. 79–81, and Bois, op. cit., pp. 211–12; Bavaria: Carsten, *Princes and Parliaments in Germany*, p. 419; Bohemia: Mejdricka, op. cit., p. 394, and H. Freudenberger, *The Waldstein Woolen Mill*, p. 3; Poland: Blum, *The End of the Old Order* ..., p. 81; Spain: Dominguez Ortiz, *La sociedad española en el siglo XVIII*, p. 303; Low Countries: Devleeshouwer, op. cit., p. 213; Sicily: Mack Smith, *History of Sicily*, p. 99, and H. G. Koenigsberger, *The Government of Sicily under Philip II of Spain*, p. 76; Scotland: Smout, op. cit., p. 120; Portugal: Silbert, *Le Portugal méditerranéen* ..., I, pp. 143–4; Lombardy: J. M. Roberts, 'Lombardy', in *The European Nobility in the Eighteenth Century*, ed. Goodwin, p. 63, and Naples: B. Croce, *A History of the Kingdom of Naples*, p. 183.

69 Blum, *The End of the Old Order* ..., pp. 93–4; Koenigsberger, op. cit., p. 76; Bloch, *French Rural History*, p. 133.

70 Ibid., pp. 82–3; Duby, op. cit., pp. 224–8; Devleeshouwer, op. cit., pp. 209 and 212; N. Salomon, *La campagne de Nouvelle Castille à la fin du XVIe siècle*, pp. 197–8; Fourquin, op. cit., p. 94; Croce, op. cit., pp. 182–3; Silbert, op. cit., I, pp. 142–3; Mackrell, op. cit., p. 49, and Brugmans, op. cit., p. 231.

71 Duby, op. cit., p. 228, and Bloch, op. cit., pp. 78–9 and 102–3.

72 Ibid., p. 78; Salomon, op. cit., pp. 198 ff; A. Dominguez Ortiz, *El regimen señorial y el reformismo borbonico*, p. 11; Roberts, op. cit., p. 63; Silbert, op. cit., I, pp. 148–9, and Kieniewicz, op. cit., pp. 75–6.

73 Sweden, see n. 98; Frisia: Duby, op. cit., p. 170; Basque provinces and Navarre: Dominguez Ortiz, *The Golden Age of Spain*, p. 160, and *La sociedad española en el siglo XVIII*, p. 304; Württemberg: Carsten, *Princes and Parliaments in Germany*, p. 4; Rhine duchies: Blum, *The End of the Old Order* ..., p. 86.

74 Ibid., pp. 86–8.

75 Carsten, op. cit., pp. 193–4 and 255, and his *The Origins of Prussia*, pp. 94–9 and 112–13.

76 Duby, op. cit., pp. 194–5; S. and B. Webb, *English Local Government*, II, pp. 24–6, and H. Cam, 'The decline and fall of English feudalism', *History*, new ser., 25 (1940–1), pp. 228–9.

77 J. K. Hyde, *Padua in the Age of Dante*, p. 19; Braudel, op. cit., p. 711; Salomon, op. cit., pp. 198 ff, and Carsten, *Princes and Parliaments in Germany*, p. 350.

78 Hungary: Király, op. cit., pp. 88–9; Bohemia: R. J. Kerner, *Bohemia in the Eighteenth Century*, p. 170; Austria: Link, op. cit., p. 18; Poland: Rutkowski, op. cit., pp. 20–2; Brandenburg: Carsten, *The Origins of Prussia*, pp. 98–100; Russia: Blum, *Lord and Peasant in Russia*, pp. 428–9; France: Bloch, op. cit., p. 78; Mackrell, op. cit., pp. 15 and 70, and Meyer, op. cit., pp. 796–7; Aragon: Dominguez Ortiz, *La sociedad española en el siglo XVIII*, pp. 307–10; Sicily:

Mack Smith, op. cit., pp. 155-6 and 343-4; Koenigsberger, op. cit., pp. 110 and 138-9, and Rosselli, op. cit., pp. 1-2; Naples: A. F. C. Ryder, *The Kingdom of Naples under Alfonso the Magnanimous*, pp. 13, 50 and 318, and Croce, op. cit., p. 212; Scotland: J. H. Burton, *The History of Scotland*, VIII, pp. 516-17; Netherlands: Brugmans, op. cit., p. 226.

79   France: Blum, *The End of the Old Order*, p. 86, and Mackrell, op. cit., pp. 68-71; Aragon: Dominguez Ortiz, op. cit., pp. 309-10; Austria: Link, op. cit., p. 18; Poland: Kieniewicz, op. cit., p. 20.

80   Blum, op. cit., pp. 86-7, and Devleeshouwer, op. cit., p. 207.

81   Miller, *The Nobility in Polish Renaissance Society* ..., pp. 67, 206 and 210; P. Dukes, *Catherine the Great and the Russian Nobility*, p. 106.

82   Fourquin, op. cit., pp. 31 and 40-41; R. Boutruche, *Seigneurie et féodalité*, I, p. 133; Duby, op. cit., pp. 187-8, and M. Bloch, *Feudal Society*, pp. 366 and 373-4.

83   Blum, *The End of the Old Order* ..., pp. 90-91.

84   Carsten, *The Origins of Prussia*, pp. 157 and 187.

85   Király, op. cit., pp. 88-90; H. Marczali, *Hungary in the Eighteenth Century*, pp. 174-5, and Blum, *Noble Landowners* ..., p. 88.

86   Wright, *Serf, Seigneur and Sovereign*, pp. 17-18 and 37; Kerner, op. cit., pp. 278 and 280-1, and G. Hanke, 'Das Zeitalter des Zentralismus', in *Handbuch der Geschichte der böhmischen Länder*, ed. Bosl, II, pp. 455-7.

87   *C.E.H.* I, pp. 261-2 (Bloch), and G. Duby, *The Chivalrous Society*, pp. 34 ff.

88   Fourquin, op. cit., pp. 39-41 and 170, and *C.E.H.* I, p. 263 (Bloch).

89   Fourquin, op. cit., pp. 29-36; *C.E.H.* I, pp 261-2 (Bloch); Boutruche, op. cit., I, p. 133; Bloch, *French Rural History*, p. 78, and Bloch, *Feudal Society*, II, pp. 362-4.

90   Duby, op. cit., pp. 34-5 and 41; Fourquin, op. cit., pp. 36-42, 68 and 92-3; Duby, *Rural Economy and Country Life* ..., pp. 187-8; *C.E.H.* I, pp. 264-5 (Bloch), and Bloch, *French Rural History*, p. 77.

91   J. Blum, 'The rise of serfdom in Eastern Europe', *A.H.R.* 62 (1957), pp. 824-6; P. Skwarczyński, 'The problem of feudalism in Poland up to the beginning of the sixteenth century', *Slavonic and East European Review*, 34 (1955-6), p. 303, and Carsten, *The Origins of Prussia*, pp. 30-2 and 94-100.

92   Bloch, *French Rural History*, p. 78.

93   Duby, *Rural Economy and Country Life*, pp. 194-5; Fourquin, op. cit., pp. 140-1; *C.E.H.* I, pp. 265-6 and 274-5 (Bloch); Ryder, op. cit., pp. 12-13; A. H. de Oliveira Marques, *History of Portugal*, I, p. 86, and J. N. Hillgarth, *The Spanish Kingdoms*, I, pp. 104-6.

94   Jones, in *Florentine Studies*, pp. 212-14; Duby, op. cit., p. 195, and Fourquin, op. cit., p. 70.

95   Meyer, op. cit., pp. 781-2; Dominguez Ortiz, *The Golden Age of Spain*, pp. 156-7, and his *La sociedad española en el siglo XVIII*, pp. 301-2.

96   Mack Smith, op. cit., pp. 155-6; Ryder, op. cit., p. 50 and 317-18, and G. Martin, *The Red Shirt and the Cross of Savoy*, p. 27.

97   Carsten, *The Origins of Prussia*, pp. 236-7.

98   P. Jeannin, *L'Europe du nord-ouest et du nord aux XVIIe et XVIIIe siècles*, p. 127 n. 2; M. Roberts, *Gustavus Adolphus*, I, p. 318, and *Sweden's Age of Greatness*, ed. M. Roberts, p. 122.

99   Blum, *The End of the Old Order* ..., pp. 88, and see n. 94. Also see Bloch, *French Rural History*, p. 103.

100 Ibid., and O. Hufton, 'The seigneur and the rural community in eighteenth-century France', *T.R.H.S.*, 5th ser., 29 (1978), pp. 32–6.

101 Brugmans, op. cit., pp. 222–3; Wright, op. cit., pp. 19–20, and Carsten, *The Origins of Prussia*, pp. 67–9.

102 For the basic distinctions between serf, freeman and slave, see *C.E.H.* I, pp. 253–4 (Bloch), Rosdolsky, op. cit., *Journal of Central European Affairs*, 12 (1952), pp. 131 ff, and Blum, op. cit., *A.H.R.* 62 (1957), pp. 808–9.
For serfdom in England, see F. Pollock and F. W. Maitland, *The History of English Law before the Time of Edward I*, I, pp. 414–15; in France, see Bloch, *French Rural History*, pp. 104–6 and 86–8; in Russia, see R. E. Jones, *The Emancipation of the Russian Nobility*, p. 291; D. Field, *The End of Serfdom*, pp. 14–15, and Blum, *Lord and Peasant in Russia*, pp. 262–5; in Hungary, see K. Benda, 'Le régime féodal en Hongrie à la fin du XVIIIe siècle', *L'abolition de la féodalité*, I, pp. 415–17; in Bohemia: Mejdricka, op. cit., pp. 395–7; Austria: Macartney, op. cit., p. 62.

103 *C.E.H.* I, pp. 251–9 (Bloch), and A. H. M. Jones, 'The Roman Colonate', *Past and Present*, 13 (1958).

104 Fourquin, op. cit., p. 179, and Duby, *Rural Economy and Country Life . . .* , pp. 249–50.

105 Jones, in *Florentine Studies*, pp. 193 ff; *C.E.H.* I, pp. 402 ff (Jones); Bloch, *French Rural History*, pp. 106–12; Smout, op. cit., pp. 36–7; H. Pirenne, *Belgian Democracy*, p. 79; A. R. Lewis, *The Development of Southern French and Catalan Society, 718–1050*, p. 388; S. G. Payne, *A History of Spain and Portugal*, pp. 121 f, and Blum, op. cit., *A.H.R.* 62 (1957), pp. 810–12.

106 Blum, *The End of the Old Order . . .* , p. 35; Bloch, op. cit., p. 112, and G. Benecke, *Society and Politics in Germany*, pp. 76–81 and 177–8.

107 M. Malowist, 'The economic and social development of the Baltic countries from the fifteenth to the seventeenth centuries', *Econ. H.R.*, 2nd ser., 12 (1959), p. 180; J. H. S. Birch, *Denmark in History*, pp. 69 and 132; B. J. Hovde, *The Scandinavian Countries*, I, p. 61, and *N.C.M.H.* VII, pp. 342–3 (Hatton).

108 Roberts, *Gustavus Adolphus*, II, p. 50, and *Sweden's Age of Greatness*, ed. Roberts, p. 69.

109 See the symposium on neo-serfdom in Eastern Europe in the *Slavic Review*, 34 (1975) (contributions by L. Makkai, W. E. Wright, A. Kamiński and B. K. Király); Malowist, op. cit., *Econ. H.R.*, 2nd ser., 12 (1959), and Blum, op. cit., *A.H.R.* 62 (1957).

110 For this thesis see ibid., pp. 809 and 822–3.

111 Poland: Miller, *The Nobility in Polish Renaissance Society . . .* , p. 217; Bohemia: *Slavic Review*, 34 (1975), p. 242; Mejdricka, op. cit., pp. 394–7; Austrian Empire: R. J. W. Evans, *The Making of the Habsburg Monarchy*, pp. 86–8. For the connexion between royal absolutism and serfdom, see n. 18.

112 For this thesis see Malowist, op. cit., *Econ. H.R.*, 2nd ser., 12 (1959).

113 Blum, *Lord and Peasant in Russia*, pp. 223–5; Carsten, *The Origins of Prussia*, ch. 8; Miller, op. cit., pp. 210–11, and *Slavic Review*, 34 (1975), pp. 242 ff.

114 For the relationship between population density and serfdom, see E. D. Domar, 'The causes of slavery or serfdom: a hypothesis', *Journal of Economic History*, 30 (1970).

115 For basic differences between the two, see Blum, op. cit., *A.H.R.* 62 (1957), pp. 820–22. For problems of peasant flight, see Miller, op. cit., pp. 211–12; Mej-dricka, op. cit., p. 395; Domar, op. cit., pp. 23–5, and Carsten, op. cit., pp. 104–

14. For demesne farming serving as a solution to depopulation, see Blum, op. cit., pp. 828, and *C.E.H.* I, p. 708 (Genicot).

116 R. Portal, 'Le régime féodal en Russie à la veille de son abolition', *L'abolition de la féodalité*, I, pp. 442–3, and E. Niederhauser, 'L'emancipation des serfs en Hongrie et en Europe orientale', ibid., p. 420.

117 Blum, *The End of the Old Order*, ch. 5; Bloch, *French Rural History*, pp. 71 and 88, Fourquin, op. cit., pp. 188–9; Macartney, op. cit., pp. 69–70; Kieniewicz, op. cit., pp. 15–17; *Slavic Review* 34 (1975), p. 273; Brugmans, op. cit., p. 223. For government protection of peasant tenures: Blum, op. cit., pp. 207–8 and 410; Macartney, op. cit., p. 48, and Blum, *Noble Landowners* . . . , pp. 82–4.

118 Blum, *The End of the Old Order*, p. 103; Kieniewicz, op. cit., pp. 15–16; *Slavic Review*, 34 (1975), p. 232; H. Rosenberg, 'The rise of the junkers in Brandenburg-Prussia, 1410–1653', *A.H.R.* 49 (1964), pp. 232 and 240; Macartney, op. cit., p. 69, and Blum, *Noble Landowners* . . . , p. 82.

119 Roberts, *Gustavus Adolphus*, II, p. 51; Tonnesson, op. cit., *L'abolition de la féodalité*, I, p. 304, and *C.E.H.* I, p. 655 (Bolin).

120 Blum, *The End of the Old Order* . . . , pp. 35–6 and 99–100; Mejdricka, op. cit., p. 398; Bloch, *French Rural History*, p. 88, and Brugmans, 'La fin de la féodalité aux Pays-Bas', *L'abolition de la féodalité*, I, p. 233.

121 *C.E.H.* I, pp. 256–8 and 261 (Bloch).

122 See above, p. 46.

123 Sweden: M. Roberts, *Essays in Swedish History*, p. 37; Denmark: Blum, *The End of the Old Order* . . . , pp. 219–20 and Tonnesson, op. cit., pp. 304–5; Russia: Blum, *Lord and Peasant in Russia*, p. 466, and A. Herzen, *Childhood, Youth and Exile*, p. 29; Prussia: J. J. Sheehan, 'Conflict and cohesion among German élites in the nineteenth century', in *Imperial Germany*, ed. Sheehan, p. 75; Bohemia-Austria: Kerner, op. cit., p. 274, and Macartney, op. cit., p. 21.

124 Roberts, *Gustavus Adolphus*, II, p. 156, and M. Roberts, 'Sweden', in *The European Nobility in the Eighteenth Century*, ed. Goodwin, p. 146.

125 Smout, op. cit., pp. 261–2.

126 T. F. Hamerow, *The Social Foundations of German Unification*, p. 60, and Lesnodorski, op. cit., *L'abolition de la féodalité*, I, p. 469.

127 Brugmans, op. cit., pp. 227–8.

128 Bloch, *French Rural History*, pp. 74–7; *C.E.H.* I, pp. 251–9, 263–6, and 273–4 (Bloch).

129 Ibid., pp. 261–2; Fourquin, op. cit., pp. 92–3, and Duby, *Rural Economy and Country Life* . . . , pp. 39 and 187–8.

130 Goubert, *The Ancien Régime*, pp. 84–5; Duby, op. cit., pp. 169–70; *C.H.E.* I, pp. 658–9 (Bolin); Carsten, *The Origins of Prussia*, pp. 160–1, and Blum, *The End of the Old Order* . . . , p. 30.

131 G. Ohlin, 'Entrepreneurial activities of the Swedish aristocracy', *Explorations in Entrepreneurial History*, 6 (1953), pp. 154–5, and Roberts, *Gustavus Adolphus*, II, pp. 51–2.

132 See n. 62.

133 Carsten, op. cit., p. 164; Blum, op. cit., *A.H.R.* 62 (1957), p. 832, and *Slavic Review*, 34 (1975), pp. 262–3.

134 See Domar, op. cit., *Journal of Economic History*, 30 (1970), passim. For a criticism of the exclusive emphasis upon demography, see Brenner, op. cit., *Past and Present*, 70 (1976), pp. 34–42.

135 Slicher van Bath, op. cit., p. 37; F. Lütge, 'The fourteenth and fifteenth centuries

in social and economic history', in *Pre-Reformation Germany*, ed. G. Strauss, pp. 353–8; Salomon, *La campagne de Nouvelle Castille* ..., pp. 189–90; Blum, op. cit., *A.H.R.* 62 (1957), pp. 814–19; *Slavic Review*, 34 (1975), pp. 240–7 and 257; Koenigsberger, *The Government of Sicily* ..., pp. 77–8, and Mack Smith, *A History of Sicily*, pp. 278–9; Király, *Hungary in the late Eighteenth Century*, pp. 9–10 and 52–3, and Kieniewicz, *The Emancipation of the Polish Peasantry*, p. 12.

136 See above, pp. 164 and 166.

137 Duby, op. cit., pp. 317 ff; for England: e.g. P. D. A. Harvey, *A Medieval Oxford Village*, pp. 15, 82 and 138–9; F. W. Maitland, 'History of a Cambridgeshire manor', *Collected Papers*, II, pp. 401–2, and G. A. Holmes, *The Estates of the Higher Nobility in Fourteenth-Century England*, pp. 119–20.

138 *C.E.H.* I, p. 708 (Genicot); *Slavic Review*, 34 (1975), p. 262, and Mejdricka, op. cit., *L'abolition de la féodalité*, I, pp. 395 ff.

139 See n. 59.

140 See vol. II.

141 Jones, in *Florentine Studies*, pp. 193–4 and 198–200 and 214; *C.E.H.* I, pp. 402 ff (Jones).

142 See above, p. 158.

143 Jones, in *Florentine Studies*, pp. 203–4; Duby, op. cit., bk IV, chs. 1 and 2, and *C.E.H.* I, pp. 709–13 (Genicot).

144 Blum, *The End of the Old Order* ..., p. 386.

145 Mejdricka, op. cit., pp. 401–5; Link, *The Emancipation of the Austrian Peasant*, pp. 17, 46–7 and 118–22; Kerner, op. cit., p. 128, and see n. 146.

146 Blum, op. cit., pp. 221–2.

147 Ibid., ch. 11; E. Cochrane, *Florence in the Forgotten Centuries*, p. 489, and J. Nicolas, 'La fin du régime seigneurial en Savoie', *L'abolition de la féodalité*, I, pp. 29–30.

148 See R. Mousnier, *Peasant Uprisings in Seventeenth-Century France, Russia and China*, pt I and conclusion, and the articles generated by this study, especially J. H. M. Salmon, 'Venality of office and popular sedition in seventeenth-century France', *Past and Present*, 37 (1967), L. Bernard, 'French society and popular uprisings under Louis XIV', *French Historical Studies*, 3 (1964), and C. S. L. Davies, 'Peasant revolt in France and England: a comparison', *Agricultural History Review*, 21 (1973).

149 See G. Lefebvre, *The Great Fear*, A. Davies, 'The origins of the French peasant revolution of 1789', *History*, 49 (1964), and R. R. Palmer, 'The peasants and the French Revolution', *Journal of Modern History*, 31 (1959). For the impact of the revolts upon the course of the revolution, see Barrington Moore junior, *Social Origins of Dictatorship and Democracy*, ch. 2, and T. Skocpol, *States and Social Revolutions*, ch. 3. Also see G. Lefebvre's 'The place of the revolution in the agrarian history of France' in *Rural Society in France*, ed. R. Forster and O. Ranum, p. 32.

150 For the significance of 1848, see Blum, *The End of the Old Order* ..., pp. 370–1, and T. Hamerow, *Restoration, Revolution and Reaction*, ch. 9. For the conservative abolition of seigneurial right, in reaction to revolution, see Lesnodorski, op. cit., *L'abolition de la féodalité*, I, pp. 470–1, and Niederhauser, op. cit., ibid., pp. 421–4.

151 Low Countries: essays by Devleeshouwer (pp. 205 ff) and Brugmans (pp. 221 ff) in *L'abolition de la féodalité*, I; Lombardy: P. Villani, 'L'abolition de la

féodalité dans le royaume de Naples', *L'abolition de la féodalité*, I, p. 265, and K.
R. Greenfield, *Economics and Liberalism in the Risorgimento*, pp. 48-9 and n.
71; Savoy: Blum, *The End of the Old Order* ..., p. 386.

152   Naples: Villani, op. cit., pp. 268-72; German states: Blum, *The End of the Old
      Order*, p. 370; Austrian territories: Blum, *Noble Landowners* ..., p. 67; Poland:
      Lesnodorski, op. cit., p. 465-6, and Kieniewicz, op. cit., p. 75.
153   Ibid, p. 59.
154   S. de Moxó, *La disolución del regimen señorial en España*, p. 16.
155   Mack Smith, op. cit., pp. 327, and Rosselli, op. cit., pp. 1-4.
156   Blum, *Lord and Peasant in Russia*, p. 419.
157   A. Silbert, 'Sur la féodalité portugaise et son abolition', in *L'abolition de la
      féodalité*, I, pp. 330-4; Netherlands: Brugmans, op. cit., pp. 227 and 230; Spain:
      Dominguez Ortiz, op. cit., *L'abolition de la féodalité*, I, p. 320; Prussia: Blum,
      The End of the Old Order ..., p. 413.
158   Poland: ibid., p. 419, and Lesnodorski, op. cit., pp. 465-6; Austria: Blum, *Noble
      Landowners* ..., p. 67; Spain: Dominguez Ortiz, op. cit., p. 320.
159   Blum's conclusion that the abolition resulted from a final victory for the Crown
      in a long struggle with the nobility seems to misconstrue the traditional rela-
      tionship between Crown and nobility (Blum, *The End of the Old Order* ..., p.
      373).
160   Ibid., p. 368.
161   It is significant that in Prussia an edict was passed allowing nobles to acquire
      peasant tenures on the same day that peasants were allowed to redeem their
      subjection to seigneurial right (ibid., p. 410). For East Prussia, Poznan and
      Estonia see: Dickler, op. cit., in *European Peasants and their Markets*, ed.
      Parker and Jones, pp. 276-85 and 292. For Poland: Lesnodorski, op. cit., pp.
      464-5 and 469-70. For Mecklenburg and Swedish Pomerania: von Hippel, op.
      cit., in *L'abolition de la féodalité*, I, p. 293. The point is more generally made in
      E. Hobsbawm, *The Age of Revolution*, ch. 8.
162   Macartney, *The Habsburg Empire*, pp. 279-81; Niederhauser, op. cit., pp. 420-
      1; Mejdricka, op. cit., pp. 404-5; Blum, *The End of the Old Order*, pp. 91 and
      311.
163   Hungary: Niederhauser, op. cit., pp. 419-22, and Blum, op. cit., p. 311; Boh-
      emia: ibid., pp. 310-11; Rumania, ibid., p. 315; Poland: Lesnodorski, op. cit.,
      pp. 463, 470 and 473, and Blum, op. cit., p. 359; Russia: ibid., p. 314; Sicily: see
      n. 155.
164   Blum, op. cit., pp. 371-2. Also see A. Soboul, 'Persistence of "feudalism" in the
      rural society of nineteenth-century France', in *Rural Society in France*, ed. R.
      Forster and O. Ranum. Soboul attributes the final disappearance of seigneurial
      exactions to the rise of agrarian capitalism; but his evidence seems to show not
      only that seigneurial exactions lingered longer in the peasant farming areas of
      the South-west and South than in the areas of capitalist farming in the North,
      but also that the extreme hostility which peasants were capable of showing
      towards seigneurial exactions was both a factor preventing their restoration
      and a cause of their eventual disappearance.
165   Mejdricka, op. cit., pp. 407, and Blum, op. cit., pp. 229-31, 409 and 413-17.
166   Netherlands: Brugmans, op. cit., pp. 228 and 230; Sweden and Denmark:
      Hovde, *The Scandinavian Countries*, I, p. 284; England: K. G. Davies, 'Vestiges
      de la féodalité en Angleterre aux XVIIe et XVIIIe siècles', *L'abolition de la
      féodalité*, I, p. 24; Scotland: J. Critchley, *Feudalism*, p. 22.

167 Blum, op. cit., p. 367.
168 Ibid., pp. 386-8.
169 Soboul, op. cit., passim.
170 Duchy of Warsaw: Blum, op. cit., pp. 368, 407 and 414. For Lombardy, see n. 151. For Austria, see n. 152.
171 Silbert, op. cit., pp. 331 ff, and Dominguez Ortiz, op. cit., pp. 320-1.
172 Blum, op. cit., pp. 398 and 405-6; Silbert, op. cit., p. 332.
173 Hovde, op. cit., II, pp. 516-17.
174 Blum, *Lord and Peasant in Russia*, pp. 554-60.
175 E.g. see Mack Smith, op. cit., p. 406, and Macartney, op. cit., p. 74.
176 Du Puys de Clinchamps, *La noblesse*, pp. 21-2.
177 Duby, *Rural Economy and Country Life* ..., pp. 227-8, and Fourquin, op. cit., p. 172.
178 Blum, *The End of the Old Order* ..., p. 164. Prussia: Carsten, *The Origins of Prussia*, ch. XI; Austria: Macartney, op. cit., pp. 67-8; Blum, *Noble Landowners* ..., pp. 74-8, and Link, op. cit., pp. 16-17; Russia: T. Emmons, *The Russian Landed Gentry and the Peasant Emancipation of 1861*, pp. 22-5; Hungary: Zs P. Pach, *Die ungarische Agrarentwicklung im 16-17 Jahrhundert*, pp. 18-23; Bohemia and Poland: *Slavic Review*, 34 (1975), pp. 248-9 and 262-3, and Freudenberger, *The Waldstein Woolen Mill*, p. 3.
179 Bois, *Crise du féodalisme*, pp. 213-14; Goubert, *The Ancien Régime*, pp. 84 and 126-7; R. Forster, *The Nobility of Toulouse* ..., pp. 38-9; Meyer, *La noblesse bretonne au XVIIIe siècle*, pp. 613 and 651-6; and A. Soboul, 'Problèmes de la féodalité d'ancien régime, *L'abolition de la féodalité, I, pp. 118-19 and 123-4.
180 See n. 58; Silbert, in *L'abolition de la féodalité*, I, p. 339; Forster, op. cit., *A.H.R.* 75 (1970), pp. 1605-7, and his 'The provincial noble: a reappraisal', *A.H.R.* 68 (1963), pp. 685-6.
181 E.g. in France, see ibid., p. 684.
182 See vol. II.
183 B. Behrens, *The Ancien Régime*, p. 40, and Hufton, op. cit., *T.R.H.S.*, 5th ser., 29 (1978), p. 33.
184 Blum, *The End of the Old Order* ..., pp. 394-8, and M. Bullock, *Austria, 1918-1938*, pp. 116-17.
185 Critchley, *Feudalism*, pp. 142 ff.
186 See n. 25.
187 Blum, op. cit., pp. 399-400.
188 For their retarding effect, see Blum, *The End of the Old Order* ..., pp. 116-17; Soboul, op. cit. *L'abolition de la féodalité*, I, pp. 126-7, Forster, op. cit., *A.H.R.* 75 (1970), passim, and Brenner, op. cit., *Past and Present*, 70 (1976), pp. 48 and 60. The tenor of the latter part of Brenner's article, however, is that the major impediment on economic development is the peasant economy rather than the seigneurial system (pp. 64-5 and 68), and especially the capacity of small farmers to protect themselves from landlord exploitation by securing proprietorial rights to their holdings.
189 Blum, *The End of the Old Order* ..., p. 299. Bohemia: Freudenberger, op. cit., p. 34, and Macartney, op. cit., p. 61; Russia: Portal, op. cit., in *L'abolition de la féodalité*, pp. 441-2.
190 Bois, op. cit., pp. 203-4; Spufford, *Contrasting Communities*, p. 46.
191 Blum, *The End of the Old Order* ..., p. 118.
192 See ibid., chs. 6 and 7; P. O'Brien and C. Keyder, *Economic Growth in Britain*

and France, 1780–1914, ch. 5, and B. Sexauer, 'English and French agriculture in the late eighteenth century', *Agricultural History*, 50 (1976).

193 Blum, op. cit. pp. 75 ff.
194 As in parts of Poland between the thirteenth and the nineteenth centuries: see Miller, *The Nobility in Polish Renaissance Society*, pp. 323–4 and 382–3.
195 E. Hobsbawm and G. Rudé, *Captain Swing*, pts. I and III.

Chapter VII. Privileges of land ownership

1 J. Blum, *The End of the Old Order in Rural Europe*, pp. 17–20. In the parts of Poland acquired by the Hohenzollerns, the re-imposed privilege lasted until 1807; in the Duchy of Warsaw (later Congress Kingdom), the Tzar accepted Napoleon's termination of the privilege; while in the part annexed by the Habsburgs, the re-imposed privilege lasted until 1848 (P. S. Wandycz, *The Lands of Partitioned Poland*, pp. 8, 15 and 48). The privilege was also imparted to Livonia when it was annexed by the Russians in 1710 and lasted until the nineteenth century (Blum, op. cit., p. 19).

2 W. Dworzaczek, 'Perméabilité des barrières sociales dans la Pologne du XVIe siècle', *Acta Poloniae Historica*, 24 (1971), pp. 24–5; J. C. Miller, *The Nobility in Polish Renaissance Society*, pp. 53–4, and A. Mączak, 'The social distribution of landed property in Poland from the 16th to the 18th century' *Third International Conference of Economic History*, I, p. 456.

3 B. K. Király, *Hungary in the late Eighteenth Century*, p. 43, n. 2; Blum, op. cit., p. 19, and K. Benda, 'Le régime féudal en Hongrie à la fin du XVIIIe siècle', *L'abolition de la féodalité*, I, p. 414.

4 J. Blum, *Lord and Peasant in Russia*, pp. 358–62.
5 Blum, *The End of the Old Order ....*, pp. 19–20.
6 Landownership in Hungary and Russia eventually became a qualification for the enjoyment of privilege, but only in conjunction with, not as an alternative to, the possession of noble status (see above, p. 95).

7 Not all the provinces of the Prussian monarchy possessed this privilege. It was absent from Silesia and West Prussia (A. Goodwin, 'Prussia', in *The European Nobility in the Eighteenth Century*, ed. Goodwin, pp. 94–5) and from Mark and Cleves (F. L. Carsten, *The Origins of Prussia*, p. 231). In addition, the reservation did not apply to very small estates (Goodwin, op. cit., p. 95). Also see Carsten, op. cit., p. 188; *The Historical Essays of Otto Hintze*, ed. F. Gilbert, pp. 55 and 58; H. Rosenberg, *Bureaucracy, Aristocracy and Autocracy*, pp. 218–19, and his 'The rise of the junkers in Brandenburg-Prussia, 1410–1653 (part II)', *A.H.R.* 49 (1944), p. 240.

8 Rosenberg, *Bureaucracy, Aristocracy and Autocracy*, pp. 218–20, and F. Martiny, 'Die Adelsfrage in Preussen vor 1806', *Vierteljahrschrift für Sozial- und Wirtschaftsgeschichte*, 1938 (Beheit 35), pp. 36–7.

9 J. Blum, *Noble Landowners and Agriculture in Austria*, pp. 23 and 61–7; C. A. Macartney, *The Habsburg Empire*, pp. 21, 126 and 515 n. 4; S. Adler, *Das adelige Landrecht in Nieder- und Oberösterreich ...*', pp. 60–1; B. Waldstein-Wartenberg, 'Österreichisches Adelsrecht, 1804–1918', *Mitteilungen des österreichisches Staatsarchivs*, 17–18 (1964–5), p. 142, and Blum, *The End of the Old Order ...*, p. 18.

10 Bavaria: F. L. Carsten, *Princes and Parliaments in Germany*, p. 419; Saxony: ibid., pp. 220 and 241.

11 Savoy: Blum, *The End of the Old Order* ..., p. 21; Sweden: M. Roberts, *Gustavus Adolphus*, II, p. 53; Roberts 'Sweden', in *The European Nobility in the Eighteenth Century*, ed. Goodwin, pp. 145–6 and 151; K. D. Tonneson, 'Les pays scandinaves', *L'abolition de la féodalité*, I, pp. 309–10, and B. J. Hovde, *The Scandinavian Countries*, p. 285; Denmark: E.-L. Peterson, 'La crise de la noblesse danoise entre 1580 et 1660', *Annales d'histoire* E.S., 23 (1968), pp. 1238 and 1244.

12 Spain: J. F. O'Callaghan, *A History of Medieval Spain*, p. 288; France: P. Contamine, 'The French nobility and the war', in *The Hundred Years' War*, ed. K. Fowler, p. 142; E. G. Barber, *The Bourgeoisie in Eighteenth-Century France*, p. 94, and R. Mousnier, *Peasant Uprisings in the Seventeenth Century*, p. 12.

13 Poland: Wandycz, op. cit., p. 8; Sweden: Hovde, op. cit., p. 285; Hungary: Macartney, op. cit., p. 291; France: J. Q. C. Mackrell, *The Attack on 'Feudalism' in Eighteenth-Century France*, pp. 146–7.

14 J. Meyer, *La noblesse bretonne*, pp. 108–10, 126–7 and 433–4; O. Hufton, *Bayeux in the late Eighteenth Century*, p. 49; E. Le Roy Ladurie, 'Family structures and inheritance customs in sixteenth-century France', in *Family and Inheritance*, ed. Goody, pp. 53–4.

15 *Ibid.*, pp. 61 ff.

16 J. P. Cooper, 'Patterns of inheritance and settlement by great landowners from the fifteenth to the eighteenth centuries', *Family and Inheritance*, ed. Goody, ch. 8; S. J. Woolf, *Studi sulla nobiltà piemontese nell' epoca dell' assolutismo*, pp. 150–1; E. E. Malefakis, *Agrarian Reform and Peasant Revolution in Spain*, p. 68; R. Forster, 'The survival of the nobility during the French Revolution', *Past and Present*, 37 (1967), p. 75, and T. F. Hamerow, *Restoration, Revolution and Reaction*, p. 206.

17 Blum, *Noble Landowners and Agriculture in Austria*, p. 63; Waldstein-Wartenberg, op. cit., p. 142, and E. Cochrane, *Florence in the Forgotten Centuries*, p. 448.

18 Hungary: C. A. Macartney, 'Hungary', in *The European Nobility in the Eighteenth Century*, ed. Goodwin, p. 125, and see ch. III n. 43; Russia: see n. 19; Poland: P. Skwarczyński, 'The problem of feudalism in Poland up to the beginning of the sixteenth century', *Slavonic and East European Review*, 34 (1955–6), p. 301; Flanders: E. Warlop, *The Flemish Nobility before 1300*, pp. 290–1; France: G. Fourquin, *Lordship and Feudalism in the Middle Ages*, p. 146.

19 R. Pipes, *Russia under the Old Regime*, pp. 51 and 96–7; R. E. Jones, *The Emancipation of the Russian Nobility*, pp. 18–21 and 282; Blum, *Lord and Peasant in Russia*, pp. 169–71 and 183–7, and M. Raeff, *Origins of the Russian Intelligentsia*, pp. 28, 53 and 116.

20 This does not mean that overlord rights were never reasserted: regalian rights were reclaimed or extended by the Crown in twelfth/thirteenth- and seventeenth-century France (Fourquin, op. cit., p. 146, and F. Loirette, 'The defence of the allodium in seventeenth-century Agenais ...', *State and Society in Seventeenth-century France*, ed. R. F. Kierstead, passim); in sixteenth- and seventeenth-century Hungary (H. Marczali, *Hungary in the Eighteenth Century*, p. 313); and in eighteenth-century Sicily and Naples under Bourbon rule (D. Mack Smith, *A History of Sicily*, p. 291, and J. Rosselli, *Lord William Bentinck and the British Occupation of Sicily*, p. 3).

21 Fourquin, op. cit., pp. 142–4; J. R. Strayer, *Feudalism*, p. 56; Warlop, op. cit.,

p. 291; W. Görlitz, *Die Junker*, p. 25; F. Graus, 'Origines de l'état et de la noblesse en Moravie et en Bohême', *Revue des études slaves*, 39 (1961), p. 54, and J. C. Holt, 'Politics and property in early medieval England', *Past and Present*, 57 (1972), passim.

22 Livonia: Blum, *The End of the Old Order* ..., p. 19; Hungary: Marczali, op. cit., p. 130; Russia, n. 19.

23 Fourquin, op. cit., pp. 141, 145–6, 148, 150–1 and 156–7.

24 Prussia: Martiny, op. cit., pp. 15–16; Hungary: Király, op. cit., pp. 70 and 183–4; Russia: Jones, *The Emancipation of the Russian Nobility*, pp. 196–7; England: P. Roebuck, 'Post-Restoration landownership: the impact of the abolition of wardship', *Journal of British Studies*, XVIII (1978).

25 *N.C.M.H.* VI, p. 603 (Stoye); Macartney, 'Hungary', in *The European Nobility in the Eighteenth Century*, ed. Goodwin, p. 125, and Mack Smith, op. cit., p. 476.

26 *N.C.M.H.* III, p. 398 (Skwarczyński), and G. Ohlin, 'Entrepreneurial activities of the Swedish aristocracy', *Explorations in Entrepreneurial History*, 6 (1953), p. 157.

27 L. Stone, *The Crisis of the Aristocracy*, pp. 338–9, and H. A. Lloyd, *The Gentry of South-West Wales*, pp. 82–3.

28 Spain: F. Sanchez Ramos, *La economía siderúrgica española*, I, pp. 49–50, and J. Nadal, 'The failure of the industrial revolution in Spain, 1830–1914', in *The Fontana Economic History of Europe*, IV (2), p. 568; Low Countries: J. Dhondt and M. Bruwier, 'The industrial revolution in the Low Countries, 1700–1914', ibid., IV (1), p. 335; Germany: W. O. Henderson, *The State and the Industrial Revolution in Prussia*, pp. 29–30 and 61; France: G. Richard, *Noblesse d'affaires au XVIIIe siècle*, p. 185; Silesia: Henderson, op. cit., p. 5; Poland: *N.C.M.H.* III, p. 398 (Skwarczyński); Sweden: Ohlin, op. cit., p. 156, and Roberts, *Gustavus Adolphus*, II, p. 36.

29 Sicily: Mack Smith, op. cit., pp. 95 and 384; Tuscany: E. Cochrane, *Florence in the Forgotten Centuries*, p. 408; Russia: Jones, op. cit., p. 282; Spain: Sanchez Ramos, op. cit., p. 74.

30 France: Richard, op. cit., pp. 185–7; Spain: Nadal, op. cit., p. 568, and Sanchez Ramos, op. cit., pp. 48–50 and 73–5; Silesia: Henderson, op. cit., p. 5; Saar: ibid., pp. xxi and 60–1; Low Countries: Dhondt and Bruwier, op. cit., p. 335, and R. Devleeshouwer, 'L'abolition des droits féodaux en Belgique', *L'abolition de la féodalité*, I, p. 213.

31 Blum, *The End of the Old Order* ..., p. 20, and see above, ch. VI.

32 Le Roy Ladurie, op. cit., pp. 61 ff.

33 See above, p. 192.

34 Meyer, op. cit., pp. 108–10 and 126–7. Also see F. Bluche, *La vie quotidienne de la noblesse française au XVIIIe siècle*, pp. 206–7.

35 Cooper, op. cit., pp. 252–3.

36 Waldstein-Wartenberg, op. cit., p. 142.

37 S. A. Hansen, 'Changes in the wealth and the demographic characteristics of the Danish aristocracy, 1470–1720', *Third International Conference of Economic History*, IV, pp. 101–2, and Blum, *End of the Old Order* ..., pp. 18–19.

38 Ibid., p. 18, and Martiny, op. cit., p. 35.

39 France: Blum, op. cit., p. 20; Sweden, E. Heckscher, *An Economic History of Sweden*, pp. 31 and 168; England: F. M. L. Thompson, 'The social distribution

of landed property in England since the sixteenth century', *Econ. H.R.*, 2nd ser., 19 (1966), passim.

40 Denmark: Hansen, op. cit., p. 102; Prussia, J. R. Gillis, 'Aristocracy and bureaucracy in nineteenth-century Prussia', *Past and Present*, 41 (1968), p. 113; Russia: E. Wolf, *Peasant Wars in the Twentieth Century*, p. 65.

41 J. J. Sheehan, 'Conflict and cohesion among German élites in the nineteenth century', in *Imperial Germany*, ed. Sheehan, p. 79; L. Cecil, 'The creation of nobles in Prussia 1871-1918', *A.H.R.* 75 (1969-70); and Waldstein-Wartenberg, op. cit., pp. 134-5.

42 Bavaria: Carsten, *Princes and Parliaments in Germany*, p. 351. For the other examples, see above, p. 181.

43 E.g. Hamerow, *The Social Foundations of German Unification*, pp. 37-8; Gillis, op. cit., p. 113, and Sheehan, op. cit., p. 79.

44 Wide-ranging study of the subject is provided by J. Critchley, *Feudalism*, Barrington Moore, *Social Origins of Dictatorship and Democracy*, and Perry Anderson, *Lineages of the Absolutist State*, section III and n. B. For Africa: J. Goody, 'Economy and feudalism in Africa', *Econ. H.R.*, 2nd ser., 22 (1969), D. N. Levine, *Wax and Gold: Tradition and Innovation in Ethiopian Culture*, ch. 5, J. Vansina, *Kingdoms of the Savanna*, pp. 28-30 and 246-7, G. Balandier, *Daily Life in the Kingdom of the Kongo*, ch. 7, and T. O. Ranger, 'The nineteenth century in Southern Rhodesia', in *Aspects of Central African History*, ed. Ranger; the Ottoman Empire: Perry Anderson, op. cit., section II (7), H. A. R. Gibb and H. Bowen, *Islamic Society and the West*, I, pp. 193-9 and ch. 5, and F. Braudel, *The Mediterranean*, pp. 718 ff; Japan: Anderson, op. cit., n. A, A. Lewis, *Knights and Samurai*, E. O. Reischauer, 'Japanese feudalism' in *Feudalism in History*, ed. R. Coulborn, and Barrington Moore, op. cit., ch. 5; the Moghul Empire: Barrington Moore, op. cit., ch. 6, D. Thorner, 'Feudalism in India', in *Feudalism in History*, ed. Coulborn, and Jagdish Raj, *The Mutiny and British Land Policy in North India, 1856-1868*, chs. 1 and 2; Imperial China: Barrington Moore, op. cit., ch. 4, and M. Elvin, *The Pattern of the Chinese Past*, chs. 1, 6 and 15; the Persian Empire: A. K. S. Lambton, *Landlord and Peasant in Persia*, ch. 13, and *Persian Land Reform, 1962-6*, ch. 1.

45 R. Mousnier and F. Hartung, 'Quelques problèmes concernant la monarchie absolue', *X Congresse Internazionale di Scienze Storici, Relazioni*, IV (1955), passim.

46 See above, pp. 153-4 and 172.

47 Mack Smith, op. cit., p. 384.

48 E.g. Poland: *Cambridge History of Poland*, I, p. 446, and *N.C.M.H.* III, p. 398 (Skwarczyński); Silesia: Henderson, op. cit., p. 20; Belgium, Dhondt and Bruwier, op. cit., p. 335; Sicily: Mack Smith, op. cit., p. 387 and 476; Sweden: Hovde, op. cit., pp. 182-3, and Roberts, op. cit., p. 36; Russia: P. Dukes, *Catherine the Great and the Russian Nobility*, p. 234; England: J. T. Ward, 'Landowners and mining', in *Land and Industry*, ed. Ward and R. G. Wilson, ch. 2.

Bibliography

A. Åberg, 'The Swedish army, from Lützen to Narva', *Sweden's Age of Greatness*, ed. M. Roberts, ch. 8.

L'abolition de la féodalité dans le monde occidental (Colloques Internationaux du Centre National de la Recherche Scientifique, Paris. 1971), two volumes.

Acts of the Parliaments of Scotland (London, 1820), VIII.

S. Adler, *Das adelige Landrecht in Nieder- und Oberösterreich und die Gerichtsreformen des XVIII. Jahrhunderts* (Vienna, 1912).

K. Ågren, 'The *reduktion*', *Sweden's Age of Greatness*, ed. M. Roberts, ch. 7.

E. N. and P. R. Anderson, *Political Institutions and Social Change in Continental Europe in the Nineteenth Century* (Berkeley, 1967).

P. Anderson, *Lineages of the Absolutist State* (London, 1974).

I. Andersson, *A History of Sweden*, trans. Carolyn Hannay (London, 1956).

A. B. Appleby, 'Agrarian capitalism or seigneurial reaction? The northwest of England, 1500-1700', *American Historical Review*, 80 (1975), pp. 574 ff.

Sven-Erik Åström, 'The Swedish economy and Sweden's role as a great power, 1632-1697, *Sweden's Age of Greatness*, ed. M. Roberts, ch. 2.

R. Auty and D. Obolensky (ed.), *An Introduction to Russian History* (Cambridge, 1976).

O. P. Backus, 'The problem of feudalism in Lithuania, 1506-1548', *Slavic Review* 21 (1962), pp. 639 ff.

G. Balandier, *Daily Life in the Kingdom of the Kongo*, trans. H. Weaver (London, 1968).

R. Baldick, *The Duel* (London, 1965).

F. E. Baldwin, *Sumptuary Legislation and Personal Regulation in England* (Baltimore, 1926).

E. G. Barber, *The Bourgeoisie in Eighteenth-Century France* (Princeton, 1955).

R. Barber, *The Knight and Chivalry* (London, 1970).

J. Bardach, 'Gouvernants et gouvernés en Pologne au moyen-âge et aux temps modernes', *Recueils de la Société Jean Bodin*, 25 (1965), ch. 10.

J. Beeler, *Warfare in Feudal Europe, 730–1200* (London, 1972).

B. Behrens, 'Nobles, privileges and taxes in France at the end of the ancien régime', *Economic History Review*, 2nd ser., 15 (1963), pp. 451 ff.

Behrens, 'A revision defended: nobles, privileges and taxes in France', *French Historical Studies*, 9 (1976), pp. 521 ff.

Behrens, *The Ancien Régime* (London, 1967).

K. Benda, 'Le régime féodal en Hongrie à la fin du XVIIIe siècle', *L'abolition de la féodalité*, I, pp. 411 ff.

G. Benecke, *Society and Politics in Germany, 1500–1750* (London, 1974).

R. M. Berdahl, 'Conservative politics and aristocratic landholders in Bismarckian Germany', *Journal of Modern History*, 44 (1972), pp. 1 ff.

J. Bérenger, *Finances et absolutisme autrichien dans la seconde moitié du XVII siècle* (Paris, 1975).

L. Bernard, 'French society and popular uprisings under Louis XIV', *French Historical Studies*, 3 (1964), pp. 454 ff.

R. R. Betts, 'Constitutional development and political thought in Eastern Europe', *The New Cambridge Modern History*, II, ch. 15.

Betts, 'The Habsburg Lands', ibid. V, ch. 20.

J. H. S. Birch, *Denmark in History* (London, 1938).

G. Birtsch, K. Kluxen, H. Roos and E. Weis, *Der Adel vor der Revolution* (Göttingen, 1971).

M. Bloch, *French Rural History*, trans. J. Sondheimer (London, 1966).

Bloch, *Feudal Society*, trans. L. A. Manyon (London, 1961), two volumes.

Bloch, 'The rise of dependent cultivation and seignorial institutions', *The Cambridge Economic History of Europe*, I (2nd ed., 1966), ch. 6.

F. Bluche, *La vie quotidienne de la noblesse française au XVIIIe siècle* (Paris, 1973).

J. Blum, *Lord and Peasant in Russia* (Princeton, 1961).

Blum, *Noble Landowners and Agriculture in Austria, 1815–1848* (Baltimore, 1947).

Blum, *The End of the Old Order in Rural Europe* (Princeton, 1978).

Blum, 'The rise of serfdom in Eastern Europe', *American Historical Review*, 62 (1957), pp. 807 ff.

Blum, 'The condition of the European peasantry on the eve of emancipation', *Journal of Modern History*, 46 (1974), pp. 395.

Blum, 'Russia', *European Landed Elites in the Nineteenth Century*, ed. D. Spring, ch. 4.

G. Bois, *Crise du féodalisme: économie rurale et demographie en Normandie orientale du début du XIVe siècle au milieu du XVIe siècle* (Paris, 1976).

S. Bolin, 'Medieval agrarian society in its prime: Scandinavia', *The Cam-*

bridge Economic History of Europe, I (2nd ed., 1966), ch. 7 (8).

G. Bonis, 'The Hungarian feudal diet, 13th–18th centuries', *Recueils de la Société Jean Bodin*, 25 (1965), ch. 11.

R. Bonney, *Political Change in France under Richelieu and Mazarin, 1624–1661* (Oxford, 1978).

K. Bosl (ed.), *Handbuch der Geschichte der böhmischen Länder* (Stuttgart, 1967), four volumes.

A. B. Boswell, 'Poland', *The European Nobility in the Eighteenth Century*, ed. A. Goodwin, ch. 9.

R. Boutruche, *Seigneurie et féodalité* (Paris, 1968–70, 2nd ed.), two volumes.

F. Braudel, *The Mediterranean* (English trans.: London, 1973), two volumes.

G. Brenan, *The Spanish Labyrinth* (2nd ed., Cambridge, 1950).

R. Brenner, 'Agrarian class structure and economic development in pre-industrial Europe', *Past and Present*, 70 (1976), pp. 30 ff.

P. A. Bromhead, *The House of Lords and Contemporary Politics, 1911–1957* (London, 1958).

N. P. Brooks, 'Arms, status and warfare in late Saxon England', *Ethelred the Unready*, ed. D. Hill (*British Archaeological Reports*, 59 (1978)).

I. J. Brugmans, 'La fin de la féodalité aux Pays-Bas', *L'abolition de la féodalité*, I, pp. 221 ff.

M. Bullock, *Austria, 1918–1938: a study in Failure* (London, 1939).

P. Burke, *Venice and Amsterdam: a Study of Seventeenth-Century Elites* (London, 1974).

Burke (ed.), *The New Cambridge Modern History* (Cambridge, 1979), XIII.

J. H. Burton, *The History of Scotland from Agricola's Invasion to the Extinction of the last Jacobite Insurrection* (2nd ed., Edinburgh, 1873), VIII.

O. Büsch, *Militärsystem und Sozialleben im alten Preussen, 1713–1807* (Berlin, 1962).

M. L. Bush, *The Government Policy of Protector Somerset* (London, 1975).

Bush, 'Place and period in the study of History', *Times Higher Education Supplement*, Sept. 1980.

W. J. Callahan, *Honour, Commerce and Industry in Eighteenth-Century Spain* (Boston, 1972).

H. Cam, 'The decline and fall of English feudalism', *History*, new ser., 25 (1940–1), pp. 216 ff.

The Cambridge Economic History of Europe, I (2nd ed., 1966), ed. M. M. Postan and H. J. Habakkuk.

The Cambridge History of Poland, ed. W. F. Reddaway, J. H. Penson, O. Halecki and R. Dyboski (Cambridge, 1941–50), two volumes.

W. Camden, *Remaines concerning Britaine* (London, 1636).

J. Cannon, *Parliamentary Reform, 1640–1832* (Cambridge, 1973).

F. L. Carsten, *The Origins of Prussia* (Oxford, 1954).

Carsten, *Princes and Parliaments in Germany from the Fifteenth to the Eighteenth Centuries* (Oxford, 1959).

Carsten, 'German estates in the eighteenth century', *Recueils de la Société Jean Bodin*, 25 (4) (1965), ch. 8.

G. J. Cavanaugh, 'Nobles, privileges and taxes in France: a revision reviewed', *French Historical Studies*, 8 (1974), pp. 681 ff, and 'Reply to Behrens', ibid., 9 (1976), pp. 528 ff.

F. A. Cazel (ed.), *Feudalism and Liberty: Articles and Addresses of S. Painter* (Baltimore, 1961).

L. Cecil, 'The creation of nobles in Prussia, 1871–1918', *American Historical Review*, 75 (1970), pp. 757 ff.

M. J. Cheke, *Dictator of Portugal: the Life of the Marquis of Pombal* (London, 1938).

F. L. Cheyette (ed.), *Lordship and Community in Medieval Europe* (New York, 1968).

S. Chrimes, C. D. Ross and R. A. Griffiths (eds.), *Fifteenth-century England, 1399–1509* (Manchester, 1972).

J. T. Cliffe, *The Yorkshire Gentry from Reformation to Civil War* (London, 1969).

P. du Puy de Clinchamps, *La noblesse* (Paris, 1959).

E. Cochrane, *Florence in the Forgotten Centuries, 1527–1800* (Chicago, 1973).

D. C. Coleman, 'Gentlemen and Players', *Economic History Review*, 2nd ser., 26 (1973), pp. 92 ff.

Coleman, 'Economic problems and policies', *The New Cambridge Modern History*, V, ch. 2.

Coleman and A. H. John (eds.), *Trade, Government and Economy in Pre-industrial England* (London, 1976).

P. Colletta, *History of the Kingdom of Naples, 1734–1825*, trans. S. Horner (London, 1858), two volumes.

G. Coniglio, *Il regno di Napoli al tempo di Carlo V* (Naples, 1951).

P. Contamine, 'The French nobility and the war', *The Hundred Years' War*, ed. K. Fowler, ch. 6.

J. P. Cooper, 'Differences between English and continental governments in the early seventeenth century', *Britain and the Netherlands*, ed. J. S. Bromley and E. H. Kossmann, I (London, 1960), pp. 62 ff.

Cooper, 'Patterns of inheritance and settlement by great landowners from the fifteenth to the eighteenth century', *Family and Inheritance*, ed. J. Goody, etc., ch. 8.

Cooper, 'General introduction', *The New Cambridge Modern History*, IV, ch. 1.

R. Coulborn (ed.), *Feudalism in History* (Princeton, 1965).

P. J. Coveney (ed.), *France in Crisis, 1620–1675* (London, 1977).

O. Crisp, *Studies in the Russian Economy before 1914* (London, 1976).

J. Critchley, *Feudalism* (London, 1978).

B. Croce, *A History of the Kingdom of Naples*, ed. H. Stuart Hughes, trans. F. Frenage (Chicago, 1970).

S. Dahlgren, 'Estates and classes', *Sweden's Age of Greatness*, ed. M. Roberts, ch. 3.

A. Davies, 'The origins of the French peasant revolution of 1789', *History*, 49 (1964), pp. 24 ff.

C. S. L. Davies, 'Peasant revolt in France and England: a comparison', *Agricultural History Review*, 21 (1973), pp. 122 ff.

K. G. Davies, 'Vestiges de la féodalité en Angleterre aux XVIIe et XVIIIe siècles', *L'abolition de la féodalité*, I, pp. 19 ff.

J. C. Davis, *The Decline of the Venetian Nobility as a Ruling Class* (Baltimore, 1962).

M. Defourneaux, *Daily Life in Spain in the Golden Age*, trans. N. Brauch (London, 1970).

K. Demeter, *The German Officer-Corps in Society and State, 1650–1945*, trans. by A. Malcolm (London, 1965).

T. K. Derry, *A History of Modern Norway, 1814–1972* (Oxford, 1973).

R. Devleeshouwer, 'L'abolition des droits féodaux en Belgique', *L'abolition de la féodalité*, I, pp. 205 ff.

P. Deyon, 'The French nobility and absolute monarchy in the first half of the seventeenth century', *France in Crisis, 1620–1675*, ed. P. J. Coveney, ch. 8.

J. Dhont, 'Estates or powers: essays in the parliamentary history of the Southern Netherlands from the twelfth to the eighteenth century', *Anciens pays at assemblées d'états*, 69 (1977).

J. Dhont, and M. Bruwier, 'The industrial revolution in the Low Countries, 1700–1914', *Fontana Economic History of Europe*, IV (2).

Diccionario de historia de España (Madrid, 1968–9), three volumes.

R. A. Dickler, 'Organisation and change in productivity in Eastern Europe', in *European Peasants and their Markets: Essays in Agrarian Economic History*, ed. W. N. Parker and E. L. Jones (Princeton, 1975), ch. 7.

E. D. Domar, 'The causes of slavery or serfdom: a hypothesis', *Journal of Economic History*, 30 (1970), pp. 18 ff.

A. Dominguez Ortiz, *The Golden Century of Spain: 1516–1659*, trans. J. Casey (London, 1971).

Dominguez Ortiz, *Politica y hacienda de Felipe IV* (Madrid, 1960).

Dominguez Ortiz, *El regimen señorial y el reformismo borbonico* (Madrid, 1974).

Dominquez Ortiz, *la sociedad española en el siglo XVII* (Madrid, 1964–70), two vols.

Dominguez Ortiz, *La sociedad española en el siglo XVIII* (Madrid, 1955).

Dominguez Ortiz, 'La fin du régime seigneurial en Espagne', *L'abolition de la féodalité*, I, pp. 315 ff.

R. Doucet, *Les institutions de la France au XVIe siècle* (Paris, 1948), two vols.

W. Doyle, *The Old European Order, 1660-1800* (Oxford, 1978).

Doyle, 'Was there an aristocratic reaction in pre-revolutionary France?', *Past and Present*, 57 (1972), pp. 97 ff.

G. Duby, *The Chivalrous Society*, trans. C. Postan (London, 1977).

Duby, *Rural Economy and Country Life in the Medieval West*, trans. C. Postan (London, 1968).

Duby, 'The nobility in eleventh- and twelfth-century Mâçonnais', *Lordship and Community in Medieval Europe*, ed. F. L. Cheyette, pp. 137 ff.

P. Dukes, *Catherine the Great and the Russian Nobility* (Cambridge, 1967).

F. Dumont, 'La noblesse et les états particuliers français', *Études présentées à la commission internationale pour l'histoire des assemblées d'états*, 11 (1950), ch. 8.

W. Dworzaczek, 'Perméabilité des barrières sociales dans la Pologne du XVIe siècle', *Acta Poloniae Historica*, 24 (1971).

P. Earle (ed.) *Essays in European Economic History, 1500-1800* (Oxford, 1974).

K. Edwards, *The English Secular Cathedrals in the Middle Ages* (Manchester, 1949).

E. Ekman, 'The Danish royal law of 1665', *Journal of Modern History*, 29 (1957), pp. 102 ff.

J. H. Elliott, *The Revolt of the Catalans: a Study in the Decline of Spain, 1598-1640* (Cambridge, 1963).

Elliott, *Imperial Spain* (London, 1963).

G. R. Elton, *Studies in Tudor and Stuart Politics and Governments* (Cambridge, 1974), two volumes.

M. Elvin, *The Pattern of the Chinese Past* (London, 1973).

T. Emmons, *The Russian Landed Gentry and the Peasant Emancipation of 1861* (Cambridge, 1968).

E. Esmonin, *Études sur la France des XVIIe et XVIIIe siècles* (Paris, 1964).

T. Esper, 'The *odnodvortsy* and the Russian nobility', *Slavonic and East European Review*, 45 (1967), pp. 124 ff.

R. J. W. Evans, *The Making of the Habsburg Monarchy, 1500-1700* (Oxford, 1979).

H. Feigl, *Die Niederösterreichische Grundherrschaft vom ausgehenden Mittelalter bis zu den theresianisch-josephinischen Reformen* (Vienna, 1964).

D. Field, *The End of Serfdom: Nobility and Bureaucracy in Russia, 1855-1861* (Cambridge, Mass., 1976).

A. Fletcher, *A County Community in Peace and War: Sussex, 1600–1660* (London, 1975).

F. L. Ford, *Robe and Sword: the Regrouping of the French Aristocracy after Louis XIV* (New York, 1965).

A. J. Forey, *The Templars in the Corona de Aragon* (London, 1973).

R. B. Forster, *The House of Saulx-Tavanes: Versailles and Burgundy, 1700–1830* (Baltimore, 1971).

Forster, *The Nobility of Toulouse in the Eighteenth Century: a Social and Economic Study* (Baltimore, 1960).

Forster, 'Obstacles to agricultural growth in eighteenth-century France', *American Historical Review*, 75 (1970), pp. 1600 ff.

Forster, 'The survival of the nobility during the French Revolution', *Past and Present*, 37 (1967), pp. 71 ff.

Forster, 'The provincial noble: a reappraisal', *American Historical Review*, 68 (1963), pp. 681 ff.

Forster and O. Ranum (ed.) *Rural Society in France: selections from the Annales: Économies, Sociétés, Civilisations* (Baltimore, 1977).

G. Fourquin, *Lordship and Feudalism in the Middle Ages*, trans. I. and A. L. L. Sells (London, 1976).

K. Fowler (ed.), *The Hundred Years' War* (London, 1971).

Fowler, *The Age of Plantagenet and Valois: the Struggle for Supremacy, 1328–1498* (London, 1967).

G. Frêche, 'Compoix, propriété, foncière, fiscalité et démographie historique en pays de taille réelle (XVIe–XVIIIe siècle)', *Revue d'histoire moderne et contemporaine*, 18 (1971), pp. 321 ff.

M. Freudenberger, *The Waldstein Woolen Mill: noble Entrepreuneurship in Eighteenth-Century Bohemia* (Harvard, 1963).

M. Gelzer, *The Roman Nobility*, trans. R. Seager (Oxford, 1969).

L. Genicot, 'Recent research on the medieval nobility', *The Medieval Nobility*, ed. T. Reuter, ch. 1.

Genicot, 'Crisis: from the middle ages to modern times', *The Cambridge Economic History of Europe*, I (2nd ed., 1966), ch. 8.

Genicot, 'The nobility in medieval Francia: continuity, break or evolution?' *Lordship and Community in Medieval Europe*, ed. F. L. Cheyette, pp. 128 ff.

J. Georgelin, *Venise an siècle des lumières* (Paris, 1978).

D. Gerhard, 'Problems of representation and delegation in the eighteenth century', *Études présentées à la commission internationale pour l'histoire des assemblées d'états*, 27 (1965), ch. 7.

H. A. R. Gibb and H. Bowen, *Islamic Society and the West* (London, 1950).

F. Gilbert (ed.) *The Historical Essays of Otto Hintze* (New York, 1975).

J. R. Gillis, 'Aristocracy and bureaucracy in nineteenth-century Prussia', *Past and Present*, 41 (1968), pp. 105 ff.

H. Gollwitzer, *Die Standesherren: die politische und gesellschaftliche Stellung der Mediatisierten, 1815–1918* (Göttingen, 1964).

A. Goodwin (ed.), *The European Nobility in the Eighteenth Century* (London, 1953).

Goodwin, 'Prussia', ibid., ch. 5.

J. Goody, 'Economy and feudalism in Africa', *Economic History Review*, 2nd ser., 22 (1969), pp. 393 ff.

Goody, J. Thirsk and E. P. Thompson (eds.), *Family and Inheritance* (Cambridge, 1976).

W. Görlitz, *Die Junker: Adel und Bauer im deutschen Osten* (Limburg, 1964).

K. Górski, 'Les débuts de la représentation de la *communita nobilium* dans les assemblées d'états de l'est européen', *Anciens pays et assemblées d'états*, 47 (1968), pp. 37 ff.

Górski, 'The origins of the Polish sejm', *Slavonic and East European Review*, 44 (1966), pp. 122 ff.

Górski, 'Les structures sociales de la noblesse polonaise au moyen âge,' *Le moyen âge* (1967), pp. 73 ff.

P. Goubert, *The Ancien Régime*, trans. S. Cox (London, 1973).

A. Grant, 'The development of the Scottish peerage', *Scottish Historical Review*, 57 (1978).

F. Graus, 'Origines de l'état et de la noblesse en Moravie et en Bohême', *Revue des études slaves*, 39 (1961).

M. Graves, 'Freedom of peers from arrest: the case of Henry second Lord Cromwell, 1571–72', *American Journal of Legal History*, 21 (1977), pp. 1 ff.

K. R. Greenfield, *Economics and Liberalism in the Risorgimento: a Study of Nationalism in Lombardy, 1814–1848* (revised ed., Baltimore, 1965).

G. Griffiths, *Representative Government in Western Europe in the Sixteenth Century* (Oxford, 1968).

V. R. Gruder, *The Royal Provincial Intendants: a Governing Elite in Eighteenth-Century France* (New York, 1968).

W. L. Guttsman, *The British Political Elite* (London, 1963).

G. M. Hamburg, 'Land, Economy and Society in Tzarist Russia' (Stanford University dissertation, 1978).

T. F. Hamerow, *Restoration, Revolution, Reaction: Economics and Politics in Germany, 1815–1871* (Princeton, 1958).

Hamerow, *The Social Foundations of German Unification, 1858–1871: Ideas and Institutions* (Princeton, 1969), I.

G. Hanke, 'Das Zeitalter des Zentralismus' in *Handbuch der Gesschichte der böhmischen Länder*, ed. K. Bosl, II, pp. 415 ff.

S. A. Hansen, 'Changes in the wealth and the demographic characteristics of the Danish aristocracy, 1470-1720', *Third International Conference of Economic History*, IV (Munich, 1965), pp. 91 ff.

G. L. Harriss, *King, Parliament and Public Finance in Medieval England to 1369* (Oxford, 1975).

N. B. Harte, 'State control of dress and social change in pre-industrial England', *Trade, Government and Economy in Pre-industrial England*, ed. D. C. Coleman and A. H. John, ch. 8.

P. D. A. Harvey, *A Medieval Oxford Village: Cuxham, 1240-1400* (London, 1965).

J. Hassell, 'Implementation of the Russian table of ranks during the eighteenth century', *Slavic Review*, 29 (1970), pp. 283 ff.

R. M. Hatton, 'Scandinavia and the Baltic', *The New Cambridge Modern History*, VII, ch. 15.

Hatton (ed.), *Louis XIV and Absolutism* (London, 1976).

H. Hauser, 'The characteristic features of French economic history from the middle of the sixteenth to the middle of the eighteenth century', *Economic History Review*, 4 (1933), pp. 257 ff.

D. Hay, *Europe in the Fourteenth and Fifteenth Centuries* (London, 1971).

E. Heckscher, *An Economic History of Sweden*, trans. G. Ohlin (Cambridge, Mass., 1954).

W. O. Henderson, *The State and the Industrial Revolution in Prussia, 1740-1870* (Liverpool, 1958).

J. B. Henneman, *Royal Taxation in Fourteenth-Century France: the Development of War Financing, 1322-1356* (Princeton, 1971).

D. Herlihy, *Pisa in the Early Renaissance: a Study of Urban Growth* (New Haven, 1958).

R. Herr, *The Eighteenth-Century Revolution in Spain* (Princeton, 1958).

F. Hertz, *The Development of the German Public Mind: a Social History of German Political Sentiments, Aspirations and Ideas*, III (London, 1975).

A. Herzen, *Childhood, Youth and Exile* (Oxford, 1980).

J. H. Hexter, 'The myth of the middle class in Tudor England', *Reappraisals in History* (London, 1961), ch. 5.

J. N. Hillgarth, *The Spanish Kingdoms, 1250-1516*, I (Oxford, 1976).

R. H. Hilton, 'Freedom and villeinage in England', *Peasants, Knights and Heretics*, ed. Hilton (Cambridge, 1976), ch. 7.

W. von Hippel, 'Le régime féodal en Allemagne au XVIIIe siècle et sa dissolution', *L'abolition de la féodalité*, I, pp. 289 ff.

E. Hobsbawm, *The Age of Revolution: Europe, 1789-1848* (London, 1962).

Hobsbawm and G. Rudé, *Captain Swing* (London, 1973).

H. Hochenegg, *Der Adel in Leben Tirols: eine soziologische Studie* (Innsbruck, 1971).

J. K. Hoensch, *Sozialverfassung und politische Reform: Polen im vorrevo-*

lutionären Zeitalter (Cologne, 1973).

H. Holborn, *A History of Modern Germany, 1840–1945* (New York, 1969).

G. A. Holmes, *The Estates of the Higher Nobility in Fourteenth-Century England* (Cambridge, 1957).

J. C. Holt, 'Politics and property in early medieval England', *Past and Present*, 57 (1972), pp. 3 ff.

B. J. Hovde, *The Scandinavian Countries, 1720–1865: the Rise of the Middle Classes* (reissue, Ithaca, N.Y., 1948), two volumes.

O. H. Hufton, *Bayeux in the Late Eighteenth Century: a Social Study* (Oxford, 1967).

Hufton, 'The seigneur and the rural community in eighteenth-century France. The seigneurial reaction: a reappraisal', *Transactions of the Royal Historical Society*, 5th ser. 29 (1978), pp. 21 ff.

S. P. Huntington, *Political Order in Changing Societies* (New Haven, 1968).

J. Hurstfield, 'Social structure, office-holding and politics, chiefly in Western Europe', *The New Cambridge Modern History*, III, ch. 5.

J. K. Hyde, *Padua in the Age of Dante* (Manchester, 1966).

F. Irsigler, 'On the aristocratic character of early Frankish society', *The Medieval Nobility*, ed. T. Reuter, ch. 5.

H. Jablonowski, 'Poland-Lithuania, 1609–48', *The New Cambridge Modern History*, IV, ch. 19 (1).

C. Jago, 'The influence of debt on the relations between Crown and aristocracy in seventeenth-century Castile', *Economic History Review*, 2nd ser., 26 (1973), pp. 218 ff.

A. János, 'The decline of oligarchy: bureaucratic and mass politics in the age of dualism', *Revolution in Perspective: Essays on the Hungarian Soviet Republic of 1919*, ed. János and W. B. Slottmann (Berkeley, 1971), ch. 1.

P. Jeannin, *L'Europe du nord-ouest et du nord aux XVIIe et XVIIIe siècles* (Paris, 1969).

A. H. Johnson, *The Disappearance of the Small Landowner* (Oxford, 1909).

A. H. M. Jones, 'The Roman colonate', *Past and Present*, 13 (1958), pp. 1 ff.

P. J. Jones, 'From manor to mezzadria: a Tuscan case-study in the medieval origins of modern agrarian society', *Florentine Studies*, ed. N. Rubinstein, ch. 5.

Jones, 'Medieval agrarian society in its prime: Italy', *The Cambridge Economic History of Europe*, I (2nd ed., 1966), ch. 7 (2).

R. E. Jones, *The Emancipation of the Russian Nobility, 1762–1785* (Princeton, 1973).

H. Kamen, *The Iron Century* (London, 1971).

Kamen, *The War of the Succession in Spain, 1700–1715* (London, 1969).

A. Kamiński, 'Neo-serfdom in Poland-Lithuania', *Slavic Review*, 34 (1975), pp. 253 ff.

J. L. Keep, *The Russian Revolution* (London, 1976).

Keep, 'Imperial Russia: Alexander II to the Revolution' in *An Introduction to Russian History*, ed. R. Auty and D. Obolensky.

H. Kellenbenz, 'German aristocratic entrepreneurship: economic activities of the Holstein nobility in the sixteenth and seventeenth centuries', *Explorations in Entrepreneurial History*, 6 (1953–4).

R. J. Kerner, *Bohemia in the Eighteenth Century* (New York, 1932).

E. Kerridge, 'The movement of rent, 1540–1640', *Economic History Review*, 2nd ser., 6 (1953), pp. 16 ff.

S. Kieniewicz, *The Emancipation of the Polish Peasantry* (Chicago, 1969).

R. F. Kierstead (ed.), *State and Society in Seventeenth-Century France* (New York, 1975).

B. K. Király, *Hungary in the late Eighteenth Century: the Decline of Enlightened Despotism* (New York and London, 1969).

Király, 'Neo-serfdom in Hungary', *Slavic Review*, 34 (1975), pp. 269 ff.

D. Knowles, *The Monastic Order in England, 940–1216* (2nd ed., Cambridge, 1963).

H. Koenigsberger, *The Government of Sicily under Philip II of Spain* (London, 1951).

Koenigsberger, 'The states-general of the Netherlands before the Revolt', *Tenth International Congress of Historical Sciences* (Rome, 1955), pp. 143 ff.

E. H. Kossmann, 'The Low Countries', *The New Cambridge Modern History*, IV, ch. 12.

J. Kovacsics, 'The population of Hungary in the eighteenth century', *Third International Conference of Economic History*, IV (Munich, 1965), pp. 137 ff.

J.-P. Labatut, *Les noblesses européennes de la fin du XVe siècle à la fin du XVIIIe siècle* (Paris, 1978).

Labatut, *Les ducs et pairs de France au XVIIe siècle: étude sociale* (Paris, 1972).

M. A. Ladero Quesada, 'Les finances royales de Castille à la veille des temps modernes', *Annales d'histoire E.S.*, 25 (1970), pp. 775 ff.

E. Le Roy Ladurie, *Carnival: a People's Uprising at Romans, 1579–1580*, trans. M. Feeney (London, 1979).

Le Roy Ladurie, 'Family structures and inheritance customs in sixteenth-century France', *Family and Inheritance*, ed. J. Goody, ch. 2.

A. K. S. Lambton, *Landlord and Peasant in Persia: a Study of Land Tenure and Land Revenue Administration* (London, 1953).

Lambton, *The Persian Land Reform, 1962–1966* (Oxford, 1969).

J. Larios Martin, *Catálogo de los archivos españoles en que se conservan fondos genealógicos y nobiliarios* (Madrid, 1960).

J. C. Lassiter, 'The defamation of peers: the rise and decline of the action of scandalum magnatum, 1497–1773', American Journal of Legal History, 22 (1978), pp. 216 ff.

G. Lefebvre, 'Urban society in the Orléanais in the late eighteenth century', Past and Present, 19 (1961), pp. 46 ff.

Lefebvre, 'The place of the revolution in the agrarian history of France', Rural Society in France, ed. R. Forster and O. Ranum, ch. 3.

Lefebvre, The Great Fear of 1789, trans. J. White (London, 1973).

P. Léon, etc., 'Régime seigneurial et régime féodal dans la France du sud-est', L'abolition de la féodalité, I, pp. 147 ff.

R. F. Leslie, Polish Politics and the Revolution of November, 1830 (London, 1956).

Leslie, 'The Polish Question', Historical Association Pamphlet, gen. ser., 57 (1964).

B. Lesnodorski, 'Le processus de l'abolition du régime féodal dans les territoires polonais aux XVIIIe et XIXe siècles', L'abolition de la féodalité, I, pp. 461 ff.

D. N. Levine, Wax and Gold: Tradition and Innovation in Ethiopian Culture (Chicago, 1970).

A. R. Lewis, The Development of Southern France and Catalan Society, 718–1050 (Austin, 1965).

Lewis, Knights and Samurai: Feudalism in Northern France and Japan (London, 1974).

P. S. Lewis, Later Medieval France: the Polity (London, 1968).

K. Leyser, 'The German aristocracy from the ninth to the early twelfth century', Past and Present, 41 (1968), pp. 25 ff.

D. Ligou, 'Quelques recherches sur les états dans le royaume de France à l'époque moderne', Anciens pays et assemblées d'états, 70 (1977), pp. 435 ff.

J. O. Lindsay, 'The Western Mediterranean and Italy', The New Cambridge Modern History, VII, ch. 12.

E. M. Link, The Emancipation of the Austrian Peasant, 1740–1798 (New York, 1949).

R. B. Litchfield, 'Demographic characteristics of Florentine patrician families, sixteenth to the nineteenth centuries', Journal of Economic History, 29 (1969), pp. 191 ff.

Litchfield, 'Les investissements commerciaux des patriciens florentins au XVIIIe siècle', Annales d'histoire E.S., 24 (1969), pp. 685 ff.

H. V. Livermore, A New History of Portugal (Cambridge, 1966).

H. A. Lloyd, The Gentry of South-west Wales, 1540–1640 (Cardiff, 1968).

F. Lourette, 'The defense of the allodium in seventeenth-century Agenais', State and Society in Seventeenth-Century France, ed. R. F. Kierstead, pp. 180 ff.

E. Lourie, 'A society organised for war: medieval Spain', Past and Present,

35 (1966), p. 54 ff.

C. Loyseau, *Traicte des Ordres* (2nd ed., Paris, 1614).

C. R. Lucas, 'Nobles, bourgeois and the origins of the French Revolution', *Past and Present*, 60 (1973), pp. 84 ff.

F. Lütge, 'The fourteenth and fifteenth centuries in social and economic history', *Pre-Reformation Germany*, ed. G. Strauss, ch. 9.

J. Lynch, *Spain under the Habsburgs*, II (Oxford, 1969).

E. Lyon and A. Wigram, *The House of Lords* (London, 1977).

C. A. Macartney, *The Habsburg Empire* (London, 1968).

Macartney, *Hungary: a Short History* (Edinburgh, 1974).

Macartney, 'Hungary', *The European Nobility in the Eighteenth Century*, ed. A. Goodwin, ch. 7.

Macartney, 'Eastern Europe', *The New Cambridge Modern History*, I, ch. 13.

W. O. McCagg, *Jewish Nobles and Geniuses in Modern Hungary* (New York, 1972).

K. B. McFarlane, *The Nobility of Later Medieval England* (Oxford, 1973).

D. Mack Smith, *A History of Sicily*, two volumes (London, 1968).

A. Mackay, *Spain in the Middle Ages: from Frontier to Empire, 1000-1500* (London, 1977).

J. Q. C. Mackrell, *The Attack on 'Feudalism' in Eighteenth-Century France* (London, 1973).

A. Maçzak, 'The social distribution of landed property in Poland from the sixteenth to the eighteenth century', *Third International Conference of Economic History*, I (Munich, 1965), pp. 455 ff.

V. Magalhães Godinho, 'Portugal and her empire, 1680-1720', *The New Cambridge Modern History*, VI, ch. 16.

Magalhães Godinho, 'Portugal and her empire', ibid., V, ch. 16.

F. W. Maitland, 'The history of a Cambridgeshire manor', *Collected Papers*, II (Cambridge, 1911), pp. 366 ff.

L. Makkai, 'Die Enstehung der gesellschaftlichen Basis des Absolutismus in den Ländern der österreichischer Habsburger', *Studia Historica Academicae Scientiarum Hungaricae*, 43.

Makkai 'Neo-serfdom: its origin and nature in East Central Europe', *Slavic Review*, 34 (1975), pp. 225 ff.

E. E. Malefakis, *Agrarian Reform and Peasant Revolution in Spain* (New Haven, 1970).

M. Malowist, 'The problem of the inequality of economic development in Europe in the later middle ages', *Economic History Review*, 2nd ser., 19 (1966), pp. 15 ff.

Malowist, 'Poland, Russia and Western trade in the fifteenth and sixteenth centuries', *Past and Present*, 13 (1958), pp. 26 ff.

Malowist, 'The economic and social development of the Baltic countries from the fifteenth to the seventeenth century', *Economic History Review*, 2nd ser., 12 (1959), pp. 177 ff.

H. Marczali, *Hungary in the Eighteenth Century* (Cambridge, 1916).

M. Marion, *Dictionnaire des institutions de la France aux XVIIe et XVIIIe siècles* (Paris, 1923).

A. Marongiu, *Medieval Parliaments: a Comparative Study*, trans. S. J. Woolf (London, 1968).

G. Martin, *The Red Shirt and the Cross of Savoy, 1748-1871* (London, 1970).

J. Martindale, 'The French aristocracy in the early middle ages: a reappraisal', *Past and Present*, 75 (1977), pp. 5 ff.

F. Martiny, 'Die Adelsfrage in Preussen vor 1806', *Vierteljahrschrift für Sozial- und Wirtschaftsgeschichte*, 1938 (Beiheft 35).

P. Mathias and P. O'Brien, 'Taxation in Britain and France, 1715-1810', *Journal of European Economic History*, 5 (1976), pp. 601 ff.

G. T. Matthews, *The Royal General Farms in Eighteenth-Century France* (London, 1958).

K. Mejdricka, 'L'état du régime féodal à la veille de son abolition et les conditions de sa suppression en Bohême', *L'abolition de la féodalité*, I, pp. 393 ff.

J. Meuvret, 'Fiscalism and public opinion under Louis XIV', *Louis XIV and Absolutism*, ed. R. Hatton, ch. 10.

J. Meyer, *Noblesses et pouvoirs dans l'Europe d'ancien régime* (Paris, 1973).

Meyer, *La noblesse bretonne au XVIIIe siècle*, two volumes (Paris, 1966).

H. Miller, 'Subsidy assessments of the peerage in the sixteenth century', *Bulletin of the Institute of Historical Research*, 28 (1955), pp. 15 ff.

J. C. Miller, 'The Nobility in Polish Renaissance Society, 1548-1571' (dissertation, Indiana University, 1977), two volumes.

A. Milward and S. B. Saul, *The Economic Development of Continental Europe, 1780-1870* (London, 1973).

G. E. Mingay, *English Landed Society in the Eighteenth Century* (London, 1963).

A. Molinie-Bertrand, 'Les "hidalgos" dans le royaume de Castille à la fin du XVIe siècle', *Revue d'histoire economique et sociale*, 52 (1974), pp. 51 ff.

B. Moore, junior, *Social Origins of Dictatorship and Democracy* (London, 1967).

R. Mousnier, *Peasant Uprisings in Seventeenth-Century France, Russia and China*, trans. B. Pearce (London, 1971).

Mousnier, 'Research into the popular uprisings in France before the Fronde', *France in Crisis, 1620-1675*, ed. P. J. Coveney, ch. 5.

Mousnier, 'The development of monarchical institutions and society in France', in *Louis XIV and Absolutism*, ed. R. Hatton.

Mousnier and F. Hartung, 'Quelques problèmes concernant la monarchie absolue', X *Congresso Internazionale di Scienze Storici, Relazioni*, IV (Florence, 1955).

S. de Moxó, *La Alcabala, sobre sus órigenes, concepto y naturaleza* (Madrid, 1963).

De Moxó, *La disolución del regimen señorial en España* (Madrid, 1965).

L. W. Muncy, *The Junker in the Prussian Administration under William II, 1888-1914* (reprint of 1944 ed., New York, 1970).

J. H. Mundy, *Europe in the High Middle Ages, 1150-1309* (London, 1973).

A. R. Myers, *Parliaments and Estates in Europe to 1789* (London, 1975).

J. Nadel, 'The failure of the industrial revolution in Spain, 1830-1914', *Fontana Economic History of Europe*, IV, ch. 9.

E. J. Nell, 'Economic relationships in the decline of feudalism', *History and Theory*, 6 (1967), pp. 313 ff.

J. Nicolas, 'La fin du régime seigneurial en Savoie, 1771-1792', *L'abolition de la féodalité*, I, pp. 27 ff.

C. Nicolet, 'Les classes dirigeantes romaines sous la République: ordre sénatorial et ordre équestre', *Annales d'histoire E.S.*, 32 (1977), pp. 726 ff.

E. Niederhauser, 'L'emancipation des serfs en Hongrie et en Europe orientale', *L'abolition de la féodalité*, I, pp. 419 ff.

L. O'Boyle, 'The middle class in Western Europe, 1815-1848', *American Historical Review*, 71 (1966), pp. 826 ff.

P. O'Brien and C. Keyder, *Economic Growth in Britain and France, 1780-1914* (London, 1978).

J. F. O'Callaghan, *A History of Medieval Spain* (Ithaca, N.Y., 1975).

G. Ohlin, 'Entrepreneurial activities of the Swedish aristocracy', *Explorations in Entrepreneurial History*, 6 (1953).

A. M. de Oliveira Marques, *History of Portugal* (New York, 1972), two volumes.

Z. P. Pach, *Die ungarische Agrarentwicklung im 16-17. Jahrhundert: Abbiegung vom westeuropäischen Entwicklungsgang* (Budapest, 1964).

S. Painter, 'Feudalism, liberty and democracy', *Feudalism and Liberty*, ed. F. A. Cazel.

F. B. Palmer, *Peerage Law in England* (London, 1907).

R. R. Palmer, 'The peasants and the French Revolution', *Journal of Modern History*, 31 (1959), pp. 329 ff.

E. Pamlenyi (ed.), *A History of Hungary* (London, 1975).

G. Parker, 'The emergence of modern finance in Europe, 1500-1730', *Fontana Economic History of Europe*, II, ch. 7.

S. G. Payne, *A History of Spain and Portugal* (Madison, 1973), two volumes.

E. Perroy, 'Feudalism or principalities in fifteenth-century France', *Bulletin of the Institute of Historical Research*, 20 (1945), pp. 181 ff.

E. L. Petersen, 'La crise de la noblesse danoise entre 1580 et 1660', *Annales d'histoire E.S.*, 23 (1968), pp. 1237 ff.

L. O. Pike, *A Constitutional History of the House of Lords* (London, 1894).

R. Pike, *Aristocrats and Traders; Sevillian Society in the Sixteenth Century* (Ithaca, N.Y., 1972).

L. G. Pine, *The Genealogist's Encyclopedia* (Newton Abbot, 1969).

W. K. Pintner, *Russian Economic Policy under Nicholas I* (Ithaca, N.Y., 1967).

R. Pipes, *Russia under the Old Regime* (London, 1974).

H. Pirenne, *Belgian Democracy* (Manchester, 1915).

F. Pollock and F. W. Maitland, *The History of English Law before the Time of Edward I* (2nd ed., Cambridge, 1968), two volumes.

R. Portal, 'Le régime féodal en Russie à la veille de son abolition', *L'abolition de la féodalité*, I, pp. 439 ff.

M. M. Postan, 'Medieval agrarian society in its prime: England', *The Cambridge Economic History of Europe*, I (2nd. ed., 1966), ch. 7 (7).

J. E. Powell and K. Wallis, *The House of Lords in the Middle Ages: a History of the English House of Lords to 1540* (London, 1968).

N. von Preradovich, *Die Führungsschichten in Österreich und Preussen, 1804–1918, mit einem Ausblick bis zum Jahre 1945* (Wiesbaden, 1955).

T. B. Pugh (ed.), *The Marcher Lordships of South Wales, 1415–1536: Select Documents* (Cardiff, 1963).

Pugh, 'The magnates, knights and gentry', in *Fifteenth-Century England*, ed. S. B. Chrimes (Manchester, 1972), ch. 5.

B. S. Pullan, *A History of Early Renaissance Italy from the Mid-Thirteenth to the Mid-Fifteenth Century* (London, 1973).

M. Raeff, *Origins of the Russian Intelligensia: the Eighteenth-Century Russian Nobility* (New York, 1966).

Raeff, 'Imperial Russia: Peter I to Nicholas I', in *An Introduction to Russian History*, ed. R. Auty and D. Obolensky, ch. 4.

R. S. Rait, *The Parliaments of Scotland* (Glasgow, 1924).

T. O. Ranger, 'The nineteenth century in Southern Rhodesia', *Aspects of Central African History*, ed. Ranger (London, 1968).

O. Ranum, *Richelieu and the Councillors of Louis XIII* (Oxford, 1963).

F. Redlich, 'European aristocracy and economic development', *Steeped in Two Cultures* (New York, 1971), pp. 65 ff.

E. O. Reischauer, 'Japanese feudalism', *Feudalism in History*, ed. R. Coulborn, ch. 3.

T. Reuter (ed.), *The Medieval Nobility* (Amsterdam, New York and Oxford, 1978).

G. Richard, *Noblesse d'affaires au XVIIIe siècle* (Paris, 1974).

J. Richard, 'Les états bourguignons', *Anciens pays et assemblées d'états*, 35

(1966), ch. 9.

K. Richter, 'Die böhmischen Länder von 1471–1740' in K. Bosl (ed.), *Handbuch der Geschichte der böhmischen Länder*, II, pp. 99 ff.

J. Riley-Smith, *The Knights of St. John of Jerusalem and Cyprus, c. 1050–1310* (London, 1967).

J. M. Roberts, 'Lombardy', *The European Nobility in the Eighteenth Century*, ed. A. Goodwin, ch. 4.

M. Roberts, *Gustavus Adolphus* (London, 1953–58), two volumes.

Roberts, *The Early Vasas* (Cambridge, 1968).

Roberts, 'Sweden', *The European Nobility in the Eighteenth Century*, ed. A. Goodwin, ch. 8.

Roberts, *Essays in Swedish History* (London, 1967).

Roberts (ed.), *Sweden's Age of Greatness, 1632–1718* (London, 1973).

G. T. Robinson, *Rural Russia under the Old Regime* (London, 1932).

P. Roebuck, 'Post-Restoration landownership: the impact of the abolition of wardship', *Journal of British Studies*, 18 (1978).

C. M. de la Roncière, 'Indirect taxes or "gabelles" at Florence in the fourteenth century: the evolution of tariffs and problems of collection', *Florentine Studies*, ed. N. Rubinstein, ch. 5.

R. Rosdolsky, 'On the nature of peasant serfdom in Central and Eastern Europe', *Journal of Central European Affairs*, 12 (1952).

Rosdolsky, 'The distribution of the agrarian product in feudalism', *Journal of Economic History*, 11 (1951), pp. 247 ff.

J. Rosén, 'Scandinavia and the Baltic', *The New Cambridge Modern History*, V, ch. 22.

H. Rosenberg, *Bureaucracy, Aristocracy, Autocracy: the Prussian Experience, 1660–1815* (Cambridge, Mass., 1958).

Rosenberg, 'The rise of the junkers in Brandenburg-Prussia, 1410–1653', *American Historical Review*, 49 (1943), pp. 1 ff, and ibid. (1944), pp. 228 ff.

J. S. Roskell, 'Perspectives in parliamentary history', *Bulletin of the John Rylands Library*, 46 (1963–4).

J. Rosselli, *Lord William Bentinck and the British Occupation of Sicily, 1811–1814* (Cambridge, 1956).

N. Rubinstein (ed.), *Florentine Studies: Politics and Society in Renaissance Florence* (London, 1968).

J. Russell Major, *Representative Institutions in Renaissance France, 1421–1556* (Madison, 1960).

Russell Major, *Representative Government in Early Modern France*, Studies Presented to the International Commission for the History of Representative and Parliamentary Institutions, LXIII (New Haven and London, 1980).

Russell Major, 'The Crown and the aristocracy in Renaissance France',

American Historical Review, 69 (1964), pp. 631 ff.

J. Rutkowski, *Le régime agraire en Pologne au XVIIIe siècle* (Paris, 1928).

A. F. C. Ryder, *The Kingdom of Naples under Alfonso the Magnanimous* (Oxford, 1976).

E. Sagarra, *A Social History of Germany, 1648-1914* (London, 1977).

J. H. M. Salmon, 'Venality of office and popular sedition in seventeenth-century France', *Past and Present*, 37 (1967), pp. 21 ff.

N. Salomon, *La campagne de nouvelle Castille à la fin du XVIe siècle* (Paris, 1964).

R. Sanchez Ramos, *La economia siderúrgica española* (Madrid, 1945).

A.-E. Sayous, 'Aristocratie et noblesse à Gênes', *Annales d'histoire E.S.*, 9 (1937), pp. 366 ff.

H. G. Schenk, 'Austria', in *The European Nobility in the Eighteenth Century*, ed. A. Goodwin, ch. 6.

F. Schevill, *History of Florence from the Founding of the City through to the Renaissance* (New York, 1936).

W. Schlesinger, 'Lord and follower in Germanic institutional history', *Lordship and Community in Medieval Europe*, ed. F. L. Cheyette, pp. 64 ff.

K. Schmid, 'The structure of the nobility in the earlier middle ages', *The Medieval Nobility*, ed. T. Reuter, ch. 2.

R. S. Schofield, 'Parliamentary Lay Taxation, 1485-1547' (Cambridge Ph.D., 1963).

H. Seton-Watson, *The Russian Empire, 1801-1917* (Oxford, 1967).

B. Sexauer, 'English and French agriculture in the late eighteenth century', *Agricultural History*, 30 (1976), pp. 491 ff.

J. J. Sheehan, 'Conflict and cohesion among German elites in the nineteenth century', in *Imperial Germany*, ed. Sheehan (New York, 1976).

J. H. Shennan, *Government and Society in France, 1461-1661* (London, 1969).

H. Siegert (ed.), *Adel in Österreich* (Vienna, 1971).

A. Silbert, *Le Portugal méditerranéen à la fin de l'ancien régime* (Paris, 1966), two volumes.

Silbert, 'Sur la "féodalité" portugaise et son abolition', *L'abolition de la féodalité*, I, pp. 323 ff.

T. Skocpol, *States and Social Revolutions* (Cambridge, 1979).

P. Skwarczyński, 'The problem of feudalism in Poland up to the beginning of the sixteenth century', *Slavonic and East European Review*, 34 (1956), pp. 292 ff.

Skwarczyński, 'Poland and Lithuania', *The New Cambridge Modern History*, III, ch. 12.

H. Slapnicka, 'Die böhmischen Länder und die Slowakei 1919-1945', *Handbuch der Geschichte der Böhmischen Länder*, ed. K. Bosl, IV, pp. 2 ff.

B. H. Slicher van Bath, *The Agrarian History of Western Europe, A.D. 500–1850*, trans. O. Ordish (London, 1963).

R. B. Smith, *Land and Politics in the England of Henry VIII: the West Riding of Yorkshire, 1530–1546* (Oxford, 1970).

T. C. Smout, *A History of the Scottish People, 1560–1830* (London, 1969).

A. Soboul, 'Persistence of "feudalism" in the rural society of nineteenth-century France', *Rural Society in France*, ed. R. Forster and O. Ranum, ch. 4.

Soboul, 'Problèmes de la féodalité d'ancien régime. Note sur le prélèvement féodal au XVIIIe siècle', *L'abolition de la féodalité*, I, pp. 115 ff.

D. Spring (ed.), *European Landed Elites in the Nineteenth Century* (Baltimore, 1977).

M. Spufford, *Contrasting Communities: English Villagers in the Sixteenth and Seventeenth Centuries* (Cambridge, 1974).

F. Stacey, *The Government of Modern Britain* (Oxford, 1968).

S. F. Starr, *Decentralisation and Self-government in Russia, 1830–1870* (Princeton, 1972).

Statutes of the Realm, ed. A. Luders, etc. (London, 1810–28).

C. Stephenson, *Medieval Institutions: Selected Essays*, ed. B. D. Lyon (Ithaca, N.Y., 1954).

L. Stone, *The Crisis of the Aristocracy, 1558–1641* (Oxford, 1965).

Stone, 'Social mobility in England, 1500–1700', *Past and Present*, 33 (1966), pp. 16 ff.

J. W. Stoye, 'The Austrian Habsburgs', *The New Cambridge Modern History*, VI, ch. 18.

G. Strauss (ed.), *Pre-Reformation Germany* (London, 1972).

J. R. Strayer, *On the Medieval Origins of the Modern State* (Princeton, 1970).

Strayer, *Feudalism* (Princeton, 1965).

Strayer and C. H. Taylor, *Studies in Early French Taxation* (Cambridge, Mass, 1939).

D. J. Sturdy, 'Tax evasion, the *faux nobles* and state fiscalism: the example of the *généralité* of Caen, 1634–35', *French Historical Studies*, 9 (1976), pp. 549 ff.

M. Szeftel, 'La participation des assemblées populaires dans le gouvernement central de la Russie depuis l'époque kiévienne jusqu'à la fin du XVIIIe siècle', *Receuils de la Société Jean Bodin*, 25 (4) (1965), ch. 13.

Szeftel, 'The representatives and their powers in the Russian legislative chambers, 1906–17', *Etudes présentées à la commission internationale pour l'histoire des assemblées d'états*, 27 (1963), ch. 11.

G. V. Tayor, 'Non-capitalist wealth and the origins of the French Revolution', *American Historical Review*, 72 (1967), pp. 469 ff.

G. Tellenbach, 'From the Carolingian imperial nobility to the German estate of imperial princes', *The Medieval Nobility*, ed. T. Reuter, ch. 7.

N. Temple, 'French towns during the ancien régime', *State and Society in Seventeenth-Century France*, ed. R. F. Kierstead, pp. 67 ff.

J. Thielens, 'Les assemblées d'états du duché de Limbourg et des pays d'Outre-Meuse au XVIIe siècle', *Anciens pays et assemblées d'états*, 43 (1968).

F. M. L. Thompson, *English Landed Society in the Nineteenth Century* (London, 1963).

Thompson, 'The social distribution of landed property in England since the sixteenth century', *Economic History Review*, 2nd ser., 19 (1966), pp. 505 ff.

Thompson, 'Britain', *European Landed Elites in the Nineteenth Century*, ed. D. Spring, ch. 2.

I. A. A. Thompson, *War and Government in Habsburg Spain, 1560–1620* (London, 1976).

D. Thorner, 'Feudalism in India', *Feudalism in History*, ed. R. Coulborn, ch. 7.

J. Z. Titow, *English Rural Society, 1200–1350* (London, 1969).

D. Tonnesson, 'Les pays scandinaves', *L'abolition de la féodalité*, I, pp. 303 ff.

J. Topolski, 'Economic development in Poland from the sixteenth to the eighteenth century', *Essays in the European Economic History, 1500–1800*, ed. P. Earle.

L. Trenard, 'Survivances féodale et régime seigneurial dans les provinces septentrionales de la France au XVIIIe siècle', *L'abolition de la féodalité*, I, pp. 181 ff.

A. S. Turberville, *The House of Lords in the Reign of William III* (Oxford, 1913).

Turberville, *The House of Lords in the Age of Reform, 1784–1837* (London, 1958).

J. Vansina, *Kingdoms of the Savanna* (Madison, 1966).

G. V. Vernadsky, *Russia at the Dawn of the Modern Age:* vol. 4 of *A History of Russia* (New Haven, 1959).

D. V. Verney, *Parliamentary Reform in Sweden, 1866–1921* (Oxford, 1957).

L. Verriest, *Noblesse, chevalerie, lignages* (Brussels, 1959).

P. Villani, 'L'abolition de la féodalité dans le royaume de Naples', *L'abolition de la féodalité*, I, pp. 263 ff.

R. Villari, *La rivolta antispagnola a Napoli: le origini, 1585–1647* (Bari, 1967).

A. R. Wagner, *Heralds and Heraldry in the Middle Ages* (London, 1959).

Wagner, *English Genealogy* (Oxford, 1960).

B. Waldstein-Wartenberg, 'Österreichisches Adelsrecht, 1804–1918', *Mittei-*

lungen des österreichisches Staatsarchivs, 17–18 (1964–5), pp. 109 ff.

I. Wallerstein, *The Modern World-System: Capitalist Agriculture and the Origins of the European World Economy in the Sixteenth Century* (New York, 1974).

P. S. Wandycz, *The Lands of Partitioned Poland, 1795–1918* (London, 1974).

E. Wangermann, *The Austrian Achievement, 1700–1800* (London, 1973).

J. T. Ward and R. G. Wilson (eds.), *Land and Industry: the Landed Estate and the Industrial Revolution* (Newton Abbot, 1971).

J. T. Ward, 'Landowners and mining', *Land and Industry*, ed. Ward and Wilson, ch. 2.

W. R. Ward, *The Land Tax in the Eighteenth Century* (Oxford, 1953).

E. Warlop, *The Flemish Nobility before 1300* (Kortrijk, 1975–6), two parts in four volumes.

S. and B. Webb, *English Local Government from the Revolution to the Municipal Corporations Act*, II (London, 1908).

R. Wellens, 'Les états généraux des Pays-Bas des origines à la fin du règne de Philippe le Beau, 1464–1506', *Anciens pays et assemblées d'états*, 64 (1972).

K. F. Werner, 'Important noble families in the kingdom of Charlemagne', *The Medieval Nobility*, ed. T. Reuter, ch. 6.

E. Wolf, *Peasant Wars in the Twentieth Century* (New York, 1969).

M. Wolfe, *The Fiscal System in Renaissance France* (New Haven, 1972).

P. Wolff, 'The Armagnacs in southern France (14th and 15th centuries)', *Bulletin of the Institute of Historical Research*, 20 (1945), pp. 186 ff.

A. Wolowski, *La vie quotidienne en Pologne au XVIIe siècle* (Paris, 1972).

S. J. Woolf, *Studi sulla nobiltà piemontese nell'epoca dell'assolutismo* (Turin, 1963).

Woolf, 'The aristocracy in transition: a continental comparison', *Economic History Review*, 2nd ser., 23 (1970), pp. 520 ff.

L. P. Wright, 'The military orders in sixteenth and seventeenth-century Spanish society', *Past and Present*, 43 (1969), pp. 34 ff.

W. E. Wright, *Serf, Seigneur and Sovereign: Agrarian Reforms in Eighteenth-century Bohemia* (Minneapolis, 1966).

Wright, 'Neo-serfdom in Bohemia', *Slavic Review*, 34 (1975), pp. 239 ff.

K. Wrightson and D. Levine, *Poverty and Piety in an English Village: Terling, 1525–1700* (New York, 1979).

G. L. Yaney, *The Systematisation of Russian Government* (Urbana, 1973).

A. Zajaczkowski, 'En Pologne: cadres structurels de la noblesse', *Annales d'histoire E.S.*, 18 (1963), pp. 88 ff.

D. E. Zanetta, 'The patriziato of Milan from the domination of Spain to the unification of Italy: an outline of the social and demographic history', *Social History*, 6 (1977), pp. 745 ff.

T. Zeldin, *France, 1848–1945*, I (Oxford, 1973).

Index